The Fountain Light

Photo by Gary Gilbert

The Fountain Light

Studies in Romanticism and Religion

In Honor of John L. Mahoney

edited by
J. ROBERT BARTH, S.J.

Fordham University Press
New York
2002

Copyright © 2002 by FORDHAM UNIVERSITY PRESS
All rights reserved.
ISBN 0-8232-2228-4 (*hardcover*)
ISBN 0-8232-2229-2 (*paperback*)
ISSN 1096-6692
Studies in Religion and Literature, no. 5

Library of Congress Cataloging-in-Publication Data

The fountain light : studies in romanticism and religion : in honor of John L. Mahoney / edited by J. Robert Barth.
    p. cm.—(Studies in religion and literature, ISSN 1096-6692 ; no. 5)
Includes bibliographical references and index.
ISBN 0-8232-2228-4 (hbk.) — ISBN 0-8232-2229-2 (pbk.)
    1. English literature—19th century—History and criticism. 2. Religion and literature—Great Britain—History—19th century. 3. Romanticism— Great Britain. I. Barth, J. Robert. II. Mahoney, John L. III. Studies in religion and literature (Fordham University Press) ; no. 5
PR468.R44 F68 2002
821'.709382—dc21   2002029487

"But for those first affections,
Those shadowy recollections,
Which, be they what they may,
Are yet the fountain light of all our day,
Are yet a master light of all our seeing."

        Wordsworth, *Ode: Intimations of Immortality*

CONTENTS

Preface   ix

John L. Mahoney: A Profile   xi

1. Religion and Animal Rights in the Romantic Era   1
   David Perkins

2. Wordsworth and St. Francis: "A meeker man than this lived never."   22
   Robert Kiely

3. Wordsworth's Abbey Ruins   37
   Dennis Taylor

4. Cowper, Wordsworth, and the Sacred Moment of Perception   54
   David J. Leigh, S.J.

5. Wordsworth between God and Mammon: The Early "Spots of Time" and the Sublime as Sacramental Commodity   73
   Charles J. Rzepka

6. Icons of Women in the Religious Sonnets of Wordsworth and Felicia Hemans   90
   John Anderson

7. Wordsworth's "Immortality Ode" and Hopkins' "The Leaden Echo and the Golden Echo": In Pursuit of Transcendence   111
   J. Robert Barth, S.J.

8. Coleridge (and His Mariner) on the Soul: "As an exile in a far distant land" 128
   James Engell

9. The Gothic Coleridge: Mythos and the Real 152
   Thomas Lloyd

10. "Sounding on His Way": Coleridgean Religious Dissent and Hazlitt's Conversational Style 176
    Jonathan Mulrooney

11. Coleridge and De Quincey on Miracles 193
    Frederick Burwick

12. Coleridge and Newman: The Centrality of Conscience 231
    Philip C. Rule, S.J.

13. "All About the Heart": The Material-Theology of Maturin's *Melmoth the Wanderer* 256
    Judith Wilt

Notes on Contributors 275

A Bibliography of the Works of John L. Mahoney 281

Index 291

PREFACE

To say that this book is a labor of love would be no exaggeration. The contributors to this collection are all colleagues and students of John Mahoney, who offer these essays as a tribute to one for whom they have deep respect and affection. Their work is an attempt not only to recognize and express gratitude for their personal debts to him, but also to celebrate publicly his distinguished career. We offer him this baker's dozen with admiration and with heartfelt gratitude.

* * *

It has often been suggested that Romanticism of its very nature has affinities with religious quest and spiritual values. These essays, ranging from broad consideration of several Romantic writers to close readings of individual poems, attempt to explore some of the many intersections of Romanticism and religion.

David Perkins' opening essay on religion and animal rights, which considers a wide range of Romantic literature, is followed by six essays on various aspects of religious experience in Wordsworth: Robert Kiely on Wordsworth and St. Francis of Assisi; Dennis Taylor discussing the re-emergence of the imagery of medieval Catholicism in his work; David Leigh tracing some of Wordsworth's religious rhetoric and imagery to the influence of William Cowper; Charles Rzepka on religious dimensions of the early *Prelude*; John Anderson comparing the religious sonnets of Wordsworth with those of Felicia Hemans; and J. Robert Barth considering the influence of Wordsworth on the Jesuit poet Gerard Manley Hopkins.

The next sequence of essays focuses on Coleridge: James Engell on Coleridge's discussions of the soul; Thomas Lloyd on the religious use of "mythos" in Coleridge; Jonathan Mulrooney discussing the influence of Coleridge's religious dissent on William Hazlitt's "conversational style"; Frederick Burwick on Coleridge and Thomas De Quincey on the subject of miracles; and Philip Rule tracing the affinities between Coleridge and John Henry Newman in their emphasis on the role of conscience in human experience. The collection closes with Judith Wilt's exploration of the exotic theology of Charles Maturin in *Melmoth the Wanderer*.

* * *

Debts in the making of this book are many, and it is a pleasure to acknowledge them here. First and foremost, I am deeply grateful for the generous contribution of the essayists, who not only readily agreed to contribute to this collection but bore patiently and generously with the demands of the editor upon their time and attention.

Also very importantly, I want to acknowledge the extraordinary help of my gifted research associate, Matthew VanWinkle, whose intelligence and careful attention to detail contributed perhaps more than he knows to the successful completion of this project and to the equanimity of the editor.

For financial support, I am happy to express my gratitude to Dean Michael A. Smyer, Dean of the Graduate School at Boston College, and to the James P. McIntyre Research Fund. I am also grateful to John L. Mahoney, Jr., who generously shared remembrances of his father, and to Ben Birnbaum, Director of the Boston College Office of Marketing Communication, for permission to quote from his article on John Mahoney in the *Boston College Magazine*.

Earlier versions of two of the essays, "Wordsworth's 'Immortality Ode' and Hopkins' 'The Leaden Echo and the Golden Echo': In Pursuit of Transcendence" and "Coleridge and De Quincey on Miracles" appeared in, respectively, *Renascence* and *Christianity and Literature*. I am grateful to the editors of these journals for allowing earlier material to be used here.

I cannot say enough about the generous support and encouragement of Dr. Mary Beatrice Schulte, Executive Editor of Fordham University Press, throughout the process of planning this book and bringing it to completion. It has been evident throughout that her work with us has been, as much as ours is, a tribute to John Mahoney.

For the rest, our deepest gratitude goes to our friend John Mahoney—and to Ann—for blessing our lives with their friendship.

Chestnut Hill, Massachusetts J. R. B.
February 4, 2002

JOHN L. MAHONEY
A Profile

Perhaps the photograph—the frontispiece of this book—says it better than my words can. There he is—the intent look, the eloquent hands, the warm and inviting smile—all at the service of the students who sit before him. John Mahoney is nowhere more himself, some would say, than when he is in the classroom. And in the classroom he is as much a listener as he is a talker, for he is invariably intent not on himself, nor even primarily on his students, but on the ideas and images and words that flow between them. No one but John was surprised when, several years ago, he was named Massachusetts Professor of the Year.

A university friend and colleague, Ben Birnbaum, wrote of John Mahoney in an elegant and eloquent article in the *Boston College Magazine*: "Even while listening, he appears to be covering ground, thought and emotion playing across his long, expressive face like landscape on the windows of a moving train." In the classroom, he goes on, "this attentive energy works like a gravitational core, drawing student thoughts and ideas, which, amplified by the professor's glosses, corrections and punctuation marks, are then shot back across the room to be inscribed as full lecture notes in student notebooks."

Birnbaum's commentary on John's classroom performance is hard to resist, so I presume to quote it again. John had told his students about a jazz recording which he found he "only liked after several hearings." However, he went on, "when you break through the complexity, you seem to see this luminous order." This was in Birnbaum's mind when he attended another of John's classes "and watched him work his charms." "What were they taken with?" he wondered of the students. "Is it the tweed-wrapped authority? The learning? The consideration with which he greets each and every remark he can squeeze out of them? The passion of his readings? Or is there something more that is responsible for his extraordinary charisma as a teacher—something he represents to students that is rarely to be found in postmodern culture or postmodern classrooms: perhaps that very old-fashioned and most uncynical possibility of finding (given luck and will) the 'luminous order' behind the confusion; that possibility of an earned wholeness?"

But this "wholeness" in John Mahoney's life is a complex reality—perhaps like the complexity of that jazz recording. One of his sons remarked of John that he has a "desire for and delight in all things beautiful." Anyone who knows him will appreciate that this is simply the veriest truth. His love of literature—in every one of its forms—is legendary and infectious, his devotion to the theatre is a lifelong passion, his love and knowledge of film is deep and passionate, and he is a serious and knowledgeable jazz afficionado. The very mention of, say, Stevie Smith or Seamus Heaney, a production of Tom Stoppard's *Arcadia* at the Huntington Theatre or a recent film of David Lynch's, a jazz recording by Bill Evans or Marian McPartland, will set him off on a wonderful riff or an intense exchange. Just try him on *My Dinner with André*, one of his favorite films—and prepare for a treat!

A student of several years ago recalls John Mahoney's class on *My Dinner with André* as a striking example of his "deep dramatic sensibility." The course was "The Poetry of Religious Experience," and John entered the class and introduced himself as André Gregory. For an hour, he *was* André Gregory, the student remembers with something approaching awe. "Never once did he break character," and by the end of the hour his students "felt they had met André Gregory."

This "dramatic sensibility" is also celebrated in a remembrance of a young Jesuit who took a course with John in the Harvard University Summer School some years ago on "Eighteenth- and Nineteenth-Century Literary Criticism. "Among the memorable moments of the course," he recalls, "were his impersonations of Samuel Johnson, which brought the old critic to life for us." He seemed, he goes on, "to have memorized half of Johnson's juiciest critical maxims, which he would recite with Johnsonian gusto."

Perhaps it should come as no surprise that the son of a printer should be so passionate about words: the written word—the poetry of Wordsworth, the sonorous prose of Dr. Johnson; or the spoken word—in conversation, in the classroom, in film or on stage. But it was a long journey that took this son of a printer from the blue-collar neighborhood of his childhood in Somerville, Massachusetts, to Harvard University in next-door Cambridge. The journey was by way of a Jesuit education, first at Boston College High School, then at its sister school,

Boston College. In local parlance that makes him—referring to the mascot of both these institutions—a "double eagle." Several years of service in the postwar U.S. Army followed, after which he returned to the banks of the Charles River for his doctoral studies.

At Harvard the aspiring scholar met such literary giants as Douglas Bush, Perry Miller, B. J. Whiting, Alfred Harbage, Herschel Baker—and Walter Jackson Bate. It was W. J. Bate in particular who was to become in many ways a model for his own scholarly career. They both began work in the literature of the eighteenth century, only to move on in the course of their careers to become respected critics of the Romantic period. And for the rest of his life, W. J. Bate and John Mahoney were to remain not only close colleagues on either side of the Charles, but close friends.

Even the most cursory look at John Mahoney's lengthy bibliography makes it clear that his intellectual roots are in the eighteenth century. His very first published article was on "The Classical Tradition in Eighteenth-Century Rhetorical Education," bringing together—one might surmise—his Jesuit rhetorical training and his eighteenth-century studies at Harvard; and his first published book was an edition of the *Essay on Original Genius* of the eighteenth-century Scottish critic William Duff. But, like those of W. J. Bate, John's interests were too broad to be confined to the eighteenth century, and he soon began to publish on Romanticism—his interest culminating in his learned anthology *The English Romantics: Major Poetry and Critical Theory*, published over twenty years ago and still in use today. There followed his major book on Hazlitt, *The Logic of Passion: The Literary Criticism of William Hazlitt*; another major anthology, still in use, on *The Enlightenment and English Literature;* a book on tragedy; and finally—spanning both his major fields of scholarship—his wide-ranging study, *The Whole Internal Universe: Imitation and the New Defense of Poetry in British Criticism and Aesthetics, 1660–1830*. Other work followed, in books and scholarly journals, leading to his recent important books on Wordsworth: first, his splendid *William Wordsworth: A Poetic Life*, which follows in the tradition of critical biography pioneered by Bate; and his most recent book, *Wordsworth and the Critics: The Development of a Critical Reputation*. And there is, of course, promise of more to come.

Besides the sheer range of his scholarship, though, one is impressed by what I can only call the "openness" of John's learning. Schooled in an earlier tradition of literary work, he is always open to fresh currents of ideas and new methodologies. He is invariably alert to the work of younger colleagues, for example, and is nurtured by their approaches to literature even—or perhaps especially—when they differ considerably from his own. As he wrote, memorably, in the introduction to his splendid book *William Wordsworth: A Poetic Life*, "while my own temperament cannot be described as deconstructive, I have learned valuable lessons about the heuristic and pleasurable possibilities of seeing varied and often conflicting meanings in the text as in the larger text of human experience" (p. xxiii). For John, methodologies—whatever they may be—are always in service of the poetry and the poet. As he said in outlining his approach to Wordsworth's "poetic life": "I look for an approach, one that eschews mere chronology, easy categories, and facile generalizations as it tries to connect life and work more closely, to develop a way of thinking about the life as it nourishes the work and the work as it illuminates the life" (xxi). In John Mahoney's work, as in his life, "openness" and "wholeness" are inextricably linked.

As anyone is aware who knows him, John Mahoney's gifts—even beyond teaching and scholarship—are many and varied. He served for several years with great success as department Chair, for example, and his leadership on major college and university committees has been frequent and highly respected. The faculty luncheons he has regularly organized for the past several years have addressed substantive issues concerning the nature of a Jesuit and Catholic university—issues he holds dear and on which he speaks with both eloquence and authority. Given his well-known and highly regarded leadership ability and organizational skills, there have been attempts to lure him into full-time academic administration, but John's heart has always been in the classroom and with his scholarly work. And it was surely in recognition not only of his teaching and scholarship but also of all his varied gifts that in 1994 John was named to the Thomas P. Rattigan Chair of English, the first endowed professorship in the history of the Department of English at Boston College.

"Attentive energy," was the phrase Ben Birnbaum used of John Mahoney. And this is perhaps a phrase that could be used to characterize every aspect of his life and work: his teaching, his scholarship, his "university citizenship," his remarkable gift for friendship, his beautiful devotion to Ann and his family. John's whole life, I suggest, is marked by this quality, for—as Birnbaum puts it—"an indefatigable interest in the lives of others is a hallmark of his sensibility." Whether it be his beloved family, his fortunate students, or such seemingly far-off figures as Dr. Johnson and William Wordsworth, he brings to them all his "attentive energy," his "indefatigable interest in the lives of others"— and his love. In return, we, his colleagues, students, and friends, offer him—on behalf of so many more who love and respect him—this tribute of our admiration and affection.

J.R.B.

1

Religion and Animal Rights in the Romantic Era

David Perkins

"BESIDES, THESE CREATURES, insignificant as they appear in your estimation, were made by God as well as you.... How then can you expect that God will send His blessing upon you if, instead of endeavouring to imitate him in being merciful to the utmost of your power, you are wantonly cruel to innocent creatures which he designed for happiness."[1] So in Sarah Trimmer's *The Robins* (1786) Mrs. Benson reproves Miss Lucy Jenkins, a visiting ten-year-old who had neglected to feed some young birds—chicks wickedly taken from their nests by her brother. Mrs. Benson's remarks were commonplaces. Similar points were made over and over in treatises, sermons, pamphlets, poems, and literature for children such as Trimmer's very popular book. But in no other age would these ideas have seemed so obvious—for example, that animals are innocent, that God designed them for happiness, and that He will punish cruelty to them.

Sympathy, compassion, and fellow feeling with and for animals had been voiced recurrently from Homer through the ages. Moralists had generally, though not invariably, condemned cruelty to animals as dangerous, because of the passions stirred, both for the person who inflicts it and ultimately for society. But in England around 1775 sympathy for animals began to be expressed with far greater frequency and emotional commitment. Arguments were brought forward that had been less available or had seemed less convincing in the past. The bearers of this increasing solicitude were mostly to be found in the 15% to 25% of the population that might be called middle class.[2] The writers who

---

[1] Sarah Trimmer, *The Robins, or, Fabulous Histories, Designed for the Instruction of Children Respecting Their Treatment of Animals* (Boston, 1822) 69–70.

[2] On the proportion of the total population that might be considered middle class,

propagated it were middle-class intellectuals—preachers, poets, philosophers, and the like.

They encountered resistance from the start, were dismissed as cranks, disturbers, molly-coddlers, effeminates, and radicals. For example, a 1772 sermon by James Granger on Proverbs 12: 10, "A righteous man regardeth the life of his beast," was heard with "almost universal disgust."[3] Humphrey Primatt knew in 1776 that he was exposing himself to "obloquy" by publishing his *The Duty of Mercy and Sin of Cruelty to Beasts*.[4] When in 1796 James Plumptre, inspired by Cowper's *The Task*, preached before the University of Cambridge, in the presence of Prince William of Gloucester, on "The Duties of Man to the Brute Creation," "the subject was then considered by many as trifling, and beneath the dignity of the pulpit, and especially that of the University."[5] As time passed, however, the hearers and readers of this discourse increasingly shared its views and emotions. Animals became a humanitarian cause like slaves, prisoners, chimney sweeps, foundlings, and other helpless victims, and the effort has continued ever since.[6] We now refer to all such pleas and political activity on behalf of animals with the covering term "animal rights." Two hundred years ago there

---

see Leonore Davidoff and Catherine Hall, *Family Fortunes: Men and Women of the English Middle Class, 1780–1850* (London, 1987) 23–24.

[3] *An Apology for the Brute Creation, or, Abuse of Animals Censured; in a Sermon on Proverbs xii 10*, 2nd ed. (London, 1773) 27.

[4] Quoted in Richard D. Ryder, *Animal Revolution* (Oxford, 1989) 67.

[5] *Three Discourses on the Case of the Animal Creation and the Duties of Man to Them* (London, 1816) v.

[6] On this eighteenth-century development see Keith Thomas, *Man and the Natural World: Changing Attitudes in England, 1500–1800* (London, 1983) 36–192. The following books deal mainly with Victorian and modern developments, but have some preliminary material on earlier periods: Ernest S. Turner, *All Heaven in a Rage* (New York, 1965); Harriet Ritvo, *The Animal Estate: The English and Other Creatures in the Victorian Age* (Cambridge, Mass., 1987); James Turner, *Reckoning with the Beast: Animals, Pain, and Humility in the Victorian Mind* (Baltimore, 1980); Hilda Kean, *Animal Rights: Political and Social Change in Britain since 1800* (London, 1998). Discussions of poems on this topic include Dix Harwood, *Love for Animals and How It Developed in Great Britain* (New York, 1928) and Dagobert De Levie, *The Modern Idea of the Prevention of Cruelty to Animals* (New York, 1947). I have written on the complex relation of certain poets and poems to the campaign on behalf of animals: "Cowper's Hares," *Eighteenth Century Life* 20 (1996): 57–69; "Wordsworth and the Polemic against Hunting: 'Hart-leap Well,'" *Nineteenth-Century Literature* 52 (1998): 421–445; "Compassion for Animals and Radical Politics: Coleridge's 'To a Young Ass,'" *ELH* 65 (1998): 929–944; "Sweet Helpston! John Clare on Badger Baiting," *Studies in Romanticism* 38 (1999): 387–407; "Animal Rights and 'Auguries of Innocence,'" *Blake Quarterly* 33 (1999): 4–11.

were also claims that animals had natural rights and should be granted legal ones. But though I adopt our contemporary term for its shorthand convenience, my focus is the growing insistence that animals ought to be treated kindly whether they have rights or not.

The sources of this changing attitude lie among cultural and social developments familiar to all students of the period: sentimentalism; the redescription of moral goodness to emphasize sympathy and kindness; the idealization of external nature, of which animals are a part; scientific discovery (partly through vivisection!) that the higher animals closely resemble humans in their physiology and hence probably also to some extent in their thought processes and passions; a growing middle class that was living in towns or cities and was not directly involved in farming or financially dependent on it; the sense, within this social group, of emerging from a Gothic past into modern civilization and refinement, so that the gruesome blood-sports of the gentry and the bull-baitings and cock-throwings of the populace seemed atavistic—"barbarian" was the common term for cruelties to animals; the spread in all classes of pet keeping, with the result that animals were seen as individuals, each with its life history, and on them were projected human motives and characteristics. Perhaps also at this time a greater modern sensitivity to pain began to emerge and a feeling that it is anomalous. Certainly, the Utilitarian equation of pain with evil surfaces in the most surprising places, for example in Mary Wollstonecraft's *Original Stories from Real Life* (1791), a book for children. "Do you know the meaning of the word Goodness?" asks Mrs. Mason of Mary, age fourteen, who has been chasing insects. "I will tell you. It is, first, to avoid hurting any thing; and then, to contrive to give as much pleasure as you can."[7]

Two hundred years ago arguments about animal rights referred habitually to religion. This, in fact, is the most striking difference in the debates then and now, for otherwise the points made then were similar to ours, pro and con. By religion I do not mean the churches, for although individual clergymen spoke out, the various churches and sects did not take a position on animal rights. The nearest thing to an exception might be found in Methodism; Wesley impressed on his preachers kindness to animals as a concern.[8]

---

[7] *Original Stories from Real Life* (1791; facsimile Oxford and New York, 1990) 5.

[8] Richard E. Brantley, *Locke, Wesley, and the Method of English Romanticism* (Gainesville, 1984) 90.

The Bible, the dictated or inspired word of God, was also mute. It was, of course, the ultimate source of religious authority for most middle-class persons, and was combed for instruction on how to treat animals. But the many pertinent texts were not harmonious; moreover, they were subject to varying interpretations. Whoever wishes to know just which passages could be cited can refer to the sermon by James Plumptre mentioned earlier, which takes up almost all of them. Undeniably God had given man dominion over the animals (Genesis 1: 26), but there was nothing to suggest that humans should be harsh or uncaring. After the flood He had made his covenant not only with Noah but with the animals also (Genesis 9: 12), and this surely implied His concern for them. There were regulations in Deuteronomy (22: 4, 6) that enjoined kindness to cattle and to nesting birds; Balaam's ass (Numbers 22: 21–34) had seen the angel when Balaam could not: Job (17: 14) had said "to the worm, Thou art my mother, and my sister." And so forth.

As an example of the earnestness and ingenuity brought to bear in interpreting, we may view William Paley's wrestling with the vegetarian question: is it right for humans to eat animals? Meat eating was often numbered among the consequences of Original Sin, an idea that in no way increased pleasure at dinner. God had certainly authorized our feeding on animals (Genesis 9: 3), but this had not been until after the flood, and it was no less certain, as Paley read his Bible, that man in paradise had lived only on vegetables (Genesis 1: 29). Might greens be preferable in God's eyes? Thus Paley was interested in knowing what the antediluvians ate, those persons who had lived between the Fall and the flood, and, so far as the Bible informs us, had not yet been given permission to eat animals. "Whether they actually refrained from the flesh of animals, is another question. Abel, we read, was a keeper of sheep; and what purpose he kept them for, but to eat, is hard to say (unless it were sacrifices): might not, however, some of the stricter sects among them [the antediluvians] be scrupulous, as to this point; and might not Noah and his family be of this description; for it is not probable that God would publish a permission, to authorise a practice which had never been disputed?"[9] Thus, inference from texts could not inspire conviction. One could not plausibly cite Balaam's ass, or Christ's riding an ass into Jerusalem (Mark 11: 1–7), or even his birth in a stable, to educe God's views on kindness to cattle.

---

[9] *The Principles of Moral and Political Philosophy*, 2 vols. (London, 1785; reprint New York, 1978) 84.

It was not from the Bible, then, that Sarah Trimmer, in the sentences I quoted at the start, derived her premises and her confidence in them. So also with the great many other writers who made more or less the same points in the same way, that is, in a "potted" fashion, briefly, without argument, as one states the generally known and accepted. For example, Thomas Paine, in *The Age of Reason* (1793), says that "the moral duty of man consists in imitating the moral goodness and beneficence of God, manifested in the creation toward all His creatures . . . everything of cruelty to animals, is a violation of moral duty";[10] Thomas Young, in *An Essay on Humanity to Animals* (1798): "The Creator wills the happiness of these his creatures, and consequently that humanity towards them is agreeable to him, and cruelty the contrary";[11] Edward Augustus Kendall in *Keeper's Travels in Search of His Master* (1799), a very popular story for children: men should "acknowledge the Rights; instead of bestowing their Compassion upon the creatures, whom, with themselves, God made, and made to be happy";[12] Wordsworth in "Hart-Leap Well" on the death of a hunted deer:

> This beast not unobserved by Nature fell;
> His death was mourned by sympathy divine.
>
> The Being, that is in the clouds and air,
> That is in the green leaves among the groves,
> Maintains a deep and reverential care
> For the unoffending creatures whom he loves.[13]

Clearly the famous "moral" of Coleridge's "The Rime of the Ancient Mariner" (1798) was not unusual in its time:

> He prayeth best, who loveth best
> All things both great and small;
> For the dear God who loveth us,
> He made and loveth all.[14]

---

[10] *The Age of Reason* (1794), ed. P. S. Foner (Secaucus, N.J., 1974) 98.
[11] Quoted in Samuel F. Pickering, Jr., *John Locke and Children's Books in Eighteenth-Century England* (Knoxville, 1981) 37.
[12] *Keeper's Travels in Search of His Master* (1799; Philadelphia, 1801) v.
[13] William Wordsworth, "Hart-Leap Well," lines 163–168, in *English Romantic Writers*, ed. David Perkins, 2nd ed. (Fort Worth, 1995) 322.
[14] Samuel Taylor Coleridge, "The Rime of the Ancient Mariner," lines 614–617, in *The Portable Coleridge*, ed. I. A. Richards (New York, 1950) 104–105.

If God intended that animals should be happy, it followed that cruelty to them was impious. Persons who urged kindness to animals did not typically believe in a God of wrath and vengeance, but He was just. "Man may dismiss compassion from his heart, / But God will never," Cowper wrote in *The Task* (1785), and whoever showed no mercy to animals would himself "seek it, and not find it."[15] Sometimes this rhetoric became alarming. Blake's Thel knew "That God would love a Worm . . . and punish the evil foot / That wilful bruis'd its helpless form," and there is Blake's much-quoted couplet in "Auguries of Innocence": "A Robin Red breast in a Cage / Puts all Heaven in a Rage."[16] We have learned to read special meanings into Blake's words, but should not ignore the literal threat. In *The Rights of Animals and Man's Obligation to Treat Them with Humanity* (1838), William Drummond waxed terrifying: "to injure, to abuse, to maim, torture, or inflict upon them [animals] any pain which can be avoided, is to act in opposition to the will of Heaven, and rise in rebellion against his Maker," the sin of Satan.[17]

That the Father loves *all* His creatures and intends them to be happy was the most powerful and usual argument of the Romantic age. If you believed it, that is, if you accepted the description of God's being and attributes that lies behind it, and the inferences from this description, it stood in the way of hunting, baiting, whipping, driving, cramming, plucking, and innumerable other practices, painful to animals, that were an ordinary, familiar part of life. In the boxing terms of the era, the argument was not a "settler," for you could claim that these practices were necessary, or, alternatively, that live geese, for example, do not mind having their quills plucked—defenses that are still usual—but at least the argument was a "facer." It made you pause and think. The burden of proof had now shifted to you.

The description of God that grounds this argument is too familiar to be rehearsed at length. In the eighteenth century an unfathomable, fearful God, who incalculably by His grace saves some persons and not others, seemed incredible to many English intellectuals. As a being

---

[15] William Cowper, *The Task*, Book VI, "The Winter Walk at Noon," *Poetical Works*, 2 vols. (London, 1830), II, 176, 181.

[16] William Blake, "The Book of Thel," Plate 5, lines 9–10; "Auguries of Innocence," lines 5–6, *Complete Writings*, ed. Geoffrey Keynes (London, 1966) 130, 431.

[17] *The Rights of Animals and Man's Obligation to Treat Them with Humanity* (London, 1836) 49.

perfectly good, God must wish the happiness of all beings, since this is intrinsic to what we mean by goodness. So much could be known *a priori*. As Thomas Reid told his students at the University of Edinburgh, "Goodness, Mercy & forbearance are evidently implied in a perfect moral character, for without it we can conceive no moral character whatever." Therefore, the laws of the universe must be and are "fitted to promote the interest of his creatures & to give all that degree of happiness of which their several natures are capable."[18] Reid was a university lecturer, but the point was a staple of moral and religious instruction at all levels. Thus Sarah Trimmer: "how excellently . . . inferior creatures . . . are informed and instructed by their great Creator for the enjoyment of happiness in their different classes of existence. . . . There is no doubt that the Almighty designed all beings for happiness"; Wollstonecraft: God made all creatures "to be happy . . . and when he made them, did not leave them to perish, but placed them where the food that is most proper to nourish them is easily found"; Kendall, quoting Blair: "One end of God in this visible creation, was, certainly, the delight of his creatures, of which the meanest reptile has undoubtedly its share."[19] The Unitarian Joseph Priestley looked forward to the collapse of the traditional religious system, for this would clear the way to the correct "simple belief, that the merciful parent of the universe . . . never meant any thing but the happiness of his creatures."[20] God, said the Earl of Shaftesbury, "is the best-natured Being in the world."[21] Thus, moral ideals of the age were projected onto God, who became the perfect exemplar of reasonableness, benevolence, and compassion. To imitate God was to cultivate these qualities.

I should emphasize that this view of God did not generally prevail in middle-class households. Here a more traditional religion would probably be found, centered on the sense of sinfulness and the experience of conversion through Christ.[22] Neither were these optimistic beliefs shared by all intellectuals—far from it. But they were the newer,

---

[18] *Lectures on Natural Theology* (1780), ed. Elmer H. Duncan (Washington, D.C., 1981) 86.

[19] Trimmer 151, 203; Wollstonecraft 3; Edward Augustus Kendall, *The Canary Bird: A Moral Story, Interspersed with Poetry* (Philadelphia, 1801) 54.

[20] Quoted in Thomas McFarland, *Coleridge and the Pantheist Tradition* (Oxford, 1969) 312, from Priestley's *Three Tracts* . . . (London, 1791) 177.

[21] Quoted in Basil Willey, *The Eighteenth Century Background: Studies on the Idea of Nature in the Thought of the Period* (New York, 1940) 11.

[22] Davidoff and Hall 87.

more modern understanding of God and His relation to His creation, and they seeped gradually into people's minds, mixing illogically with other beliefs and modifying them. Whether or not Sarah Trimmer had read John Locke, Samuel Clarke, Matthew Tindal, Willliam Wollaston, the Earl of Shaftesbury, and other shapers of the modern faith I do not know. But she would not have needed to. Their thoughts were echoed in sermons, journal articles, and poems. They were, as we say, in the air.

Since fatherhood was a usual analogy for God, we may note that fatherly behavior seems also to have been in transition during the eighteenth century. The father was still very much the household figure of authority. He was usually older than his wife, had the advantage of experience in the world, and controlled the finances. Women and children were dependent. However, in middle-class households fathers were generally not distant parents. They might take care of children when the mother was ill or away, nurse them when they were sick, tell them stories, teach them, and play games with them, and as the boys grew older, the father would settle them in business or a career. In short, fathers were likely to be much involved with their children and to be caring.[23] I mention this because the ways of earthly fathers would modify conceptions of the heavenly one—perhaps quite as much as the reverse process.

Traditionally it had been said that God created animals for the convenience and use of man, that is, presumably, so that they could be eaten, be made to pull carriages, and so forth.[24] But as had long since been pointed out, God created many animals of which man can make no use, animals, even, of which we have no knowledge. Was it possible that God produced animals for His own sake or for the sake of the creatures themselves? We are touching on what A. O. Lovejoy calls "the principle of plenitude," the idea that it belongs to the perfection of God to create all the kinds of living things that are possible. Along with its correlate, the great Chain of Being—that is, the hierarchical, continuous scale of beings from the lowest to God—the idea of plenitude had, says Lovejoy, its "widest diffusion" in the eighteenth century.[25] In this light it appeared that the animal species were not created

---

[23] Davidoff and Hall 329–333.

[24] For quotations and discussion see A. O. Lovejoy, *The Great Chain of Being* (1936; New York, 1960) 187–188.

[25] Lovejoy 183.

for the benefit of man, and the opinion that they were was satirized by Pope[26] and many other writers.

Because the perfect goodness of God entailed, for some reasoners, His intention that animals should be happy, it further required that animal souls be immortal. Expressions of this belief might be mainly wishful or sentimental, as when Alexander Pope told Spence that dogs must have souls "as imperishable in their nature as ours. . . . Where would be the harm to us in allowing them immortality."[27] Robert Southey, grieving for a dead spaniel, wrote that "there is another world, / For all that live and move—a better one."[28] The immortality of human souls could be inferred without biblical revelation, and the same arguments were cogent for animals. Wollaston, for example, observed that the world bursts with innocent suffering: "how can we acquit the *justice* and *reasonableness* of that Being . . . if there be no *future state*, where the proper amends may be made."[29] Wollaston does not mention animals, but others pointed out that their innocent lives may also contain a huge excess of pain over pleasure. Moreover, some of the traditional rationalizations of evil and suffering did not apply very well to animals, such as that suffering improves moral and spiritual character and redirects attention toward God. In his consideration of *Scriptural and Philosophical Arguments . . . that Brutes Have Souls* (1824), Peter Buchan concluded that since a just God must recompense "undeserved pain," He must have appointed "a future state" for animals.[30] Richard Dean, a clergyman, tried to prove this by the Bible, relying on such passages as Romans 8: 21 and Isaiah 65: 25. But in his *Essay on the Future Life of Brute Creatures* (1768) he also used the rationalist argument: animals suffer in this world; if they are not compensated in the next world, "I know not whether we shall not be obliged to . . . impeach the divine Goodness."[31]

Like other ideas that weakened the distinction between humans and

---

[26] Alexander Pope, *An Essay on Man*, I, 131–140, ed. Maynard Mack (New Haven, 1950).

[27] Joseph Spence, *Observations, Anecdotes, and Characters of Books and Men*, ed. J. M. Osborn, vol. 1 (Oxford, 1966) 118–119.

[28] *Poems* (1797; Oxford, 1989), "On the Death of a Favourite Old Spaniel," 133.

[29] William Wollaston, *The Religion of Nature Delineated* (1724; New York, 1978) 203.

[30] *Scriptural and Philosophical Arguments . . . that Brutes Have Souls* (Peterhead, 1824) 17.

[31] *An Essay on the Future Life of Brute Creatures*, 2 vols. (London, 1768), I, 21.

animals, the immortality of animal souls was objectionable on emotional, moral, and religious grounds as well as on practical, economic ones. For thinkers like Samuel Taylor Coleridge, who maintained that the truth of immortality is known by self-awareness, the possession of such ideas constituted the humanity in human beings in contradistinction to animals.[32] Even "a common man would startle at hearing talk of the *Souls* of Brutes: for he connects with the word the faculty of Self-consciousness, and (on the strength of this) believes in immortality."[33] For Samuel Johnson, to take another example, the promotion of animals to immortality would, I think, have activated latent doubts about that of humans. When Richard Dean's book was mentioned in conversation by a "gentleman" (probably Boswell), Johnson "discouraged this talk" and was "offended at its continuation."[34] Boswell calls animal immortality a "curious speculation," and no doubt for most people it was merely that. Yet it had weighty support even among religious thinkers. Wesley believed it, and so did Bishop Joseph Butler, whom Coleridge thought one of "the three greatest, nay, only three *great* Metaphysicians which this Country *has* produced."[35]

In the eyes of the age, the main achievement of modern religious thought was the elaboration, through empirical study of the natural world, of the traditional argument from design. Observation of nature proved the existence and at least some attributes of its Creator. When stated in smug, popular ways, the argument from evidences of design in nature was easy to parody and laugh away. But when carefully stated, even so powerful a logician as Kant found it almost impossible to resist, though Kant believed he had refuted it. Few persons yet thought that species had evolved under the pressure of natural selection. Each species, it seemed, and each organ and instinct of a species, must have originated in a separate act of creation. Hence one could infer a Creator, and the marvelous intricacy and functional effectiveness of the

---

[32] *On the Constitution of the Church and State*, ed. John Colmer (Princeton, 1976) 47n.

[33] *Shorter Works and Fragments*, ed. H. J. Jackson and J. R. de J. Jackson, 2 vols. (Princeton, 1995), II, 958n. Anya Taylor, *Coleridge's Defense of the Human* (Columbus, 1985) 35–60, emphasizes how firmly Coleridge maintained that there is an essential distinction between humans and animals.

[34] James Boswell, *Life of Johnson*, ed. George Birkbeck Hill, rev. L. F. Powell, 6 vols. (Oxford, 1934) II, 54.

[35] Samuel Taylor Coleridge, *Collected Letters*, ed. Earl Leslie Griggs, 6 vols. (Oxford, 1956–1971) II, 703.

designs in nature proved His power and intelligence. I quote Cleanthes in David Hume's *Dialogues Concerning Natural Religion*, which was first published in 1779, three years after Hume's death: "Look round the world.... The curious adapting of means to ends, throughout all nature, resembles exactly, though it much exceeds, the productions of human contrivance—of human design, thought, wisdom, and intelligence. Since therefore the effects resemble each other, we are led to infer, by all the rules of analogy, that the causes also resemble, and that the Author of Nature is somewhat similar to the mind of man."[36] Whether Hume himself accepted this argument is uncertain. Perhaps he allowed it to prove the existence and so forth of God but not His so-called moral attributes, His goodness, His benevolence.

However, for more than two hundred years, through William Paley's *Natural Theology* (1802), which marks more or less the culmination of this discourse, the benevolence of God was evidenced by study of nature. The method of argument was to describe, often with lavish detail, the physical character and functioning of an organ or bodily part of humans or animals, to point out the necessity or use of this part for the creature, and hence to infer God's care for the creature, for its well-being. Paley describes eyes, ears, joints, and so on for pages. For brevity I quote him on the "oil with which *birds* preen their feathers.... On each side of the rump of birds is observed a small nipple, yielding upon pressure a butter-like substance, which the bird extracts by pinching the pap with its bill. With this oil or ointment, thus procured, the bird dresses his coat."[37] In this and the "vast plurality of instances in which contrivance is perceived," it "is *beneficial*" to the animal.[38]

Moreover, God had often made gratuitous provisions for creatures, that is, He had given more than mere existence would require. In Hume's *Dialogues Concerning Natural Religion* Philo somewhat anticipates the subsequent argument of natural selection: "no form ... can subsist unless it possess those powers and organs requisite for its subsistence; some new order or economy must be tried, and so on, without intermission, till at last some order which can support and maintain itself is fallen upon." To this Cleanthes replies by pointing to the generosity of the "economy": "But according to this hypothesis, whence arise

---

[36] *Dialogues Concerning Natural Religion*, ed. Nelson Pike (New York, 1970) 22.
[37] *Natural Theology* (New York, n.d.) 163.
[38] Paley, *Natural Theology* 295.

the many conveniences and advantages which men and all animals possess? Two eyes, two ears are not absolutely necessary for the subsistence of the species. . . . Though the maxims of nature be in general very frugal, yet instances of this kind are far from being rare; and any one of them is a sufficient proof of design—and of a benevolent design—which gave rise to the order and arrangement of the universe."[39] Paley makes the same argument. Capacities that "according to the established course of nature, . . . must have been given, if the animal" was to exist at all, do not "prove the goodness of God." But "there is a class of properties which may be said to be superadded from an intention expressly directed to happiness—an intention to give a happy existence . . . capacities for pleasure in cases wherein, so far as the conservation of the individual or of the species is concerned, they were not wanted, or wherein the purpose might have been secured by the operation of pain."[40] Paley mentions the pleasures of eating as an example.

However, Paley has in mind a broader truth, if it is a truth, that for most individual creatures, most of the time, existence is happy. This estimate was a necessary inference from the goodness of God, but if a reasoner took the preponderance of happiness in experience as a fact, it would tend to demonstrate God's goodness. Paley believes, as *mutatis mutandis* most intellectuals had believed for a hundred years, that nature or the Creator had attached a feeling of pleasure to the most ordinary sensations and doings of living beings—to seeing, hearing, moving, feeding, sleeping, and, generally, being alive and using their capacities. Wordsworth called it the "pleasure that there is in life itself."[41] To modern readers Wordsworth's "Lines Written in Early Spring" have been a scandal, but they went beyond the common opinions of most advanced thinkers mainly with respect to plants:

> The birds around me hopped and played,
> Their thoughts I cannot measure:—
> But the least motion which they made,
> It seemed a thrill of pleasure.
>
> The budding twigs spread out their fan,
> To catch the breezy air;

---

[39] Hume 72–73.
[40] Paley, *Natural Theology* 311–312.
[41] William Wordsworth, "Michael," line 77, in *English Romantic Writers* 324.

> And I must think, do all I can,
> That there was pleasure there.⁴²

The sober, rational Paley was hardly less visionary. "It is a happy world after all," he concludes: "Swarms of new born *flies* . . . Their sportive motions . . . testify their joy . . . in their lately discovered faculties. A *bee* among the flowers . . . so busy, and so pleased . . . fish . . . their leaps out of the water, their frolics in it . . . show their excess of spirits. . . . What a sum, collectively, of gratification and pleasure have we here before our view."⁴³ To all this happiness, gratitude was the right response.

With the argument from design so firmly in mind, to consider any natural thing, from the stars in their courses to the well-adapted, happy aphids on a leaf, might bring to mind the Author of this and all. And, as many a scholarly study has shown, the transition from this quasi-inferential knowledge of God through nature to a more emotional communion with God in nature came quickly, spread widely, and lasted well into the nineteenth century. I quote a few passages in illustration. For Henry Needler, in 1724, every part of the natural world "abounds with manifest Proofs and Instances of the Wisdom, Power, and Goodness of its Maker"; hence when Needler wanders "into the fields," his thoughts "take a Solemn and Religious Turn."⁴⁴ This solemn turn, Addison adds, "consecrates every Field and Wood"; Addison is still talking about "rational Admiration" of the "Wonders of Divine Wisdom" in natural forms, but in this passage the admiration is so intense that it consecrates the natural forms.⁴⁵ The divine is moving into the landscape, and, in the process, is endowing it with the immense appeal and significance that it retained throughout the Romantic age. In nature, as James Thomson wrote, "we feel the *present* Deity,"⁴⁶ a feeling that famously culminated, so far as poetic utterance is concerned, in Wordsworth's "Lines Composed a Few Miles above Tintern Abbey": "I have felt / A presence" in the mountains and streams, a "something far more deeply interfused . . . a spirit" that "rolls through all things."⁴⁷ So far as statement is concerned, Wordsworth

---

⁴² William Wordsworth, lines 13–20, in *English Romantic Writers* 289.

⁴³ Paley, *Natural Theology* 296–297.

⁴⁴ "Letter to D," *Works* (London, 1724) 201–202.

⁴⁵ Joseph Addison, *Spectator* 393 (1712), quoted in Willey 65.

⁴⁶ *The Seasons*, "Spring," in *Complete Poetical Works*, ed. J. Logie Robertson (London, 1908) 37.

⁴⁷ William Wordsworth, lines 93–94, 96, 100–102, in *English Romantic Writers* 302.

was actually more cautious than earlier poets on this theme. His achievement was to convey, or seem to convey, personal experience rather than doctrine—this and his grandeur of phrasing. In *An Essay on Man* Pope had written that "All are but parts of one stupendous whole, / Whose body Nature is, and God the soul." Pope admitted privately that this might "at first glance be taken for heathenism," though he denied that it was.[48] The pious Cowper equally affirmed in *The Task* that "there lives and works / A soul in all things, and that soul is God," and, going further, he added that He "is the life of all that lives."[49] In this context, Blake's "For every thing that lives is Holy" sounds neither unusual nor unorthodox.[50] To find God in "all that lives" places Him in the animals also, whose happiness is thus doubly grounded: in the first place, God made them to be happy, and we cannot think that His design is aborted; and, secondly, the happiness of animals is ultimately that of the Divine Life in them.

These religious beliefs and intuitions explain why Romantic poets usually described animals as happy—"O happy living things!" as Coleridge's Mariner said of the water snakes.[51] As with Paley's flies and fish, their happiness was signified in their motions—"they coiled and swam" (line 280)—and generally animal flights, frisks, bounds, and sounds were interpreted as expressions of delight. Thus in Wordsworth's "Resolution and Independence" the hare is "running races" and the poet assumes it is "in her mirth."[52] In Cowper's *The Task* the "bounding fawn . . . darts across the glade . . . through mere delight of heart, / And spirits buoyant with excess of glee," and the awkward gambols of cows give "such act and utt'rance as they may / To ecstasy too big to be suppress'd."[53] Similarly in the "Immortality Ode" Wordsworth takes the songs of birds and the leaps of lambs as "joyous." Wordsworth's skylark, like Shelley's, pours forth its "joy divine" in soaring and singing, and "joy awaits" his butterfly when the breeze "calls you forth again." The green linnet is the happiest among all the birds, butterflies, and flowers in the poet's orchard, as he knows by its flutters, flits,

---

[48] Pope 47, lines 267–68 and n.
[49] William Cowper, *The Task*, Book VI, "The Winter Walk at Noon," 167–168.
[50] William Blake, *The Marriage of Heaven and Hell*, in *Complete Writings* 160.
[51] Samuel Taylor Coleridge, "The Rime of the Ancient Mariner," line 282, in *The Portable Coleridge* 92.
[52] William Wordsworth, line 11, in *English Romantic Writers* 335.
[53] William Cowper, *The Task*, Book VI, "The Winter Walk at Noon," 226–227.

and trills. Though usually in eighteenth-century poetry owls had been melancholy mopers in church towers, the owls in Wordsworth's "There Was a Boy," shout a "concourse wild / Of jocund din."[54] Blake writes in *Songs of Innocence*:

> Birds delight
> Day and Night
> Nightingale
> In the dale
> Lark in Sky
> Merrily.

This vision would now be interpreted as perspectival, as belonging to the character of innocence, but, as I said, it was the usual view of Blake's time.[55] The nightingale is especially telling, for in this case ideology triumphed over poetic tradition. The conventionally lamenting nightingale or Philomela continued to sorrow in poems by Ann Radcliffe, Charlotte Smith, and Mary Robinson. But Coleridge, in his poem on the bird, replied that "In Nature there is nothing melancholy," and to his ear the bird's song was "merry."[56] Keats needed a happy bird in his "Ode to a Nightingale" and Romantic assumptions provided for it. Generally, however, Keats' poetry yields a mixed report on the happiness of animals and of nature. In "I Stood Tip-Toe" the minnows in their streams experience "sweet delight," and even the watery ripples "seem right glad" (line 81). On the other hand, there is the chilling vision of predation and "eternal fierce destruction" in the "Epistle to John Hamilton Reynolds." The suffering of animals in winter had long been a poetic topic, and Keats alludes to it in the owl and "limping hare" of "The Eve of St. Agnes."[57]

At sight of the water snakes "a spring of love" (line 284) gushed from the Mariner's heart, and this love, this sympathy, yearning, and blessing were of course the usual and the approved response to happy

---

[54] William Wordsworth, "Ode: Intimations of Immortality," line 19; "To a SkyLark" ("Up with me!"), line 12; "To a Butterfly" ("I've watched you now . . ."), line 7; "The Green Linnet"; "There Was a Boy," lines 15–16, in *English Romantic Writers* 332, 334, 343, 303.

[55] William Blake, "Spring," lines 3–9, in *Complete Writings* 123.

[56] Samuel Taylor Coleridge, "The Nightingale," lines 15, 43, in *The Portable Coleridge* 145–146.

[57] John Keats, "I Stood Tip-Toe," lines 72–80," "Epistle to John Hamilton Reynolds," line 97, "The Eve of St. Agnes," lines 2–3, in *English Romantic Writers* 1196, 1220, 1241.

animals. One "feels their happiness augment his own," said Cowper, or one longs to share it, as Wordsworth does in the "Immortality Ode," as Shelley does in "To a Skylark"— "Teach me half the gladness / That thy brain must know"—and as Keats does in his ode.[58] In Blake's *Milton* the sun becomes a surrogate of the poet observer: the "little throat" of the lark "labours with inspiration; every feather . . . vibrates with the effluence Divine," and the sun

> Stands still upon the Mountain looking on this little Bird
> With eyes of soft humility & wonder, love & awe.[59]

But this happiness belonged only to animals in their natural state, to wild animals and to domestic animals such as cattle and sheep when they were free in the fields, not being driven, branded, docked, castrated, and the like. When humans tormented animals by hunting, shooting, spurring, whipping, beating, baiting, maiming, and starving them, the happiness God willed for them was intercepted and destroyed. For religious persons mankind's ideal relation to animals was modeled in the garden of Eden, when, as Cowper described it, Adam and Eve felt "the law of universal love": "No cruel purpose lurk'd within his heart, / And no distrust of his intent in theirs"—in the hearts of animals.[60] Kindly relations with animals, which especially could be enacted with pets, might be a gesture at restoring this unfallen world.

But for wild animals the best hope, in the world as it is, was to be far off, or hidden, or at least elusive. This was one of the motivations of the many poems on wild birds. With some forgetting of fact, poets could represent in them a nature man cannot subjugate or harm, the compensatory dream of Romantic poetry. If we ask how, in general, birds are seen in this poetry, they are unseen. The owls in Wordsworth's "There Was a Boy" call out of darkness from across a lake. In Wordsworth's "To the Cuckoo" the bird is sought but "never seen," a conventional thought in poems about this bird. In Wordsworth's "The Green Linnet" the bird "deceives" the eye, cannot be followed as it flits among the leaves. Keats' nightingale is perceived only by the ear and

---

[58] William Cowper, *The Task*, Book VI, "The Winter Walk at Noon," *Poetical Works* 172; Percy Bysshe Shelley, "To a Skylark," lines 101–102, in *English Romantic Writers* 1095.

[59] William Blake, *Milton*, plate 31, lines 34–38, in *Complete Writings* 520.

[60] William Cowper, *The Task*, Book VI, "The Winter Walk at Noon," *Poetical Works* 173.

the imagination. Shelley's skylark is lost in distance and light. Felicia Hemans' "Sea-Bird Flying Inland" is visible but uncatchable and so is her "Freed Bird." Thus wild birds could represent nature as poets dearly wished it to be—inviolable.

But in fact the eggs of birds or the young chicks were regularly taken from nests and sold; the adults were netted and then eaten or imprisoned. Many a parlor kept a caged bird for the sake of its song. Estimates of the number of birds destroyed in these ways are given by Henry Mayhew for London at mid-century and are astonishing.[61] Which brings me back from poems that imagined a world without cruelty to animals to the more voluminous discourse that sought to correct it.

Those who believed that cruelty to animals was impious and would be punished were merely applying the religious teaching of their time with respect to any offense against God. But in other writings of the age a view is implicit that, as I think, has greater relevance now. We may turn again to the Mariner in Coleridge's profound poem. Critics have often mentioned that he has no motive for shooting the albatross, and this indeed seems the point. It was simply an act and expression of his own being, an instance of the unmotivated malignity that Coleridge attributed to Iago. What befalls the Mariner after the shooting is often described as a punishment. If it is, the punishment is not a consequence of the Mariner's deed. It is, again, a manifestation of his being, of his isolation (214–215, 232–233), fear (193–194, 204–205), self-contempt (lines 238–239, 246–247), death-longing (lines 261–262), and of his projection of all this into the world around him, so that the world seems foul to him. It represents the inner and outer world of a person who would shoot an albatross. His punishment is to be himself.[62] Other writers, in their pleas for sympathy with animals, did not analyze so deeply, but they perfectly understood that our relations with animals express ourselves in our attitude to the world. They did not have in mind merely that we should be compassionate, as when Christopher Smart says of his cat Jeoffry, "he is of the Lord's poor and so indeed is

---

[61] *London Labour and the London Poor*, 4 vols. (London, 1861–1862) II, 66–74. Mayhew's estimates give a total of 300,000 caged birds sold annually in London as parlor pets.

[62] For further discussion of this point see David Perkins, "The 'Ancient Mariner' and Its Interpreters: Some Versions of Coleridge," *Modern Language Quarterly* 57 (1996) 435–436.

he called by benevolence perpetually—Poor Jeoffry! poor Jeoffry!" We must also see and feel, as Smart does, that "the divine spirit comes about his body to sustain it in compleat cat."[63]

Works Cited

Addison, Joseph. *Spectator* 393 (1712).
Blake, William. *Complete Writings*. Ed. Geoffrey Keynes. London: Oxford University Press, 1966.
Boswell, James. *Life of Johnson*. Ed. George Birkbeck Hill. Rev. L. F. Powell. Vol. 2. Oxford: Clarendon Press, 1934.
Brantley, Richard E. *Locke, Wesley, and the Method of English Romanticism*. Gainesville: University Presses of Florida, 1984.
Buchan, Peter. *Scriptural and Philosophical Arguments . . . that Brutes Have Souls*. Peterhead: n.p., 1824.
Coleridge, Samuel Taylor. *Collected Letters*. Ed. Earl Leslie Griggs. Vol. 2. Oxford: Clarendon Press, 1956.
———. *The Collected Works of Samuel Taylor Coleridge*. Ed. Kathleen Coburn. 16 vols. Bollingen Series 75. Princeton: Princeton University Press, 1969–. Cited as *CC*.
———. *On the Constitution of the Church and State*. Ed. John Colmer. Princeton: Princeton University Press, 1976. *CC* Vol. X.
———. *The Portable Coleridge*. Ed. I. A. Richards. New York: Penguin, 1950.
———. *Shorter Works and Fragments*. Ed. H. J. Jackson and J. R. de J. Jackson. Vol. 2. Princeton: Princeton University Press, 1995. 2 vols. *CC* Vol. XI.
Cowper, William. *The Task. Poetical Works*. Vol. 2. London: William Pickering, 1830.
Davidoff, Leonore, and Catherine Hall. *Family Fortunes: Men and Women of the English Middle Class, 1780–1850*. London: Hutchinson, 1987.
Dean, Richard. *An Essay on the Future Life of Brute Creatures*. 2 vols. London: G. Kearsley, 1768.
De Levie, Dagobert. *The Modern Idea of the Prevention of Cruelty to Animals*. New York: S. F. Vanni, 1947.

---

[63] *Rejoice in the Lamb (Jubilate Agno)*, ed. W. F. Stead (London, 1939) 134–135.

Drummond, William H. *The Rights of Animals and Man's Obligation to Treat Them with Humanity*. London: John Mardon, 1836.

Granger, James. *An Apology for the Brute Creation, or, Abuse of Animals Censured; in a Sermon on Proverbs xii 10*. 2nd ed. London: T. Davies, 1773.

Harwood, Dix. *Love for Animals and How It Developed in Great Britain*. New York: n.p., 1928.

Hume, David. *Dialogues Concerning Natural Religion*. Ed. Nelson Pike. New York: Bobbs-Merrill, 1970.

Kean, Hilda. *Animal Rights: Political and Social Change in Britain since 1800*. London: Reaktion, 1998.

Keats, John. "Epistle to John Hamilton Reynolds," "I Stood Tip-Toe," "The Eve of St. Agnes." *English Romantic Writers*. Ed. David Perkins. 2nd ed. Fort Worth: Harcourt Brace College Publishers, 1995. 1219–1220, 1196, 1241–1246.

Kendall, Edward Augustus. *The Canary Bird: A Moral Story, Interspersed with Poetry*. Philadelphia: B. and J. Johnson, 1801.

———. *Keeper's Travels in Search of His Master*. Philadelphia: B. and J. Johnson, 1801.

Lovejoy, A. O. *The Great Chain of Being*. New York: Harper, 1960.

McFarland, Thomas. *Coleridge and the Pantheist Tradition*. Oxford: Clarendon Press, 1969.

Mayhew, Henry. *London Labour and the London Poor*. Vol. 2. London: Charles Griffin, 1861–1862.

Needler, Henry. "Letter to D." *Works*. London: J. Watts, 1724.

Paine, Thomas. *Age of Reason*. Ed. P. S. Foner. Secaucus, N.J.: Citadel, 1974.

Paley, William. *Natural Theology*. New York: American Tract Society, n.d.

———. *The Principles of Moral and Political Philosophy*. 2 vols. London: R. Faulder, 1785. New York: Garland, 1978.

Perkins, David. "The 'Ancient Mariner' and Its Interpreters: Some Versions of Coleridge." *Modern Language Quarterly* 57 (1996): 425–448.

———. "Animal Rights and 'Auguries of Innocence.'" *Blake Quarterly* 33 (1999): 4–11.

———. "Compassion for Animals and Radical Politics: Coleridge's 'To a Young Ass.'" *ELH* 65 (1998): 929–944.

———. "Cowper's Hares." *Eighteenth Century Life* 20 (1996): 57–69.

———. "Sweet Helpston! John Clare on Badger Baiting." *Studies in Romanticism* 38 (1999): 387–407.

———. "Wordsworth and the Polemic against Hunting: 'Hart-leap Well.'" *Nineteenth-Century Literature* 52 (1998): 421–445.

Pickering, Samuel F. Jr. *John Locke and Children's Books in Eighteenth-Century England.* Knoxville: University of Tennessee Press, 1981.

Plumptre, James. *Three Discourses on the Case of the Animal Creation and the Duties of Man to Them.* London: Darton, Harvey, and Darton, 1816.

Pope, Alexander. *An Essay on Man.* Ed. Maynard Mack. New Haven: Yale University Press, 1950.

Primatt, Humphry. *The Duty of Mercy and Sin of Cruelty to Beasts.* London: Cadell, 1776.

Reid, Thomas. *Lectures on Natural Theology.* Ed. Elmer H. Duncan. Washington, D.C.: University Press of America, 1981.

Ritvo, Harriet. *The Animal Estate: The English and Other Creatures in the Victorian Age.* Cambridge, Mass.: Harvard University Press, 1987.

Ryder, Richard D. *Animal Revolution.* Oxford: Basil Blackwell, 1989.

Shelley, Percy Bysshe. "To a Skylark." *English Romantic Writers.* Ed. David Perkins. 2nd ed. Fort Worth: Harcourt Brace College Publishers, 1995. 1094–1095.

Smart, Christopher. *Rejoice in the Lamb (Jubilate Agno).* Ed. W. F. Stead. London: Jonathan Cape, 1939.

Southey, Robert. *Poems.* Bristol: Joseph Cottle, 1797. Oxford: Woodstock Books, 1989.

Spence, Joseph. *Observations, Anecdotes, and Characters of Books and Men.* Ed. J. M. Osborn. Oxford: Clarendon, 1966.

Taylor, Anya. *Coleridge's Defense of the Human.* Columbus: Ohio University Press, 1985.

Thomas, Keith. *Man and the Natural World: Changing Attitudes in England, 1500–1800.* London: Allen Lane, 1983.

Thomson, James. *The Seasons. Complete Poetical Works.* Ed. J. Logie Robertson. London: Oxford University Press, 1908.

Trimmer, Sarah. *The Robins, or, Fabulous Histories, Designed for the Instruction of Children Respecting Their Treatment of Animals.* Boston: Munroe and Francis, 1822.

Turner, Ernest S. *All Heaven in a Rage.* New York: St. Martin's, 1965.

Turner, James. *Reckoning with the Beast: Animals, Pain, and Humility in the Victorian Mind*. Baltimore: Johns Hopkins University Press, 1980.

Willey, Basil. *The Eighteenth Century Background: Studies on the Idea of Nature in the Thought of the Period*. New York: Columbia University Press, 1940.

Wollaston, William. *The Religion of Nature Delineated*. 1724. New York: Garland, 1978.

Wollstonecraft, Mary. *Original Stories from Real Life*. 1791. Oxford and New York: Woodstock Books, 1990.

Wordsworth, William. Selections in *English Romantic Writers*. Ed. David Perkins. 2nd ed. Fort Worth: Harcourt Brace College Publishers, 1995. 259–470.

2

Wordsworth and Saint Francis: "A meeker man than this lived never..."

Robert Kiely

SHOULD IT ASTONISH Wordsworthians that the great poet of nature would understand and admire the great apostle of nature, Francis of Assisi?

For several reasons it should. Francis was a thirteenth-century Italian Catholic whose piety, asceticism, and literal adherence to the gospels was in strong contrast with Wordsworth's moderate, English, post-Enlightenment Christianity. Though the love of Francis had never faltered on the continent, the Order of Friars Minor had suffered internal divisions and persecution since the saint's death. In England the stereotypical friar was not thin and holy, but fat, jolly, and worldly. In Ecclesiastical Sonnet XX Wordsworth writes of "Bacchus, clothed in semblance of a Friar."[1]

Most of the time, except for a reference here and there to nuns who "fret not" or a lonely hermit in the woods, Wordsworth, like most Englishmen of his time and place, gave little thought to the figures of ancient Catholic tradition. When he did think of them, he rarely departed far from the Protestant stereotypes of decorative figures from the medieval past or of melancholy, morose wraiths who had given themselves over to a living death.

And yet when it comes to Francis, there are reasons beyond the conventional and historical ones that would seem to bind the two together. It is not simply that they loved nature, but that they loved it and experienced it in particular ways. Neither was attracted to a senti-

---

[1] From *Ecclesiastical Sonnets*, in *The Poetical Works of William Wordsworth*, ed. Ernest De Selincourt and Helen Darbishire (Oxford, 1963) 371.

mental, picturesque view of nature. In fact, though Wordsworth wrote famous "vista" poems and it is said that Francis loved looking up to the mountain on the slopes of which Assisi was built, what is striking about both is their immersion in the natural world, not their distance from it. Both encountered the awesome, sublime, destructive power of nature, yet both also reveled in the fragile details, the "little flowers" and the birds. True, Shelley and Keats wrote about birds, but did any of the Romantic poets write so often and with such fondness and intimacy about birds as Wordsworth did? Francis' way with birds had become so legendary over the centuries that it may well have been the one thing Wordsworth knew about him before his visit to Assisi in 1837 at the age of sixty-seven.

Both Francis and Wordsworth have been called pantheists and both were deeply conscious of the suspicions of orthodox Christians of their times. Yet both clung to Christianity *and* to the experiences that persuaded them of a divine presence in natural phenomena. Furthermore, both believed not only that nature spoke of God, but that it also contained lessons for the moral formation of human beings. One of Francis' favorite gospel references was to Matthew 6: 26–31, "Behold the birds of the air: for they sow not. . . . Consider the lilies of the field . . . they toil not, neither do they spin."[2] Since Francis was hardly lazy, he obviously did not take Jesus' words to be advocating sloth, but as a warning against excessive anxiety about material things. Francis was made to realize, as the son of a rich merchant, that prayer was not considered real work, just as several hundred years later it would be made clear to Wordsworth that writing poetry was, in some eyes, an idle pastime.

Francis and Wordsworth were perceived by their "practical" contemporaries not only as avoiding work, but, more particularly, as shying away from the "manly" professions of war, business, and law. By all accounts, both were characters of strong will and considerable physical courage, yet they were attracted to a human quality often held up to ridicule: meekness. Though it is also in Matthew (5: 5) that Jesus says, "Blessed are the meek, for they shall inherit the earth," in the minds of many, associations of hypocrisy, spinelessness, Uriah Heapishness have crept into the connotative atmosphere of the word.

---

[2] See *The Little Flowers of Saint Francis*, trans. Raphael Brown (New York, 1958) 76–77.

Not so for Francis. And evidently not so for Wordsworth, who sketched a moral portrait in Book IX of *The Prelude* so meek and Francis-like that it could serve as an introduction to the saint's life:

> A meeker man
> Than this lived never, or a more benign—
> Meek, though enthusiastic to the height
> Of highest expectation. Injuries
> Made *him* more gracious, and his nature then
> Did breathe its sweetness out most sensibly,
> As aromatic flowers on Alpine turf
> When foot has crushed them. He through the events
> Of that great change wandered in perfect faith
> As through a book, an old romance, or tale
> Of fairy, or some dream of actions wrought
> Behind the summer clouds. By birth he ranked
> With the most noble, but unto the poor
> Among mankind he was in service bound
> As by some tie invisible, oaths professed
> To a religious order. Man he loved
> As man, and to the mean and the obscure,
> And all the homely in their homely works,
> Transferred a courtesy which had no air
> Of condescension, but did rather seem
> A passion and a gallantry.... (*1805* IX, 298–318)[3]

In fact, this beautiful and clearly heartfelt passage is not about Francis of Assisi but about Michel Beaupuy, a young French nobleman whom Wordsworth befriended in France in 1792 and who persuaded the poet of the justice of the Revolution.[4] That the portrait is not of Francis and that, as has often been suggested, Wordsworth might have been thinking of Chaucer's knight makes its applicability to Francis all the more intriguing. True, there is a line in The Prologue to *The Canterbury Tales* that describes the knight as "meeke as is a mayde," but Wordsworth's sketch has little else in common with Chaucer's, which mainly lists the knight's battles and describes his dress. But it has al-

---

[3] All references to *The Prelude* will be to William Wordsworth, *The Prelude: The Four Texts (1798, 1799, 1805, 1850)*, ed. Jonathan Wordsworth (London, 1995).

[4] See Juliet Barker, *Wordsworth: A Life* (London, 2000) 107–109. It is thought that when Wordsworth wrote the lines in praise of Beaupuy, he feared that his friend had been killed in battle, whereas, in fact, the young officer was only wounded and went on to become a general.

most everything in common with what is known about Francis. His mother was of French nobility and his father was rich, but he "was in service . . . bound unto the poor . . . as by some tie invisible . . . to a religious order." Well before Francis wrote a simple Rule and founded an Order, he devoted himself to the poorest of the poor. His own father and most of Assisi thought him mad and hurled abuse at him as he wandered the streets begging, but "injuries made *him* more gracious." In one of Francis' most famous teachings, he equates "perfect joy" with the ability to endure injury with patience and love.[5]

Meekness for Francis, as for the idealized Beaupuy of Wordsworth's poem, did not mean weakness or passivity, but patience, resilience, and a refusal to hate one's injurers. Finally, Wordsworth's claim that his admired friend "wandered in perfect faith / As through a book, an old romance" could also be an apt description of Francis, who grew up with French romances of gallantry and applied their courtly conventions to his religious life, his devotion to "Lady Poverty," and his encouragement to his followers to treat the poor and suffering with *cortesia*, "a courtesy which had no air of condescension."

Wordsworth may have known little or nothing about Saint Francis when he wrote Book IX of *The Prelude*, but in his own way he seems to have known and loved the peculiar combination of virtues that in the Catholic world are invariably associated with Francis. We could leave the matter there as a nice coincidence of feelings and expressions. But there is at least one more chapter to the story. In 1837 Wordsworth traveled with his friend Henry Crabb Robinson to Italy, visited several of the great Franciscan holy places, including Assisi and La Verna, and wrote a poem about a bird, about Francis, and, as always, about his own response to new surroundings. With Beaupuy, the French Revolution, and much of his life and career behind him, Wordsworth still seemed ready to learn. Sometimes.

The trip was not a complete success. Though he had known Robinson for many years, the old friends were not altogether compatible travelers. Robinson liked to sleep late; Wordsworth was an early riser. Robinson loved classical antiquities; Wordsworth found them boring: "I am unable from ignorance to enjoy these sights. I receive an impression, but that is all."[6] Robinson was five years younger than Words-

---

[5] *Little Flowers* 58–60.
[6] Barker, *Wordsworth: A Life* 685.

worth, who became increasingly homesick and conscious of his age as the weeks of sightseeing wore on. From Rome he wrote to his family: "Of churches and pictures and statues in them I am fairly tired—in fact, I am too old in head, limbs and eyesight for such hard work."[7] But like all sensitive tourists, Wordsworth had his moments: watching a sunset over the Pincio; meeting Keats' friend Joseph Severn; he even admired the interior of St. Peter's (unlike George Eliot and her heroine Dorothea Brooke, who were depressed by it).

Though he was weary and a little sick of sights, Assisi and La Verna clearly touched Wordsworth and awakened an interest in and sympathy for Francis that must have surprised him and his traveling companion. Robinson recalled: "He made inquiries for St. Francis' biography, as if he would dub him his Leibheiliger (body-saint), as Goethe (saying everyone must have one) declared St. Philip Neri to be his."[8] Goethe and a clumsy translation from the German seem a roundabout way, in Italy of all places, to refer to a patron saint, but both Robinson and Wordsworth were always at pains to retain their Protestant distance even while taking an interest in a Catholic hero. Indeed, the hero that Wordsworth had most in mind while visiting monastic sites in Italy was his own most Protestant, most English "body-poet," Milton. In May, while still abroad, he placed at the top of a letter to Dora the opening lines of *Stanzas, Composed in the Simplon Pass*:

> Vallombrosa! I longed in thy shadiest wood
> To linger reclined on the moss-covered floor. (1–2)

Wordsworth's visit to Vallombrosa did not live up to expectations. He quarreled with Robinson, who preferred to sleep in rather than get up at five to climb another mountain. Wordsworth went alone with an Italian guide, who got lost. When he finally arrived at the monastery, he did not find it in a shady valley but on a promontory that did not fit at all with his imagined Miltonic picture.

The trip to La Verna was another matter altogether. The small friary sits at the edge of a steep precipice of vast rock outcroppings that appear to have been thrust up from the earth and split into weird shapes by some prehistoric geological upheaval. There is no way to approach,

---

[7] *The Letters of William and Dorothy Wordsworth, Second Edition, VI, The Later Years, Part III, 1835–1839*, ed. Alan G. Hill (Oxford, 1982) 399–400.
[8] *Poetical Works* 496.

still today, except through a thick forest of beech and pine. No Miltonic or other English literary allusions are associated with the spot, but for Franciscans it is, next to Assisi, the holiest of places, because it was there that Francis received the stigmata, the five wounds of Christ on the cross. It is also on the path leading through the woods below the sanctuary that there is a small chapel marking the spot where Francis is said to have preached to the birds.

Wordsworth's poem "The Cuckoo at La Verna, May 25, 1837" recollects, like some of his greatest lyrics, the poet's reaction to a natural setting that somehow has the power to arouse strong feelings in the beholder. But what emotion could the aging English Lake poet feel en route to a Franciscan holy place revered by Catholics as the site of a bloody miracle that repelled most Protestants as a grotesque fiction?

At the poem's outset, the poet is aroused not by strangeness, but by familiarity, not by the Franciscan sublime (or ridiculous or grotesque), but by a homely, modest, almost English sound:

> List—'twas the Cuckoo, O with what delight
> Heard I that voice! And catch it now, though faint,
> Far off and faint, and melting into air,
> Yet not to be mistaken. Hark again! (1–4)[9]

There is a triple poignancy in this opening of the poem. The homesick poet is like a grateful child who encounters a friendly, familiar voice in an alien land: "Thanks, happy Creature, / For this unthought-of greeting!" (7–8). He goes on to say that he has heard nightingales and thrushes during his Italian trip "blending as in a common English grove" (23), but until this moment the "vagrant Voice" (27) of the cuckoo "was wanting" (line 28). Robinson later reported that, in fact, he had heard the bird first and "that it absolutely fretted [Wordsworth] that my ear was first favored; and that he exclaimed with delight, 'I hear it! I hear it!'"[10] Already feeling his age earlier in the Italian trip, Wordsworth—always sensitive to the meaningful moment—must have felt a mixed sensation of pleasure in hearing the reassuringly familiar sound and sadness (as well as fretfulness) that he did not hear it as

---

[9] All quotations from "The Cuckoo at La Verna" are from De Selincourt and Darbishire 218–222. For a discussion of religious elements in Wordsworth's earlier poem "To the Cuckoo," see John L. Mahoney, *William Wordsworth: A Poetic Life* (New York, 1997) 173–174.

[10] *Poetical Works* 496.

quickly or perhaps as clearly as his companion. "Faint, far off, and faint" describes not only the bird's call but the poet's hearing, and perhaps, by extension, the poet's sensibility.

But there is another element in the poet's response that lifts the poem toward a narrative goal and away from its lyrical opening of mixed delight and sadness. By this time in his trip, Wordsworth knew the story of Francis preaching to the birds and that his encounter with the cuckoo had occurred in very nearly the same place as Francis' sermon was supposed to have occurred. Robinson wrote: "It was at La Verna too, that he had led me to expect that he had found a subject on which he would write; and that was the love which birds bore to St. Francis."[11] The sound of the cuckoo brings the poet momentarily back to England, to himself as an old man a little hard of hearing, and now, too, to the little Italian beggar-saint who also had a special relationship with birds:

> And he went toward the birds that were on the ground. And as soon as he began to preach, all the birds that were on the trees came down toward him. And all of them stayed motionless even though he went among them, touching many with his habit. But not a single one of them made the slightest move, and later they did not leave until he had given them his blessing. . . . "My little bird sisters, you owe much to God your Creator, and you must always and everywhere praise Him, because He has given you freedom to fly anywhere. . . . Be careful not to be ungrateful, but strive always to praise God."[12]

Though written nearly a hundred years after the death of Francis, this episode from *The Little Flowers of Saint Francis* (*I Fioretti*) captures the tone and flavor of much that was recalled and written about the saint by those who knew him. There is a deliberate innocence, simplicity, fairy-tale quality throughout, and the homily is clear. Francis' love of life extended to every living creature and gave him an extraordinary ability to draw the natural world into a peaceful and *silent* witness to his goodness and into his sermon. Not the birds' song but the preacher's words are what are featured here. Though monks and nuns are frequently assumed in post-Reformation literature to be "imprisoned" behind walls and in cells, Francis celebrates the "freedom" of the birds and, by association, his own freedom and that of his followers (who

---

[11] *Poetical Works* 496.
[12] *Little Flowers* 76–77.

were listening too) from the burden of material possessions. The birds do finally sing in this story ("and in the air they sang a wonderful song") but only after Francis has blessed them and tuned them up, as it were, to praise God.

Unless we think of early poems like "We Are Seven," "Anecdote for Fathers," or "The Idiot Boy," this does not sound much like Wordsworth or indeed like anything that the Wordsworth of 1837, tired, out of sorts, fed up with Robinson, sick of Italian piety, would have liked. And, sure enough, after hearing the cheering note of the cuckoo, the poet turns his sights up to the "far-famed Pile" (29) and does not especially like what he sees, "a Christian fortress" (32), and imagines inside it, "a stern society, / Dead to the world" (34–35). Hardly what Wordsworth admired or Francis had in mind. Yet, as in his most characteristic and greatest poems, the poet reflects a *movement* of mind and heart and language. His mood softens and with it his vision of the place. To his and perhaps the reader's surprise, Francis enables the change:

> His milder Genius (thanks to the good God
> That made us) over these severe restraints
> Of mind, that dread, heart-freezing discipline,
> Doth sometimes here predominate, and works
> By unsought means for gracious purposes;
> For earth through heaven, for heaven, by changeful earth,
> Illustrated, and mutually endeared. (42–48)

For a moment, we almost hear ("though faint, far off and faint") the younger Wordsworth in these lines that transform abstraction into feeling, prosaic detachment into lyrical empathy.

As he continues his meditation on Francis, the poem becomes more and more private and for Wordsworth more immediate. He surely knew that English readers of the time would have been unfamiliar with the details of Francis' life and with his great poem "The Canticle of Brother Sun." Yet he weaves the praises and acts of Francis into his verse as though they were Miltonic echoes resonating in and lending inspiration to his own thoughts:

> Rapt though he were above the power of sense,
> Familiarly, yet out of the cleansed heart
> Of that once sinful being overflowed
> On sun, moon, stars, the nether elements,

>   And every shape of creature they sustain,
>   Divine affections; and with beast and bird
>   (Stilled from afar—such marvel story tells—
>   By casual outbreak of his passionate words,
>   And from their own pursuits in field or grove
>   Drawn to his side by look or act of love
>   Humane, and virtue of his innocent life)
>   He wont to hold companionship so free,
>   So pure, so fraught with knowledge and delight,
>   As to be likened in his Followers' minds
>   To that which our first parents, ere the fall
>   From their high state darkened the earth with fear,
>   Held with all Kinds in Eden's blissful bowers. (49–65)

True, Milton does creep in at the end, but the passage is really an astonishing tribute to Francis and a mark of Wordsworth's awe and perhaps envy of the saint, as though he were a younger, purer, happier self in such harmony with the earth as to have resembled Adam before the Fall, the original poet who "by casual outbreak of his passionate words," named every living animal and made them his companions. Having read or heard that Francis had sown his own wild oats as a young man, Wordsworth finds another unexpected bond with the holy man, "that once sinful being," who, with innocence restored, could respond to nature with a poet's rapture. Though he does not quote Francis' "Canticle," Wordsworth distills and paraphrases certain of its lines:

>   Be praised, my Lord, with all your creatures,
>   Especially Sir Brother Sun.
>   By whom you give us the light of day!
>   And he is beautiful and radiant with great splendor.
>   Of You, Most High, he is a symbol.
>   Be praised, my Lord, for Sister Moon and the Stars. . . .
>   Be praised, My Lord, for Brother Wind. . . .
>   Be praised, My Lord, for Sister Water. . . .
>   Be praised, My Lord, for Brother Fire.
>   Be praised, My Lord, for our Sister Mother Earth. . . .[13]

His mood mellowed, almost sweetened by the example of Francis, whose meekness (*dolcezza*) was renowned, the English poet becomes

---

[13] *Little Flowers* 317–318.

open to the possibility that despite his prejudice, some of the friars may also be similarly inspired by the saint:

> Then question not that, 'mid the austere Band,
> Who breathe the air he breathed, tread where he trod,
> Some true partakers of his loving spirit
> Do still survive.... (66–69)

The poet seems at least momentarily persuaded that the "loving spirit" of the saint can turn these apparently stern and austere "monks" into human beings. (Though Franciscans are friars, not monks, Wordsworth uses the generic term for male members of religious orders.) As usual, Wordsworth, unlike Francis, is also thinking of himself. After all, he, too, is breathing the air the saint breathed while at La Verna; he, too, treads where the saint trod. If a weary poet past his prime can be touched and enlivened here, why shouldn't it be possible for a few Italian Franciscans living on the mountain to be flesh-and-blood persons rather than stereotypes out of a Gothic romance by Mrs. Radcliffe? In a sudden moment of self-knowledge, the poet seems to be thinking, "If it can happen to me, it can happen to anyone!"

Wordsworth makes peace and poetry out of the place because all at once he can see himself in it:

> Thus sensitive must be the Monk, though pale
> With fasts, with vigils worn, depressed by years,
> Whom in a sunny glade I chanced to see,
> Upon a pine-tree's storm-uprooted trunk,
> Seated alone, with forehead skyward raised.... (74–78)

The cuckoo may have reminded him of home, but in the sensitive monk sitting alone on a stump, the poet and the reader are reminded of one of Wordsworth's favorite figures, of himself and of those he most responded to, the solitary immersed in thought, alone in nature, mysterious and apart, yet somehow linked to the observer in a moment of time and space.

As Wordsworth lets his imaginative sympathy rather than his fatigue and his prejudice lead him on, he moves closer and closer to an identification with another friar he sees:

> A young Ascetic—Poet, Hero, Sage,
> He might have been, Lover belike he was—
> If they received into a conscious ear

> The notes whose first faint greeting startled me,
> Whose sedulous iteration thrilled with joy
> My heart. . . . (86–91)

The thought that a friar might have had the same pleasure, the same sensation of joy that he did in hearing the cuckoo is almost too much for the poet to contemplate for more than a moment. The empathic mood is abruptly broken, "Ah! not like me." But why not like him? Is this a failure of the older poet's imagination? A failure of faith in the "loving spirit" of Francis? A return to reserve and skepticism about the human nature of monks? The poem's answer is somewhat confused. The poet wonders not only whether the young friar's heart was thrilled by the bird's call, but whether he

> . . . may have been moved like me to think,
> Ah! not like me who walk in the world's ways,
> On the great Prophet, styled *The voice of one
> Crying amid the wilderness.* . . . (91–94)

How did John the Baptist suddenly get into the picture? The poet's imaginative sympathy is broken, and the poetry's momentary fusion of identities becomes a syntactical and logical tangle. While wondering whether a monk is as thrilled by the birdsong as he is, the poet (a little strangely) associates that song with a familiar biblical text and then performs a double somersault, first attributing the thought to himself *and* the friar, and then extricating himself on the grounds that he is too worldly for such an idea. But, of course, it *is* his poem and his analogy. Neither he nor we have any idea what the solitary friars are thinking when they hear the cuckoo. It may be prayerful musing; it may be visions of the next meal rather than the next world.

Wordsworth's quoting the King James Version of John the Baptist's quoting Isaiah sounds a false note, a wordy intrusion on this otherwise peaceful scene, an English and Protestant way of assuming how "religious" people think. This is perhaps just another way of saying that the poet's reverie is broken and he has returned to his ordinary self. Why does it sound more like a stumble than a smooth step back? After all, the analogy does make a certain kind of sense. Cuckoos are woodland creatures; their song can be heard from great distances; or, as in the case of the poet, not heard at all amid the creaking of branches and the inattention of a pilgrim-tourist. Perhaps it is the neat logic of the analogy that is the problem. It seems *thought* rather than *heard*.

In the end, the poet does think himself pleasantly out of the place, the poem, the dilemma. "Fare-thee-well; sweet Bird! / If that substantial title please thee more" (103–104). The bird has returned to being just a bird. Instead of a Franciscan blessing, the poet takes leave of the cuckoo with a friendly "good wish," an almost Shakespearean epilogue:

> . . . from bower
> To bower as green, from sky to sky as clear,
> Thee gentle breezes waft—or airs that meet
> Thy course and sport around thee softly fan—
> Till night, descending upon hill and vale,
> Grants to thy mission a brief term of silence.
> And folds thy pinions up in blest repose. (106–112)

If Wordsworth had not been old and worried about his health and if the occasion for this poem had not been La Verna and the inspiration had not been Saint Francis, as well as the song of the cuckoo, this lovely, conventional ending would be easier to read. But Wordsworth was feeling his age and thinking more and more about death, not as an abstraction but as something that was going to happen to him. Furthermore, having come to La Verna filled with curiosity about Francis, he had to have known that the very reason that the place was so revered by Franciscans was its association with Francis' greatest suffering and most mysterious visionary experience of the crucified Jesus. No doubt the specifics of the miracle would have been puzzling to Wordsworth as they have been even to Francis' most devout followers. But the fact that Francis faced suffering and death so directly, so fearlessly, so physically and emotionally *present* cannot have escaped Wordsworth.

Yet the poem touches on none of this. Indeed, at the very moment of strongest identification with a friar, another Francis, "a young ascetic—Poet, Hero, Sage," the poet rears back, "Ah! not like me." And it as this point that the *"voice of one crying amid the wilderness"* is heard. There is an emotional logic to the moment after all. The poet who, in the conclusion of *The Prelude*, spoke of himself and Coleridge as "prophets of nature" recalls his role as one bringing good news to an inattentive world. "Crying" seems more applicable to the Baptist and to the aging Wordsworth than to the faint call of the cuckoo or the silent rapture of Francis at La Verna. Wordsworth is not ready—even in his imagination—to go all the way with his "body-saint," but prefers, with some regret, to comfort his reader and himself with thoughts of "a brief term of silence" and "blest repose."

* * *

According to Kierkegaard in "Of the Difference Between a Genius and an Apostle," we have no business comparing a poet with a saint, a "genius" with an "apostle." Geniuses are born; apostles are called. Geniuses derive their momentary authority from their talents; apostles derive their permanent authority from God.[14] In the conclusion to his essay, Kierkegaard draws the contrast in a way of particular interest for this discussion of Francis and Wordsworth:

> The lyrical author is only concerned with his production, enjoys the pleasure of producing . . . but he has nothing to do with others, he does not write *in order that*: in order to enlighten men or in order to help them along the right road. . . . No genius has an *in order that*; the Apostle has, absolutely and paradoxically, an *in order that*.[15]

Wordsworth would have had trouble with this distinction. In the conclusion to *The Prelude*, he speaks of himself and Coleridge as "joint labourers in a work." In the 1805 version (XIII, 441) the work is "redemption"; in the 1850 version (XIV, 443), "deliverance." Either way, the intended labor has a powerful, "inspired" *in order that*:

> Though men return to servitude as fast
> As the tide ebbs . . .
>   we shall still
> Find solace in the knowledge which we have,
> Blest with true happiness if we may be
> United helpers forward of a day
> Of firmer trust, joint labourers in a work—
> Should Providence such grace to us vouchsafe—
> Of their redemption, surely yet to come.
> Prophets of nature, we to them will speak
> A lasting inspiration, sanctified

---

[14] Søren Kierkegaard, "Of the Difference Between a Genius and an Apostle," in *The Present Age*, trans. Alexander Dru (London, 1969) 107–110.

[15] "Of the Difference Between a Genius and an Apostle" 127.

> By reason and by truth. What we have loved
> Others will love, and we may teach them how.... (*1805* XIII, 433–445)

In Kierkegaard's terminology, Wordsworth was a "genius" trying to be an "apostle" whereas Francis was an "apostle" called by God to speak and act with divine authority. And though Wordsworth refers to the saint's "milder Genius" in his poem, Francis preferred to call himself a fool. "Reason and truth" were not unknown to him, but "love" and "joy" came more readily to his mind, as "faith" and "grace" come more readily to ours when we think of him. We need not accept Kierkegaard's definitions rigidly to see that Francis and Wordsworth do finally belong to different "spheres," not merely different eras, cultures, and languages, but to different conceptions and experiences of the intersection of the divine and the human. The important and interesting question, especially for historians and literary scholars, is whether and how the two can meet. Wordsworth's trip to La Verna and the poem that resulted provide one answer. While not one of the poet's great works, "The Cuckoo at La Verna" is one of the most charged and provocative of his later pieces. It shows the poet reaching yet again into another realm, warming to familiarity in difference, and retreating, a little clumsily, but not altogether without grace or reason, when the demand becomes too great.

As for what Francis might have thought of Wordsworth, it is not hard to say. The saint was not a great reader, but he was an early riser and he had to have loved another birdwatcher.

Works Cited

Barker, Juliet. *Wordsworth: A Life*. London: Viking Press, 2000.
Brown, Raphael, trans. *The Little Flowers of Saint Francis*. New York, Doubleday, 1958.
Kierkegaard, Søren. "Of the Difference Between a Genius and an Apostle." *The Present Age*. Trans. Alexander Dru. London: The Fontana Library, 1969.
Mahoney, John L. *Wordsworth: A Poetic Life*. New York: Fordham University Press, 1997.
Wordsworth, William. *The Poetical Works of William Wordsworth*. Ed.

Ernest de Selincourt and Helen Darbishire. 5 vols. Oxford: Clarendon Press, 1963–1966.

———. *The Prelude: The Four Texts*. Ed. Jonathan Wordsworth. London: Penguin, 1995.

———, and Dorothy Wordsworth. *The Letters of William and Dorothy Wordsworth*. Ed. Alan G. Hill. Vol. VI. 2nd ed. Oxford: Clarendon, 1982.

3

Wordsworth's Abbey Ruins

Dennis Taylor

ONE OF THE PERENNIAL QUESTIONS in Wordsworth criticism is: where is the abbey in "Tintern Abbey"? The easiest answer is that it is merely a place in Wordsworth's title, "Lines Composed a Few Miles above Tintern Abbey, on Revisiting the Banks of the Wye during a Tour. July 13, 1798." Though Wordsworth called the poem "Tintern Abbey," the abbey is arguably merely a place used to identify the spot on the river Wye that Wordsworth revisited in 1798. Presumably the poem might have been subtitled "A few miles above Chichester Common" or "Above Birnum Woods" if these had been the nearby places.

One oddity is that Wordsworth's tour at this time included several visits to the abbey itself. Another is that the nature scene described in the poem might well have been inspired by Wordsworth's early experience in the Lake Country, by the river Derwent celebrated in *An Evening Walk*. Another oddity is that Wordsworth referred to the poem as "Tintern Abbey," though this may have been simple shorthand. And still another is simply the fact that Tintern Abbey is the major signifying marker for the poem in the minds of generations of readers.

But there is occasional speculation that the abbey does in fact cast its shadow in the poem, if only by its absence.[1] Indeed an influential new historicist interpretation of recent years argues that Wordsworth forcibly keeps out of the poem the beggars and industrial pollution associated with the abbey in 1798 and described by William Gilpin in his *Observations on the River Wye* (1782). Thus the vagrants and smoke in the first verse paragraph indicate a reality that Wordsworth has chosen to suppress in favor of the imaginative subjectivity of the poem.[2]

---

[1] See Peter A. Brier, "Reflections on Tintern Abbey," *The Wordsworth Circle* 5 (1974): 5–6.

[2] See Marjorie Levinson, *Wordsworth's Great Period Poems* (Cambridge, 1986) 37–38.

But I would argue that the real question is not "Where are the beggars?" but rather "Where is the Abbey?" Tintern Abbey is, like Poe's purloined letter, visible throughout but unseen by the untrained eye. We need to look, once more, at the opening lines:

> Five years have past; five summers, with the length
> Of five long winters! and again I hear
> These waters, rolling from their mountain-springs
> With a soft inland murmur.—Once again
> Do I behold these steep and lofty cliffs,
> That on a wild secluded scene impress
> Thoughts of more deep seclusion; and connect
> The landscape with the quiet of the sky.
> The day is come when I again repose
> Here, under this dark sycamore, and view
> These plots of cottage-ground, these orchard-tufts,
> Which at this season, with their unripe fruits,
> Are clad in one green hue, and lose themselves
> 'Mid groves and copses. Once again I see
> These hedge-rows, hardly hedge-rows, little lines
> Of sportive wood run wild: these pastoral farms,
> Green to the very door; and wreaths of smoke
> Sent up, in silence, from among the trees!
> With some uncertain notice, as might seem
> Of vagrant dwellers in the houseless woods,
> Or of some Hermit's cave, where by his fire
> The Hermit sits alone.[3] (1–22)

I would argue that the Abbey is all through these lines, but first we need to look at an unnoticed part of Wordsworth's career, his empathy for the Catholic spirituality especially associated with monasteries and convents. I should caution that this argument is not of the "Shakespeare was an Irish Catholic" school of thought. Wordsworth thought of himself as a good Protestant, nationalistic, loyal (increasingly) to the Church of England, deeply suspicious of papal power and priestly superstition. He is rightly thought of as the poet of imaginative liberty, of natural landscape, even at his best as a poet who secularizes the religious tradition into a celebration of "the very world which is the

---

[3] Quotations from Wordsworth's poetry, except *The Prelude*, are taken from Wordsworth, *The Poems*, ed. John O. Hayden (New Haven, 1981).

world / Of all of us, the place in which, in the end, / We find our happiness, or not at all."[4] But this is only half the story.

If we simply numbered the Catholic images, or Catholic words, in Wordsworth, he would seem the most Catholic of poets. His poems abound with images of monasteries, hermitages, hermits, Catholic shrines, Catholic processions, nuns, saints, the Virgin Mary, priests. A few of these are, of course, Anglican, but the vast majority are specifically papist. Many of these images occur in poems that are not much discussed in Wordsworth criticism, and therefore the images and their importance go unnoticed. But they also abound in the canonical poems, so much so that there almost seems a conspiracy of silence about them. For what it is worth, a simple check of the concordance[5] shows how frequently Wordsworth uses Catholic terms and their cognates with positive connotation, like *nun* (17), *convent* (30), *Mass* (11), *cell* (81), *cloister* (19), *anchorite* (4), *abbey* (17), *recluse* (6), *Virgin* (12), *monk* (35) (though *monkish* occasionally carries a negative weight), *hermit* (34) and manifold references to the Virgin Mary and to Catholic saints. *Hermit*, incidentally, carries for Wordsworth a specifically Catholic association, as in "The Excursion" (7.302–305):

> The hermit, lodged
> Amid the untrodden desert, tells his beads,
> With each repeating its allotted prayer
> And thus divides and thus relieves the time....

In addition to these words are a host of terms which often take on Catholic associations: hallowed, litany, sainted, saint, altar, church, prayer, chapel, priest, holy, shrine, pilgrim, retreat, Madonna, benediction, altar, sacred, grace, sanctity, votary, angels, temple, blessed, rite, prayer, etc. Distinguishing the Catholic, Anglican, and secularized associations of these words is, of course, part of the critical task.

What was the importance of Catholicism for Wordsworth? I would argue that it offered him a major analogy for his most important psy-

---

[4] Wordsworth, *The Prelude* (*1805*), X, 725–727. Quotations from *The Prelude* are taken from *The Prelude 1799, 1805, 1850*, ed. Jonathan Wordsworth, M. H Abrams, and Stephen Gill (New York, 1979).

[5] See Lane Cooper, ed., *A Concordance to the Poems of William Wordsworth* (London, 1911). This concordance does not include some poems like "The Tuft of Primroses" which is laden with the relevant words.

chological experience, the experience of "spots of time." The analogy is that of the solitude of contemplation experienced by the monk or hermit. We can illustrate this by glancing at one of Wordsworth's earlier poems, written before his career took a more overtly religious turn after 1805. "Descriptive Sketches," written in 1790–1792, after his first trip to France, begins (I am quoting the revised version of 1836):

> Were there, below, a spot of holy ground,
> Where from distress a refuge might be found,
> And solitude prepare the soul for heaven;
> Sure, nature's God that spot to man had given
> Where falls the purple morning far and wide
> In flakes of light upon the mountain-side,
> Where with loud voice the power of water shakes
> The leafy wood, or sleeps in quiet lakes. (1–10)

This is a generic description which could apply to Wordsworth's early experience of the Lake Country, as well as the French and Swiss countryside of his walking tour. Wordsworth is larger than his critics because his poetry defines the sacred moment in a way much richer than any critic has been able to parse. In these opening lines, we can simply point to the idea of a sacred place, a refuge, where a deeply religious solitude is experienced, a sense of "peculiar grace, / A leading from above, a something given" (in the words of "Resolution and Independence") in a setting often surrounded by mountains, as if by walls, creating a valley filled with light, both physical and spiritual.

But these lines are only a beginning. Where they lead is not to Paris, the scene of revolutionary liberty (which Wordsworth then applauded), but to a place not often discussed in Wordsworth criticism: the Cistercian monastery of La Grande Chartreuse in France. To describe the effect of the monastery on Wordsworth at this time, I will use later lines from the 1850 *Prelude*:

> . . . an awful *solitude*:
> Yes, for even then no other than a place
> Of soul-affecting *solitude* appeared
> That far-famed region, though our eyes had seen,
> As toward the sacred mansion we advanced,
> Arms flashing, and a military glare
> Of riotous men commissioned to expel
> The blameless inmates, and belike subvert

> That frame of social being, which so long
> Had bodied forth the ghostliness of things
> In silence visible and perpetual calm.
> —'Stay, stay your sacrilegious hands!'—The voice
> Was Nature's, uttered from her Alpine throne;
> I heard it then and seem to hear it now—
> 'Your impious work forbear, perish what may,
> Let this one temple last, be this one spot
> Of earth devoted to eternity!'
> She ceased to speak, but while St. Bruno's pines
> Waved their dark tops, not silent as they wave,
> And while below, along the several beds,
> Murmured the sister streams of Life and Death,
> Thus by conflicting passions pressed, my heart
> Responded....
> '... be the house redeemed
> With its unworldly votaries, for the sake
> Of conquest over sense, hourly achieved
> Through faith and meditative reason, resting
> Upon the word of heaven-imparted truth,
> Calmly triumphant; and for humbler claim
> Of that imaginative impulse sent
> From these majestic floods, yon shining cliffs,
> The untransmuted shapes of many worlds,
> Cerulean ether's pure inhabitants,
> These forests unapproachable by death,
> That shall endure as long as man endures,
> To think. to hope, to worship, and to feel,
> To struggle, to be lost within himself
> In trepidation, from the blank abyss
> To look with bodily eyes, and be consoled.'
> (VI, 414–436, 451–466)

The 1850 version intensifies and expands the experience given in "Descriptive Sketches" and again in the 1805 *Prelude*. "Solitude" is italicized, as though being discovered clearly for the first time. The monastery, about to be stripped, has "bodied forth the ghostliness of things," an embodiment of those eternal intersections characterizing the more personal spots of time, but a ghostly one, eerily Gothic in some respects. And Nature enforces the parallel with the other spots of time by insisting: "be this one spot / Of earth devoted to eternity!"

There are various complications to the passage, and to Wordsworth's experience of Catholicism generally. On the one hand, these places of monastic solitude are the "real thing," in Henry James' sense, where monks contemplated nature and God, and where their contemplation was authenticated by centuries of religious practice. On the other hand, Chartreuse is also a stern and forbidding place, with its history of harsh penitence, "conquest over sense, hourly achieved." This aspect of monastic discipline threatens Wordsworth's liberty of imagination, and indeed underscores for him the more sinister aspects of Catholicism, its cold power, its tyranny, its Gothic dark. But even in these lines, Wordsworth puts the harsher silence next to a softer mode, for he also credits the Chartreuse with the "humbler claim / Of that imaginative impulse sent / From these majestic floods, yon shining cliffs / . . . These forests." So Catholic solitude can go either into the richness of gentle personal contemplation in a natural setting, or into something threatening to Wordsworth's sense of his own individuality, not to speak of his loyalty to his beloved English countryside, dotted with Anglican spires.

There are at least two things that connect the passage with "Tintern Abbey." One is the use of the word *mansion*, used here to describe the "sacred mansion" of Chartreuse, and in "Tintern Abbey" to describe the imaginative mind, in this case Dorothy's:

> . . . thy mind
> Shall be a mansion for all lovely forms,
> Thy memory be as a dwelling-place
> For all sweet sounds and harmonies. . . . (139–142)

Another connection is the very shape of the setting, where the "imaginative impulse" is "sent / From these majestic floods, yon shining cliffs / . . . These forests." This sense of enclosure connects with lines from "Tintern Abbey":

> these steep and lofty cliffs,
> That on a wild secluded scene impress
> Thoughts of more deep seclusion; and connect
> The landscape with the quiet of the sky. (5–8)

The Chartreuse experience contains another theme of profound importance to Wordsworth, a theme increasingly important in recent "revisionist" discussions of English Reformation history. It is a theme embodied in Eamon Duffy's title, *The Stripping of the Altars*, a book that describes the destruction of English Catholic culture and religion during the Elizabethan years.[6] This theme is not just confined to the English Reformation; it extends itself in other recent works into discussions of the way modern Protestant culture is haunted by its destroyed Catholic past. A preeminent example of this latter discussion is Jenny Franchot's *Roads to Rome*, which discusses how nineteenth-century Protestant culture in America is haunted by its Catholic 'other,' the alien Italianate Christianity that both attracts and repels writers like Longfellow and Hawthorne.[7] In alluding so briefly to an immense body of scholarship, of which Duffy and Franchot are only the tips of the iceberg, I simply want to suggest how the topic of Wordsworth and Catholicism is part of a much larger topic of growing importance: English (and American) Catholic and Protestant relations. Wordsworth, I would argue, is an unnoticed major participant in this discussion, as suggested by this passage from *The Prelude*:[8]

> —'Stay, stay your sacrilegious hands!'—The voice
> Was Nature's, uttered from her Alpine throne;
> I heard it then and seem to hear it now—
> 'Your impious work forbear, perish what may,
> Let this one temple last, be this one spot
> Of earth devoted to eternity!' (*1850* VI, 425–430)

The warning against sacrilege comes not from the Church, but from Nature. The symbiosis between the abbey and the natural setting is so close that to destroy one is to destroy the other. The stripping of the altars becomes a stripping of nature, a destruction of the sacred place where the spot of time occurs.

So we see another connection with "Tintern Abbey." The poem does not refer to a living monastery, like the ones Wordsworth experienced in France, but to a ruin, a set of gutted rooms, an outline only of chapel and dormitory, "bare ruined choirs where late the sweet birds sang," now overgrown with moss and ivy and brush. Wordsworth had

---

[6] *The Stripping of the Altars: Traditional Religion in England c. 1400–c. 1850* (New Haven, 1992).

[7] *Roads to Rome: The Antebellum Protestant Encounter with Catholicism* (Berkeley, 1994).

[8] Wordsworth's *Ecclesiastical Sonnets* are also an important part of this tradition. Although the sonnets defend Protestantism, "yet the negative always seems tinged with some regret that the delicate balance of reforming and preserving had not been maintained"; John L. Mahoney, *William Wordsworth: A Poetic Life* (New York, 1997) 249.

experienced such abbeys before he went to France; and one of them, Furness Abbey, was a companion to some of his earliest spots of time. But Wordsworth's trip to the continent taught him an astonishing lesson. What was now happening to the monasteries on the continent had happened to the monasteries in England. The raw ragged ruins of the freshly destroyed buildings in France were the same as those in the English countryside, but these English ruins had been overgrown, had become picturesque, had become the setting of paintings and poems and a whole school of melancholy. Startlingly, so I would argue, Wordsworth realized the parallel between the continent now and England then. Chartreuse now was Tintern Abbey then.

William Gilpin's book, a likely source for Wordsworth and one invoked by the new historicists, can be our guide here:

> A more pleasing retreat could not easily be found. The woods, and glades intermixed; the winding of the river; the variety of the ground; the splendid ruin, contrasted with the objects of nature; and the elegant line formed by the summits of the hills, which include the whole; make all together a very inchanting piece of scenery. Every thing around breathes an air so calm, and tranquil; so sequesterd, a man of warm imagination, in monkish times, might have been allured by such a scene to become an inhabitant of it. . . . Nature has made it [the abbey] her own. Time has worn off all traces of the rule; it has blunted the sharp edges of the chissel; and broken the regularity of opposing parts. . . . To these [windows] are superadded the ornaments of time. Ivy, in masses uncommonly large, has taken possession of many parts of the wall. . . . Mosses of various hues, with lychens, maiden-hair, penny-leaf, and other humble plants, overspread the surface. . . . The pavement is obliterated: the elevation of the choir is no longer visible: the whole area is reduced to one level . . . covered with neat turf, closely shorn.[9]

There follows the description of the homeless inhabitants of the abbey, including one poor woman who had taken over "the remnant of a shattered cloister. . . . It was her own mansion." Again the word, mansion!

The parallels with the first stanza of "Tintern Abbey" should now be more clearly coming into view:

> These plots of cottage-ground, these orchard-tufts,
> Which at this season, with their unripe fruits,
> Are clad in one green hue, and lose themselves

---

[9] *Observations on the River Wye* (1782; Oxford, 1991) 32–34.

> 'Mid groves and copses. Once again I see
> These hedge-rows, hardly hedge-rows, little lines
> Of sportive wood run wild: these pastoral farms,
> Green to the very door; and wreaths of smoke
> Sent up, in silence, from among the trees!
> With some uncertain notice, as might seem
> Of vagrant dwellers in the houseless woods,
> Or of some Hermit's cave, where by his fire
> The Hermit sits alone. (11–22)

The scene here is one of effaced outlines, hedgerows overgrown and losing themselves in one green hue, running wild like sportive woods, the boundary between nature and the human habitation blurred; and behind this screen of overgrown outlines, the sense of someone dwelling there, in silence, a hermit telling his beads. Tintern Abbey itself is a palimpsest in the first verse paragraph of "Tintern Abbey."

So half our job is done. But why is the abbey there? What function does it serve? The plot of the poem moves quickly away from the opening setting and into the subject of Wordsworth's imagination. We need to look at those ruins more closely.

What made the ruins? The answer is given in other lines from the Chartreuse passage quoted above:

> Thus by conflicting passions pressed, my heart
> Responded; 'Honour to the patriot's zeal,
> Glory and hope to new-born Liberty!
> Hail to the mighty projects of the time!
> Discerning sword that Justice wields, do thou
> Go forth and prosper; and, ye purging fires,
> Up to the loftiest towers of Pride ascend,
> Fanned by the breath of angry Providence.
> But oh! if Past and Future be the wings
> On whose support harmoniously conjoined
> Moves the great spirit of human knowledge, spare
> These courts of mystery.... (*1850* VI, 435–446)

What made the ruins was the spirit of "new-born Liberty" to which Wordsworth wholeheartedly aspired, but with "conflicting passions." Wordsworth could see how "Liberty" threatened tradition and order. He could see this not just in political terms, but in personal terms. Geoffrey Hartman, in *Wordsworth's Poetry*, has discussed how Wordsworth fears the overweening power of a self-sufficient imagination and needs to bind that imagination into some sense of natural continuity.[10] In his own imagination, Wordsworth could feel the same dazzling power that led to the destruction of the monasteries. When he discusses the "sacrilege" that threatens the monastic silence, he knows he is capable of the same thing in homefelt terms.

The situation is complicated. Spots of time are experienced by the free imagination that finds itself wandering—going on a pilgrimage, in a sense—in a natural setting. In the sacred solitude, the imagination finds its sustenance. But it does so out of a sense of its own freedom, a freedom that contributes to the sense of blessing, of being an imagination finding its home in a sacred place. It experiences the blessing of having a mind able to perceive a beautiful world, fitting and being fitted. But that freedom fears something about the solitude—namely: its potential stasis, its capability of paralyzing the imagination, of imprisoning it like Ariel in a tree. The solitude can turn Gothic, superstitious, soul-destroying. It can become Roman Catholicism.

So what Wordsworth discovered at Chartreuse was a prime analogy, which connected a massive cultural fact with a personal experience: the analogy between the Protestant stripping of Catholic sacred places and the imagination's violation of its sacred sources. To see this analogy more clearly in "Tintern Abbey," we need once again to consider part of its title: "July 13, 1798." Critics have puzzled over the fact that the date is not July 14, the great anniversary of the Bastille (whose celebrations Wordsworth witnessed on his 1790 trip to Chartreuse). However, the date, July 13, does signal the date of Wordsworth's first visit to France, on July 13, 1790, and also the date of the assassination of Marat, July 13, 1793, which some see as the beginning of the Terror.[11] What is puzzling is the way Wordsworth describes his memory of 1793 as he looks back in 1798:

> here I stand, not only with the sense
> Of present pleasure, but with pleasing thoughts
> That in this moment there is life and food
> For future years. And so I dare to hope,
> Though changed, no doubt, from what I was when first
> I came among these hills; when like a roe

---

[10] *Wordsworth's Poetry, 1787–1814* (New Haven, 1964) 41–42, 212.

[11] See J. R. Watson, "A Note on the Date in the Title of 'Tintern Abbey,'" *The Wordsworth Circle* 10 (1979): 379–380.

> I bounded o'er the mountains, by the sides
> Of the deep rivers, and the lonely streams,
> Wherever nature led: more like a man
> Flying from something that he dreads, than one
> Who sought the thing he loved. For nature then
> (The coarser pleasures of my boyish days,
> And their glad animal movements all gone by)
> To me was all in all.—I cannot paint
> What then I was. The sounding cataract
> Haunted me like a passion: the tall rock,
> The mountain, and the deep and gloomy wood,
> Their colours and their forms, were then to me
> An appetite; a feeling and a love,
> That had no need of a remoter charm,
> By thought supplied, nor any interest
> Unborrowed from the eye. (62–83)

What is curious is that if this refers to five years previous, it refers to a time, 1793, when Wordsworth was twenty-three and a revolutionary sympathizer, not fourteen and bounding about in the Lake Country. In 1793, Wordsworth was a very sophisticated young man, back from his second trip and long stay in France, back from Annette Vallon and Michel Beaupuy (whose influences on his Catholic sympathies were very important), back in London for several months and perhaps revisiting Paris where he may have witnessed an execution of one of the Girondists, the more conservative of the republicans, and also the year when Wordsworth wrote his republican "Letter to the Bishop of Landaff." Sometime between 1793 and 1798 he became profoundly disillusioned with revolutionary politics, a disillusionment recorded in "Tintern Abbey," which attempts to recover the sacred sources of his imagination.

In his memory, Wordsworth points to several stages of his joy, from late childhood (a time of "coarser pleasures") when he bounded over the mountains, through adolescence when he played truant from school and rode to Furness Abbey, to his young adulthood, when he strode across France and felt the winds of freedom. The five-year-old joy, really five- and ten- and twenty-year-old joy, is in modern parlance "overdetermined." But somehow a loss has occurred, a stripping of the imaginative altars; so that all he has left are "beauteous forms" but empty, only "a picture of the mind," an outline, like the abbey outline, needing to be filled in. He needs to recover La Grande Chartreuse.

We need to discern yet another palimpsest, that of Chartreuse, in the following lines:

> for such loss, I would believe,
> Abundant recompence. For I have learned
> To look on nature, not as in the hour
> Of thoughtless youth; but hearing oftentimes
> The still, sad music of humanity,
> Nor harsh nor grating, though of ample power
> To chasten and subdue. And I have felt
> A presence that disturbs me with the joy.... (87–94)

Wordsworth learned this lesson at Chartreuse. I say this because of a passage in *The Prelude* where Wordsworth identifies the moment when he turned consciously from nature to humanity. In Book VIII of *The Prelude*, Wordsworth praises the figure of the shepherd, and draws upon the memory of his 1790 visit to Chartreuse:

> His form hath flashed upon me glorified
> By the deep radiance of the setting sun;
> Or him have I descried in distant sky,
> A solitary object and sublime,
> Above all height, like an aërial cross,
> As it is stationed on some spiry rock
> Of the Chartreuse, for worship. Thus was man
> Ennobled outwardly before mine eyes,
> And thus my heart at first was introduced
> To an unconscious love and reverence
> Of human nature.... (*1805* VIII, 404–414)

And at the end of this passage, Wordsworth praises "the mind / That to devotion willingly would be raised, / Into the temple and the temple's heart" (469–471), thus enforcing the parallel of nature's temple, the mind's temple, and the monastic temple. The passage is very important for crediting Chartreuse, and the worshipping shepherd, with the move to "love and reverence / Of human nature."

Now, this connection with Chartreuse is hardly explicit in "Tintern Abbey," where the Tintern Abbey outlines fade in and out like the Cheshire cat's smile. But one thing that is explicit in the poem is the constant uncertainty and tentativeness of several moments of the poem: "If this / Be but a vain belief," "And so I dare to hope," "for such loss, *I would believe*, abundant recompense" (emphasis added), "Nor perchance if I were not thus taught." These hesitancies have been much remarked, and they are indeed odd since Wordsworth has been describing an experience of blessed joy, not merely a hope for it. But what we are seeing is the dialectic of the free imagination—able to doubt and fly away from its moorings—and the original sacred place of holy seclusion experienced in nature and confirmed in the abbey setting. Wordsworth must somehow re-create this joy and this monastic setting in a new subjective way. Though he has the experience, he needs to see if the experience is permanent and embodies an immortal value. This need is what made him so grateful to discover the monastic equivalent to his early spots of time, for the abbey spirituality provided a religious mooring for his private experience. So in the poem, he needs to recontact that support for his early experience. He needs to re-experience the abbey.

He does so by turning to his sister Dorothy. Dorothy in the poem has characteristics that we find in other distinctive characters in Wordsworth:

> Therefore let the moon
> Shine on thee in thy solitary walk;
> And let the misty mountain-winds be free
> To blow against thee: and, in after years,
> When these wild ecstasies shall be matured
> Into a sober pleasure; when thy mind
> Shall be a mansion for all lovely forms,
> Thy memory be as a dwelling-place
> For all sweet sounds and harmonies; oh! then,
> If solitude, or fear, or pain, or grief,
> Should be thy portion, with what healing thoughts
> Of tender joy wilt thou remember me,
> And these my exhortations! (134–146)

What Wordsworth here says of Dorothy is similar to what he says of the "Old Cumberland Beggar" in that poem also written in this year:

> Be his the natural silence of old age!
> Let him be free of mountain solitudes;
> And have around him, whether heard or not,
> The pleasant melody of woodland birds. . . . (182–185)

The old Cumberland beggar has connections with the leech-gatherer in "Resolution and Independence," whose connection with the hermit is discussed by Geoffrey Hartman in *The Unmediated Vision*.[12] Dorothy's "mansion" also connects here with Gilpin's description of one of the inhabitants of the abbey, the old pauper woman whom he describes: "She could scarce crawl; shuffling along her palsied limbs, and meagre, contracted body, by the help of two sticks" (36). So also the leech-gatherer, whose body was "bent double, feet and head / Coming together in life's pilgrimage" (66–67): "Himself he propped, limbs, body, and pale face, / Upon a long grey staff of shaven wood" (71–72). Gilpin's poor woman serves as the tour guide who had taken over "the remnant of a shattered cloister. . . . It was her own mansion."

Dorothy is connected with the Cumberland beggar, with the leech-gatherer, with Gilpin's beggar woman, and thus becomes the re-encountered hermit in the poem. She internalizes in herself the monk's mansion, now a mental mansion "for all lovely forms."[13] Just as Wordsworth is supported by nature and by the abbey setting in his spots of time, now he is supported by Dorothy: "with what healing thoughts / Of tender joy wilt thou remember me"—a phrase meant as encouragement to her, but in fact carrying the personal accent of his own appeal. With Dorothy, he will reconstitute a monastic community, as "worshipper[s] of Nature . . . Unwearied in that service . . . with far deeper zeal / Of holier love." The moment will recover "these steep woods and lofty cliffs," the enclosing setting of the sacred place, for which the abbey is a prime symbol, and where worship, service, holier love is carried out in ancient traditional style.

There is another example that reinforces the parallel of Dorothy to the monastic hermit. Years later, in 1835, Wordsworth was to compose a poem, "Written after the Death of Charles Lamb," in which he speaks not only of Lamb but of his sister Mary, who may be seen as parallel to Dorothy:

> O gift divine of quiet sequestration!
> The hermit, exercised in prayer and praise,
> And feeding daily on the hope of heaven,

---

[12] *The Unmediated Vision: An Interpretation of Wordsworth, Hopkins, Rilke, and Valéry* (New Haven, 1954) 33–35.

[13] A related passage is *The Prelude* (*1805*) II, 294–296, "The props of my affections were removed, / And yet the building stood, as if sustained / By its own spirit!" This passage is discussed as a symbol of the imagination by J. Robert Barth, S.J., "'The Props of My Affections': A Note on *The Prelude* II, 276–281," *The Wordsworth Circle* 10 (1979): 344–345.

> Is happy in his vow, and fondly cleaves
> To life-long singleness; but happier far
> Was to your souls, and, to the thoughts of others,
> A thousand times more beautiful appeared,
> Your *dual* loneliness. The sacred tie
> Is broken; yet why grieve? ... (121–129)

There are many further questions that cannot be adequately considered here: the relation of Wordsworth's Catholic sympathies to his high church Anglicanism; their consistency with his furious anti-papalism at the time of the Catholic Emancipation Act; their relevance to the question of the continuity and discontinuity of his career; their relation to the question of Romantic escapism from social ills (like the Tintern Abbey beggars); their consistency with the secularized Wordsworth of the modern critical tradition. Let me only say a concluding word about this last topic.

M. H. Abrams has argued influentially, in *Natural Supernaturalism*, that Wordsworth secularized the religious—so influentially in fact that it constitutes current orthodoxy:

> The Christian theodicy of the private life, in the long lineage of Augustine's Confessions, transfers the locus of the primary concern with evil from the providential history of mankind to the providential history of the individual self, and justifies the experience of wrongdoing, suffering, and loss as a necessary means toward the greater good of personal redemption. But Wordsworth's is a secular theodicy—a theodicy without an operative *theos*—which retains the form of the ancient reasoning, but translates controlling Providence into an immanent teleology, makes the process coterminous with our life in this world, and justifies suffering as the necessary means toward the end of a greater good which is nothing other than the stage of achieved maturity.[14]

Such Wordsworthian theodicy, he goes on, "translates the painful process of Christian conversion and redemption into a painful process of self-formation, crisis, and self-recognition, which culminates in a stage of self-coherence, self-awareness, and assured power that is its own reward." About this view, I have written elsewhere: "The distinction is familiar, but because of it, the old religious theodicy seems flat and conventional, the new secular theodicy seems bland and aimless. In any

---

[14] *Natural Supernaturalism: Tradition and Revolution in Romantic Literature* (New York, 1971) 95–96.

event, New Historicism has hatcheted Wordsworth's 'self-discovery' into a thing of shreds and patches. In fact, might there be a way of reinvigorating both religious and psychological traditions by bringing them into new forms of contact with each other?"[15]

I am quoting myself here because at the time I did not see the way through the disabling alternatives of old orthodoxy and secular blandness. But I would now argue that Wordsworth keeps returning to the religious as a base from which he can spring, again and again. He needs to keep returning to the sources and mainstay of his imaginative life, sources that are associated with natural solitude, and whose prime analogy is with the experience of Catholic monks and hermits. And we are speaking of the religious not in some vague sense, but in the specific historical sense of the Catholicism of pre-Reformation England and pre-Revolutionary France, but continuing in "Roman Catholic" form into Wordsworth's time. The scope of Wordsworth is immense in that he takes on the whole span of English religious history—thus the importance of his long look at the subject in *Ecclesiastical Sonnets*. Because of revisionist Reformation history, we are beginning to see the power of the Catholic past in England, and can now see it here in the most famous English poet of nature and imagination.

Works Cited

Abrams, M. H. *Natural Supernaturalism: Tradition and Revolution in Romantic Literature*. New York: Norton, 1971.

Barth, J. Robert, S.J. "'The Props of My Affections': A Note on *The Prelude* II, 276–281." *The Wordsworth Circle* 10 (1979): 344–345.

Brier, Peter A., "Reflections on Tintern Abbey." *The Wordsworth Circle* 5 (1974): 5–6.

Cooper, Lane, ed. *A Concordance to the Poems of William Wordsworth*. London: Smith, Elder, 1911.

Duffy, Eamon. *The Stripping of the Altars: Traditional Religion in England c. 1400–c. 1580*. New Haven: Yale University Press, 1992.

Franchot, Jenny. *Roads to Rome: The Antebellum Protestant Encounter with Catholicism*. Berkeley: University of California Press, 1994.

---

[15] Dennis Taylor, "The Need for a Religious Literary Criticism," *Religion and the Arts* 1 (1996): 142.

Gilpin, William. *Observations on the River Wye* 1782. Oxford, England: Woodstock Books, 1991.

Hartman, Geoffrey. *The Unmediated Vision: An Interpretation of Wordsworth, Hopkins, Rilke, and Valéry*. New Haven: Yale University Press, 1954.

———. *Wordsworth's Poetry, 1787–1814*. New Haven: Yale University Press, 1964.

Levinson, Marjorie. *Wordsworth's Great Period Poems*. Cambridge: Cambridge University Press, 1986.

Mahoney, John L. *William Wordsworth: A Poetic Life*. New York: Fordham University Press, 1997.

Taylor, Dennis. "The Need for a Religious Literary Criticism." *Religion and the Arts* 1 (1996): 124–150.

Watson, J. R. "A Note on the Date in the Title of 'Tintern Abbey'." *The Wordsworth Circle* 10 (1979): 379–380.

Wordsworth, William. *The Poems*. 2 Vols. Ed. John O. Hayden. New Haven: Yale University Press, 1977, 1981.

———. *The Prelude 1799, 1805, 1850*. Ed. Jonathan Wordsworth, M. H. Abrams, and Stephen Gill. Norton Critical Edition. New York: Norton, 1979.

4

Cowper, Wordsworth, and the Sacred Moment of Perception

David J. Leigh, S. J.

THE INFLUENCE of William Cowper remains one of the paradoxes of early English Romanticism. In the minds of the first-generation romantics, Cowper was "the best modern poet"; in the writings of most twentieth-century critics, he is, at best, an eccentric forerunner whose influence is seen by contrast in a few scattered passages in Wordsworth's or Coleridge's conversational poems.[1] The present essay at-

---

[1] Cf. M. H. Abrams, "Structure and Style in the Greater Romantic Lyric," in *From Sensibility to Romanticism*, ed. Frederick W. Hilles and Harold Bloom (London, 1965), 527–560; J. Robert Barth, S.J., *The Symbolic Imagination: Coleridge and the Romantic Tradition*, rev. ed. (New York, 2001); T. E. Blom, "Eighteenth-Century Reflexive Process Poetry," *Eighteenth-Century Studies* 10 (1976): 52–72; "The Structure and Meaning of *The Task*," *Pacific Coast Philology* 5 (1970): 12–18; Marshall Brown, "The Pre-Romantic Discovery of Consciousness," *Studies in Romanticism* 17 (1978): 387–412; P. M. S. Dawson, "Cowper's Equivocations," *Essays in Criticism* 33 (1983): 19–35; William N. Free, *William Cowper* (New York, 1970); Tim Fulford, "Wordsworth, Cowper and the Language of Eighteenth-Century Politics," in *Early Romantics: Perspectives in British Poetry from Pope to Wordsworth*, ed. Thomas Woodman (Cambridge, 1998), 117–147; Dustin Griffin, "Cowper, Milton, and the Recovery of Paradise," *Essays in Criticism* 31 (1981): 15–26; "Redefining Georgic: Cowper's *Task*," *ELH* 57 (1990): 865–879; Deborah Heller, "Cowper's *Task* and the Writing of a Poet's Salvation," *Studies in English Literature* 35 (1995): 575–599; Humphrey House, *Coleridge* (London, 1953) 71ff.; Myrddin Jones, "Wordsworth and Cowper: The Eye Made Quiet," *Essays in Criticism* 21 (1971): 236–247; Frank D. McConnell, *The Confessional Imagination: A Reading of Wordsworth's "Prelude"* (Baltimore, 1974), Appendix I; W. G. Marshall, "The Presence of 'the Word' in Cowper's *The Task*," *Studies in English Literature* 27 (1987): 475–487; Joseph F. Musser, Jr., "William Cowper's Rhetoric: The Picturesque and the Personal," *Studies in English Literature* 19 (1979): 515–531; Vincent Newey, "Cowper and the Description of Nature," *Essays in Criticism* 23 (1973): 102–108; "Wordsworth, Bunyan, and the Puritan Mind," *ELH* 41 (1974): 212–232; and *Cowper's Poetry: A Critical Study and Reassessment* (Totowa, N.J., 1982); W. J. B. Owen, "Literary Echoes in *The Prelude*," *The Wordsworth Circle* 5 (1972): 3–16; A. F. Potts, *Wordsworth's "Prelude": A Study of Its Literary Form* (Ithaca, 1953) 350ff.; Martin Priestman, *Cowper's "Task": Structure and Influence* (Cambridge, 1983);

tempts to show the complex but pervasive influence of Cowper on Wordsworth. In particular, the essay examines similarities in central themes and motifs of Cowper's *The Task* and Wordsworth's *The Prelude* and other major poems, especially the theme of "sacred perception." The entire study suggests not only important historical connections but also some complications in theories of literary influence. Furthermore, the Cowper-Wordsworth connection alerts critics to the need for a reassessment and reinterpretation of the recently much-neglected major poetry of Cowper. As Richard E. Brantley has shown in his *Wordsworth's "Natural Methodism,"* Wordsworth was affected in a fundamental way by the precise movement of which Cowper was the major poetic voice—the evangelical revival in the Anglican Church.[2] It is no accident that Cowper's prophetic shadow over Wordsworth and the early Romantics is consciously mingled with that of Milton. For Cowper's visionary verse reunites the Miltonic ritual of inspiration with what George Eliot called Cowper's evangelical "truthfulness of perception." But the unrivaled importance of *The Task* in mediating and transforming seventeenth-century poetry of inspiration into the new visionary poetry of the first-generation Romantics has been largely neglected by critics.

The general influence of inspirational Protestantism on the rise of Romantic politics and literature is, of course, a commonplace. Frederick C. Gill wrote a book entitled simply *The Romantic Movement and Methodism*.[3] T. B. Shepherd could say in a similar study of the eighteenth century, "In so far as Romanticism is closely bound up with a love of liberty, a deeper interest in man, a love of Nature and simple domestic joys, a freer expression of emotions, and an outburst of lyrical poetry, Methodism encouraged it, or was part of the same spirit."[4] Norman Nicholson extended the same generalization to the evangelical revival, which, he said, "was, in fact, not so much a symptom of the Romantic Movement as the Movement itself in so far as it affected a

---

Maurice Quinlan, *William Cowper: A Critical Life* (Minneapolis, 1953); Max F. Schulz, *The Poetic Voices of Coleridge* (Detroit, 1963), ch. 5; Rachel Trickett, "Cowper, Wordsworth, and the Animal Fable," *Review of English Studies*, New Series, 34 (Nov. 1983): 471–480. Among these critics, only Blom, Brown, House, Newey, Potts, and Priestman emphasize the positive aspects of Cowper's influence through *The Task* on Wordsworth.

[2] *Wordsworth's "Natural Methodism"* (New Haven, 1975).
[3] *The Romantic Movement and Methodism* (London, 1937).
[4] *Methodism and the Literature of the Eighteenth Century* (London, 1940) 266.

large class and section of the population. . . . For these the Revival was all they ever saw or heard of Romanticism."[5] H. W. Piper traced Romantic patterns in the late eighteenth-century Unitarians who influenced the young Wordsworth and Coleridge.[6] All these studies echo Stopford A. Brooke's 1874 thesis concerning the transition from a humanized to a devotional to an organic nature in poets leading into the early Romantics.[7] More recently, Vincent Newey has suggested the importance of Cowper's reading of James Hervey's meditations as an impetus toward the poet's "sense of the spiritual value and content of perceptual acts in the presence of nature."[8]

None of these standard approaches, however, deals adequately with the uniquely poetic structures of either Protestant or Romantic poetry. Most of the studies merely provide lists of similar subject matter or extrinsic circumstances in the movement from Milton to Wordsworth. More recent critics, however, while doing justice to the poetic nuances of Protestantism in poetry at either end of the journey (especially in Milton–Vaughan–Traherne and Blake–Wordsworth–Coleridge), have failed to travel the intervening distance.[9] As a consequence, one hears even Northrop Frye asserting that "Blake was the first and the most radical of the Romantics who identified the creative imagination of the poet with the creative power of God."[10] Or one reads Martin Price's suggestion that all religious epic action disappeared from poetry between Milton and Wordsworth.[11] Harold Bloom, in his introduction to the enlarged edition of *The Visionary Company*, takes a few tentative steps through the eighteenth century in an effort to link up the tradition of Protestant dissent with its Romantic consequences. Yet even Bloom mentions little in the intervening period, other than Collins in the Miltonic revival of the 1740s, in which to discover traces of this transition from inspirational to visionary poetry. When speaking of Protestantism itself, Bloom leaps from Milton's search for liberty to Fox's radical whiggery, or from the early Quakers to the Unitarians

---

[5] *William Cowper* (London, 1951) 10.

[6] *The Active Universe: Pantheism and the Concept of the Imagination in the English Poets* (London, 1962).

[7] *Theology in the English Poets* (London, 1874).

[8] Newey 150.

[9] Blom, Newey, and Priestman are the best among the few who have explored Cowper's structure or related the patterns of *The Task* to Wordsworth.

[10] *The Stubborn Structure* (Ithaca, 1970) 172.

[11] *To the Palace of Wisdom* (New York, 1964) 353.

Price and Priestley. The intervening period is mentioned primarily as an age of madness in which poets fearful of psychic energy "sought to return to the intellectual and aesthetic daring of Milton, with results in their lives, at least, which bore out Johnson's melancholy warnings."[12] Bloom admits this prevalence of a "perilous balance" from 1740 to 1770 is still an unsolved problem.

Even M. H. Abrams repeatedly leaps from Wordsworth to Milton and back without touching Cowper or his contemporaries.[13] This omission is even more remarkable, for the Romantic schemata that Abrams finds in Wordsworth are similar to the structural patterns of Cowper's *The Task*. In fact, nearly every secularized religious pattern, theme, and mode that Abrams finds in the conversational poems of Wordsworth and Coleridge is prefigured in Cowper's major poem. These very patterns are made possible by the tendencies within evangelical theology and its devotional literature known to both Cowper and Wordsworth. The immanent versions of the evangelical premises of individuality, inwardness, and divinization of self-in-nature are the unquestioned assumptions of the early Romantics.

Thus, Cowper's high reputation among the Romantics is less mysterious if we recognize that both he and Wordsworth are related to the most influential popular movement in England in the late eighteenth century—the evangelical and Methodist revivals. Richard Brantley is the first to show the widespread influences of evangelical and Methodist patterns in both Wordsworth's life and his poetry. Although he overstretches the evidence in places, Brantley demonstrates many obvious parallels between evangelical theology of the Spirit or of the Book of Nature, and the autobiographical patterns of *The Prelude* and *The Excursion*. What Brantley omits completely, however, is that these thematic patterns are the very heart of the major poet of the Anglican evangelical movement—William Cowper.

---

[12] *The Visionary Company*, rev. ed. (Ithaca, 1971) xviii.

[13] Abrams does suggest James Hervey as one who carried on the meditative tradition, but fails to develop Hervey's relationship to evangelicalism and Cowper. Abrams mentions Cowper only as a secondary influence on Coleridge. Cf. "Structure and Style," 543–556. In *Natural Supernaturalism*, Abrams discovers the following imaginative patterns in Wordsworth and Romantic poetry: the self-moving system, the Romantic spiral, an immanent teleology, unity lost and regained, progressive self-education, and the homeward journey (175–192). Unfortunately, Abrams does not connect these with similar patterns in Cowper. Priestman provides the only extensive study of parallel schemata in *The Task* and *The Prelude*.

Before tracing the details of these thematic parallels, however, it will be helpful to take a brief look at the major devotional theme of Cowper—what I call "the moment of sacred perception." For it is this precise devotional theme that will reappear in a wide number of forms in Wordsworth. John Newton, Cowper's pastor at Olney, provides a clue to this devotional practice he calls "meditation":

> The chief means for attaining wisdom, and suitable gifts for the ministry, are the holy scriptures and prayer. . . . Next these, and derived from them, is meditation. By this I mean . . . a disposition of mind to observe carefully what passes within us and around us; what we see, hear, and feel; and to apply all for the illustration and confirmation of the written word to us.[14]

This method of religious musing takes a subtle twist in the context of evangelical piety. For it becomes a self-authenticating mode of contemplation, subject only to Scripture, which in turn is privately interpreted. God is now available for contemplation in every perceptual act of the individual. In the hands of a precise craftsman and in conjunction with a further evangelical doctrine (the inner Spirit), such "meditation" comes to undergird authentic poetry—if it can reach the concrete.

The difficulty of reaching the concrete world of nature was doubly problematic for the evangelical Anglican. He was trapped not only by the outer wall of Lockean epistemology but also by the inner wall of natural spiritual blindness. For him only a radical inner transformation of faculties could break through this double perceptual barrier and make contact with concrete nature. Another letter of Newton's in the same series provides a clue to the process of illumination and its poetic consequences (which will be great for Cowper and through him for Wordsworth): "The enlightened man's great business is to behold the glory of God in Christ; and by beholding, he is changed into the same image. . . . I can think of no single word more descriptive of the state of the enlightened than contemplation."[15] The fusion of this "contem-

---

[14] "Letters on Religious Subjects," in *The Works of Rev. John Newton* (New York, 1847), I, 115.

[15] Newton 136. In this essay I presuppose a coherent reading of *The Task* as an "epic of retreat," composed of six books, each consisting of several major eighteenth-century modes. Within each of the first four books, the narrator moves from a fallen solution for the chaotic flux of evil to the start of a transcendent solution in a higher poetic mode. The final stage of each of these books is in turn absorbed into the final two books as an element of revelation, where the sacred moment of perception occurs.

plation" with the previous method of perceptual "meditation" on Nature brings about what may be Cowper's major contribution to religious (and Romantic) poetry—the sacred moment of perception. For the enlightened person, changed from within by the Spirit, now contemplates God in every experience and "by beholding" "is changed into the same image."

Since *The Task* is the story of the narrator's progress toward this state of the sacred moment of perception, only a close analysis of the poem can authenticate these contentions. For the present study, however, a review of major passages in the fifth book can suggest the importance of this moment for Cowper and Wordsworth. For instance, Cowper describes the enlightened one as a student of the concrete:

> So reads he nature whom the lamp of truth
> Illuminates. Thy lamp, mysterious word!
> Which whoso sees no longer wanders lost,
> With intellect bemaz'd in endless doubt,
> But runs the road of wisdom. . . . (*Task*, V, 845–849).

Here an important image of the creative imagination—the lamp—indicates the creative role of the new light in the soul of the narrator. Now that his perception is renewed from within, his very act of seeing constitutes its images as moments of revelation. The divine but inward nature of this process is reinforced by an auditory metaphor that reverses the traditional process to make the same point: "In vain thy creatures testify of thee / Till thou proclaim thyself" (856–857). The silent universe of Addison again proclaims the glory of God—but from an inner divine voice. The transformation is interior but active, producing new faculties:

> Liberty, like day,
> Breaks on the soul, and by a flash from heav'n
> Fires all the faculties with glorious joy.
> A voice is heard that mortal ears hear not
> Till thou hast touch'd them. (*Task*, V, 883–887)

Newey also emphasizes the importance of visionary perception as related to some of Cowper's religious sources, but fails to work out the details of the journey of the narrator or show the influence of John Newton. Priestman relates the up-and-down patterns in *The Task* to Cowper's manic-depressive personality, and explores imagery of land and sea, earthquakes, and prospects, but does little more than admit that Cowper includes a "clarified perception theme" and a millennial prophecy in the final book. Priestman is at his best in exploring the structural influences of Cowper's satirical passages on Wordsworth.

This brief digression into evangelical creative perception in Newton and Cowper should prevent us, of course, from being surprised at the extensive thematic parallels between *The Task* and *The Prelude* or *The Excursion*. For both poets, the "sacred moment of perception" was a central religious and poetic doctrine. However complicated Wordsworth's struggle was by his acquaintance with Hartley's associationist psychology or Lockean epistemology, his evangelical background was nevertheless significant enough to provide him with dozens of echoes of Cowper's *Task*.

But echoes of this theme in the poetry are not the only link between the two poets. For Wordsworth in an early letter describes a doctrine very close to that of Newton and Cowper on the moment of perception:

> In a word, if I were disposed to write a sermon, and this is something like one, upon the subject of taste in natural beauty, I should take for my text the little pathway in Lowther Woods, and all that I had to say would begin and end in the human heart, as under the direction of the divine Nature conferring value on the objects of the senses, and pointing out what is valuable in them.[16]

Here is the evangelical stress on inwardness ("human heart"), the creative perception process ("conferring value on the objects of the senses"), all under divine guidance at particular moments ("under the direction of the divine Nature"). Both Cowper and Wordsworth are on a similar immanent visionary quest.

The sacred moment of perception is for both poets the summing up of a complex process. Both can put the matter simply and in similar phrases. "All we behold is miracle," says Cowper's narrator in *The Task* VI, 132; "All which we behold is full of blessings," echoes the poet in

---

[16] "William Wordsworth, to Lord Beaumont, 1805," *Letters of William and Dorothy Wordsworth*, 2d ed., rev. Chester L. Shaver (Oxford, 1967) I, 627–628. All references to William Cowper's poetry will be to *The Poems of William Cowper*, ed. John D. Baird and Charles Ryskamp, 3 vols. (New York, 1980–). References to his letters and prose will be to *The Letters and Prose Writings of William Cowper*, ed. James King and Charles Ryskamp. 5 vols. (New York, 1979–1986). For Wordsworth's poetry, I use the following texts: *Early Poems and Fragments, 1785–1797*, ed. Carol Landon, The Cornell Wordsworth (Ithaca, 1997); *"Lyrical Ballads," and Other Poems, 1797–1800*, ed. James Butler and Karen Green, The Cornell Wordsworth (Ithaca, 1992); *"Home at Grasmere": Part First, Book First of "The Recluse,"* ed. Beth Carlington, The Cornell Wordsworth (Ithaca, 1977); *The Fourteen Book Prelude*, ed. W. J. B. Owen, The Cornell Wordsworth (Ithaca, 1985); and for *The Excursion*, *The Poetical Works of William Wordsworth*, ed. Ernest de Selincourt and Helen Darbishire (Oxford: Clarendon, 1940–1945), vol. 5.

"Tintern Abbey," 133–134 or *The Prelude*: "All / That I beheld respired with inward meaning" (III, 131–132). In the "Prospectus," as Abrams notes, Wordsworth links the sacredness of this perceptual moment with echoes from Milton's *Paradise Lost*:

> The discerning intellect of Man
> When wedded to this goodly universe
> In love and holy passion, shall find these
> A simple produce of the common day. (52–55)

A similar wedding of mind and universe occurs in *The Prelude* in moments of concrete perception of a "new world" "in life's everyday appearances":

> . . . a world, too, that was fit
> To be transmitted and to other eyes
> Made visible, as ruled by those fixed laws
> Whence spiritual dignity originates,
> Which do both give it being and maintain
> A balance, an ennobled interchange
> Of action from without and from within;
> The excellence, pure function, and best power
> Both of the object seen, and eye that sees. (XIII, 369–377)

The complexity of this passage shows Wordsworth's expansion of Cowper's fundamental sacred moment.

A study of various aspects of this common theme reveals that Cowper's influence was pervasive but not stifling. In the following section, we will examine several peculiarly Cowperian themes from *The Task*—*interiority*, *prophetic harp*, the *inward light*, *spiritual blindness*, *second birth*, *moments of time*, and *reading the book of nature*—and recognize how each theme is absorbed and transformed by Wordsworth.

The notion of *interiority* is so commonplace as to be easily taken for granted in Wordsworth. Numerous critics have traced the focus of *The Prelude* ("my theme has been / What passed within me" III, 172–173) back to Milton's "Paradise within" (*Paradise Lost* XII, 587), but few have noted the transmission of this focus through Cowper's "his warfare is within" (*Task* VI, 935.) Within this warring paradise, the image of the poet as *harp* is often associated with Wordsworth and Coleridge. In the opening of *The Prelude*, the poet tells us that, despite "Aeolian visitations" within his soul, "the harp / was soon defrauded" (I, 96–97) and he cannot grapple with the "noble theme." When he tries to write an epic "seated harp in hand," he fails and ends up telling "a tale from my own heart" on an "Orphean lyre" (I, 172, 222, 233). At the climax of Cowper's poem, however, the narrator sings in similar tone "how sweet is the harp of prophecy" when he touches on "some theme divinely fair" (VI, 747, 754). For Wordsworth, of course, the harp is not so easily tuned, and may at times, as Hartman notes about an early poem from 1787, become part of the resistance of nature and the inner warfare:

> Deep sighs his harp with hollow groan
> He starts the dismal sound to hear
> Nor dares revert his eyes for fear
> Again his harp with grating thrill
> Shrieks at his shoulder sharp and shrill ("Vale of Esthwaite," 58–62).[17]

This rebellious harp is not so far from Cowper as Hartman suggests, for, in "Retirement," Cowper describes the fallen man in terms of an untuned harp:

> Man is an harp whose chords elude the sight,
> Each yielding harmony dispos'd aright;
> The screws reversed . . .
> Ten thousand strings at once go loose,
> Lost, till he tune them all their pow'r and use. (325–330)

The consequences of such an unstrung harp are explicitly described in terms of the failure of the sacred moment of perception: "his faded eye, / That passes all he sees unheeded by" ("Retirement" 339–340). In a later poem composed in 1828, "On the Power of Sound," Wordsworth is more optimistic about the power of the harp in time of struggle: "But lead sick Fancy to a harp, / That hath in noble tasks been tried" (89–90). Here, he finds Cowper's theme of "noble tasks" amenable to the power of the "prophetic harp."

The prophetic theme of the inner harp is an elaboration of a more common and more explicitly evangelical theme in Cowper and Wordsworth, that of the inner spirit enlightening the imagination against *blindness*. In Cowper, of course, the theme of divine *inner light* is commonplace (e.g., *Task* III, 242, 272; V, 810; VI, 802, etc.). Wordsworth

---

[17] Cited by Geoffrey Hartman, *Wordsworth's Poetry, 1787–1814* (New Haven, 1964) 85.

is usually less explicit, except in such passages as *Excursion* I, 94ff.: "as the mind was filled with inward light."[18] For Wordsworth, as Hartman observes, is hesitant throughout *The Prelude* to place too much emphasis on either Nature or the Soul in the visionary process. At times, such as in *Home at Grasmere* or *Prelude* II, 401–405, he can come out strongly for creative perception—"There is creation in the eye." But more often he hedges enough to leave the balance intact, as in "Tintern Abbey": ". . . all the mighty world / Of eye and ear,—both what they half create, / And what perceive."[19] Wordsworth in all these instances is much less comfortable with the explicit language of evangelical theology of enlightenment by the Spirit, but, as we shall see, he moves toward a more immanent theory of the imagination as its Romantic derivative.

The entire process of reaching this moment of sacred perception for both poets is the matter of their major poems. In *The Task*, the first four books present the narrator searching through a series of inadequate visions for the prospect he is to find in the revelatory moments of the final two books. In Book I, in particular, the limitation of secular prospects is seen repeatedly on his rural walk. Once again, Hartman has given us an excellent account of the stages in Wordsworth's struggle with the visual that is analogous to the struggle in Cowper. In *Prelude* VI, for instance, Hartman finds the poet experiencing "a power in the mind independent of sight" but called forth by a "supremely visual moment" after the Crossing of the Alps. And like Cowper, Wordsworth resorts to the image of blindness as characteristic of his normal state of questing.[20]

This state of blindness leading to vision does not terrify Cowper as thoroughly in *The Task* as the overwhelming power of Imagination threatens Wordsworth. And yet the related problem of delusive vision and of dreaming arises in *The Task* in passages that may have influenced Wordsworth. In particular, the theme of the deluded mariner occurs in both major poems. In Cowper, the mariner of Book I is "possess'd / With visions prompted by intense desire" and falls pathetically into the sea (I, 447); but the mariner of Book V, 832ff. "darts an eye / Radiant

---

[18] Cited by Brantley 113. For a more theological reading of *The Task*, see my article "Images of God in Pre-Romantic English Poetry," *Ultimate Reality and Meaning* 9 (1986): 37–55.
[19] Hartman discusses this complex issue: 114, 180ff.
[20] Cf. Hartman 240–241; and Priestman ch. 9.

with joy towards the happy land." The difference between the two is, of course, the sacred moment of perception. The early mariner is an image of unenlightened vision; the happy mariner, that of enlightened visionary. Wordsworth picks up this image of the mariner only to use it as a simile illustrating the fortunate blindness toward the past: "If the mariner, / When at reluctant distance he hath passed / Some tempting island, could but know the ills / That must have fallen upon him had he brought / His bark to land upon the wished-for-shore . . ." (*Prelude* III, 483–487). In a variant on this theme, Wordsworth speaks in a nearby passage of the shepherd dreaming as he views the sea—"and rather makes than finds what he beholds" (III, 510ff.). This, too, may be an echo of Cowper's portrait of Kate's dream of her longed-for lover returning on the sea (*Task* I, 539ff.), a dream that is "delusive most where warmest wishes are."

For Cowper, the evangelical notion of the *second birth* is another aspect of the sacred moment of perception. In Cowper, the notion appears in a major passage in "Retirement," but as a consequence in Nature following the moment of illumination:

> Then heav'n, eclips'd so long, and this dull earth,
> Shall seem to start into a second birth;
> Nature, assuming a more lovely face,
> Borrowing a beauty from the work of grace,
> Shall be despis'd and over look'd no more. (355–359)

Hartman has pointed out a fragment written by Wordsworth in 1797 or 1798 that perhaps parallels in reverse this crucial evangelical passage of Cowper's:

> And in this season of his second birth,
> He feels that, be his mind however great
> In aspiration, the universe in which
> He lives is equal to his mind, that each
> Is worthy of the other; if the one
> Be insatiate, the other is inexhaustible.[21]

What in Cowper is the second birth of nature following the inner birth of the light of the Spirit becomes in Wordsworth the second birth of the visionary, making him equal to the infinite without and within. Later, reflecting in *The Prelude* on the French Revolution, Wordsworth

---

[21] Hartman 170.

says, "All things have second birth," but he finds that this thought does not bring him "soft peace" or "repose" (X, 83ff.).

The practical result, so to speak, of the second birth and the new inward light is the ability to "read" the *book of Nature*. For Cowper, this traditional power (with its evangelical interpretation) enables one to "read" various aspects of Nature—events ("Expostulation," 312–313), the world ("Hope," 426ff.), and concrete objects in nature (*Task* V, 798ff., 845ff.; VI, 617). The source of this reading is, as always, interior: "So reads he nature whom the lamp of truth illuminates." As Brantley, Marshall, and others have shown, this ability to "read" nature is a recurrent theme in Wordsworth. In some passages, the poet of *The Prelude* sounds like John Newton's enlightened man of meditation (III, 121ff.); in others, he becomes the full man of contemplation, especially in the famous Simplon moment of revelation: "With such a book / Before our eyes, we could not choose but read / Lessons of genuine brotherhood" (VI, 543–545).[22]

This moment of perception is not, however, wholly unprepared for. In both Cowper and Wordsworth, we find a notion that suggests a common belief in unconscious, almost archetypal, imaginative patterns fashioned in terms of Nature. In Cowper, whose narrator tells us that his "very dreams were rural," the doctrine of an innate structural pattern of nature is implied:

> Tis born with all: the love of Nature's works
> Is an ingredient in the compound man,
> Infus'd at the creation of the kind . . .
> . . . this obtains in all,
> That all discern a beauty in his works,
> And all can taste them. (*Task* IV, 700, 731ff.)

This almost transcendental bias toward nature is similar to what Hartman suggests is developed by the scenes of beauty or fear in the early books of *The Prelude*. For Hartman this "mythical or transcendental" point of view is often at odds with an associationist view in Wordsworth.[23]

All these aspects of the sacred moment of perception are summed up in Wordsworth's doctrine of "*spots of time*." Although Hartman connects this notion with that of *genius loci*, it seems more likely to derive

---

[22] Brantley ch. 4.
[23] Hartman 219ff.

directly from the evangelical moment of perceptual revelation. In these "spots of time," the particular concrete objects as seen and remembered become the media of an imaginative insight into their more profound, and often religious, meaning. Wordsworth usually interprets in more psychological or philosophical terms what Cowper openly calls "the unambiguous footsteps of the God / Who gives its luster to an insect's wing" (*Task* V, 811–812). Cowper too recognizes the need not only for instantaneous perception but also for reflection and remembrance: "Meditation here / May think down hours to moments" (*Task* VI, 84–85). The guiding light of the Spirit may become the Wordsworthian transforming Imagination, but the pattern of the visionary moment is strikingly similar.[24]

Clustering around this central motif of sacred perception are a variety of themes peculiar to both Cowper and Wordsworth. The sacred moment is, of course, a spot of time in a visionary quest both within and beyond nature, a quest in which the narrator is both fascinated by nature's revelatory beauty and fearful of the consequences of a transcendent imagination. The narrator of *The Task* I–IV well fits Hartman's description of the early Wordsworth as "a mind in search (primarily through the eye) of a nature adequate to its idea." And the narrator in *The Task* V–VI strongly resembles the "borderer" between the natural and the divine of *Prelude* XIV.[25] Both Cowper's narrator and the Wanderer of *The Excursion* come to see in sublime terms their goal as a "sacred city" (see *Task* V, 1ff.; VI, 799ff,: *Excursion* II).

What is surprising to find in Wordsworth, however, is his borrowing on occasion of the titular theme of Cowper's poem—the theme of "task" and "repose." We have seen this motif appear momentarily at the beginning and ending of both *The Task* and *The Prelude*, but we did not point out that Wordsworth uses language of "task" or "repose" in more than sixty passages in his two major long poems. For example, Wordsworth says that early efforts at his quest are "baffled and plagued by a mind that every hour / Turns recreant to her task" and thus must

---

[24] Other instances of the moment of sacred perception in *The Prelude* are: II, 348ff.; VIII, 365ff.; IV, 160ff.; VII, 619ff.; VI, 76; XII, 208ff.; XIII, 368ff.; XIII, 283ff.; also, cf. *Excursion* III, 101ff. Priestman (191) points out that both Cowper and Wordsworth associate early spots of time with the deaths of their fathers.

[25] See Hartman 103ff., 197ff. For an insightful overview of Wordsworth's "quest for transcendence in the midst of immanence" in his poetry, see John L. Mahoney, "William Wordsworth: Nature, Imagination, and Ultimate Reality," *Ultimate Reality and Meaning* 13 (1990): 177–200.

"seek repose / In listlessness from vain perplexity" (*Prelude* I, 257–258, 265–266). Wordsworth, in his approach to the revelatory moment of the Simplon crossing, pauses momentarily to describe the scenes of pastoral life that fascinate him on his walk. He speaks of "sanctified abodes of peaceful man . . . pleased with his daily task" who is "called forth to industry" and later returns when "evening shadows lead him to repose" (*Prelude* VI, 508ff.). Later, in Book XIII, both "task" and "repose" in Nature become united for Wordsworth as he foresees his future as a poet: "If future years mature me for the task, / . . . my theme / No other than the very heart of man / . . . In Nature's presence" (233, 240–241, 245). This interest in the retired life appears also in *The Excursion* III, 392ff., when the solitary describes the contemplative life in language similar to Cowper's:

> The universal instinct of repose,
> The longing for confirmed tranquility
> Inward and outward, humble yet sublime.

This interplay of both task and repose is part of a larger pattern of Romantic "harmony of discordance." For Cowper this harmony seems at first to require the rural life, where "discordant motives in one center meet" ("Retirement," 173). But later, in *Task* V–VI, this same harmony occurs in a transcendent state that is primarily interior, in which "antipathies are none" and "all is harmony." Wordsworth attributes such harmony to the "Immortal spirit" whose "dark inscrutable workmanship . . . reconciles / Discordant elements" (*Prelude* I, 340ff.). Although primarily an inner state for Wordsworth also, this harmony works best in solitude rather than society, in country rather than city (*Prelude* I, 219ff.; II, 110ff.). The images of such harmony, of course, contrast with the irrational flood images of disorder in London life (*Task* II; *Prelude* VII).[26]

Beyond harmony, however, lies the ultimate goal of both the evangelical and the Romantic imagination—"liberty." Both Cowper and Wordsworth lament the failure of political systems to bring about authentic freedom (*Task* V; *Prelude* X–XI), most tragically in England. Both poets employ the image of "wings" to portray the process of liber-

---

[26] Blom stresses the "irreconcilable nature of the polarized issues" in Cowper's "reflexive process poetry" in *The Task*. This dialectic applies quite nicely to the first four books of the poem, but fails to take account of the final two books. Blom, "Eighteenth-century" 72.

ation (*Task* V, 771; *Prelude* XI, 253). And, for both, their major poem is a panegyric of interior liberty (*Task* V, 538ff.; *Prelude* XIV, 130ff.).

Our wide-ranging survey of thematic parallels between Cowper and Wordsworth allows us to draw some tentative, but highly suggestive, conclusions. First, we can see that Brantley is correct in placing Wordsworth in the evangelical tradition. But, as our analysis of Cowper shows, this late evangelical tradition is much closer to the immanentized Christian patterns of M. H. Abrams' *Natural Supernaturalism* than Brantley permits. For the very changes in Christian patterns described by Abrams as peculiar to Wordsworth are very often those he absorbed and transformed from Cowper's *Task*. And although Cowper tried to incorporate traditional evangelical doctrine in several passages, his overall stress in the later books on the sacred moment of perception and the immanent presence of the divine in nature led him further toward Romantic theology than his premises might allow. When he fuses poetry and prophecy so intimately in the ending of *The Task* that a divine revelation occurs within the poet's submission to the soul of nature, then he is difficult to distinguish from the early Wordsworth.[27]

Second, and more tentatively still, we can conjecture that Wordsworth's dependence on Cowper is that of an uncomfortable younger son in the shadow of a neurotic older brother, who himself is a victim of an overpowering father-figure, John Milton. Wordsworth's comments on and attitude toward Cowper—with their combination of admiration, resentment, neglect, and ultimate transcendence—are reflected in the scattered use and misuse of his forerunner in the themes and motifs of *The Prelude* and *The Excursion*.

Here we might find Harold Bloom's elaborate "map of misreading" suggestive. For *The Task* can be read as fitting precisely the three-part division of great Wordsworthian and modern poems:

> First, an initial vision of loss or crisis, centering on a question of renewal or imaginative survival; second, a despairing or reductive answer to the question, in which the mind's power, however great, seems inadequate

---

[27] See Newey on Cowper's descriptions as " undermining the claims of Christian orthodoxy," *Cowper's Poetry* 161. I do not agree with Abrams that Wordsworth fully "secularizes" Christian patterns, but he does "immanentize" many of them by emphasizing the presence and power of God in nature. For a recent study of Wordsworth's varying relations to Christianity in his early period, see William A. Ulmer, "The Christian Wordsworth: 1798–1800," *Journal of English and German Philology* 95 (1996): 336–358 and *The Christian Wordsworth: 1798–1805* (Albany, 2001).

to overcome the obstacles both of language and of the universe of death, of outer sense; third, a more hopeful or at least ongoing answer, however qualified by recognitions of continuing loss. Historically, this is certainly a displacement of a Protestant pattern, and traces back to similar triads of the spirit in the Psalms and the Prophets, and in Job.[28]

The Task begins with two books of crisis, the first of which is a vision of frustration and loss as the narrator breaks from the patterns of his Miltonic predecessors, the second a complete reversal of the sublime in satire and apocalypse. In Book Three, the narrator presents a counter-sublime in an excessive and desperate panegyric of the georgic life. And in Book Four, he empties his vision completely and reduces the entire quest to an isolated interior withdrawal. The final two books, in language mixing evangelical with Romantic imagery, simultaneously project the divine resolution into nature and introject its reception back into the self. This occurs, of course, in the sacred moment of perception, which is expressed in the early/late images of a revelation that both takes place within and goes beyond time.

Thus, Cowper, in the words of Blake, like Wordsworth spent his soul in prophecy. His prophetic words in *The Task* broke through the psychic and poetic barriers between the bards of sensibility and the Romantic prophets of the commonplace. His central poem contains the major themes and motifs of his most important successor, who was to succeed in drawing out the consequences of *The Task*. In this epic of repose, Cowper created a new mode that revolutionized the voice of poetry for the following century. He succeeded not only in recovering and transforming the voice of Milton, not merely in chastening and developing his own tones with post-Augustan precision, but also was able to find "proportionate praise" for a visionary theme of the sacred moment of perception. Through Wordsworth, Cowper was to inform a new spirit for a new age.

Works Cited

Abrams, M. H. *Natural Supernaturalism: Tradition and Revolution in Romantic Literature*. New York: Norton, 1971.

---

[28] *A Map of Misreading* (New York, 1975) 9.

———. "Structure and Style in the Greater Romantic Lyric." Hilles and Bloom 527–560.
Barth, J. Robert, S.J. *The Symbolic Imagination: Coleridge and the Romantic Tradition*. Rev. ed. New York: Fordham University Press, 2001.
Blom, T. E. "Eighteenth-Century Reflexive Process Poetry." *Eighteenth-Century Studies* 10 (1976): 52–72.
———. "The Structure and Meaning of *The Task*," *Pacific Coast Philology* 5 (1970): 12–18.
Brantley, Richard. *Wordsworth's "Natural Methodism."* New Haven: Yale University Press, 1975.
Brooke, Stopford A. *Theology in the English Poets*. London: J. M. Dent, 1874.
Brown, Marshall. "The Pre-Romantic Discovery of Consciousness." *Studies in Romanticism* 17 (1978): 387–412.
Cowper, William. *The Letters and Prose Writing of William Cowper*. Ed. James King and Charles Ryskamp. 5 vols. New York: Oxford University Press, 1979–1986.
———. *The Poems of William Cowper*. Ed. John D. Baird and Charles Ryskamp. 3 vols. New York: Oxford University Press, 1980–.
Dawson, P. M. S. "Cowper's Equivocations." *Essays in Criticism* 33 (1983): 19–35.
Free, Norman N. *William Cowper*. New York: Twayne, 1970.
Frye, Northrup. *The Stubborn Structure*. Ithaca: Cornell University Press, 1970.
Fulford, Tim. "Wordsworth, Cowper, and the Language of Eighteenth-Century Politics." Woodman 117–133.
Gill, Frederic C. *The Romantic Movement and Methodism*. London: Epworth, 1937.
Griffin, Dustin. "Redefining Georgic: Cowper's *Task*," *ELH* 57 (1990): 865–879.
———. "Cowper, Milton, and the Recovery of Paradise." *Essays in Criticism* 31 (1981): 15–26.
Hartman, Geoffrey. *Wordsworth's Poetry, 1787–1814*. New Haven: Yale University Press, 1964.
Heller, Deborah. "Cowper's *Task* and the Writing of a Poet's Salvation," *Studies in English Literature* 35 (1995): 575–599.
Hilles, Frederick W., and Harold Bloom, eds. *From Sensibility to Romanticism*. London: Oxford University Press, 1965.

House, Humphrey. *Coleridge.* London: Oxford University Press, 1953.
Jones, Myrddin. "Wordsworth and Cowper: The Eye Made Quiet." *Essays in Criticism* 23 (1973): 102–108.
Leigh, David J. "Images of God in Pre-Romantic English Poetry," *Ultimate Reality and Meaning* 9 (1986): 37–55.
McConnell, Frank D. *The Confessional Imagination: A Reading of Wordsworth's "Prelude."* Baltimore: Johns Hopkins University Press, 1974.
Mahoney, John L. "William Wordsworth: Nature, Imagination, and Ultimate Reality." *Ultimate Reality and Meaning* 13 (1990): 177–200.
Marshall, W. G. "The Presence of 'the Word' in Cowper's *The Task*." *Studies in English Literature* 27 (1987): 475–487.
Musser, Joseph F. "William Cowper's Rhetoric: The Picturesque and the Personal," *Studies in English Literature* 19 (1979): 515–531.
Newey, Vincent. "Cowper and the Description of Nature." *Essays in Criticism* 23 (1973): 102–108.
———. *Cowper's Poetry: A Critical Study and Reassessment.* Totowa, N.J.: Barnes & Noble, 1982.
———. "Wordsworth, Bunyan, and the Puritan Mind." *ELH* 41 (1974): 212–232.
Newton, John. *The Works of the Rev. John Newton.* 2 vols. New York: R. Carter, 1847.
Nicholson, Norman. *William Cowper.* London: J. Lehman, 1951.
Owen, W. J. B. "Literary Echoes in *The Prelude*." *The Wordsworth Circle* 5 (1972): 3–16.
Piper, H. W. *The Active Universe: Pantheism and the Concept of the Imagination in the English Poets.* London: Athlone Press, 1962.
Potts, A. F. *Wordsworth's Prelude: A Study of Its Literary Form.* Ithaca: Cornell University Press, 1953.
Price, Martin. *To the Palace of Wisdom.* New York: Doubleday, 1964.
Priestman, Martin. *Cowper's Task: Structure and Influence.* Cambridge: Cambridge University Press, 1983.
Quinlan, Maurice. *Willliam Cowper: A Critical Life.* Minneapolis: University of Minnesota Press, 1953.
Schulz, Max F. *The Poetic Voices of Coleridge.* Detroit: Wayne State University Press, 1963.
Shepherd, T. B. *Methodism and Literature and the Eighteenth Century.* London: Epworth Press, 1940.

Trickett, Rachel. "Cowper, Wordsworth, and the Animal Fable," *Review of English Studies*, New Series 34 (Nov. 1983): 471–480.

Ulmer, William A. "The Christian Wordsworth, 1798–1800." *Journal of English and German Philology* 95 (1996): 336–358.

———. *The Christian Wordsworth: 1798–1804*. Albany: State University of New York Press, 2001.

Woodman, Thomas, ed. *The Early Romantics: Perspectives in British Poetry from Pope to Wordsworth*. Cambridge: Cambridge University Press, 1998.

Wordsworth, William. *Early Poems and Fragments, 1785–1797*. Ed. Carol Landon. *The Cornell Wordsworth*. Ithaca: Cornell University Press, 1997.

———. *The Fourteen Book Prelude*. Ed. W. J. B. Owen. *The Cornell Wordsworth*. Ithaca: Cornell University Press, 1985.

———. *"Home at Grasmere": Part First, Book First of "The Recluse."* Ed. Beth Darlington. *The Cornell Wordsworth*. Ithaca: Cornell University Press, 1977.

———. *Letters of William and Dorothy Wordsworth*. 2d ed. Rev. Chester L. Shaver. Oxford: Oxford University Press, 1967.

———. *"Lyrical Ballads," and Other Poems, 1797–1800*. Ed. James Butler and Karen Green. *The Cornell Wordsworth*. Ithaca: Cornell University Press, 1992.

———. *The Poetical Works of William Wordsworth*. Ed. Ernest de Selincourt and Helen Darbishire. 5 vols. Oxford: Clarendon, 1940–1945.

Wu, Duncan. *Wordsworth's Reading: 1770–1799*. Cambridge: Cambridge University Press, 1993.

5

Wordsworth Between God and Mammon: The Early "Spots of Time" and the Sublime as Sacramental Commodity

Charles J. Rzepka

BEGINNING with the earliest drafts of *The Prelude*, in the two-part version of 1798–99, Wordsworth's "spots of time" play a vital role in his retrospective self-fashioning at mid-life. They seem to him revelatory not only of the sources of his mature poetic power, but also of the obscure influence of a supervening intelligence—what he will later call, in "Resolution and Independence," a "peculiar grace, / A leading from above" (50–51)[1]—on the course of his creative life. These pre-potent events, writes Wordsworth in 1799,

> with distinct pre-eminence retain
> A fructifying virtue, whence, depressed
> By trivial occupations and the round
> Of ordinary intercourse, our minds—
> Especially the imaginative power—
> Are nourished, and invisibly repaired;
> Such moments chiefly seem to have their date
> In our first childhood. (I, 289–296)[2]

---

[1] All quotations from Wordsworth's poetry, except for *The Prelude*, are taken from Stephen Gill, ed. *The Oxford Authors: William Wordsworth* (Oxford, 1984).

[2] All quotations from *The Prelude* are taken from the two-part version of 1798–99, unless otherwise noted. Quotations of material from all versions of *The Prelude*, 1798–1799, 1805, and 1850, come from *The Prelude 1799, 1805, 1850*, ed. Jonathan Wordsworth, M. H. Abrams, and Stephen Gill (New York, 1979).

While religion has not played a very important part in critical reflections on the "spots of time,"[3] it did provide the poet with an important trope by which to convey the sense of poetic mission or election often accompanying the "imaginative power" that the spots invisibly nourish and repair. Thus, referring to the opening lines that serve as a "glad preamble" (VII, 4) to the 1805 *Prelude*, Wordsworth writes, "To the open fields I told / A prophecy; poetic numbers came / Spontaneously, and clothed in priestly robe / My spirit, thus singled out, as it might seem, / For holy services" (I, 60–63). In Book III, a similarly elevating experience occurs during his first summer vacation from Cambridge, on a lonely country road at sunrise: "I made no vows," says the poet, "but vows / Were then made for me: bond unknown to me / Was given, that I should be—else sinning greatly— / A dedicated spirit" (*1805* III, 341–344).

As the language of "bond" and "sinning" suggests, being singled out for poetic election—being led "from above"—entails a profound sense of spiritual indebtedness and its corresponding anxieties. While the sense of election is often accompanied by the "miraculous gift" (*1805* I, 22) of visionary insight and creative power—"a gift that consecrates my joy" (*1805* I, 40), as Wordsworth puts it—this gift brings with it high, often fearful, obligations. The "bond unknown" of the poet's early years became known, and thus fell due (as it were) only when he came to recognize, primarily with the help of his sister, Dorothy, "his true self" (*1805* X, 915) and, therein, his true "office upon earth" as "a poet" (*1805* X, 919–920). His consequent sense of spiritual obligation, and fear of "sinning greatly" by neglecting to fulfill it, are nowhere more clearly announced than in the denouement of indecision that appears not long after the "glad preamble" of 1805:

---

[3] For instance, neither Nancy Easterlin, *Wordsworth and the Question of "Romantic Religion"* (Lewisberg, 1996), nor Robert Ryan, *The Romantic Reformation: Religious Politics in English Literature, 1789–1824* (Cambridge, 1997) makes any connection between the "spots" and Wordsworth's religious sensibility. J. R. Watson, *Wordsworth's Vital Soul: The Sacred and Profane in Wordsworth's Poetry* (Atlantic Highlands, N.J., 1982) 133, finds in "spots" like the bird's nesting episode (I, 57–66) a resemblance to "manifestations of the sacred—hierophanies—in primitive religion," but does not develop the idea. Richard E. Brantley, *Wordsworth's "Natural Methodism"* (New Haven, 1975) 41–42, like M. H. Abrams, *Natural Supernaturalism: Tradition and Revolution in Romantic Literature* (New York, 1971) 385–390, links the "spots" to the Augustinian/Calvinist tradition of "spiritual autobiography." On the relation of the "spots of time" to biblical notions of temporality, see J. Robert Barth, S.J., "The Temporal Imagination in Wordsworth's *Prelude*: Time and the Timeless," *Thought* 66 (1991): 148–149.

> This is my lot; for either still I find
> Some imperfection in the chosen theme,
> Or see of absolute accomplishment
> Much wanting—so much wanting—in myself
> That I recoil and droop, and seek repose
> In indolence from vain perplexity,
> Unprofitably travelling towards the grave,
> Like a false steward who hath much received
> And renders nothing back. (*1805* I, 263–271)

Wordsworth here alludes to the parable of the false steward in Matthew 25: 14–30, who hid away the money—the "talent"—he was given by his master instead of improving and increasing it: "Take therefore the talent from him," the master commands his servants, "and give it unto him that hath ten talents, for unto everyone that hath shall be given, and he shall have abundance: but from him that hath not shall be taken away even that which he hath" (Matthew 25: 28–29).[4]

Wordsworth knew that to invest and make spiritually profitable the gift of his own "talent" would require the writing of more than ordinary poetry. As his sunrise dedication scene indicates, it would demand nothing less than "prophecy," and prophets are not often respected in their own country. The 1798 "Advertisement" to the first edition of *Lyrical Ballads* conveys the poet's awareness that his commitment to a prophetic, spiritually revolutionary kind of poetry will require his readers to "struggle with feelings of strangeness and awkwardness": "they will look round for poetry, and will be induced to inquire by what species of courtesy these attempts can be permitted to assume that title."[5]

The consequences for poets who set up as prophets can be more than just humiliating, whether or not they eventually succeed in finding listeners with ears to hear. More often than not that audience, though fit, will be few. However much Wordsworth deprecated a life of "getting and spending" ("The world is too much with us," 2), he understood the necessity, indeed the responsibility, of making a gainful living. "Resolution and Independence," reflecting the poet's state of mind on the day he explained to Mary Hutchinson that he would have to come to an understanding with his former French mistress, Annette

---

[4] All biblical references are to the King James Version.
[5] *Lyrical Ballads*, ed. R. L. Brett and A. R. Jones (New York, 1963) 7.

Vallon, before he and Mary could wed,[6] reveals the poet's long-standing worries over financial as well as spiritual and emotional independence. He is beset by "Dim sadness, and blind thoughts" (28) of "distress, and poverty" (35):

> My whole life I have lived in pleasant thought,
> As if life's business were a summer mood;
> As if all needful things would come unsought
> To genial faith, still rich in genial good;
> But how can He expect that others should
> Build for him, sow for him, and at his call
> Love him, who for himself will take no heed at all? (36–42)

Echoes, again, of Matthew's Gospel resound here, specifically the Sermon on the Mount, 6: 25–34, when Jesus tells his disciples, "Take no thought for your life, what ye shall eat, or what ye shall drink; nor yet for your body, what ye shall put on." He then goes on to cite, as examples, "the fowls of the air: for they sow not, neither do they reap . . . yet your heavenly Father feedeth them."

As I have observed elsewhere,[7] from 1798 to 1802, that is, from the year he published *Lyrical Ballads* to the year he wrote "Resolution and Independence," Wordsworth was haunted by two conflicting anxieties. On the one hand, in continuing to ignore or to delay work on his magnum opus, the great philosophical poem of *The Recluse*, he was defaulting on the spiritual obligations entailed by his poetic "talent." On the other hand, he was seriously questioning whether or not poetry, and especially the kind of poetry he wished to write, could provide what the leech-gatherer in "Resolution and Independence" calls "an honest maintenance" (112), not only for himself, but for his present and prospective household. This conflict between spiritual obligation and material need surfaces not long after the publication of *Lyrical Ballads*, in early drafts of the 1798–99 two-part *Prelude*, and it specifically informs one of the two original "spots of time" introduced as such in that poem. Unpacking the implications of this particular "spot," we can discern some of the psychological obstacles impeding Words-

---

[6] Mary Moorman, *William Wordsworth: A Biography*, vol. 1, *The Early Years, 1770–1803* (Oxford, 1957) 540.

[7] Charles J. Rzepka, "A Gift that Complicates Employ: Poetry and Poverty in 'Resolution and Independence,'" *Studies in Romanticism* 28 (1989): 225–247.

worth's prophetic commitment to share with his readers what he had come to call, a few months before in "Tintern Abbey," his "sense sublime, / Of something far more deeply interfused" (96–97): a spiritual presence immanent in the natural world, yet reverberating with "the still, sad music of humanity" (92). By the summer of 1798, this "sense sublime" had become the foundation of both his mission and his identity as a poet, the very point of his "office upon earth."

In the second of the original "spots of time," Wordsworth describes himself at thirteen years of age, "feverish, and tired, and restless" (I, 332), awaiting the arrival—"impatient for the sight" (I, 333)—of his father's horses to take him and his two brothers home for the Christmas holidays.

> Ere I to school returned
> That dreary time, ere I had been ten days
> A dweller in my Father's house, he died,
> And I and my two Brothers, orphans then,
> Followed his body to the grave. The event
> With all the sorrow which it brought appeared
> A chastisement; and when I called to mind
> That day so lately passed, when from the crag
> I looked in such anxiety of hope,
> With trite reflections of morality,
> Yet with the deepest passion, I bowed low
> To God who thus corrected my desires;
> And afterwards the wind, and sleety rain,
> And all the business of the elements,
> The single sheep, and the one blasted tree,
> And the bleak music of that old stone wall . . .
> All these were spectacles and sounds to which
> I often would repair, and thence would drink
> As at a fountain. (I, 349–370)

This scene is famously under- rather than over-determined in the context of *The Prelude* itself. We can, like Richard Onorato or Don Johnson,[8] seek to understand Wordsworth's mysterious feelings of "chastisement" by resorting to textbook Freudian versions of Oedipal

---

[8] Richard J. Onorato, *The Character of the Poet: Wordsworth in "The Prelude"* (Princeton, 1971) 253–254; Don Johnson, "The Grief Behind the Spots of Time," *American Imago* 45 (1988): 302–303.

rage and guilt, an explanation that has by now become so obvious, says Richard E. Matlak, that it "hardly requires further confirmation."[9] Or we might, like Richard Brantley and Nancy Easterlin,[10] read the episode in the light of Evangelical convictions that any form of impatience, especially when it is directed at a parent, is opposed to God's will and in need of divine "chastisement."

However, as David Ellis points out, "hostility towards the father" is neither stated nor implied within the episode itself. It is an "addition" that the reader must "supply as a logical extension of the boy's mood." Without that addition, "the wait on the summit is deficient in any special appropriateness as a focus or collecting point for Wordsworth's responses to his father's death."[11] To put it another way: the patently bad fit between the boy's impatient "anxiety of hope" to return *to* his "Father's house" and the oddly triangulated form of God's "chastisement" for his having had such hopes (why kill the father to chastise the son for wanting to be with him?) drives readers to search for explanations outside the text. Appeals to repressed Oedipal rage and to "screen memories," however, help little to advance understanding. The "desires" that God "corrected" were clearly conscious, not repressed, and thus inconsistent with the theory of repressed hostility that would explain them. Perhaps, Ellis suggests, the boy's "anxiety" is "no more than an eagerness to go home. In which case, the 'desires' [Wordsworth] speaks of (and which God 'corrected') would be the normal holiday projects and schemes of a boy tired of school."[12]

I believe Ellis is right to focus on "holiday . . . schemes," but that focus needs to be sharpened (what are these "schemes"?) and redirected away from active "hostility" altogether. As we shall see, the "desires" giving rise to Wordsworth's "anxiety of hope" are not difficult to locate within the abbreviated two-part *Prelude* itself, and they are worthy of "chastisement" only because they have displaced emotions more appro-

---

[9] *The Poetry of Relationship: The Wordsworths and Coleridge, 1797–1800* (New York, 1997) 186. By contrast, Alan Richardson, "Wordsworth at the Crossroads: 'Spots of Time' in the 'Two-Part *Prelude*,'" *The Wordsworth Circle* 19 (1988): 15–20, finds here an instance of pre-Oedipal magical thinking, in which the boy, mistaking his father's death as consequence, interprets his "hope" as "an act of apparent omnipotence" (18).

[10] See Brantley 42–44 and Easterlin 105–106.

[11] *Wordsworth, Freud, and the Spots of Time: Interpretation in "The Prelude"* (Cambridge, 1985) 20.

[12] Ellis 20–21.

priate to the Christmas season, such as filial affection and gratitude. Moreover, these "desires" are clearly related to the anxieties over indebtedness, election, and obligation that Wordsworth was experiencing at the time he wrote this passage. The precise nature of these anxieties is made evident by several New Testament passages echoing within this spot of time.[13] Let us begin with the phrase, "my Father's house."

Wordsworth's decision to capitalize "Father's" is consistent with his capitalization of other familial epithets throughout the 1798–99 *Prelude*—"Brothers" (I, 335, 352) or "Child" later on (I, 394), or in Part Two, "Mother's eye" (II, 273). But in this context, where the whole point seems to be that the boy has experienced "chastisement" by God, his heavenly "Father," for "desires" and hopes directed at "the house" of his earthly father, the word's upper-case initial seems more than just a typographical eccentricity.

In particular, the phrase corresponds to John 2: 16, where Jesus, having arrived in Jerusalem at Passover, overthrows the money-changers' tables in the Temple, saying, "Take these things hence; make not my Father's house an house of merchandise." Later, in John 14: 12, when Jesus bids farewell to his disciples at his last Passover supper, he tells them, "In my Father's house are many mansions: if it were not so, I would have told you. I go to prepare a place for you" (14: 2). Taken together, the two allusions seem to suggest that this originary spot of time has something to do with choosing spiritual over material values and a heavenly as opposed to an earthly path, as well as accepting one's destined role as leader, teacher, and prophet—as the one who must "go before" to "prepare a place" for the rest of us. Closely allied to these two references, "all the business of the elements," which Wordsworth later identifies with "the workings of [his] spirit" (I, 374), points us to still another New Testament passage, this time from Luke: "How is it that ye sought me?" the young Jesus asks his worried parents when they discover him teaching the elders in the Temple, "wist ye not that I must be about my Father's business?" (Luke 2: 49).

The spot of time associated with his father's death, then, would seem to encapsulate, in a memory taken to be profoundly self-formative, the struggle between God and mammon that Wordsworth felt himself to be facing in 1798, not long after he had formally embarked on his

---

[13] I wish to thank Father J. Robert Barth, S.J., for helping me with these allusions.

poetic career, and several years after he had rejected the "office" of the Anglican ministry intended for him by his guardians.[14]

As I have just indicated, we do not need to look beyond the two-part *Prelude* itself in order to make sense of the relationship between these biblical echoes and the "feverish," "restless" "desires" informing young William's "anxiety of hope" in the Christmas-homecoming spot of time. Christmas is the season of gift-giving, and among the gifts that Wordsworth and his two brothers received each year were "purses more profusely filled" to take back to school in order to supplement their "little weekly stipend." Robert Woof's appendices to T. W. Thompson's *Wordsworth's Hawkshead* itemize several examples of such seasonal largesse,[15] lacking which Wordsworth was forced (so he says) to live for most of the year "in pennyless poverty":

> More than we wished we knew the blessing then
> Of vigorous hunger, for our daily meals
> Were frugal, Sabine fare—and then, exclude
> A little weekly stipend, and we lived
> Through three divisions of the quartered year
> In pennyless poverty. But now to school
> Returned from the half-yearly holidays,
> We came with purses more profusely filled,
> Allowance which abundantly sufficed
> To gratify the palate with repasts
> More costly. . . .[16]
> Hence inroads into distant vales, and long
> Excursions far away among the hills,
> Hence rustic dinners on the cool green ground—
> Or in the woods, or by a river-side
> Or fountain—festive banquets, that provoked
> The languid action of a natural scene
> By pleasure of corporeal appetite. (II, 79–97)

Meals *al fresco*, "rustic" or "festive," were not the only luxuries made possible by these extra funds.

---

[14] See Stephen Gill, *William Wordsworth: A Life* (Oxford, 1989) 40–41, 84, and 116–117, and John L. Mahoney, *William Wordsworth: A Poetic Life* (New York, 1997) 27–29, for an account of the pressures shaping this decision and its consequences.

[15] See *Wordsworth's Hawkshead*, ed. Robert Woof (Oxford, 1970) 253–254.

[16] "than the dame of whom I spake, / That ancient woman, and her board, supplied." The "ancient woman" referred to here was an old woman—"Nanny" or Ann Holme, by name—who sold her "huckster's wares" (II, 44) in the Hawkshead marketplace. See Thompson 253.

> Nor is my aim neglected if I tell
> How twice in the long length of those half-years
> We from our funds perhaps with bolder hand
> Drew largely, anxious for one day at least
> To feel the motion of the galloping steed;
> And with the good old innkeeper, in truth
> I needs must say, that sometimes we have used
> Sly subterfuge, for the intended bound
> Of the day's journey was too distant far
> For any cautious man. (II, 98–107)

By the end of the two-part *Prelude* we have probably forgotten that his father's holiday supplements underwrote the thrilling horseback rides with his school-fellows that Wordsworth singles out for special attention: day-long excursions to the "sequestered ruin" (114) of Furness Abbey—"a holy scene" (111) haunted by the sound of "the murmuring sea" (116), by Gothic effigies like "the cross-legged knight / And the stone abbot," and by "that single wren / Which one day sang so sweetly in the nave" (120–122). At nightfall, as they rode homeward, says Wordsworth, "Lightened by gleams of moonlight from the sea, / We beat with thundering hoofs the level sand" (137–139). From the adult perspective of 1798–99, as the poet faced the difficulties of making spiritually profitable the stewardship of his poetic "office upon earth," these youthful quests in search of sublime experiences appeared to have played an indispensible role in his development as "a *creative* soul" (*1805*, XI, 256).

They were also, to a certain degree, transgressive, based as Wordsworth admits on "sly subterfuge": the innkeeper who owned the horses had no idea the boys intended to travel so far, "too distant far / For any cautious man." Indeed, there is something similarly "sly" and transgressive in many of the earlier boyhood incidents Wordsworth recounts in the fragments of Part One written approximately from October to November 1798, well before the "spots of time" passage itself. Typically, these incidents involve solitary, surreptitious appropriations of things that do not belong to the boy: stealing from others' woodcock snares, secretly borrowing a boat, or raiding birds' nests. By the time the first continuous draft of Part One was written in January 1799, these incidents, along with several others dating mainly from Wordsworth's Hawkshead school years and including the Christmas episode, come to bear a generic resemblance that fits them comfortably under the rubric of the "spots of time" broadly defined: sublime moments, often tinged with some degree of fear, anxiety, or awe, that the poet took to be formative in what he later called the "history of [his] poet's mind" (*1805* XIII, 408).

That acts of misappropriation should appear so prominently in the earliest "spots of time" suggests that at the childhood origin of the Wordsworthian sublime there lies a fundamental conflict between the hard facts of material dependency and an urgent need to assert spiritual autonomy. The antinomian sense of entitlement informing these early "spots" and the thrill of anticipated retribution confirming their transgressive self-affirmations are adumbrations of the sublime that the poet will later interpret as early signs of his prophetic election. As I have already observed, this conflict between the fact of dependency and the need for autonomy has traditionally been subsumed by fundamentally Oedipal readings of the poem.[17] In certain respects, however, it seems to respond better to discursive, Lacanian versions of Freudianism where the Law of the Father, expressed in the alienated but self-empowering symbolic registers of language and exchange-value, disciplines the subjective imaginary and forces the Self and its experiences to emerge as objects of discourse and exchange in a community of others.[18]

The symbolic exchange-form assumed by the child's imaginary encounters with the sublime as he entered young manhood appears in Part Two of the 1798–99 *Prelude*, when Wordsworth begins to share these experiences with a group of like-minded communicants. Some of these group experiences were even collaboratively staged. When Robert Greenwood perched himself on a rock at the edge of Lake Windermere to play his flute and, as Wordsworth puts it, "the calm / And dead still water lay upon my mind / Even with a weight of pleasure, and the sky, / Never before so beautiful, sank down / Into my heart and held me like a dream" (II, 210–214), it no doubt helped that Greenwood, accustomed to his role as "the minstrel of our troop" (209), had agreed

---

[17] See, e.g., Matlak's interpretation, in which "the natural landscape of Wordsworth's youth becomes a shadowy world for a confrontation between father and son over identity and control" (177).

[18] This approach was expressed in the psycho-semiotic interpretation of Thomas Weiskel, *The Romantic Sublime* (Baltimore, 1976). See, e.g., ch. 6, "Absence and Identity in the Egotistical Sublime," 136–164, and ch. 7, "Wordsworth and the Defile of the Word," 167–204.

to be left there to perform as the others "rowed off gently" in their "pinnace" over "the dusky lake" (205–209).

Whether staged or not, the group opportunities for "momentary trance" (II, 177) that Wordsworth singles out were activities wholly subsidized by the "purses more profusely filled" that the boys received at half-yearly holidays: "*Hence* inroads" and "excursions," writes Wordsworth, "*Hence* rustic dinners" and "festive banquets." Riding to Furness Abbey on rented horses (II, 100–139), floating in a rented boat in the "cloister"-like "gloom" of "ancient trees" along Coniston water and viewing sunsets through their "horizontal boughs" (II, 140–178), listening to Greenwood's magic flute after luxurious picnics of strawberries and cream at the "splendid" White Horse Inn (II, 179–214)—all were fetishized commodifications of the sublime, what Marx would call "sublimates" of the young man's "material life process."[19]

The sublimation of paternal largesse that enabled the sublime itself to assume, for the young Wordsworth, a fetishized commodity-form is registered in the older poet's description of the ride to Furness Abbey. Here the boys' "sly *sub*terfuge" concerning the "intended *bound* / Of the day's journey (105–106) marks the experience they have purchased as "*sub-limin*al," the result of their having crossed "under" the "limen" or threshold of adult restriction. Indeed, the boys define themselves as a group set off from the official school community by the free exercise of their surplus buying-power to cross boundaries—geographical, academic, class, or generational—that are maintained pragmatically through adult restrictions on their allowance. By occasionally transgressing these boundaries in like-minded company and converting the money-form of the Father's gift into an object of aesthetic consumption, the adolescent poet and his peers achieve momentary independence from the Law of the Father, which ordinarily demands repayment of paternal support for a son's education in the form of an implicit bond committing him to the culturally capitalized (and of course lucrative) fields of law, religion, or medicine.[20]

---

[19] Karl Marx and Friedrich Engels, *The German Ideology, Parts I and III*, ed. R. Pascal (New York, 1947) 14.

[20] On the academic transformation of economic into cultural capital, see Pierre Bourdieu, *Distinction: A Social Critique of the Judgement of Taste*, trans. Richard Nice (Cambridge, Mass., 1984) 11–96. For an explanation of how literary production came to assume a central role in effecting this transformation during the Romantic period, see John Guillory, *Cultural Capital: The Problem of Literary Canon Formation* (Chicago, 1993).

Later, Wordsworth came to recognize that another "bond unknown" to him had been "given": that he "should be—else sinning greatly . . . dedicated" to "prophecy" and "holy services" as a poet, not a preacher. Prophecy and holy services, however, require a chosen people, a congregation of communicants. At Hawkshead, the commodity-form of the sublime purchased with their fathers' gifts united the young Wordsworth and his circle of friends into an aesthetic congregation, providing them with a shared object of sublime communion, a sacramental commodity of which all could partake.[21]

The poet's integration of "repasts," "rustic dinners," and "festive banquets" into his account of these shared "spots of time," his reiterated focus on meals that "provoked / The languid action of a natural scene / By pleasure of corporeal appetite," underscores this sacramental dimension of the boys' consumption of the sublime as spiritual communion. It also helps to contextualize Wordsworth's general tendency to figure sublime experience as ingestion, a feeding on or drinking in of the natural scene, as at the end of Part Two when the poet credits "ye mountains, and ye lakes / And sounding cataracts" with having "fed / My lofty expectations" (II, 470–471, 492–493). "The gift is yours," he tells them, twice (478, 491). In fact, it was John Wordsworth's gift, sublimated and disguised.

A sketch of the two-part *Prelude*'s chronology of composition reveals the central importance of the Christmas spot of time in the adult poet's imaginative reconstruction of these corporate sublimations of his father's pecuniary power as "spots of time" in their own right. By the end of 1799 they will emerge as sources of spiritual nourishment that are both imaginatively "fructifying," like their earlier counterparts, and portentous of the aesthetically re-attuned and empathic community that Wordsworth hopes his prophetic poetry can create for its own reception.

The order of composition of the episodes that will eventually be subsumed under the title "spots of time" is as follows:[22] from October to November 1798 Wordsworth writes, in MS JJ, what Stephen Parrish

---

[21] For the phenomenology of this process of aesthetic sublimation and its relationship to the textual sublime, see Charles J. Rzepka, *Sacramental Commodities: Gift, Text, and the Sublime in De Quincey* (Amherst, Mass., 1995) 1–66.

[22] The earliest drafts of Part One of the two-part *Prelude* are to be found in MS JJ, the "Christabel Notebook," and the Goslar faircopy MS 18A, while those of Part Two appear principally in MS RV. See *The Prelude*, ed. Jonathan Wordsworth, et al. 514–15.

calls "a coherent passage of about 150 lines,"[23] including vignettes of himself as a "naked savage" at Cockermouth, when he was four (I, 1–26), bird's nesting (I, 50–66), and woodcock snaring (I, 28–49). The boat-borrowing episode (I, 82–129) appears separately in this MS, while the ice-skating episode (I, 150–187) seems also to have been written separately at about this time. The "Christabel Notebook" (Dove Cottage MS 15) shows that by mid-December—roughly the fifteenth anniversary of the date, December 19, on which Wordsworth had waited for his father's horses near Borwick Lodge—the poet had completed a version of Part I that included boat-borrowing, but not skating. I think it is safe to characterize all of the episodes included in MS JJ by mid-December as solitary, antinomian experiences of the sublime.

Between this point and the end of January 1799, Wordsworth composed the earliest draft of the passage including the "spots of time" (I, 234–374), beginning with a few lines (234–246) describing quotidian solitary activities—nutting, fishing, and kite-flying—leading up to the "drowned man" episode" (I, 258–287). The lines specifically characterizing the "spots of time" (I, 288–296) are immediately followed by two examples. In the first, an early, pre-Hawkshead memory, young William, only five years old and just learning to ride, becomes separated from his guide, a servant of his father's. The second is the Christmas homecoming memory associated with John Wordsworth's death. Also during this period, according to the editors of the Norton *Prelude*,[24] Wordsworth first thinks of introducing group activities into the poem itself: "Not uselessly employed, / I might pursue this theme through every change / Of exercise and sport to which the year / Did summon us. . . . We were a noisy crew . . ." (I, 198–202).[25] It is not until much later, however, in the fall and winter of 1799, that the card-playing (I, 206–233) and ice-skating sequences are incorporated into Part One.

Viewed in the context of the two-part *Prelude*'s early stages of composition, the fifteenth anniversary of the waiting-for-horses episode and of John Wordsworth's subsequent death on December 30 seems pivotal in the poet's imaginative reconstruction of what would eventually be called the "spots of time." The memory of these events put

---

[23] Stephen Parrish, ed. *The Prelude, 1798–1799 by William Wordsworth* (Ithaca, 1977) 4.

[24] See *The Prelude*, ed. Jonathan Wordsworth, et al. 514.

[25] Parrish gives no indication that these lines were written at this time.

Wordsworth in mind of his father's half-yearly holiday gifts and the group activities on which he had spent them in pursuit of shared sublime experiences.[26]

The waiting-for-horses spot plays a correspondingly pivotal role in the poem itself, as we can see if we examine the theme of horseback riding. Wordsworth's memories of learning to ride a horse and then waiting to ride a horse, which immediately follow the "spots of time" passage in Part One, are thematically completed, early in Part Two, by the first of the three group experiences of the sublime made possible by supplementary paternal funds. In the trips to Furness Abbey, the poet and his friends actually ride horses, entirely under their own power and direction, "in wantonness of heart," and "beat[ing] with thundering hoofs the level sand."

Horses are traditional symbols of male autonomy, mastery, and self-empowerment. It is not unimportant to our understanding of the boy's sense of "chastisement" at his father's death that he should be waiting for his father's horses, or that these horses, unlike those that he and his companions hired by "sly subterfuge" to carry them to the hidden recesses of Furness Abbey or the wide expanse of Leven Sands, will be taking him back to his earthly "Father's house." As a "dweller" (I, 351) there, he will temporarily lose his freedom to roam at will with his companions in deliberate quest of sublime experiences. However, he will also acquire the financial wherewithal for further transgressions of the multiple boundaries implicitly inscribed around the scene of intellectual labor at Hawkshead by his "little weekly stipend."

To the adolescent Wordsworth the death of his earthly father, the

---

[26] The ice-skating scene, written earlier than the "spots" passages, is out of sequence in this gradual transition from solitary to corporate experiences of the sublime. But it is an exception that proves the rule, for it expresses a desire to test the boundary between solitude and solidarity that the memory of events surrounding his father's death will help Wordsworth cross, imaginatively, several weeks later. Beginning with his refusal to return at dusk to the home where he was staying while attending school (I, 153), Wordsworth seques into equine self-characterization and then moves on, via an allusion to horseshoes, to include group activity: "I wheeled about / Proud and exulting, like an untired horse / That cares not for its home. All shod with steel / We hissed along the polished ice in games / Confederate" (I, 152–156). The poet ends with three acts of separation leading to a private experience of sublimity: "Not seldom from the uproar I retired," he says, "into a silent bay," or "Glanced sideway, leaving the tumultuous throng," or spinning away, "at once / Have I . . . Stopped short—yet still the solitary cliffs / Wheeled by me, even as if the earth had rolled / With visible motion her diurnal round" (I, 170–182).

"half-yearly" source of "purses more profusely filled," seemed to be a "chastisement" from God, his heavenly father, for letting his greed get the better of his affections. The boy's selfishness, augmented by the desire to burst the restrictive boundaries then circumscribing his life within the limits of his father's allowance, had eclipsed his sense of filial love and gratitude. Whatever lessons we may learn from Freud, young William's "desires" were neither violent nor directed at his father: they were acquisitive and directed at his "Father's house," the seat of paternal wealth and power. The boy's "anxiety of hope" was centered in the man's money, not the man. Now that the man was dead, his son was forced to recognize which of the two had been the more beloved, and he felt "chastise[d]" for having ever allowed himself to forget the difference. His "desires," thus "corrected," had been turned, belatedly, in the right direction.

At twenty-nine, however, Wordsworth also recalled what he owed to John Wordsworth's ampler funds: they had enabled him to transform his solitary and fearful experiences of the sublime into shared encounters. To disobey the Law of the Father—particularly when one's father literally professed the law—was, as the child had already discovered, to challenge and momentarily usurp his might, exciting delightfully terrifying sensations of guilty self-empowerment. At Hawkshead, drawing on his father's "half-yearly" gifts, Wordsworth had expanded his childhood experiences of the sublime into a new, group configuration, a communion set apart from, and yet sublating the hidden power of, the symbolic registers of the paternal law of exchange. From the perspective of 1798 and 1799, those "purses more profusely filled" must have looked like a good spiritual investment, paying off as they had in the "fructifying virtue" the poet now felt nourishing and repairing his imagination as he began his prophetic mission. And yet, the feeling of "chastisement" for his pecuniary desires seems to have persisted, reawakened perhaps by a nagging, and what many would consider irrational, sense of financial urgency that vexed his commitment to a prophetic sort of poetry.[27]

The choice between God and mammon facing Wordsworth in 1798 thus finds its paradoxical expression and imaginative resolution in this otherwise baffling spot of time. In looking back over his earliest memo-

---

[27] On Wordsworth's actual and imagined economic difficulties, and his concern to make his poetry profitable, see Rzepka, "A Gift" 227–232.

ries of natural sublimity, Wordsworth alighted on one in particular that seemed to provoke his deepest anxieties concerning the temptation to choose profit over prophecy, as well as his concurrent sense of obligation to choose the reverse. Returning to the moments in his past that he hoped would enable him to make good on the "bond" enjoined by the poetic gifts he had received, Wordsworth sought reaffirmation that it was not, after all, his earthly "Father's business" that he had been destined to pursue, not the business of lawyer or clergyman or schoolteacher for which his Hawkshead tuition had supposedly been preparing him, but "all the business of the elements," all "the workings of my spirit" (I, 374), as Wordsworth called it, in that haunting scene just north of Borwick Lodge. Presumably, he found the reaffirmation he sought, for to this imaginatively re-worked memory, as he wrote near the anniversary of his father's death, "I often would repair, and thence would drink / As at a fountain" (I, 369-370).

Works Cited

Abrams, M. H. *Natural Supernaturalism: Tradition and Revolution in Romantic Literature.* New York: Norton, 1971.

Barth, J. Robert, S.J. "The Temporal Imagination in Wordworth's *Prelude*: Time and the Timeless," *Thought* 66 (1991): 139-150.

Bourdieu, Pierre. *Distinction: A Social Critique of the Judgement of Taste.* Cambridge, Mass.: Harvard University Press, 1984.

Brantley, Richard E. *Wordsworth's "Natural Methodism."* New Haven: Yale University Press, 1975.

Easterlin, Nancy. *Wordsworth and the Question of "Romantic Religion."* Lewisberg: Bucknell University Press, 1996.

Ellis, David. *Wordsworth, Freud, and the Spots of Time: Interpretation in "The Prelude."* Cambridge: Cambridge University Press, 1985.

Gill, Stephen, ed. *The Oxford Authors: William Wordsworth.* Oxford: Oxford University Press, 1984.

———. *William Wordsworth: A Life.* Oxford: Clarendon Press, 1989.

Guillory, John. *Cultural Capital: The Problem of Literary Canon Formation.* Chicago: The University of Chicago Press, 1993.

Johnson, Don. "The Grief Behind the Spots of Time," *American Imago* 45 (1988): 287-307.

Mahoney, John L. *William Wordsworth: A Poetic Life*. New York: Fordham University Press, 1997.
Marx, Karl, and Friedrich Engels. *The German Ideology, Parts I and III*. Ed. R. Pascal. New York: International Publishers, 1947.
Matlak, Richard E. *The Poetry of Relationship: The Wordsworths and Coleridge, 1797–1800*. New York: St. Martin's, 1997.
Moorman, Mary. *William Wordsworth: A Biography*, vol. 1. *The Early Years, 1770–1803*. Oxford: Clarendon, 1957.
Onorato, Richard J. *The Character of the Poet: Wordsworth in "The Prelude."* Princeton: Princeton University Press, 1971.
Richardson, Alan. "Wordsworth at the Crossroads: 'Spots of Time' in the 'Two-Part *Prelude.*'" *The Wordsworth Circle* 19 (1988): 15–20.
Ryan, Robert. *The Romantic Reformation: Religious Politics in English Literature, 1789–1824*. Cambridge: Cambridge University Press, 1997.
Rzepka, Charles J. "A Gift that Complicates Employ: Poetry and Poverty in 'Resolution and Independence,'" *Studies in Romanticism* 28 (1989): 225–247.
———. *Sacramental Commodities: Gift, Text, and the Sublime in De Quincey*. Amherst, MA: University of Massachusetts Press, 1995.
Thompson, T. W. *Wordsworth's Hawkshead*. Ed. Robert Woof. Oxford: Oxford University Press, 1970.
Watson, J. R. *Wordsworth's Vital Soul: The Sacred and Profane in Wordsworth's Poetry*. Atlantic Highlands, N.J.: Humanities Press, 1982.
Weiskel, Thomas. *The Romantic Sublime*. Baltimore: Johns Hopkins University Press, 1976.
Wordsworth, William. *The Prelude 1798–1799*. Ed. Stephen Parrish. *The Cornell Wordsworth*. Ithaca: Cornell University Press, 1977.
———. *The Prelude 1799, 1805, 1850*. Ed. Jonathan Wordsworth, M. H. Abrams, and Stephen Gill. Norton Critical Edition. New York: Norton, 1979.
———, and Samuel Taylor Coleridge. *Lyrical Ballads*. Ed. R. L. Brett and A. R. Jones. New York: Methuen, 1963.

6

Icons of Women in the Religious Sonnets of Wordsworth and Hemans

John M. Anderson

I. THIS LIVID INTERVIEW: WORDSWORTH AND HEMANS

> His voice decrepit was with Joy—
> Her words did totter so
> How old the News of Love must be
> To make Lips elderly
> That purled a moment since with Glee—
> Is it Delight or Woe—
> Or Terror—that do decorate
> This livid interview[1]

WHY READ Wordsworth's *Ecclesiastical Sonnets* now? Such poems, the peripheral works of a supremely canonical poet, are often cited as usurping the attention of scholars who might instead be acquainting themselves with the many neglected works of intriguing, newly canonical writers like Felicia Hemans.

Why read Hemans' "Female Characters of Scripture" now, when Susan J. Wolfson's magisterial new edition of Hemans' selected works demands our attention, and this sonnet sequence is not included in that work?

One answer to both questions, perhaps the most important, is delight. I am surprised by the joy I have gained from reading these nearly forgotten works closely and in each other's context. *Ecclesiastical Sonnets* and "Female Characters of Scripture" offer quiet pleasures but real

---

[1] Emily Dickinson, *Complete Poems*, ed. Thomas H. Johnson (Boston, 1960), poem # 1746.

ones—and reading them together we discover undertones, cross-lights otherwise unapparent. Some of these delights are aesthetic, but many are intellectual: these poets present ideas of religion that rival our own in their self-contradictory passions and complacencies. These works are interesting because of their frank ambitiousness and their strategies for reconciling the intimately personal and the vastly impersonal—a great aim of religious thought but also of any politically or socially engaged poetry. Wordsworth explores the dauntingly complex and august institutions and history of the English church; Hemans writes about still more revered institutions and histories—the ones that make up the stories of the Bible—often quite as dauntingly simple. These sonnet sequences are interesting for their very flaws, and so are many of the individual sonnets, showing us the most popular poet of the period (Hemans) and the most influential and critically acclaimed (Wordsworth) in late-career difficulties.

Some of these subjects have been broached recently by Julie Melnyk, who argues that in Hemans' late "turn to God she attempts to restore to women's poetry a vatic power, often represented by Wordsworth's early work, which she almost compulsively re-works—a power that affectional poetry, in becoming acceptably 'feminine,' had lost."[2] I want to consider Hemans in relation to Wordsworth's late poetry—poetry nearly contemporaneous with Hemans' and in the same form—and I want to do a closer reading of a few poems than the broad scope of Melnyk's pioneer work allows her to do. I am grateful for Melnyk's informative and insightful work, though my conclusions regarding Hemans' image of the Virgin Mary and of Mary Magdalene differ considerably from hers.

The commonly accepted idea of "Romanticism and Religion" can perhaps be summed up in another little passage from Dickinson:

Some keep the Sabbath going to church,
I keep it staying at home,
With a bobolink for a chorister
And an orchard for a dome. (#324.1–4)

If so, these two series of Romantic sonnets suggest that the subject requires something like church-going after all. The sheer size of

---

[2] "Hemans' Later Poetry: Religion and the Vatic Poet," *Felicia Hemans: Reimagining Poetry in the Nineteenth Century* (Houndsmill, England, 2001) 74.

Wordsworth's sequence forebodes the sustained discipline involved in this approach to religion. A recent critic has argued that *"Ecclesiastical Sonnets* play a significant role in completing and unifying the Wordsworth canon. The Church, at its best, serves as a synthesizing force within the characteristically Wordsworthian interdynamic of God, nature, and humanity."[3] But because *Ecclesiastical Sonnets* has attracted little critical attention, it perhaps requires a bit of introduction. The sequence is divided into three Parts, whose very earnest, dry, and ambitious titles give a not entirely misleading sense of the whole. Part 1 covers the historical period "From the Introduction of Christianity into Britain to the Consummation of the Papal Dominion"; Part 2 continues this history "To the Close of the Troubles in the Reign of Charles I"; Part 3, "From the Restoration to the Present Time," includes sonnets concerning such things as the various Sacraments, certain "Aspects of Christianity in America," even a sonnet called "Forms of Prayer at Sea." At the same time, it is a measure of the unpredictable glories of this decidedly prosy sketch of a plan that Part 3 also contains two of Wordsworth's most beautiful and famous sonnets, "Mutability" and "Inside of King's College Chapel, Cambridge."

"It is a sweeping poetic quest that he undertakes"—John L. Mahoney says in his recent, quite sympathetic discussion of what he calls "the massive sequence of the *Ecclesiastical Sonnets*"—"uneven, prosaic, even discontinuous at times, but at special moments catching, in Moorman's words, the Church 'felt as poetry.'"[4] These sonnets are far too many and too varied for us to look at them all. "Fortunately for Wordsworth and for us," Lee M. Johnson writes, "his decision to cast the materials best suited to a prose tract as a series of sonnets facilitates the resurrection of individual pieces of true distinction. Had he chosen another form, such as prose or blank verse, the wheat in all likelihood would still be buried beneath the chaff."[5] But perhaps different readers would disagree about what constitutes chaff. None of the sonnets I want to address has ever been very famous.

Considering the *Ecclesiastical Sonnets* in the light of Hemans' "Female Characters of Scripture" we notice that Wordsworth addresses three female characters most prominently: the Virgin Mary, Queen

---

[3] Anne L. Rylestone, *Prophetic Memory in Wordsworth's "Ecclesiastical Sonnets"* (Carbondale, Il., 1991) 3.

[4] *William Wordsworth: A Poetic Life* (New York, 1997) 247, 245.

[5] *Wordsworth and the Sonnet* (Copenhagen, 1973) 169–170.

Elizabeth I, and his own daughter Dora. Johnson believes that these neglected sonnets are central to the series as a whole. "The theme of mutability," he argues, "is at the heart of the *Ecclesiastical Sonnets* and generally binds together its three parts." He goes on to specify that "[b]esides those on ecclesiastical architecture, the sonnets which are closest in images and themes to 'Mutability' concern female figures" (146, 167). These three sonnets, read in the light of Hemans' own religious sonnets dedicated to women characters, yield unexpected insight into the workings of Wordsworth's religious thought.

Hemans' religious sonnets demand attention beyond their interest as a lens for reading Wordsworth's, though for a long time there was active resistance to such an idea. Roger Lonsdale, for example, collecting the works of Hemans' immediate female forebears, intentionally limits space devoted to "their efforts in the more ambitious or morally earnest genres . . . paraphrases of the Scriptures, hymns."[6] Some years later, William McCarthy showed evidence of a critical sea change when he caught some of the appeal of such poems in his discussion of one of those forebears, Anna Barbauld. "Perhaps the only undisplaced form in which a young woman would feel licensed to articulate emotional turbulence in the first person was the religious poem. . . . [This poem's] public discourse of God is an envelope for Barbauld's fantasies of happier relations with her parents."[7] While I am not interested in psychoanalyzing either Wordsworth or Hemans, I do find compelling the idea that a public discourse of God can be used to explore unmentionable experience—including unmentionable religious experience. Both these poets have done such exploring in these sequences of sonnets. Wordsworth's sonnet series presents religion as the intersection between individual conscience and the institutions of the National Church. Hemans' sonnets present religion as an intersection between the individual believer and the characters of the Bible as models, as identity figures, and as sympathetic fellow-sufferers.

"Female Characters of Scripture" is a far less extensive work than *Ecclesiastical Sonnets*, but its scope is still ambitious. A cycle of fifteen sonnets, it presents two invocations, four characters from the Old Testament, and nine New Testament stories. These nine divide into three

---

[6] *Eighteenth-Century Women Poets* (Oxford, 1989) xliv.

[7] "'We Hoped the Woman Was Going to Appear': Repression, Desire, and Gender in Anna Letitia Barbauld's Early Poems," *Romantic Women Writers: Voices and Countervoices* (Hanover, N.H., 1995) 124–125.

subgroups: the first two concern the Virgin Mary, the last two concern Mary Magdalene, and the middle five concern minor characters from the Gospels. For the purposes of this essay I have taken all my Hemans sonnets from the New Testament poems; from each of the three subgroups I have chosen one sonnet that has not already been discussed by Melnyk, pairing each with one of the Wordsworth poems.

I have thought of these pairs of poems in terms of the monastic vows of poverty, chastity, and obedience—and in terms of the vows' worldly counterparts, wealth, adultery, and power. The poems address these religious disciplines and secular satisfactions as such; moreover, their form and content suggest literary equivalents. Poverty and wealth suggest, for instance, simplicity of story, imagery, and theme—and, conversely, richness of allusion, of source material, of verbal patterning. Chastity and adultery suggest faithfulness to sources but also freedom to follow inspiration. Obedience and power have special significance in this specifically gendered selection of Romantic-era sonnets. The sonnet form itself demands a kind of obedience, but these poets are writing in a time when such literary obedience is beginning to be suspect, and both these series of sonnets strive to expand the arena of what is possible in the form. Women of the period still vowed obedience to their husbands, but such social conventions are brought into question by the power of the women examined in these sonnets. I will begin with a consideration of two sonnets under the rubric of this third binary.[8]

II. OBEDIENCE/POWER:
"The Song of the Virgin" and "The Virgin"

The Song of the Virgin

Yes, as a sunburst flushing mountain-snow,
    Fell the celestial touch of fire ere long
On the pale stillness of thy thoughtful brow,
    And thy calm spirit lightened into song.
    Unconsciously, perchance, yet free and strong
Flowed the majestic joy of tuneful words,

---

[8] It pains me instinctively that I violate the canonical ordering of poverty, chastity, and obedience by beginning with obedience, but this violation accords well with Wordsworth's and Hemans' own freedoms in such matters—and this ordering allows me to examine their poems in their proper order.

> Which living harps the choirs of heaven among
> Might well have linked with their divinest chords.
> Full many a strain, borne far on glory's blast,
> Shall leave, where once its haughty music passed,
>   No more to memory than a reed's faint sigh;
> While thine, O childlike Virgin! through all time
> Shall send its fervent breath o'er every clime,
>   Being of God, and therefore not to die.

This sonnet represents Hemans' response to the *Magnificat*, a biblical canticle sung in the Anglican ritual of evensong. Thus, even apart from its inspiration in Wordsworth, this poem is more than usually dialogic—it speaks to the other poems in this series, to the song from Luke 1: 46–55, which is itself an echo of Old Testament songs like the "Song of Miriam" to which Hemans devotes a sonnet earlier in this series, and to the daily-repeated liturgy of evensong. The poem addresses Mary, moreover, at the moment in the gospels when she most resembles a poet. The *Magnificat* is a lyric that itself recalls biblical precedent in something like the way that Hemans' poem does. Hemans lifts lyrical vignettes from the gospel narrative; in the same way, Mary's song freezes the action of the story of Christ's birth.

> Luke now introduces a pause. . . . Mary's vocalized response . . . actually brings the movement of the story to a complete halt. This is a reminder that Luke is not interested merely in *events*—past, present, and future—but especially in their *meaning*. The purpose of this narratological 'time out,' then, is hermeneutical.[9]

As the commentator must examine Luke's motives when he explains Mary's song, we are aware of Hemans' as we read her version. The sonnet's title underscores the poem's echoing effects—Hemans has called her own song by a name more appropriate to Mary's.

Hemans' emphatic opening "Yes" (line 1), signaling the continuation of the layered dialogues in which this sonnet nests, is the essence of the Virgin's song in one word. But this is Hemans' own "yes." Addressing the virgin throughout, the speaker takes both roles—the role of the creator addressing her creation and that of the receptive woman, affirming the divine message. With the phrase "ere long" (2), Hemans collapses the 1800 years of intervening time and puts herself in the

---

[9] Joel B. Green, *The Gospel of Luke* (Grand Rapids, Mich., 1997) 98.

biblical moment—Mary has just received the Annunciation and is preparing to sing. The word "thy" (3) marks this sonnet as an apostrophe, a form particularly suited to poems concerning the Virgin, who is so often addressed in prayers petitioning her intercession. But this speaker does not address the Virgin for such a purpose; she does not address her even as the mother of God. The speaker addresses Mary first as the idealized beloved of a Petrarchan sonnet and then as an epitome of the inspired singer. The poem thus marks a liberation, melting the snow of a latent power with an activating sunburst.

The power of this transformation is present from the start, but after the "Yes" and the sunburst the sonnet quiets into a cool passivity with a conventional Petrarchan blazon of the Virgin, including the "warm snow" oxymoronic forms of many such blazons. Oxymoron is, of course, the essence of the virgin mother, and Hemans' snow is emblematic of virginity as its warmth is of motherhood. Hemans may be conscious of conventions of ecclesiastical tradition as well: sunburst warming snow recalls the vernal-equinox timing of the Annunciation in the Christian Year—with a bit of excited anticipation of the glorious snow that will be back (in England, if not in Palestine) at Christmas time. Such liturgical references remain beneath the surface in this sonnet; the institution of Church Year inhabits the future here, though it is a future emphatically prophesied by the confident conclusions both of the *Magnificat* and of the sonnet.

Despite her obedience to the dictates of such convention, Hemans shows a remarkable confidence and freedom with her source. This Conception seems to be accomplished by light rather than by sound. The "celestial fire" (line 2) on the Virgin's "thoughtful brow" (3) recalls (or anticipates) the fires on the apostles' brows at Pentecost, the day of the coming of the Holy Spirit. This is an unorthodox presentation, and especially remarkable because, as I have elsewhere written, it is very unlike Hemans' own usual understanding; she emphasizes voice over vision throughout her poetry.[10] Both Hemans' reliance upon a source and her freedom in interpreting it raise the central question behind power, that of free will and determinism. She has already raised that question in the sonnet about the Annunciation that precedes this one.

---

[10] See my essay "The Triumph of Voice in Felicia Hemans' *The Forest Sanctuary*," *Felicia Hemans: Reimagining Poetry in the Nineteenth Century*, ed. Nanora Sweet and Julie Melnyk (Houndsmill, England 2001) 55–73.

She hints at it here with the words "free" (5) and "linked" (8)—and possibly a pun on "cords" ("chords" line 8)—leading to the "not to die" (14) of the poem's conclusion.

Yet perhaps this sunburst reflects Luke after all. Was it suggested by the divine gaze of "For he hath regarded the low estate of his handmaiden" (Luke 1: 48)? If so, Hemans has reversed the order of Mary's own imagery, placing "regarded" before "spirit." The word "lightened" (4) signifies both set afire (enlightened in the most palpable, life-altering way) and eased of a burden—a pun that suggests a paradox: Mary's spirit is lightened as her body takes on the burden of a child. Singing when touched by the "celestial . . . fire" (2), Hemans' Mary seems empowered like Shakespeare's lark that "at break of day arising . . . sings hymns at heaven's gate." She bears a more uncomfortable resemblance to the passive image of Memnon's statue at Thebes, which was said to make a musical sound at daybreak, when Memnon greeted his mother, the goddess of dawn.

Mary's song is about power, of course, but Hemans emphasizes the oxymoronic nature of that divine power invested in a quintessentially powerless figure. The phrase "Unconsciously, perchance" (5) may contain a note of irony. Mary may not be singing consciously, but there is glory in being an inspired singer. As the wind of inspiration grows in the poem, so does Hemans' identification of herself with Mary. The "memory" (11), with its elements of fame and imagination, has extra power here—prophetic power, predicting the later hegemony of Christianity. (It recalls Mary's prophecy, "For behold from henceforth, all generations shall call me blessed"—Luke 1: 48.) The multiple Aeolian "living harps" (line 7) of the unconscious are linked with the angels' harps. The wind of "spirit" (line 4) carries through the rest of the poem, its insistent unifying element, in forms from "blast" (line 9) through "sigh" (line 11) to "fervent breath" (line 13) that combines them. The "reed" (line 11), a ubiquitous image in Hemans' poetry, conflates the musical instrument and the biblical image of the human person as a fragile, hollow, ephemeral creature. The word "Strain" (line 9) introduces a Dickinsonian pun, having to do with the difficulties of poetic composition; "borne" (line 9) introduces another, having to do with the difficulties of childbirth. Hemans seems to want humbly to identify her own poetry with the passing, insignificant verse of lines 9–11. But even if this is so, she has placed herself among the worldly powerful who present such a contrast to the "childlike" (line 12) Mary and her genuine literary, historical, and spiritual power. The lone phrase "haughty music" (line 10) represents about all that is left here of Mary's anti-establishment lines like "the rich he hath sent empty away."

Hemans wrote this sonnet some years after Wordsworth had written his own tribute to the Virgin Mary, but Wordsworth's is set many years later in time. It is a shock to move from the immediacy of Hemans' biblical context to the historically explicit context in which Wordsworth addresses his own apostrophe to the same figure.

The Virgin

> Mother! whose virgin bosom was uncrost
> With the least shade of thought to sin allied;
> Woman! above all women glorified,
> Our tainted nature's solitary boast;
> Purer than foam on central ocean tost;
> Brighter than eastern skies at daybreak strewn
> With fancied roses, than the unblemished moon
> Before her wane begins on heaven's blue coast;
> Thy Image falls to earth. Yet some, I ween,
> Not unforgiven the suppliant knee might bend,
> As to a visible Power, in which did blend
> All that was mixed and reconciled in Thee
> Of mother's love with maiden purity,
> Of high with low, celestial with terrene!

Wordsworth calls his poem "The Virgin" with no reference to her song, but his poem concerns the Virgin herself less than her "Image" (9) as reflected in icons. The *Sonnets'* early editor suggests that "The numerous Cistercian abbeys with which Wordsworth was familiar would suggest a sonnet upon the Virgin, to whose service this order was devoted."[11] Wordsworth is especially interested in the ecclesiastical and national power struggles that put these icons up and brought them down. "'The Images of our Lady of Walsingham and Ipswich were brought up to London, with all the jewels that hung about them, and divers other images both in England and Wales, whereunto any common pilgrimage was used, for avoiding of idolatry.'"[12] The meek "some" (9) who had been accustomed to "bend the knee" (10) before these icons were inferior in worldly terms to the kings and bishops who

---

[11] William Wordsworth, *The Ecclesiastical Sonnets of William Wordsworth: A Critical Edition*, ed. Abbie Findlay Potts (New Haven, 1922) 263.

[12] Stow, quoted in Potts 263.

manipulated the icons. These meek were ironically close to the Virgin herself, whose purity the sonnet celebrates.

Wordsworth's sonnet contains archaisms ("I ween" line 9), awkward musical touches ("in which did blend" 11), and a flattened iconic image of the Virgin ("uncrost / With the least shade" 1–2) to recall these primitive images. But his use of such devices is as purposeful and innovative as Mary's and Hemans' uses of their inherited traditions. When Wordsworth depicts the peasant kneeling before the icon, he says: "As to a visible Power" (11). His figurative language is complicated by ironically literal elements.

While it alludes to primitive forms, in fact, Wordsworth's sonnet is a highly sophisticated network of interconnecting sounds, images, allusions, and ideas, recalling the rose-window complexity of Dante's tribute to Mary in *Paradiso* XXXIII. "Uncrost" (1), for example, suggests genetic purity, but it alludes as well to the cross to which such purity leads, a cross itself the symbol of quite intermixed shame and glory. Wordsworth rhymes three times with this fundamental word, and the sonnet's final turn pivots on its conceptual opposite, "mixed" (10). When Wordsworth changes Mary's epithet from "Mother!" (1) to "Woman!" (3), we prepare for the allusion to Eve that arrives with his mention of "our tainted nature" (4). And the word "all" (3) reverberates through the rest of the poem, whether by contrast ("solitary" 4), ironic echo ("falls" 9), or repetition ("All" 12). When Wordsworth alludes to "nature" (4) he introduces a quatrain of natural images, from the sea "foam" (5) to "heaven's blue coast" (8). But this nature is thoroughly mythologized. This foam recalls Aphrodite, these "roses" are "fancied" (7). This "moon" (7), perhaps the throne of the Queen of Heaven, is "unblemished" (7).

Such devices unify a poem of lists, a poem of fragments, built around the simple statement "Thy Image falls to earth" (line 9). In addition, the pure power emphasized by this artistic unity arises out of fragments, and the figure of the Virgin that Wordsworth here constructs will break again into the fragments of Queen and daughter as the sonnet sequence continues.

III. CHASTITY/ADULTERY:
"Elizabeth" and "Mary Magdalene at the Sepulchre"

Though it is perhaps no more political than his sonnet to "The Virgin," Wordsworth's tribute to Elizabeth I presents an example of what Mahoney calls "a notable tempering of the poetic spirit by the demands of history in the *Ecclesiastical Sonnets*. . . .The poet, now more overtly in search of monuments more lasting, beacons of hope and security, has found a magnificent one in the Christian Church of England." This is hardly a spontaneous overflow of religious emotion. "The price paid is candidly sketched in Wordsworth's Fenwick observation that 'there is unavoidably in all History,—except as it is mere suggestion— something that enslaves the fancy.'"[13] "Elizabeth" explores, more exclusively than "The Virgin," profoundly social and political elements of religion. *Ecclesiastical Sonnets* "is simply the most thoroughly researched work he ever composed. It is a veritable bibliography of sources for English church history. Wordsworth noted thirteen (there are more)."[14] But poetry is not dead in "Elizabeth"; it has only gone underground. It can still be heard deep down in the independent, ironic harmonics of these lines. It is, for instance, ironic that this sonnet should begin with the "Ave!" that Wordsworth withheld from his poem to the Virgin Mary; he seems to be rendering his praise here to a descendant of Caesar's.

> Hail, Virgin Queen! o'er many an envious bar
> Triumphant, snatched from many a treacherous wile! (lines 1–2)

Despite the sonnet's forthright title, this language lacks from the first the primitive clarity of Wordsworth's address to the Virgin Mary. The opening formula of address is far thornier and more tangled here, as is clear from the poet's delaying of the word "Triumphant" to the beginning of the second line. The insistently singular nouns—mother, bosom, thought, sin, woman—leading to "solitary boast" in the previous poem accorded with the unbroken simplicity of the subject. They are here replaced by a couple of nouns—"bar" (line 1) and "wile" (2) that are singular only in appearance, each preceded by the treacherous phrase "many a." No immaculate conception has brought this queen into the world; the poet hails instead a figure embroiled in political intrigues inherited from her troubled forebears. The honorific "Virgin" (1) functions in her case less as a symbol of purity than as a badge of complete independence.

Any implied parallels to the Virgin Mary are of course especially

---

[13] Mahoney 252.
[14] Johnson 151.

ironic when their object is a queen who made England again a Protestant nation, and whose Roman Catholic sister and predecessor was herself named Mary. Wordsworth inherited these parallels (and their ironies) from Spenser, but his later perspective allows him to employ the ironies more bluntly, to emphasize the worldliness of a less-than-faery queen.

> All hail, sage Lady, whom a grateful Isle
> Hath blest, respiring from that dismal war
> Stilled by thy voice! (3–5)

These blessings are all political not religious, but they are no less real for that. Elizabeth has not done a literal miracle, hushing only a war not the waves with her voice. And not heaven but England blesses her in return. Such blessings, Wordsworth implies, play an important role in the history of the Church. When he says "All hail" (line 3) he may smile a bit ironically at thus blithely sweeping aside the tangle of faction with which he began, but he seems, at least briefly, to mean it.

> But quickly from afar
> Defiance breathes with more malignant aim;
> And alien storms with home-bred ferments claim
> Portentous fellowship. (5–8)

These gathering storms, anticipating and indeed perhaps inspiring the gathering winds in Hemans' poem to the Virgin, are masterfully rendered. The sighing respiration of line 4—which we seem to hear anticipated in the line's first word, "Hath"—is met and ruffled by a harder breathing, sounded in the word "Defiance" at the beginning of line 6. Mere breath rises quickly to hurricane, but Elizabeth is not troubled.

> Her silver car,
> By sleepless prudence ruled, glides slowly on;
> Unhurt by violence, from menaced taint
> Emerging pure, and seemingly more bright. (8–11)

The word *taint* (10) recalls again the earlier sonnet—with its reference to "Our tainted nature's solitary boast"—and the reference to "pure" (11) recalls the imagery of virginity. But there is something disturbing in that word "seemingly (line 11). This is an earthly kingdom, and Elizabeth is not the Queen of Heaven. We cannot be surprised when the sonnet ends as it does, with portents of post-Elizabethan revolution.

> Ah! wherefore yields it to a foul constraint
> Black as the clouds its beams dispersed, while shone,
> By men and angels blest, the glorious light? (lines 12–14)

The sexual imagery of purity and foulness is not quite entirely allegorical here—much of the troubling power of "Elizabeth" resides in its failure to harness all its erotic energy into politics. Perhaps it is the sexual politics inherent in its subject that makes Hemans' ambitious sonnet "Mary Magdalene at the Sepulchre" so strangely unsuccessful. Its very flaws, fascinating in this regard, may serve as a foil for Hemans' more successful religious verse.

"Mary Magdalene at the Sepulchre" refers to that climactic yet tender and intimate moment in the Gospel when the risen Christ addresses Mary Magdalene, echoing verbatim the question already asked by the angels at the tomb: "Woman, why weepest thou? whom seekest thou?" (John 20: 15). Christ says "Woman," and we have seen that this is the term of address that Wordsworth uses in his sonnet to "The Virgin." Christ's epithet emphasizes for us the Magdalene's representative status, and it delays for her the sudden recognition a moment later when he uses her name. Hemans has compressed Christ's speech into a still more formal (but less universal), public address: "Weeper!" the poem begins, "to thee how bright a morn was given." The contrived and awkward epithet and the apostrophe it introduces thrust the speaker into a presumptuous relationship with the Magdalene. This public rhetoric persists in the somewhat more sympathetic second line: "After thy long, long vigil of despair," in which the phrase "long, long" seems a merely formal acknowledgment of Mary's suffering over the forty hours since Christ's death. And the awkwardness increases when Jesus' voice is characterized, many lines before he speaks the name that compels recognition:

> When that high voice which burial rocks had riven
> Thrilled with immortal tones the silent air! (3–4)

To call Jesus' voice "high" is to introduce an uneasy touch of gender confusion to take the place of the confusion Hemans does not mention—that Mary mistakes her Lord for the gardener. (Hemans perhaps thought that this humble mistake could not be reconciled with the majestic tone of her poem, a sign of the greater intimacy of John's Gospel.)

The image of the voice riving burial rocks is itself a rather oddly mixed reference, biblically. It recalls the voice of Genesis that created these rocks; the battle of Jericho in which voices (along with trumpets and other noise) rive the walls; the rock that Moses strikes with his staff for water about which Paul says, "That rock was Christ." But none of these images exactly fits the case here. And there is no mention in Scripture of a voice riving the actual burial rocks, though in Matthew 28: 2 an earthquake does. So the "immortal tones" that rive these rocks are apparently Hemans' own invention.

These lines are followed by an epic simile, for Hemans is interested, as the Evangelist was, in delaying the moment of recognition, though she accomplishes this effect with far more ceremony.

> Never did clarion's royal blast declare
> Such tale of victory to a breathless crowd. (5–6)

This passage again recalls the battle of Jericho—though that crowd was breathless from having helped to bring about the victory. Hemans compares the voice of Jesus to the voice of a trumpet. This comparison underscores the kingly grandeur that John's Gospel downplays, but it is a sophisticated move, illustrating the ambitious detail-work of Hemans' poem. For the voice of Hemans' trumpet sends us back to Exodus, for an ironic and entirely appropriate anticipation of this moment in the Gospel.

> And he said unto the people, Be ready against the third day: come not at your wives. And it came to pass on the third day in the morning, that there were thunders and lightnings, and a thick cloud upon the mount, and the voice of the trumpet exceeding loud. . . . And when the voice of the trumpet sounded long, and waxed louder and louder, Moses spake, and God answered him by a voice. (Exodus 19: 15–16, 19)

If we have such a passage in our minds, all the pomp of Hemans' sonnet seems hushed and intimate by comparison. Yet even here, John's Gospel is more muted; John alludes to this passage by the mere structures of the story he tells, without any such blaring hints as Hemans' "clarion" (line 5).

And Hemans is only beginning the organ swell of her poem's conclusion. She completes her simile with a repetitive and italicized emphasis on Jesus' simplicity of expression.

> As the deep sweetness of *one* word could bear
> Into thy heart of hearts, O woman! bowed

> By strong affection's anguish! one low word—
> "*Mary!*" and all the triumph wrung from death
> Was thus revealed. (7–11)

The character of Christ's voice, even before we have heard it in the poem, has changed; it is no longer "high," it is now "deep" and "low." And the voice of Hemans' speaker, though its crescendo contrasts with Jesus' diminuendo—though it has begun to adopt exclamation points—is still a bit awkward and formal in the presence of this scene of intimacy. She desires to sum up (as the Gospel resists summing up) the complex relationship between these two passionate figures, but can find no more rhapsodic phrase than "strong affection" (9).

The narrative dips at this point into a brief allusion to Mary Magdalene's past sin, a figurative death from which Jesus has raised her.

> and thou, that so hadst erred,
> So wept and been forgiven, in trembling faith
> Didst cast thee down before the all-conquering Son,
> Awed by the mighty gift thy tears and love had won! (11–14)

Yet even this triumphal ending strikes a series of wrong notes. Christ the conqueror seems all-too irresistible in his might; the subtextual allegory of sexual domination (a theme explored more explicitly in Donne's "Batter my heart" sonnet, for example) is off-putting when it is displaced upon the figure of the repentant whore. Worse still is the confused financial negotiation of the final line, where the benefit this overpowering Christ bestows is called a gift but seems to have been earned by "tears and love."

This fascinating failed sonnet outdone by its own sexual undercurrents thus ends in a conflict concerning the distribution of wealth. Hemans was to write a far more successful sonnet addressing the same theme more directly.

IV. POVERTY/WEALTH:
"The Penitent Anointing Christ's Feet" and "I saw the figure of a lovely Maid"

The Penitent Anointing Christ's Feet

> There was a mournfulness in angel eyes,
>   That saw thee, woman! bright in this world's train,

> Moving to pleasure's airy melodies,
>   Thyself the idol of the enchanted strain.
>   But from thy beauty's garland, brief and vain,
> When one by one the rose-leaves had been torn;
>   When thy heart's core had quivered to the pain
> Through every life-nerve sent by arrowy scorn;
> When thou didst kneel to pour sweet odours forth
>   On the Redeemer's feet, with many a sigh,
> And showering tear-drop, of yet richer worth
>   Than all those costly balms of Araby;
> *Then* was there joy, a song of joy in heaven,
> For thee, the child won back, the penitent forgiven.

Hemans' retelling of the familiar Gospel story makes the traditional conflation of the stories of the woman taken in adultery (John 8) and of Mary anointing Christ's feet (John 12). Hemans' version further recalls Christ's saying (Luke 15: 10): "There is joy in the presence of the angels of God over one sinner that repenteth." The moral of John 12 is not this passage about joy in heaven but the much less optimistic "The poor always ye have with you" (John 12: 8). Poverty and wealth are certainly the chief themes of the Gospel passage, though these have been driven a bit underground in Hemans' version.

This sonnet is unlike the others in the silence of its subject, a kind of poverty unavailable to the poet. The penitent does not speak in any of the biblical versions of the story, but the apostles (and, in John, specifically Judas) interpret her action; Jesus corrects their interpretation and offers one of his own ("against the day of my burying hath she kept this"). This language of gesture, subject to conflicting interpretation, presents a far more complex allegory for the poet's life than the previous sonnets. Further, Hemans continues this language of gesture beyond the limits set by the Gospel. Aging and the world's scorn have brought this woman to repentance—are we to understand that her own gesture is the triumph of these earthly processes? Neither is mentioned in the Gospel story. Both are forms of poverty.

But Hemans' sonnet does not accept the discipline of gestures. It forges a wealth of verbal connections to the other sonnets in the sequence. That the penitent's "pleasure" (3) should be figured as "airy melodies" (3), for instance, seems once again, as in "The Song of the Virgin," to be obliquely autobiographical—as if Hemans is repenting her own more secular poetry. In support of this link, the word "strain"

(4) is repeated here from "The Song of the Virgin," as the summarizing phrase "thyself the idol" (4) recalls the snow-statue image with which that earlier sonnet began. Such echoes pour out of this poem and make those around it richer.

At the same time, Hemans contents herself with rendering the Gospel story through stock images, with a rather suspect poverty of the imagination. The fabled wealth of Orientalism apparent in the "balms of Araby" (12), for example, contrasts with the homely "sigh / And showering tear-drop" (10–11). This particular usage of all-too-familiar imagery ironically offers the poem's most explicit presentation of the theme of poverty and wealth. Hemans makes the scene a parochial pageant in which the Gospel story is savory with mystery.

Yet we must not accept Hemans' show of poverty too readily. Her verbal play in this sonnet suggests hidden riches after all. This poem's "rose leaves" (6) wrung implicitly into ointment exquisitely anticipate Dickinson's "Essential Oils—are wrung—" (# 675). The rose-leaves are like blood; "vain" (line 5) puns on "vein," anticipating the "heart's core" (7). "Quivered" (7) quibblingly anticipates "arrowy" (8), and the Penitent becomes a kind of female St. Sebastian, emptied and fulfilled at once.

Finally, we might notice that she is addressed as "woman!" (2) when she is in sin, but as "child" (14) when she is "the penitent forgiven" (14). Wordsworth's sonnets to women move in a similar way, from mother to daughter.

The sonnet of Wordsworth with which I will conclude is by far the most conventional of the six in terms of what we ordinarily expect from a sonnet. But it is the least characteristic of these two sequences. It is the only directly autobiographical one of these sonnets, the least conventionally religious. The poet included it despite such objections, but he had to prepare a way for it.

> To justify the inclusion of manifestly personal sonnets, he placed one appropriately entitled 'Latitudinarianism' near the beginning of the third section. . . . [T]he sonnet establishes the principle that individual conscience can complement external authority when both are united in the service of truth.[15]

By placing this anomaly as the first sonnet of the sequence's final Part, Wordsworth gave it a structural importance that critics have endorsed.

---

[15] Johnson 149.

"Although there are only three overtly autobiographical sonnets in this series of 132 (I.22, III.1, and III.22), the importance of the personal role of the poet in the narrative is asserted from the start and affirmed throughout. The history of Christianity will be filtered through the poet; he will be the measure of nearly two thousand years of human drama."[16]

Wordsworth's third sonnet about a virginal woman is not formed as an apostrophe. Its subject is neither biblical nor historical but familial and psychological. He names the woman in a note rather than in the poem itself. He does not employ the word Virgin, but the humbler, Anglo-Saxon word "Maid." He begins this poem with himself, and its form is built around his faulty, halting perception.

> I saw the figure of a lovely Maid
> Seated alone beneath a darksome tree,
> Whose fondly-overhanging canopy
> Set off her brightness with a pleasing shade.
> No Spirit was she; that my heart betrayed,
> For she was one I loved exceedingly;
> But while I gazed in tender reverie
> (Or was it sleep that with my Fancy played?)
> The bright corporeal presence—form and face—
> Remaining still distinct grew thin and rare,
> Like sunny mist;—at length the golden hair,
> Shape, limbs, and heavenly features, keeping pace
> Each with the other in a lingering race
> Of dissolution, melted into air.

According to Wordsworth's note, this poem was composed, just as it now stands, in a single walk on the road from Grasmere to Ambleside. This story of its composition, Mahoney observes, "evokes memories of his account of the composition of *Tintern Abbey*, spontaneous composition while walking and finally rendered verbatim in writing."[17] The story is a testament to the poem's sincerity, its inspiration, its relation to its author's most successful previous works, its independence from historical sources. And this poem is still more personal than "Tintern Abbey," as it recounts a dream. The content is perhaps only secular, but the implications of this compositional history are decidedly religious.

---

[16] Rylestone 22.
[17] Mahoney 251.

The reason that the story of the poem's composition is so remarkable is that Wordsworth has made the poem so formally complex, so laden with literary effects. If anything, it is more intricately structured than his highly ornate sonnet to "The Virgin" that we have already examined. Consider the number of chiming repetitions, variations, and parallel constructions, for instance: lovely (1)/loved (6); brightness (4)/bright (9); pleasing shade (4)/sunny mist (11); shade (4)/Spirit (5); form (9)/shape (12); shade (4)/shape (12); face (9)/features (12). Consider the fact that "The appearance of the word *dissolution* in only this sonnet and in Mutability emphasizes the similarity of their theme."[18] Consider the graceful oxymoron of "lingering race" (13). Finally and most tellingly, consider the graceful rivulet of the independent clause that tumbles from line 7 onward, lingering and racing at once to the end.

This wealth of literary resources Wordsworth employs in expressing the profound spiritual richness of his dream. Unlike the more famous tributes to ecclesiastical architecture that conclude his sonnet sequence, this humble poem has no foundations except in the literary tradition and the poet's own emotions.

Wordsworth's opening trope of the dream contrasts with his closing cathedrals, as Coleridge's dream of Xanadu contrasts with the pleasure dome that Kubla Khan built in that country. Dreams have ever been a locus of religious experience. The wholly personal, symbolic, and vivid world of dreams is inexhaustibly rich. It is of course very like poetry, a likeness not limited to the kind of poetry Coleridge brought to *Lyrical Ballads*. "I saw the figure of a lovely maid" offers a vision of religious experience that might be called domestic supernaturalism. It would have found a congenial reader in St. Luke, and it had great appeal for Felicia Hemans.

> Hemans' Wordsworth is not the Romantic conqueror of our mythology ... but the poet of household affections, of family and hearth. Hemans praises Wordsworth for the very qualities for which she was admired. ... [And] he did see himself in the 1830s in the same way Felicia Hemans ... saw him: as a poet who celebrated domesticity and sought to find his way into the hearts of his countrymen (and women) through his poetry.[19]

---

[18] Johnson 167.

[19] Judith W. Page, *Wordsworth and the Cultivation of Woman* (Berkeley, 1991), 142–143.

So we end our journeying through these ambitious and unfamiliar works with a celebration of domesticity. The most uncanny moments in any of these works of miracles and historical upheaval are undoubtedly the moments that come closest to revealing the everyday.

> Elysium is as far as to
> The very nearest Room
> If in that Room a Friend await
> Felicity or Doom—
>
> What fortitude the Soul contains,
> That it can so endure
> The accent of a coming Foot—
> The opening of a Door—[20]

Works Cited

Anderson, John. "The Triumph of Voice in Felicia Hemans' *The Forest Sanctuary*." Sweet and Melnyk 55–73.

Dickinson, Emily. *Complete Poems*. Ed. Thomas H. Johnson. Boston: Little, Brown, 1960.

Green, Joel B. *The Gospel of Luke*. Grand Rapids, Mich.: Eerdmans, 1997.

Hemans, Felicia. *Felicia Hemans: Selected Poems, Letters, Reception Materials*. Ed. Susan J. Wolfson. Princeton: Princeton University Press, 2000.

———. "Female Characters of Scripture." *The Poetical Works of Mrs. Hemans, Reprinted from the Early Editions. With Memoir, Explanatory Notes, &c*. New York: R. Worthington, n.d.

Johnson, Lee M. *Wordsworth and the Sonnet*. Copenhagen: Rosenkilde and Bagger, 1973.

Lonsdale, Roger, ed. *Eighteenth-Century Women Poets*. Oxford: Oxford University Press, 1989.

Mahoney, John L. *William Wordsworth: A Poetic Life*. New York: Fordham University Press, 1997.

McCarthy, William. "'We Hoped the *Woman* Was Going to Appear': Repression, Desire, and Gender in Anna Letitia Barbauld's Early

---

[20] Dickinson, # 1476.

Poems." *Romantic Women Writers: Voices and Countervoices.* Ed. Paula Feldman and Theresa M. Kelley. Hanover, N.H.: University Press of New England, 1995. 113–137.

Melnyk, Julie. "Hemans' Later Poetry: Religion and the Vatic Poet." Sweet and Melnyk 74–92.

Page, Judith W. *Wordsworth and the Cultivation of Women.* Berkeley: University of California Press, 1994.

Rylestone, Anne L. *Prophetic Memory in Wordsworth's "Ecclesiastical Sonnets."* Carbondale: Southern Illinois University Press, 1991.

Sweet, Nanora, and Julie Melnyk, eds. *Felicia Hemans: Reimagining Poetry in the Nineteenth-Century.* Houndsmill, England: Palgrave, 2001.

Wordsworth, William. *The Ecclesiastical Sonnets of William Wordsworth: A Critical Edition.* Ed. Abbie Findlay Potts. New Haven: Yale University Press, 1922.

7

Wordsworth's "Immortality Ode" and Hopkins' "The Leaden Echo and the Golden Echo": In Pursuit of Transcendence

J. Robert Barth, S.J.

AT THE END of the elegantly textured argument of *Real Presences*, George Steiner concludes:

> It is, I believe, poetry, art, and music which relate us most directly to that in being which is not ours.... The arts are most wonderfully rooted in substance, in the human body, in stone, in pigment, in the twanging of gut or the weight of wind on reeds. All good art and literature begin in immanence. But they do not stop there. Which is to say, very plainly, that it is the enterprise and privilege of the aesthetic to quicken into lit presence the continuum between temporality and eternity, between matter and spirit, between man and "the other."[1]

Since the beginning of human history, Steiner argues, there has been a covenant between the artist's expression and the world he inhabits, a covenant that undergirds this belief in the transcendent dimension of the work of art. This "covenant between word and world" (93) has been broken in modern times, Steiner believes—beginning with the period of the 1870s—but the basis of the covenant, the innate relationship between immanent and transcendent, remains fundamental to the human conditions of artistic creation. Even today, when for so many the divine is an irrelevance, the transcendent is present by indirection, in what Steiner calls "the density of God's absence, the edge of presence in that absence" (229). "The phenomenology," he goes on, "is

---

[1] *Real Presences* (Chicago, 1989) 226–227.

elementary: it is like the recession from us of one whom we have loved or sought to love or of one before whom we have dwelt in fear. The distancing is, then, charged with the pressures of a nearness out of reach, of a remembrance torn at the edges" (229–230). He finds it in Kierkegaard, in Beckett's *End Game*, in the poetry of Célan, and in Kafka—where "the futile light flashes on the execution of Joseph K.," where "the helper is no longer the help," but is "still resonant with recent receding" (23).

Long before the 1870s, however, this "receding" had been experienced, albeit temporarily, for it was what prompted Wordsworth—in his "Ode: Intimations of Immortality"—to search for the vanished light. But let me begin with a letter of Gerard Manley Hopkins' in praise of Wordsworth's Ode, as a starting point for consideration of two poems that that letter, perhaps coincidentally, juxtaposes. These two poems can teach us much about the search for a lost transcendence, the recovery of that reality which is "still resonant with recent receding."

The letter in question was written on October 23, 1886, to Hopkins' friend Canon R. W. Dixon. In August of that year, evidently in reply to a comment of Dixon's about "Wordsworth-worship," Hopkins had remarked that "Wordsworth's particular grace, his *charisma*, as theologians say, has been granted in equal measure to so very few men since times was—to Plato and who else? I mean his spiritual insight into nature" (141).[2] In a belated reply in October (October 18, 1886), Dixon acknowledges that Wordsworth's "healing power" is "very great," but goes on to complain of "the extravagance of some of the claims made for him" (144–145), pointing specifically to Mark Pattison's view that the Immortality Ode is "the second poem in the language," after *Lycidas*.

The result was a letter from Hopkins, a few days later (October 23, 1886), of extraordinary power and feeling in praise of the Immortality Ode. "There have been in all history," he says, "a few, a very few men, whom common repute . . . has treated as having had something happen to them that does not happen to other men, as having *seen something*, whatever that really was. Plato was the most famous of these." He

---

[2] Quotations from Hopkins' letters are taken from *The Correspondence of Gerard Manley Hopkins and Richard Watson Dixon*, ed. Claude Colleer Abbot, rev. ed. (London, 1955).

continues: "Human nature in these men saw something, got a shock; wavers in opinion, looking back, whether there was anything in it or no; but is in a tremble ever since." What follows is worth quoting at length:

> Now what Wordsworthians mean is, what would seem to be the growing mind of the English speaking world and may perhaps come to be that of the world at large / is that in Wordsworth when he wrote that ode human nature got another of those shocks, and the tremble from it is spreading. This opinion I do strongly share; I am, ever since I knew the ode, in that tremble. You know what happened to crazy Blake, himself a most poetically electrical subject both active and passive, at his first hearing: when the reader came to 'The pansy at my feet' he fell into a hysterical excitement. Now commonsense forbid we should take on like these unstrung hysterical creatures: still it was a proof of the power of the shock. (148)

Hopkins goes on at some length about the Ode, but two of his comments should not be overlooked. First he notes that "the interest and importance of the matter were here of the highest, his insight was at its very deepest, and hence to my mind the extreme value of the poem" (148). We might recall his phrase of several months earlier about the Ode: "spiritual insight into nature" (141). Secondly, Hopkins speaks of Wordsworth's diction throughout the Ode as "so charged and steeped in beauty and yearning." Insight and yearning: words to which we shall have to recur.

All this is of course "flannel to the heart" for Wordsworthians. But there is a brief coda to this letter which is curious and intriguing—and which was the genesis of this essay. At the end of his lengthy encomium of the Immortality Ode, Hopkins concludes his letter by asking: "Have you my song for my play of *St. Winefred* called *The Leaden Echo and the Golden Echo*? If not I will try to copy it as time serves: I never did anything more musical" (149). Is this an accidental juxtaposition, or did Hopkins see—or feel—some connection between these two poems?

First of all, both these poems clearly have to do with the "spiritual insight into nature" and, further, both of them look beyond nature toward immortality, the transcendent. Both of them begin, too, with loss and despair, then swerve, suddenly and dramatically, to a clear affirmation of hope and joy—"O joy! That in our embers / Is something that doth live" and "Spare / There is one, yes I have one (Hush there!)." It is not difficult to imagine why the Immortality Ode might have put Hopkins in mind of his own poem. One might even speculate that Wordsworth's Ode may have been an inspiration for Hopkins' poem. I shall make no such claim here, however, but I would like to go on to ask what these two poems, which have so much in common, finally affirm about immortality and the transcendent.

That the Immortality Ode held pride of place in Wordsworth's view of his own poetry seems to me beyond question. In his own arrangement of his poetry—not that, of course, of Stephen Gill—Wordsworth places the Ode apart from the rest of his poetry, as the concluding poem of his shorter poetry, immediately following "Poems Referring to the Period of Old Age" and "Epitaphs and Elegiac Pieces." It has been pointed out more than once that the progression is from old age to death to life after death, and that the place of the Immortality Ode—at the end of Wordsworth's poetic work—is meant to function as "Crossing the Bar" does for Tennyson. Personally, I find it regrettable that Wordsworth's judgment and wishes have not been more respected in this regard.

In any event, even apart from its placement in the canon of Wordsworth's poetry, the poem clearly holds a special place—not always recognized, I think—in the development of Wordsworth's religious sensibility. No one has, to my mind, better situated the Ode in the development of Wordsworth's thought than Alan Grob, in a book of nearly thirty years ago, *The Philosophic Mind,* a book unjustly neglected in recent years.[3]

It is difficult to do justice in short compass to Grob's sophisticated and detailed argument. It would be fair to say, however, that Grob attempts—successfully, I think—to mediate between "the rival claims of empiricism and transcendentalism" (Preface, x) that had long been made for Wordsworth. Writing in the wake of Geoffrey Hartman's magisterial book, *Wordsworth's Poetry, 1787–1814,*[4] Grob finds himself—for all his admiration for Hartman—finally dissatisfied with his view of Wordsworth's poems as "records of defeated yearnings for apocalypse, the thwarting of consciousness in its aspirations" (Hart-

---

[3] *The Philosophic Mind: A Study of Wordsworth's Poetry and Thought, 1797–1805* (Columbus, 1973).

[4] *Wordsworth's Poetry, 1787–1814* (New Haven, 1971).

man, Preface, x). Rather, Grob sees genuine development in Wordsworth's thought, from an essentially empiricist view during the period from 1797 to 1800; to a period, from 1800 to 1804, of questioning and challenge of his empirical ontology; to, finally, in the 1804 stanzas of the Immortality Ode, the beginning of his acceptance of and commitment to a "metaphysics of transcendence" (232).

"Tintern Abbey" may fairly be taken, Grob believes, as paradigmatic of the earlier period. Here the process the poet undergoes is fundamentally naturalistic and empirical, and what the poet has experienced is—according to the poem's "empirical premises"—"universally accessible and universally beneficial, available to any and all who would submit themselves," as the poet has and as his sister will, to the great forces of nature (31). All will be well if we can "bring our lives into conformity with nature's own essential being" (36).

A crucial poem for the middle phase of Wordsworth's development is "Resolution and Independence," which—like other poems of the period from 1800 to 1804—challenges the earlier, more optimistic view of the "benevolence of nature and the development of man" (190). During the earlier period, between 1797 and 1800, Wordsworth's belief had been, "whether expressed in poems as assured as *Tintern Abbey* or as somber as *The Ruined Cottage*, that the effects of nature, acting upon mankind through the associative memory, must necessarily be productive of human happiness" (191). Many of the poems of this middle period, however, are "poems of challenge that call into question the most fundamental of Wordsworth's convictions about nature, the self, and the ethical life" (191).

"Resolution and Independence"—typical of this "transitional" period—calls explicitly into question the very foundation of Wordsworth's earlier belief in the adequacy and permanence of nature as ground and motive force for human life and action. At the beginning of the poem, with the passing of rain and dawn the moor resumes what seems its natural form: "a lonely place." What is revealed to the poet then—through the old leech-gatherer—is "the possibility for man of a spiritual existence alien to and transcending the processes of nature, a source of permanence in the midst of flux" (227). Grob makes no claim for this as a "poem of conversion." The religious experience is observed but not shared; the faith is that of the old man, not the poet. The poem does, however, point the way to an even greater poem to come, in which the poet's own faith will be revealed.

Against this background, it comes as no surprise to be reminded that the opening four stanzas of the Immortality Ode—in which the poet laments the loss of the "visionary gleam," his joy in nature—were written in 1802; these stanzas clearly share in the doubts and questionings of the period.[5] The opening lines enunciate, beautifully and movingly, the poet's sense of loss:

I

> There was a time when meadow, grove, and stream,
> The earth, and every common sight,
>   To me did seem
>   Apparelled in celestial light,
> The glory and the freshness of a dream.
> It is not now as it hath been of yore;
>   Turn wheresoe'er I may,
>   By night or day,
> The things which I have seen I now can see no more.

II

> The Rainbow comes and goes,
> And lovely is the Rose,
> The Moon doth with delight
> Look round her when the heavens are bare,
>   Waters on a starry night
>   Are beautiful and fair;
>   The sunshine is a glorious birth;
>   But yet I know, where'er I go,
> That there hath past away a glory from the earth. (1–18)

And then:

> Whither is fled the visionary gleam?
> Where is it now, the glory and the dream? (56–57)

These stanzas seem to question the very sufficiency of the poet's previous modes of perception—of eye and ear—and the sensual beauties that nature can offer.

If the 1802 stanzas are an eloquent expression of the problem—the

---

[5] Quotations of Wordsworth's poetry are taken from *Poetical Works*, ed. Thomas Hutchinson, rev. ed. Ernest de Selincourt (London, 1950).

poet's bafflement at this loss of joy in the face of the world's beauty, and of the inadequacy of his own modes of apprehension—the stanzas of 1804 are an explanation of his own history and his own deepest feelings and beliefs. It is a quest for personal identity even as it is a search for something beyond himself. And it is a search for what is perhaps beyond the capacity of eye and ear to know. Although it is necessarily expressed in images of sight and sound, we find the poet groping to articulate what is clearly beyond what eye and ear can discern: "the Soul that rises with us," "clouds of glory," "from God, who is our home." The light the child beholds is, at least in its origin, no earthly light. It may be revealed as sunrise or sunset—or even as "the light of common day"—but it is a light that "cometh from afar."

But the first stage of the poet's exploration of his history—in stanzas V to VIII—reveal the loss of the "vision splendid," as the glory attending his birth gradually gives way to the burdens of human life, the distractions of human envy and ambition, and especially the loss of even the power of seeing beyond what the senses can offer.

> Full soon thy Soul shall have her earthly freight,
> And custom lie upon thee with a weight,
> Heavy as frost, and deep almost as life! (130–132)

Looking back at stanzas V to VIII, however, I must stress—and here I stand again with Alan Grob—that what is most important about them is not the fact that they conclude with a powerful sense of loss, moving though it is, but that they affirm—especially in Stanza V, though the affirmation is implicit throughout—"the existence of a reality that is ideal, eternal, and the true dwelling place of the human spirit" (251). It is crucial to understand that, as Grob expresses it, "by concentrating his quest for identity within the realm of the ideal and changeless, Wordsworth was also assuming the existence of a component of self whose being must extend beyond life's temporal boundaries. Hence any claim for continuity in man's spiritual nature was also inevitably a claim for immortality" (240–241).

This, then, is the crucial background for the dramatic "turn" at the beginning of Stanza IX:

> O joy! that in our embers
> Is something that doth live,
> That nature yet remembers
> What was so fugitive!

> The thought of our past years in me doth breed
> Perpetual benediction: not indeed
> For that which is most worthy to be blest;
> Delight and liberty, the simple creed
> Of Childhood, whether busy or at rest,
> With new-fledged hope still fluttering in his breast:—
>   Not for these I raise
>   The song of thanks and praise;
>   But for those obstinate questionings
>   Of sense and outward things,
>   Fallings from us, vanishings;
>   Blank misgivings of a Creature
> Moving about in worlds not realized,
> High instincts before which our mortal Nature
> Did tremble like a guilty Thing surprised:
>   But for those first affections,
>   Those shadowy recollections,
>   Which, be they what they may,
> Are yet the fountain-light of all our day,
> Are yet a master-light of all our seeing. . . . (133–156)

It is in this passage of the poem—especially the much-vexed lines about "those obstinate questionings / Of sense and outward things, / Fallings from us, vanishings"—that so many readers, myself included, have been led astray. The confusion may be due in part to Wordsworth's own comments to Isabella Fenwick about this passage, especially the striking image of the schoolboy Wordsworth grasping at a wall or tree "to recall myself from this abyss of idealism to the reality." We often do not note, however, that he immediately goes on to say:

> At this time I was afraid of such processes. In later periods of life I have deplored, as we have all reason to do, a subjugation of an opposite character, and have rejoiced over the remembrances, as is expressed in the lines "Obstinate questionings / Of sense and outward things, / Fallings from us, vanishings."[6]

It seems clear, then, that Wordsworth is celebrating the time when his perceptions were not limited to "sense and outward things," when the child could "obstinately question" the evidence of the senses and affirm what was unseen, unheard. Unlike the adult, who has traveled

---

[6] Quoted in *English Romantic Writers*, ed. David Perkins (New York, 1967) 279.

"farther from the East," the child can still "move about in worlds not realized." No wonder the poet raises "the song of thanks and praise" for this memory, since the child's affirmation of this unseen, transcendent reality can be for him "the fountain-light of all our day," "the master-light of all our seeing."

And what is it that can mediate for the adult between these two worlds, the empirical world of the senses and the unseen world of transcendent reality? The child instinctively knows these two worlds coexist—the world of sense reality and an unseen world beyond—but the grown-up poet has lost this instinct. What can bring these two worlds together, and allow the poet to affirm what he does not directly experience? It is the power of thought, a word that recurs tellingly throughout the last three stanzas of the poem (emphasis added in these quotations): "The *thought* of our past years in me doth breed / Perpetual benediction" (137–138); "We in *thought* will join your throng, / Ye that pipe and ye that play" (175–176); "the soothing *thoughts* that spring / Out of human suffering" (187–188); and "To me the meanest flower that blows can give / *Thoughts* that do often lie too deep for tears" (206–207).

What has happened to the poet in the dramatic "turn" of Stanza IX is that—and here I return to Alan Grob—he has "shifted attention from concern with a state of being and mode of knowing admittedly lost beyond recovery, at least for this life, to consideration of the objects of knowledge, the central truths, then apprehended" (254). A new mode of knowing was required—a mode of knowing that was not accessible to the child—by which those early instinctive intuitions could be articulated and made permanently available to the adult. Thought, and thought alone, can cross the boundary between sensory knowledge and the transcendent reality of spirit. He need not—nor can he—rely on the instinctive knowledge of childhood, which is gone forever, but it has been replaced with something more lasting and ultimately more valuable: the gift of human thought—"the philosophic mind" (line 190)—carefully nurtured and cultivated through the years. It is this gift that sets the human person apart from the world of nature. Nature can inspire and delight, but it is finally the properly human attributes that imply thought and self-awareness—"human suffering," "man's mortality," and "the human heart by which we live"—that point us, through our human experiences and our human yearnings, toward a world of spirit, toward immortality.

The poet is not transported, to be sure, into another world. He does not yet experience the "glory" that is to come—a "glory" of which he had intimations during the innocence of childhood. He is back in the ordinary world of human suffering, of the human heart with all "its tenderness, its joys, and fears" (205). But through the gift of memory and the power of thought he has discovered "the faith that looks through death" (189), a faith that can make even "Our noisy years seem moments in the being / Of the eternal Silence" (158–159). He has had—and has—"intimations of immortality."

Wordsworth's poem has proceeded largely by way of visual imagery, especially light. He has moved from the "celestial light" of the opening lines—"the visionary gleam"—into the "light of common day"; he is at times "in darkness lost, the darkness of the grave"; but he emerges at last into the more sober but still beautiful light of "the setting sun." It is no doubt true that Wordsworth has not recovered the "celestial light," but he has clearly come to recognize that the light of this world, even the sunset, is a reflection of the heavenly light; that the light we see each day—the very light that enables us to see—is one with the greater light beyond. The world we live in is ultimately translucent to the light of heaven.

The title of Hopkins' poem, "The Leaden Echo and the Golden Echo," alerts us at once that it will be a poem focused on sound, and it does indeed proceed—characteristically for Hopkins—not only by incremental visual imagery but also by the studied concatenation of sounds, from the heavy and foreboding sounds of the "Leaden Echo" to the swifter and more "lifted," at times even exalted, sounds of the "Golden Echo." At St. Winefred's Well, each bell gives off the sound most proper to it, "speaks its name," as in the sonnet "As kingfishers catch fire":

> As tumbled over rim in roundy wells
> Stones ring; like each tucked string tells, each hung bell's
> Bow swung finds tongue to fling out broad its name.[7]

Perhaps implicit here is a reminder of the medieval custom, still alive in many places, of naming significant bells. One might say that ulti-

---

[7] Quotations of Hopkins' poetry are taken from *The Poems of Gerard Manley Hopkins*, ed. W. H Gardner and N. H. MacKenzie, 4th ed. (London, 1967).

mately the name of the leaden bell is "despair," while the name of the golden bell is "yonder."

The poem is of course the "Maidens' song from St. Winefred's Well," part of an unfinished play on the seventh-century saint, niece of the Welsh St. Beuno. Winefred was beheaded by the chieftain Caradoc as she defended her chastity. St. Beuno restored her to life, and a spring of water sprang up from the place where her head had struck the ground. She went on to become an abbess, living for another fifteen years after her resurrection. Because it is a "maidens' song," the imagery is taken from—in Hopkins' Latin phrase to Robert Bridges—the "mundus muliebris," the world of women.

While Wordsworth's Ode begins with a time of light and joy, even though only recollected ("There was a time"), the opening of Hopkins' poem is dominated by dread and seemingly unremitting loss.

The Leaden Echo

How to kéep—is there any ány, is there none such, nowhere known
   some, bow or brooch or braid or brace, lace, latch or catch or key to keep
Back beauty, keep it, beauty, beauty, beauty, . . . from vanishing away?
Ó is there no frowning of these wrinkles, rankèd wrinkles deep,
Dówn? no waving off of these most mournful messengers, still
   messengers, sad and stealing messengers of grey?—
No there's none, there's none, O no there's none,
Nor can you long be, what you now are, called fair,
Do what you may do, what, do what you may.
And wisdom is early to despair:
Be beginning; since, no, nothing can be done
To keep at bay
Age and age's evils, hoar hair,
Ruck and wrinkle, drooping, dying, death's worst, winding sheets, tombs
   and worms and tumbling to decay;
So be beginning, be beginning to despair.
O there's none; no no no there's none:
Be beginning to despair, to despair,
Despair, despair, despair, despair.

At first, it could be argued, there may be some hope, as the poet wonders "how to keep . . . beauty . . . from vanishing away?" But this hope itself vanishes quickly: "No there's none"—and the imagery swiftly descends to death, winding sheets, worms—and despair, the word itself repeated again and again like the hollow echoes within a leaden tomb. And the movement of the lines is clearly and ineluctably downward, punctuated by such words and phrases as "deep," "down"— these words placed at the end of one line and the beginning of the next, for maximum emphasis—"drooping," "tombs," and "tumbling to decay." This movement is in turn heightened by the heavy "m" sounds ("most mournful messengers"), the ominous sibilants ("sad and stealing messengers"), and the dull thud of the repeated "d" of death and decay and despair. The finality seems definitive.

The movement to the "Golden Echo," however, seems equally definitive.

The Golden Echo

     Spare!
Thereís one, yes I have one (Hush there!);
Only not within seeing of the sun,
Not within the singeing of the strong sun,
Tall sun's tingeing, or treacherous the tainting of the earth's air,
Somewhere elsewhere there is ah well where! one,
Oné. Yes I cán tell such a key, I dó know such a place,

Where whatever's prized and passes of us, everything that's fresh and
 fast flying of us, seems to us sweet of us and swiftly away with, done
 away with,
undone,
Úndone, done with, soon done with, and yet dearly and dangerously
 sweet
Of us, the wimpled-water-dimpled, not-by-morning-matchèd face,
The flower of beauty, fleece of beauty, too too apt to ah! to fleet,
Never fleets móre, fastened with the tenderest truth
To its own best being and its loveliness of youth: it is an ever-lastingness
 of, O it is an all youth!
Come then, your ways and airs and looks, locks, maidengear, gallantry
 and gaiety and grace,
Winning ways, airs innocent, maiden manners, sweet looks, loose locks,
 long locks, lovelocks, gaygear, going gallant, girlgrace—
Resign them, sign them, seal them, send them, motion them with
 breath,
And with sighs soaring, soaring sighs, deliver

Them; beauty-in-the-ghost, deliver it, early now, long before death
Give beauty back, beauty, beauty, beauty, back to God, beauty's self and
   beauty's giver.
See; not a hair is, not an eyelash, not the least lash lost; every hair
Is, hair of the head, numbered.

The "Golden Echo" is in fact an echo of the sound made by the "Leaden Echo": "despair" becomes "spare," as the echo picks up the last syllable of the echoing word. The two "echoes" are thus deeply interconnected: it is not a vision of death followed by a vision of life, but rather death transformed into life; the leaden echo *becomes* the golden echo. As the words "despair" and "spare" are organically related, the one containing the other, so death and life are intrinsic to one another; they are not opposites but cognates, both part of a single process in the history of our human world.

The shift from despair to affirmation is quite as dramatic as the "turn" to joy in Wordsworth's Ode, and it is underscored in the most lovely and touching way by the parenthetical "Hush there!"—as the maidens comfort someone weeping, much as one might hush tenderly a child in tears.

There is comfort and hope because there is a key: "Yes I can tell such a key, I do know such a place." Paul Mariani has written, with some justice, that "it is not too much to say that the lyric is, at least in part, generated on a gigantic but not quite serious pun: the search for a lock to keep our locks."[8] The "place" is where whatever is "fleeting" in our being "Never fleets more, fastened with the tenderest truth / To its own best being and its loveliness of youth: it is an everlastingness of, O it is an all youth!" Where Wordsworth had been able to intimate immortality from the human spirit, Hopkins affirms—as does the constant Christian tradition—even the resurrection of the body.

But to achieve this kind of immortality, the price is to let go of earthly beauties now, giving beauty "back to God, beauty's self and beauty's giver." Here we find Hopkins in tension, as he often is, between the profoundly incarnational theology dictated by his own Christology and by his formation in the Spiritual Exercises of Saint Ignatius Loyola—according to which God works in and through all created being—and the eschatological pole of Christian theology: "We have not here a lasting city." It is a tension that is at the center of any serious Christian's experience, and we shall return to it before we close.

---

[8] *Commentary on the Poems of Gerard Manley Hopkins* (Ithaca, 1970) 189.

There are three scriptural passages that are part of the fabric of the "Golden Echo," but they have not all been equally taken into account. The first is Matthew 10: 29–31 (and its parallel in Luke 12: 6–7): "Are not two sparrows sold for a penny? And not one of them will fall to the ground without your Father's will. But even the hairs of your head are all numbered. Fear not, therefore; you are of more value than many sparrows." Thus the poet can offer these comforting words: "See; not a hair is, not an eyelash, not the least lash lost; every hair / Is, hair of the head, numbered."

And the following passage introduces still another important biblical echo:

> Nay, what we had lighthanded left in surly the mere mold
> Will have waked and have waxed and have walked with the wind what while we slept,
> This side, that side hurling a heavyheaded hundredfold
> What while we, while we slumbered.

The reference here is to the parable of the sower in Matthew 13: 1–23 (with its parallel in Mark 4: 1–20)—including the sowing on good ground that brings forth a bounteous hundredfold. But in order fully to understand the poet's sowing imagery, I believe we must look as well to a passage shortly afterward in Mark's gospel (Mark 4: 26–29), where the work of the sower is contrasted sharply with the work of God: the sower plants the seed but—in St. Paul's words—God gives the increase. "And Jesus said, 'The kingdom of God is as if a man should scatter seed upon the ground, and should sleep and rise night and day, and the seed should sprout and grow, he knows not how. The earth produces of itself, first the blade, then the ear, then the full grain in the ear." The emphasis in Hopkins is on the priority of God in the process of salvation: even in the face of our ignorance or inattention, even as we "slumber," God is working to give us a "heavyheaded hundredfold." The seeds we cast into the "dull furrow" (as Hopkins calls it in a letter to Bridges) will have awakened and have grown—through a power beyond our own in ways beyond our knowing—into a whole field of grain blowing in the wind: "Will have waked and have waxed and have walked with the wind what while we slept." The "heavyheaded hundredfold" will have come to us even as we slumbered.

There is one other scriptural passage—John 12: 24–25—that is often overlooked in discussions of the "Golden Echo" because it is not so explicitly present, but which I believe is of extraordinary importance for this poem: "Truly, truly, I say to you, unless a grain of wheat falls into the earth and dies, it remains alone; but if it dies, it bears much fruit. He who loves his life loses it, and he who hates his life in this world will keep it for eternal life." Surely this is at the heart of the poem: eternal life reached precisely by the passage through death, death leading to life—the leaden echo being transformed into the golden echo.

After this vision of the eternal harvest to come, the closing lines of the poem bring us for a moment back into the care-ridden world of ordinary human life:

> O then, weary then whý should we tread? O why are we so haggard at
> the heart, so care-coiled, care-killed, so fagged, so fashed, so cogged,
> so cumbered? O then, weary then whý should we tread?

But it is only for a moment, as the heart is quickly drawn back to its yearning for beauty that will last:

> When the thing we freely fórfeit is kept with fonder a care,
> Fonder a care kept than we could have kept it, kept
> Far with fonder a care (and we, we should have lost it) finer, fonder
> A care kept.—Where kept? Do but tell us where kept, where.—
> Yonder.—What high as that! We follow, now we follow.—
>   Yonder, yes yonder, yonder,
>   Yonder.

And it is indeed the heart that is drawn, for the "cares" of the world that weigh us down ("care-coiled," "care-killed") are transmuted into the loving care of "fonder a care," while "fonder"—four times spoken—leads to "yonder," the end-point and culmination of the poem and of the maidens'—and the poet's—longing. For the reader also, it is with the heart as well as the ear that one must listen to "The Golden Echo."

What Hopkins praised in Wordsworth's Ode—its "insight into Nature" and its imagery "charged and steeped with beauty and yearning"—is surely true of both these remarkable poems. Both of them, by seeing into Nature, see beyond Nature to a reality transcending the evidence of the senses. Both of them, in images of incomparable beauty, express the human yearning for life and beauty that will not fade and die.

But for all his love of sense beauty, for its own sake and as a manifestation of God's beauty—"beauty's self and beauty's giver"—Hopkins remained at times fearful of it. He could write exultantly: "The world is charged with the grandeur of God" and "Glory be to God for dappled things," but when he asks "To what serves Mortal Beauty?" he must admit that it is "dangerous." Mortal beauty is, to be sure, a gift from God, a gift that "keeps warm / Men's wits to the things that are," but it cannot be allowed to distract from the giver of the gift.

> What do then? how meet beauty? ' Merely meet it; Own,
> Home at heart, heaven's sweet gift; ' then leave, let that alone.
> Yea, wish that though, wish all, ' God's better beauty, grace.

What we see then in Hopkins—in "The Leaden Echo and The Golden Echo," as in his poetry generally—is the tension between incarnational and eschatological poles, the immanent and the transcendent, that marks the central tradition of Christianity. Both these realities are integral parts of God's plan; both must be cherished. The practical problem is to keep them properly in balance: not allowing our delight in the present reality—or our pain in it—to make us forget that it is not all; not allowing our yearning for life beyond the senses to keep us from loving the beauty that is before us.

If "The Leaden Echo and the Golden Echo" ends with the poet's yearning for the "yonder" of the transcendent, Wordsworth's Immortality Ode ends back in the material world, without the "visionary gleam," where a flower—even the "meanest flower that blows"—gives "thoughts that do often lie too deep for tears." But the tension that underlies the poem—between the immanent reality of the material world and the transcendent world of which the poet has had "intimations"—is the same as that of Hopkins. Whatever the differences in imagery and rhetoric, the experience of the two poets is essentially the same: the experience of being a traveler between two worlds—one world whose passing beauty is dearly loved, the other whose lasting beauty is deeply longed for.

Works Cited

Grob, Alan. *The Philosophic Mind: A Study of Wordsworth's Poetry, 1797–1805*. Columbus: Ohio State University Press, 1973.

Hartman, Geoffrey. *Wordsworth's Poetry, 1787–1814*. New Haven: Yale University Press, 1971.

Hopkins, Gerard Manley. *The Correspondence of Gerard Manley Hop-*

kins and Richard Watson Dixon. Ed. Claude Colleer Abbot. Rev. ed. London: Oxford University Press, 1955.

———. *The Poems of Gerard Manley Hopkins*. Ed. W. H. Gardner and N. H. MacKenzie. 4th ed. London: Oxford University Press, 1967.

Mariani, Paul. *Commentary on the Poems of Gerard Manley Hopkins*. Ithaca: Cornell University Press, 1970.

Perkins, David, ed. *English Romantic Writers*. New York: Harcourt, Brace, and World, 1967.

Steiner, George. *Real Presences*. Chicago: The University of Chicago Press, 1989.

Wordsworth, William. *Poetical Works*. Ed. Thomas Hutchinson. Rev. ed. Ernest de Selincourt. London: Oxford University Press, 1950.

8

Coleridge (and His Mariner) on the Soul: "As an exile in a far distant land"

James Engell

I

EXTENDING A large intellectual pattern of the modern West, prominent thinkers in the century prior to Coleridge dissect the soul into many faculties. In an impassioned section of *The Excursion* (IV, 951–992), as well as in *The Prelude* and his lyrics, Wordsworth decries this method: "We murder to dissect." He echoes Pope, who in the "Epistle to Cobham" had articulated the problem this way: "Like following life thro' creatures you dissect, / You lose it in the moment you detect." Yet the dissecting method supports new discoveries that transform natural philosophy and give rise to modern empirical science. These changes, and the tensions they create, produce what one critic, Paul Ilie, calls "the key idea that bridges eighteenth-century philosophy and science, namely, the changing notion of a vital force or 'soul.'"[1] Some experiments to locate the soul prove heroic. In an attempt to establish that it actually resides in the chest, the physician and philosopher Jean-Baptiste van Helmont administers wolfsbane to himself. The soul is often no longer regarded in purely theological terms. In common usage, it now potentially includes, and overlaps with, whatever is meant by mind, spirit, life, self, self-consciousness, and identity.

Coleridge recognizes this broader usage throughout his writings and notes it a number of times, for example, when he says, "we use the word 'mind' in this place as nearly equivalent to the soul, as the sum of

---

[1] Rev. of *Nature's Enigma: The Problem of the Polyp in the Letters of Bonnet, Trembley and Réaumur*, by Virginia P. Dawson, *Eighteenth-Century Studies* 24 (1991): 518.

all our faculties, whether active, passive or spontaneous" (*Logic* 153).[2] The whole, too, is greater than its aggregated parts, for "there is *the idea* of the Soul with its undefined capacity and dignity, that gives the sting to any absorption of it by any one pursuit" (*Lects 1808–1819*, II, 172). To define the capacity of the soul seems inherently to fail to realize its worth and potential. As Samuel Johnson said of any attempt to circumscribe poetry with a definition, it shows only the "narrowness of the definer." Of course, this doesn't stop Coleridge. With a new urgency prompted by modern science, the problem of the soul confronts poets, critics, natural philosophers, psychologists, and theologians. And it fascinates Coleridge, which is to say the same thing.

A few thinkers Coleridge admires in the 1790s, especially Hartley, arrived at the soul and religious concerns by starting with "vibrations" of mental tissues and nerves. But Coleridge soon believes that vibrational Associationism means starting with the material and ending with the spiritual. For him, the process is backward. As an explanation of the human spirit he abhors materialism and hylozoism, the doctrine that the organization of matter alone explains life. Everyone perceives and associates the particulars of the material world. But, Coleridge insists, what explains the existence of that material world in the first place? Isn't there, in human nature, separate from the five outward senses, a moral sense, a type of reason, and a freedom of the will that together determine the worth and dignity of the individual? And isn't such an invisible, supersensuous sense just as real as touch, taste, or sight? It is an "undue degradation of the human soul" to subject "all truth to conceptions formed by the senses, or to the notions which the understanding marks for itself by reflection on its own processes" (*Logic* 197). Coleridge objects to "Voltaire, D'Alembert, Diderot" because he sees in their writings the high tide of an old misconception: "the Human Understanding ... was tempted to throw off all reverence to the spiritual and even to the moral powers and impulses of the soul" (*SM* 75). Another method of knowing—and of knowing the self in its relationship to nature—is needed.

---

[2] Parenthetical citations are to standard editions of Coleridge's collected works, letters, and notebooks (see list of Works Cited). Abbreviations are: *Aids to Reflection* (*AR*); *Biographia Literaria* (*BL*); *Collected Letters* (*CL*); *Essays on His Times* (*EOT*); *A Lay Sermon* (*LS*); *Lectures 1795: On Politics and Religion* (*Lects 1795*); *Lectures 1808–1819: On Literature* (*Lects 1808–1819*); *Lectures 1818–1819: On the History of Philosophy* (*Lects 1818–1819*); *Marginalia* (*CM*); *Notebooks* (*CN*); *Shorter Works and Fragments* (*SW&F*); *The Statesman's Manual* in *LS* above (*SM*); *Table Talk* (*TT*).

As so often, Coleridge finds ultimate authority for his position, this method of the soul, in Scripture. On the immortality of the soul, he claims, "Read the first chapter of Genesis without prejudice, and you will be convinced at once. . . . And in the next chapter," Coleridge goes on, Moses "repeats the narrative:—'And the Lord God formed man of the dust of the ground, and breathed into his nostrils the breath of life;' and then he adds these words,—'*and man became a living soul.*' Materialism will never explain those last words" (*TT*, II, 36; see I, 31–32). These words are so important to Coleridge that he quotes them, too, in the "Theory of Life" (1816) and in *Aids to Reflection* (1825). In philosophy, the starting-point so often matters, and Coleridge does not want that starting-point to be matter or nature. He credits Plato with being "the first who supported the immortality of the Soul upon arguments solid and permanent . . . he felt convinced that the diseases and the death of the body could not injure the principle of life or destroy the soul which of itself was of divine origin and of an uncorrupted and immutable essence" (*Lects 1818–1819* 205). The more we regard Coleridge's idea of the soul, the more we see his Platonism.[3] Later, Coleridge is fond of repeating that the pith of his system, if one could call it so fine a thing, is to make the senses out of the mind—not the mind out of the senses, as Locke did (e.g., *TT*, I, 312).

Coleridge is probably regretting youthful errors. For instance, in the earlier *Notebooks* he speculates on the nature of the soul in terms related to motion, time, space, and resistance. His language assumes a cast of logical deduction and draws on the vocabulary of nascent modern physics and the terminology of Locke: "I believe that what we call *motion* is our consciousness of motion, arising from the interruption of motion = the acting of the Soul resisted" (*CN*, I, 1771). Little more than a year later, in January 1805, he continues in a similar vein: "Space <is one of> the Hebrew names for God /& it is the most perfect image of *Soul, pure Soul*—being indeed to us nothing but unresisted action." He then deduces that, "thus all body necessarily presupposes soul, inasmuch as all resistance presupposes action" (*CN*, II, 2402).

If Coleridge's thinking here seems strained, it is because, earlier in his career, he wants to use the language of logic and deduction to

---

[3] Douglas Hedley, *Coleridge, Philosophy and Religion: "Aids to Reflection" and the Mirror of the Spirit* (Cambridge, 2000) 97–99, 105–116, 160–161. Hedley throughout pays close attention to the idea of the soul and traces in detail Coleridge's knowledge of it in earlier thinkers.

elucidate religious belief or conviction. He attempts to bridge the widening fissures between religion, philosophy, and science by setting their realms of discourse together, by using the same realm of discourse—the same method—for each, and then by determining, by way of a kind of syllogism, the primacy of the spiritual world: "and thus all body *necessarily* presupposes soul."

But this sort of attempt, as Coleridge soon recognizes, remains unconvincing. When younger and imitating the methods of empirical science or of logical dissection and deduction, he is drawn onto that battleground and there has difficulty sustaining his spiritual flank. Later, in *Biographia Literaria*, he no longer takes up concepts of space and time with reference to the soul. And in the "Theory of Life," his whole account of the living creation, although anticipatory of Darwin's theory of evolution in some ways, nevertheless consciously refuses a unity or even *continuity* of approach between the natural and the human when it comes to the problem of the soul. That is, the soul cannot be accounted for in nature.[4]

Sometime around 1806 Coleridge begins explicitly to credit "revelation" as convincing him "that I have a rational and responsible soul," and that by virtue of that soul there exists a "wide chasm between man and the noblest animals of the brute creation, which no perceivable or conceivable difference of organization is sufficient to *overbridge*" (*SW& F* 501). He will assert, eventually, on the last day of March 1832, that "All Religion is revealed; revealed religion is in my judgment, a mere pleonasm" (*TT*, I, 276). As early as 1806 he writes to Thomas Clarkson, who inquired about the nature of the soul, that "Reason is therefore most eminently the Revelation of an immortal soul, and it's best Synonime—it is the forma formans, which contains in itself the law of it's own conceptions" (*CL*, II, 1198).

Thus, in a real sense, the conception of one completely unified system of nature and God, spirit and matter, science and religion, founders on this very point, the soul. It cannot be demonstrated or verified in any empirical or logical manner. As James Boulger points out, Coleridge's ontological arguments about the soul contain an "open admission of circularity . . . dwelt upon to a surprising extent."[5] It was to

---

[4] W. J. Bate, *Coleridge* (New York, 1968) 194–195. Bate points out Coleridge's difficulties in accounting for the special nature of the human and ventures that, on that very point, "The essay falls apart" (195).

[5] *Coleridge as Religious Thinker* (New Haven, 1961) 163.

become a theme, one reiterated in a later *Notebook* entry of May 1826: "The characteristic Formula of all *Spiritual* Verities or Ideas is an apparent *Circle*—" (*CN*, IV, 5377). For it, there exists no proof. As Anya Taylor comments, Coleridge in the *Opus Maximum* "makes the best of a difficult situation by arguing that the proof must be indemonstrable by definition; for to demonstrate a thing is to find its antecedent, and whatever is prior can have no antecedent; therefore the Idea of God or of Soul is indemonstrable and rightly so."[6] The method of knowing nature and the method of knowing spirit cannot be one, at least not one simple unity. Such an identity would lead to pantheism, which, as Coleridge explicitly recognizes, does not easily accommodate the idea of the soul. In 1817 he sniffs that Spinoza needed to "supply a Soul" to his system (*SW&F* 567). Taken together, the advances of science and the convictions of revelation hardly seem to conform to one unitary system, no matter how much the dream of it—"a total and undivided philosophy" where "philosophy would pass into religion, and religion become inclusive of philosophy" (*BL*, I, 282, 283)—haunts Coleridge. Even Joseph Henry Green, admirer, collaborator, and literary executor, would confess about one of Coleridge's unfinished projects, apparently the *Opus Maximum*, that "the main portion of the work is a philosophical *Cosmogony*, which I fear is scarcely adapted for scientific readers, or corresponds to the requirements of modern science."[7] Members of Coleridge's family agreed that his science was out of date. In the *Philosophical Lectures*, Coleridge could make unsatisfactory statements, which, even if their ultimate direction might be grasped sympathetically, in literal application would wreak havoc in the laboratory. For example, in claiming to draw on Bacon, though the source is not apparent, he states: "all science approaches to its perfection in proportion as it immaterializes objects" (*Lects 1818–1819* 489).

The temptation attracting Coleridge, especially in his earlier thinking, entices several other Romantic writers, too. Coleridge accuses the *Naturphilosophen* of this weakness. Yet at times he himself conflates the methods and aims of *Naturwissenschaft*, the study of the natural world and the establishment of universal, ahistorical laws, with the methods and aims of *Geisteswissenschaft*, the knowledge and exploration of the

---

[6] *Coleridge's Defense of the Human* (Columbus, 1986) 163.
[7] H. J. Jackson, "Coleridge's Collaborator, Joseph Henry Green," *Studies in Romanticism* 21 (1982): 178.

human spirit caught up in history and dependent on will, genius, and moral action.[8] To act, one must yoke together and make co-present in consciousness these two kinds of knowledge. But to gain these two kinds of knowledge by the *same* method is not possible, nor can they be wrestled into one seamless system. To do so, Wilhelm Dilthey would argue, is an intellectual aspiration of the Romantic era already suspect at that time, and soon thereafter impossible.[9]

In his mature thought, Coleridge does refuse that aspiration. He treats the soul as a postulate or belief of distinctly human experience, of *Geisteswissenschaft*, rather than as an empirical observation of the natural world. The soul is a fact of the human spirit, not something the human mind can properly conceive of or analyze. Again, in his 1806 letter to Clarkson, he makes this clear: "What the Spirit of God *is*, and what the Soul *is*, I dare not suppose myself capable of *conceiving*: according to my religious and philosophical creed they are *known* by those, to whom they are revealed. . . . *Datur*, non intelligitur" (*CL*, II, 1193). As Stephen Prickett explains, the mind cannot properly conceive of the soul itself; rather, "Man, made in God's image as a living and creative soul, is at his *proper* activity . . . when acting as a mirror to God's enlightenment."[10]

This approach is not, of course, scientific. Yet it need not oppose science. There are parallels and interdependencies between the method of the soul and the methods of science. In November 1801 Coleridge quotes approvingly Sir Kenelm Digby's translation of Plato's *Phaedrus* (270c): "Do you suppose the nature of the soul can be sufficiently understood without the knowledge of the whole of nature?" (*CN*, I, 1002). As Anthony Harding notes, for Coleridge "the point . . . is that our comprehension of Nature's processes is a progressive thing, just as is our moral and religious being."[11] (We shall consider the idea of the soul's growth and progression momentarily.) But the moral and relig-

---

[8] For general discussion, see Hans Eichner, "The Rise of Modern Science and the Genesis of Romanticism," *PMLA* 97.1 (1982): 8–30.

[9] *Selected Writings*, ed. and trans. H. P. Rickman (Cambridge, 1976) 122–130. Dilthey states: "no metaphysics can satisfy the demand for a scientific proof," arguing that while philosophy retains its respective valences in science, in the search for meaning, and in the study of human conduct, it can not unify these: "We can notice, as it were, only one side of our relationship" to the world at a time (123).

[10] *Coleridge and Wordsworth: The Poetry of Growth* (Cambridge, 1970) 181.

[11] Anthony John Harding, *Coleridge and the Inspired Word* (Kingston and Montreal, 1985) 39.

ious being begins with an act of the soul. In this sense, Coleridge remarks, "Faith is a *total* act of the soul: it is the *whole* state of the mind, or it is not at all!" (*Friend*, II, 314). R. J. White identifies this as "the key" to all of Coleridge's "lay preaching" (*LS*, xliii). In *The Statesman's Manual*, Coleridge expresses it this way: "Even so doth Religion finitely express the *unity* of the infinite Spirit by being a total act of the soul" (*SM*, 90). (This is a unity of spirit, not of matter with spirit.) As he explains in *The Friend*, "The aim, the method throughout was, in the first place, to awaken, to cultivate, and to mature the truly *human* in human nature, in and through itself, or as independently as possible of the notices derived from sense, and of the motives that had reference to the sensations; till the time should arrive when the senses themselves might be allowed to present symbols and attestations of truths, learnt previously from deeper and inner sources" (*Friend*, I, 500–501). The soul, he reaffirms in the "Theory of Life," is that "which I believe to constitute the peculiar nature of man" and has no connection with, nor is the cause of, "functions and properties, which man possesses in common with the oyster and the mushroom" (*SW&F*, 501). This spiritual method, then, Coleridge claims, is to start from within and proceed dialectically to the external world. He can ally this sense of the soul's dialectical method with Fichte's *Ich bin weil ich bin* and *nicht-Ich* or with Kant's concept of self-apperception. Evident Platonic sources exist as well, many of them familiar to Schelling and Fichte. Coleridge also appeals for the existence of the soul and its method to Christian doctrine and revelation, to Jehovah's "I AM that I AM" and to the passages he quotes from Genesis. He is aware of all of these, as it were, simultaneously.

Yet, as Coleridge comes to realize that attempts to *identify* the method of the soul with the method of science do not quite square, he moves to *reconcile* advances in the method of science with reflection on the method of spiritual life. We should perhaps more often seek for this reconciliation in his thought than insist on its putative or final unity.[12] Near the end of this essay, in the context of "The Rime of the Ancient Mariner" and Coleridge's comments on the power of the

---

[12] For excellent treatment of the tension inherent in Coleridge's search for unity amidst his recognition of diversity, see Seamus Perry, *Coleridge and the Uses of Division* (Oxford, 1999). Perry emphasizes Coleridge's attempts at reconciliation in his literary criticism (233–274), but the theme is apparent throughout, including on the subject of religion.

imagination, we shall return to the *activity* of reconciliation as distinguished from unity itself, for this activity is vital in understanding how Coleridge deals with both a natural world subject to science and a specifically human world of spirit, conscience, and the moral life. In the vein of such active connection and reconciliation, he praises Thales as the first thinker to perceive that there is "a relationship between the Soul of Man and the laws of Nature" even though the primacy of knowledge comes from "the mind of Man," from "Reason" (*Lects 1818–1819* 101). For this position, Coleridge invokes at least three times, in *Biographia*, the *Philosophical Lectures*, and "On the Prometheus of Aeschylus," Milton's lines from *Paradise Lost* that climb the scale of being from natural to spiritual: ". . . whence the soul / Reason receives, and reason is her being" (V, 486–487). Nature and the soul cannot be left to go their separate ways, for they are not separate. If they become entirely so, the result will be a dehumanized society driven by mechanistic technology, a society in which individuals sacrifice their own souls or, worse, enslave the souls of others for material gain. Whether the result is the Faustian bargain of material control over nature in the first instance, or slavery and exploitation in the second instance, matters little. One leads to the other.

Coleridge's dialectical method thus starts in a way different from the dissecting method that he believes has monopolized human energy and gained the upper hand of knowledge. "In short," as he outlines it, first, "all the organs of sense are framed for a corresponding world of sense; and we have it." Yet in pursuing those senses exclusively we cannot help but become materialists. In contrast, "all the organs of spirit are framed for a correspondent world of spirit; tho' the latter organs are not developed in all alike. But they exist in all, and their first appearance discloses itself in the *moral* being." This moral being presupposes a spiritual ground of human life. In the same chapter of *Biographia Literaria*, Coleridge restates this idea by paraphrasing Schelling: "besides the language of words, there is a language of spirits (sermo interior) and . . . the former is only the vehicle of the latter" (*BL*, I, 242, 290). As early as 1805 Coleridge identifies the soul itself as an organ of spiritual or supersensuous perception (*SW&F* 154). The soul possesses the ability to modify and become one with ideas, connecting itself to the natural, external world through those ideas. In 1816, he conveys this with a strikingly poignant image: "At the annunciation" of supersensuous "*principles*, of *ideas*, the soul of man awakes, and starts up, as an exile in a far distant land at the unexpected sounds of his native language, when after long years of absence, and almost of oblivion, he is suddenly addressed in his own mother-tongue" (*SM* 24). Using the very line from Shakespeare's sonnets that John Livingston Lowes quotes from one of Coleridge's notebooks to launch discussion in *The Road to Xanadu*, Owen Barfield remarks that such a relationship between ideas and the soul is the foundation for what Coleridge "understands by method. Because ideas are the permanence and self-circling energies of reason, they are also in an almost literal sense 'the prophetic soul / of the wide world dreaming on things to come' and it is therefore only *their* presence in the mind that can give rise to a knowledge effective for the future as well as analytical of the past; and (which is much the same thing) only that which can produce any radically *new* knowledge."[13]

II

From such starting-points or postulates concerning the "organs of spirit" and "the language of spirits," as well as from Coleridge's belief in the "peculiar" nature of the human endowed with a soul, several points emerge:

(1) Everyone possesses a soul, which is something different and also something more than the mere sum of material senses and the mental operations we perform on the experiences that those material senses supply. Rather than derive the spiritual from models provided by physics, Lockean philosophy, or science, Coleridge concludes that "whatever originates its own acts, or in any sense contains in itself the cause of its own state, must be *spiritual*, and consequently *super-natural*; yet not on that account necessarily *miraculous*. And such must the responsible WILL in us be, if it be at all" (*AR* 251; see *Friend*, II, 79). If we follow *this* line of Coleridge's thought, we are not caught in the trap of using the soul as a bridge that must satisfy the traffic of science, philosophy, and religion all in the same one lane. Now the soul remains essentially outside the realm of science—science can neither find nor murder to dissect it. Yet the soul is able to subsume the results of science in order to inform human feeling and action, particularly to

---

[13] *What Coleridge Thought* (Middletown, 1971) 119.

direct our moral being. Apparently unlike the poetic and philosophic imaginations, and unlike genius, the power of the soul is, at least in potential, in every human being. The soul is potentially democratic, with deep implications, as we shall touch on in a minute, for Coleridge's social and political thought. In his later career he highlights these concerns, bolstered by an emphasis on the will, the free agency of the soul to act.

(2) If we develop our spiritual organs, the soul will grow. This growth is by no means a new idea. It is found in Plato, and in earlier English writers well known to Coleridge,[14] and he stresses it constantly. By developing the spiritual organs, we shall realize our best selves, come to know our selves, and adopt a process, a continuing "method" of spiritual quest and pilgrimage, the all-important, ancient command "Know Thyself" (*BL*, I, 252, 291). This is Coleridge's plea on behalf of an organic vision of the human spirit. Even as he believes that the individual soul is inherently flawed, he also believes that it matures by a process of self-evolution or self-actualization, "a growth of consciousness," "a reflex consciousness of it's own continuousness" (*CL*, II, 1196, 1197).[15] The soul he thus describes "as a self-conscious personal Being" (*SW&F* 427). Whatever is latent in the soul is what the self *might* become. The soul is "saved" in part by its own self-realization, which requires an act of will.

To foster this growth and realization is, in a significant way, the chief purpose of *Aids to Reflection*. Some of these ideas he seems to have met also in Fichte and Schelling, but the sense of process and growth in the soul marks much Romantic thought. It is clear that in this regard Coleridge influenced Emerson, not only through the Kantian distinction between reason and understanding in *The Friend*, but also through the Essays on Method there, and through *Aids to Reflection*. Coleridge's dialectical method informs the growth of the soul set out in Emerson's *Nature*.[16] Emerson's fourth chapter, "Language," ends by quoting

---

[14] For example, see Patricia Meyer Spacks, "The Soul's Imaginings: Daniel Defoe, William Cowper," *PMLA* 91 (1976): 420–435. Spacks sees growth and self-realization taking place in Crusoe's soul (429). Connections between Coleridge's Mariner and Crusoe are well established. Coleridge read Defoe's book as a child.

[15] Although he does not dwell specifically on the soul, for treatment of moral growth and realization of the self, see Laurence S. Lockridge, *Coleridge the Moralist* (Ithaca, 1977) 146–198.

[16] See Barry Wood, "The Growth of the Soul: Coleridge's Dialectical Method and the Strategy of Emerson's *Nature*," *PMLA* 91 (1976): 385–397. Wood credits Cole-

Coleridge's *Aids to Reflection*: "Every object rightly seen, unlocks a new faculty of the soul." Coleridge also is the presiding spirit for passages on the soul in "Self-Reliance."[17] If J. H. Green could worry that readers might find Coleridge's science unacceptable, he also expresses, in his "Introduction to the Philosophical Remains of S. T. Coleridge," that Coleridge's philosophic thought at its best traces "the growth of the soul" (*SW&F* 1533) from its spring tide to the mature vision of the moral philosopher, a growth Green illustrates with quotations from Wordsworth, whose theme of the growth of the soul is his greatest and most original. This adds resonance to the name Wordsworth habitually employed for *The Prelude*: "the poem to Coleridge."

Like other contemporaneous thinkers (Keats, Blake, Wordsworth, Schiller, and Schelling), Coleridge conceives of the soul as organic and growing, not a static entity, nor one predestined for redemption or damnation. The soul registers—it constantly creates from within—the moral worth and fate of the individual. Coleridge seems to have this quality in mind when he refers to the "abidingness of the Soul" (*CM*, III, 39). Yet, while retaining this capacity, it is flawed with the potential for sin, for evil. Imagination cannot save the self from that flaw. Salvation comes from God, and to receive it the soul must be simultaneously open to experience and open to an inner realization of its own "moral being." This requires neither genius nor extraordinary imaginative power. This process of spiritual growth exists in humankind as well as in individuals, a topic that intrigues Coleridge (as it intrigues Kant and others) and constitutes one aim of the *Philosophical Lectures*. Again, in that seminal letter to Clarkson of 1806, Coleridge states that the "growth of reflex consciousness" in the individual soul "is not conceivable without the action of kindred souls on each other.... Man is truly altered by the co-existence of other men.... Therefore the human race not by a bold metaphor, but in a sublime reality, approach to, & might become, one body whose Head is Christ (the Logos)" (*CL*, II, 1197). The individual soul, then, develops in a community, and that community itself develops. In this respect, as Anthony Harding notes, "Coleridge shared with the Enlightenment thinkers their respect for science

---

ridge with "most profound" influence (388) and argues that Coleridge's method of the soul "duplicated the process of the mind during its organic assimilation of the universe" (395), a dialectical method that Emerson adopts.

[17] See David Vallins, "Self-Reliance: Individualism in Emerson and Coleridge," *Symbiosis* 5 (2001): 51–68, esp 59.

and scholarship and their trust in the ability of the human race to develop from infancy to maturity."[18]

Coleridge perhaps exerts his greatest influence in the nineteenth century in religious questions. During his lifetime and for decades afterward, his best-selling book is *Aids to Reflection*. His meditations on the soul anticipate many developments in theology of the next century and a half. He joins Schleiermacher, for example, in seeking the ultimate concern of human consciousness; scientific data can neither prove nor disprove its existence. No such proof exists for reason: it requires a personal act of self-constructive free will. Rudolf Bultmann later champions faith as a self-authenticating act of the soul. Coleridge also anticipates some elements of Kierkegaard's existentialism and of experiential approaches to Christianity; he speaks directly of "experimentative faith" (*AR* 9). Human history as bound up with the development of a collective human soul—the Holy Spirit in humankind—preoccupies Coleridge as it will Karl Barth. Another connection links Coleridge with Paul Tillich and the concept of "the ground of being," not surprising given Tillich's deep reading in Schelling. Yet sharp differences exist, too, between Coleridge and each of these thinkers. (For example, Schleiermacher's views on revelation are not the same as Coleridge's; Kierkegaard and Barth see a virtual gulf between the human and the divine, compared with Coleridge's belief in a much more intimate relationship—where the human has its being *in* the divine). While Coleridge's influence on religious thought in Britain is well recognized, a full study of Coleridge's theological work and speculation in light of later European developments waits to be written.[19] Among other sources, the later *Notebooks* would provide considerable material.

(3) Language at its best is more than a vehicle to express direct sensations and mental reflections on the ideas formed by objects of sense. Originally, the language of words is a vehicle of the organs of spirit, of inner spiritual life: it is language that humanizes the universe

---

[18] *Inspired Word* 38.

[19] For suggestive remarks on various connections with later theologians, see J. Robert Barth, S.J., *Coleridge and Christian Doctrine* (1969; New York, 1987) 196–198. Among other things, Barth underscores Coleridge's prescient ability to grapple with "the old radical discontinuity between the natural and the supernatural" (196); see also Claude Welch, *Protestant Thought in the Nineteenth Century*, 2 vols. (New Haven, 1972), I, 108–126. Hedley (291–300) sees chiefly a "surface affinity" among Coleridge, Kierkegaard, and Barth, and stresses key differences. Still, while their answers sometimes differ, the questions are frequently the same.

and connects it to the human spirit. For Coleridge, then, true poetic language does not rest in so-called poetic diction or in wrangles over vocabulary and decorum, as much as in the imagery and music and rhythm capable of expressing the inner drama of the soul as it encounters the world at a particular time and place and in a particular mood. Both a realistic psychological dimension and a spiritual sensibility are at work, a duality pertinent to the original plan for *Lyrical Ballads*, and to "The Rime of the Ancient Mariner" in particular. The poems in *Lyrical Ballads* would deal with the commerce between natural and supernatural. Beyond this, the vehicle of language is, or at least can be, the instrument of free will and the soul's free agency, and hence of spiritual and political freedom. Certain great poets are justifiably linked with ideas of liberty. One of them, Milton, likens a book to the soul. Coleridge states, in his famous definition, that "the poet, described in *ideal* perfection, brings the whole soul of man into activity." But it is also helpful to recall his claim that the whole of his literary criticism in *Biographia* is tied to principles in "Politics, Religion, and Philosophy" (*BL*, II, 15–16; I, 5).

(4) In *The Statesman's Manual* and *A Lay Sermon*, Coleridge posits that not only individual salvation and liberty but social justice and right government ultimately depend on an understanding of, and a reverence for, the soul. Governments must respect and encourage its intrinsic moral worth and its potential for growth. Those gifted or privileged enough to enjoy the leisure and education necessary to develop the language of the spirit and the growth of the soul are expected to foster and encourage this attitude. They are the clerisy. If everyone cannot exercise creative imagination, everyone does possess a soul and the power of free will. Society and its institutions should protect and awaken these potentials of the spirit.

Coleridge's claim has practical economic and social consequences, ones not properly or purely utilitarian. His principles here are simple and profound. They inform Mill's remark that the two greatest presences of his age are Bentham and Coleridge. Coleridge's claim, fully exemplified in *A Lay Sermon* and *On the Constitution of Church and State*, that his political principles derive from religious principles, is cogent. He argues for it with passion because it is true. His idea of the soul does not lead him to espouse pure democracy, but he insists on genuine safeguards against exploitation and oppression. We can recall his long-standing, vehement opposition to the slave trade (his Greek ode on the subject won a prize at Cambridge). He repeatedly and explicitly connects slavery with slavery of the soul. He harbors a prescient fear that industrialization will treat the modern laborer as a soulless person, a commodity used to produce commodities. As early as 1795, he puts labor exploitation in these terms: "those institutions of society which should condemn me to the necessity of twelve hours daily toil, would make my *soul* a slave, and sink *the rational* being in the mere animal" (*Lects 1795* 11). Later, with regard to Napoleon, he protests that the public degrades itself "in an inward prostration of the soul before enormous POWER." The Irish, he notes, could have been "firm and able friends," but were treated so ill that they became "a people, into whose souls the <Iron-> ferocity of slaves had at last entered" (*EOT*, II, 75; III, 240). He displays acute understanding of the oppressive forces that are identified, blasted, and ridiculed by others from Blake to Charlie Chaplin to Marcuse. In middle age, Coleridge agitates for the passage of child labor laws.

III

"The Rime of the Ancient Mariner" recounts the Mariner's odyssey and trial of soul. About that the poem is explicit, though very few critics are.[20] Coleridge composes it within a year or so of Wordsworth's "Tintern Abbey" and the Prospectus to *The Excursion*, both of which dramatize the wonder of becoming a "living soul"—"an impulse to herself." The text indicates that the theme of Coleridge's poem centers in the soul. To see this we do not even need to accord crucial importance to the Albatross hailed "as if it had been a Christian soul" (65), or to the bird that "made the breeze to blow" (94). As in the "Eolian Harp," the opening of *The Prelude*, and other Romantic poems, the soul is associated with a correspondent breeze between the natural world and the interior self: *anima*, breath, inspiration, spirit, soul. The death of two hundred sailors prompts this image: "The souls did from their

---

[20] See James Engell, "The Soul, Highest Cast of Consciousness," *The Cast of Consciousness: Concepts of the Mind in British and American Romanticism*, ed. Beverly Taylor and Robert Bain (New York, 1987) 8–9; also J. Robert Barth, S.J., "'A Spring of Love': Prayer and Blessing in Coleridge's 'Rime of the Ancient Mariner,'" *The Wordsworth Circle* 30 (1999): 75–80. Barth writes: "In the poem, clearly the struggle is acute and for very high stakes: the Mariner's very soul" (78).

bodies fly ... And every soul, it passed me by, / Like the whizz of my cross-bow" (220, 222–223). In these instances, "soul" might seem a stock term, despite the fact that identifying it with the Albatross is significant. But at this very point in the poem, the Mariner is left "Alone, alone, all, all alone"; in this state he says, "never a saint took pity on / My soul in agony" (232, 234–235). By its root sense, agony denotes a struggle, as for a prize. In 1827, Coleridge refers to prayer itself as a "wrestling" (*Notebook* 34, ff. 10–12). The prize in the "Rime" is a soul remade—or trying to remake itself.

This plight of subjective self-enclosure, of remorse, existential agony, and despair, changes, or at least seems to change, precisely when his soul is freed by love. The Mariner watches "God's creatures of the great calm" (gloss at 272) and, in awe of their beauty and happiness, he cannot speak, he has yet *no* power of speech. Then, suddenly, "A spring of love gushed from my heart, / And I blessed them unaware" (284–285). It is at this moment that "Sure my kind saint took pity on me" (286). Even if we find "Sure" less than reassuring, we should note that in *Aids to Reflection*, Coleridge explicitly states, "The best, the most *Christianlike* pity thou canst show, is to take pity on thy own soul" (*AR* 53). And at this moment the Mariner ceases, at least in one sense, to be alone: "The self-same moment I could pray" (288). He can now communicate with God; the Albatross falls from his neck, like lead, into the sea. A gentle sleep, he reports, slid "into my soul" (296), and rain revives his body. If the lines near the beginning of Part V are read with the idea in mind, it will not seem far-fetched that the Mariner's soul experiences rebirth in this sleep: "—almost / I thought that I had died in sleep ..." (306–307).

Returning, the Mariner meets the "Hermit good," who habitually sings godly hymns in the forest. The Mariner's hope concerning the hermit is simple and direct: "He'll shrieve my soul, he'll wash away / The Albatross's blood" (512–513). The shriving involves a continual repeating of the Mariner's tale; he turns poet, and his soul is shriven not only by a priest but by the telling of his story. This also means that the Mariner's identity, his self-realization, tortured as it is, can finally be exposed. For, when he says, "'O shrieve me, shrieve me, holy man!'" (574), the hermit asks the question of spiritual identity: "'What manner of man art thou?'" This is, in the profound sense, a *personal* question. It is to our wholeness as persons that Coleridge so often points. Mary Anne Perkins ventures that he "believed immortality belonged to *persons*, rather than to rational souls,"[21] an observation confirmed at least once, in the long, late *Notebook* entry on the nature of the soul. There Coleridge says that what is at stake is not the resuscitation "of a Soul or Spirit but *of the Man*" (*CN*, IV, 5377). Facing the hermit's personal question, the Mariner, the person whose "soul hath been / Alone on a wide wide sea" (597–598), gains strange power of speech. He begins to repeat his tale, communicating to others his story, his own identity, and the lesson of "love and reverence to all things" (gloss at 610).

This love, reminiscent of the love that gushed from his heart unaware when he blessed the water creatures (who presumably do not have souls), indicates a primacy of love above reason, higher even than the conscious will.[22] It is at this moment of love, too, that the kind saint takes pity on him. Despite repeatedly quoting from Milton that the soul "reason receives, and reason is her being," Coleridge revisits this idea and concludes instead "that there is an Antecedent even to the Reason and that his Name is *Love*" (*Notebook* 41, f. 12). This is Christ.

In a marginal note to copy H of *Aids to Reflection*, a note written in or after 1825, Coleridge ventures ideas remarkably and eerily pertinent to the Mariner's love of the snakes and his newfound ability to pray, and to the God who "made and loveth all." Coleridge writes, "I would be satisfied to love the Creator in the Creatures, provided *I* love the creatures . . . *chiefly* in reference to the Creator, and as excitements of gratitude to him. . . . God is a pure Act: and it can only be in the purest Acts of the Soul that the Love of God can have its essential Being. . . . Lastly the answer can only be rightly sought for in prayer." To repeat, before the Mariner loved the snakes, no saint "took pity on / My Soul"; afterward, "Sure my kind saint took pity on me," and the Mariner finds that he can pray, and prayer is reaffirmed at the end of the poem (596, 606). (Whatever one thinks of the stated "moral" of the poem, it is often overlooked that it inextricably links the act of love with the act of prayer, and that prayer is not only an act of individual will but an act enabled by God.) In the same long note to *Aids* just quoted, Coleridge expresses revulsion that, despite being lovers of God, men of the Inqui-

---

[21] *Coleridge's Philosophy: The Logos as Unifying Principle* (Oxford, 1994) 225.
[22] See John Beer, *Coleridge's Poetic Intelligence* (London, 1977) 160–161; also J. Robert Barth, S.J., *Coleridge and the Power of Love* (Columbia, Mo., 1988) 61–75.

sition, when carried away by zealotry, lacked "all feeling of pity" (*AR* 213n). The question remains, though, does the Mariner ever take pity on his own soul, "the most Christianlike pity thou canst show"? He seems inwardly stuttering to voice spiritual self-knowledge but, despite his power of speech, never fully articulating it.

In a manner, then, that is *not* particularly understandable or reasonable—and perhaps why Coleridge jokingly intimates that the poem is "incomprehensible" (*BL*, I, 28*)—the "Rime" enacts one realization of love, love "Antecedent even to the Reason," love linked to prayer. Elsewhere, Coleridge suggests that original sin itself is an abstract excess of the unbalanced "rational instinct" (*SM* 61) over the affective. As J. Robert Barth remarks in his study of the poet's religious thought, "For Coleridge, as for St. John and for Dante, the last thing of all is love,"[23] meaning, in the context here, that love is also the first thing.

The "Rime" dramatizes several elements of Coleridge's thought about the soul: inner spiritual awareness, love, prayer, and suffering both merited and unmerited. The narrative seems to reveal the power of the soul to grow, to seek its way out of the worst existential loneliness. (Presumably, the Mariner prefers his perpetual wandering and tale-telling to remaining all alone on the ocean, even though, at least briefly, he has the community in the kirk.) As elsewhere in Coleridge's thought, the act of prayer—one version of "a language of spirits"—links the soul to God. The Mariner is enjoined to take up the haunted task of telling his story in order to awaken in others the organs of the spirit and the "language of spirits." Each time his agony returns, he retells the tale and attempts, once again, to remake his own soul. The soul in its agony seeks the prize of atonement, which Coleridge regards, in plausible, though not original, etymological terms, as at + one + ment (*SM* 55; see *CM*, III, 47n).

Yet, ever since Leslie Stephen's comments on the poem, it is hardly news to say that the "Rime" appears to have too easy a moral,[24] one that, paradoxically, the narrative cannot easily justify, and it has become

---

[23] Barth, *Doctrine* 195.

[24] The objections heat up with E. E. Bostetter, "The Nightmare World of 'The Ancient Mariner,'" *Studies in Romanticism* 1 (1962): 241–254. He states that Robert Penn Warren's famous 1946 interpretation of crime, punishment, love, and redemption "entirely ignores the capricious and irrational elements in the universe of *The Ancient Mariner*" (244). George Watson, *Coleridge the Poet* (London, 1966), insists that the moral is the Mariner's, not Coleridge's, and that "The truth of the poem . . . is a dramatic truth" (99).

common to cite Coleridge's own dissatisfaction with it (*TT*, I, 272–273). If the Mariner is saved, it is a curious salvation: there is much unjust suffering, others die, and the traumas seem endless. Even granting that love comes before reason, the Mariner's love seems inexplicably spontaneous, not a product of the conscious will but simply of looking at the snakes intently. Is it grace, and, if so, what kind of grace?[25] His agony of retelling the tale is forced on him; after horrors mount and subside, the Mariner is doomed to an agonizing, repetitive existence that no one would envy. It is hard to accept the story as fully unified, and there seems no moral or spiritual resolution.[26]

Part of the explanation for the Mariner's repeated agony is frequently put in terms of guilt, and certainly what is called "survivor's guilt" is also at work. To this is often added remorse, "the *implicit* Creed of the Guilty" (*AR* 128). Coleridge himself is, of course, often wracked with guilt, for instance, when he confesses to his brother George how his own behavior led to a desperate enlistment in the army: "my soul sickens at it's own guilt" (*CL*, I, 74; see I, 65). But making the Mariner into Coleridge, although virtually authorized, is too common an interpretive mode.[27] Besides, if the Mariner feels guilty, Coleridge himself could counter that, through Christ, sin is "no longer imputable as Guilt" (*AR*, 310*).[28]

Thinking of Cain or the Wandering Jew as a precursor to the Mariner is another option, but no one ploy gives the poem the satisfying unity that many readers find lacking. Many discordant qualities remain. In fact, the idea of poetry as potentially *discordant* is one Coleridge encounters when Wordsworth rejects *Christabel*. Coleridge writes in October 1800 that Wordsworth has recently rejected the poem as "disproportionate both in size & merit, & as discordant in it's character.—" Wordsworth had the same word in mind, too, for he wrote the publisher of the 1800 edition that, regarding *Christabel*, "the Style . . . was

---

[25] For grace as habitual, actual, or prevenient, see Barth, *Doctrine* 148–149 and note.

[26] See Stephen Prickett, *Romanticism and Religion* (Cambridge, 1976) 16–17; also Lockridge 145, and Perry 281–291.

[27] I realize, however, that, as most critics do, I am reading the poem through the index and context of an interpretation of Coleridge's thought expressed outside the poem, an interpretation with justifications but also liabilities. See David Perkins, "The 'Ancient Mariner' and Its Interpreters: Some Versions of Coleridge," *Modern Language Quarterly* 57 (1996): 425–448.

[28] For treatment generally, see David Miall, "Guilt and Death: The Predicament of the Ancient Mariner," *Studies in English Literature, 1500–1900* 24 (1984): 633–653.

so discordant from my own that it could not be printed along with my poems with any propriety" (*CL*, I, 643 and n.). Whether in the "Rime" or in his relations with Wordsworth over the rejection of *Christabel*, "discordant" for Coleridge could harbor significant resonances.

A return to the idea of reconciliation rather than unity may prove fruitful. When Coleridge describes the poet as bringing "the whole soul of man into activity," a remark noted above, he does not then say that the poet unifies every faculty and quality in question. While the poet diffuses a "spirit of unity," the power of imagination does not necessarily reveal itself in final unity, but rather "in the balance or reconciliation of opposite or discordant qualities" (*BL*, II, 16). There is that word discordant again. Now, the "Rime" is a poem Coleridge calls "a work of pure imagination" (*TT*, I, 273n), and so we might expect a balance or reconciling of opposite or discordant qualities. This emerges, too, in the way Coleridge glosses the power of the imagination in the Scriptures: "that reconciling and mediatory power" (*SM* 29). If the Mariner's tale offers one moral that is too neat while any other seems inscrutable, if no clear unity seems to arise from the poem, its deeper imaginative and moral power rests in a constant activity—a compulsion almost as great as the one driving the Mariner—of reconciliation and mediation.[29] For the Mariner, it is a task apparently never completed, as it may also be for the reader. Passing from "land to land," the Mariner is that figure of the soul: "an exile in a far distant land," an image of human agony and hope.

IV

In his consideration of the soul, Coleridge tries to reconcile and mediate, not strictly to unify, natural philosophy, science, psychology, moral philosophy, political economy, and all these together with theology. It is significant that he ends the "Theory of Life" with mention of the soul, and again claims for it a supernatural and primary quality. "Nature

---

[29] Although not relying on the characterization of the imagination as a reconciling and mediatory power, David Jasper, "The Two Worlds of Coleridge's 'The Rime of the Ancient Mariner,'" *An Infinite Complexity: Essays in Romanticism*, ed. J. R. Watson (Edinburgh, 1983) 125–144, sees two worlds in the poem not compatible with each other, and calls upon the imagination to "focus and bring coherence to the different levels of experience" (140).

did not assist" when "her sovereign Master" finally "made Man in his own image, by superadding self-consciousness and self-government, and breathed into him a living soul." The final words are, literally, "concerning the Soul, as the principle both of Reason and Conscience" (*SW&F* 550, 557). Beginnings and endings are revealing. Coleridge begins *The Friend* with an epigraph, an invocation to the soul (I, 2), and he closes *Biographia* with the image of the "Soul . . . in its pure *Act* of inward Adoration to the great I AM, and to the filial WORD that re-affirmeth it from Eternity to Eternity, whose choral Echo is the Universe" (*BL*, II, 247–248).

Alfred North Whitehead once remarked that we should seek not only to learn what Plato thought, but also to imagine what he would think were he alive today. Since Coleridge's death, the theory of Darwinian evolution has become widely accepted. Though many variations of it exist and scientists disagree about its operation, the mass of evidence securely supports it. What would Coleridge think today if he were to confront this fact? He might continue to hold that the soul was at some time in the creation implanted or breathed into human life by divine fiat. Or, he might view that fiat itself more as a process than as an instant of realization, a process directed and sanctioned by the divine. He might elaborate on his numerous suggestions that not only the individual soul but also the idea of the soul in the human race does evolve. After all, he credits Thales and Plato with realizations about the soul that no previous thinker had entertained. If that is so, then there would be no reason why later realizations might not contribute more. Even as we understand more about the origins of the human in nature, we might also understand better what does seem to separate us from other forms of life, even if that separation arose over time rather than in a flash. Coleridge might employ a more elaborate argument from the "Analogy of Being" and modify his proto-evolutionary thinking about life to include an explicitly Darwinian sense of change in species.[30] Thinking about such evolution might lead to a greater real-

---

[30] For a related discussion, see Anthony John Harding, "Coleridge, Natural History, and the 'Analogy of Being,'" *History of European Ideas* 26 (2000): 143–158. Harding explores Coleridge's "attempt to show how the findings of contemporary science might support a philosophical account of a rationally ordered universe" (143). While recognizing that Coleridge's view is not "Darwinian," Harding explores how Coleridge regards the unique nature of humanity as analogous to—and therefore connected with—other forms of being (152). Yet human life, the soul, "needs to be actualized" (156) in a manner not shared by other beings.

ization of the peculiar nature of the human. It is a tricky proposition, but Coleridge's sense of process and his conviction about organic growth in the soul, in the soul of the individual and of humanity at large, might fairly be applied to an idea of the self-realization of the soul over long periods of biological time. At any event, it is hard to imagine that Coleridge, facing the issue, would become reactionary.

Entering into an agonized contest with the spiritual crises and dehumanizations of his era, as well as with its accompanying fragmentation of knowledge, Coleridge displays such penetration, often in a sentence or phrase, that his struggles, false starts, self-doubt, and contradictions are punctuated with soaring insights and hope. Spiritual life remains for him always a personal struggle uphill, not an Olympian survey. He starts, after all, with some remarkable attitudes. In 1787, only fourteen, he writes in one of his first preserved letters, jocularly but a little dismissively, to his brother Luke, "Heaven would not be large enough to hold all the souls of all men, who have ever liv'd" (*CL*, I, 2). He quips almost a decade later to John Thelwall that "Ferriar believes in a *Soul*, like an orthodox Churchman—So much for Physicians & Surgeons" (*CL*, I, 295). He lives his own odyssey, his own self-realization, his own agony. This experience is at once the strength and the vulnerability of his genius. He is a reconciling and mediatory spiritual thinker, and the spiritual dimension comes to suffuse all his thought. Convincing or not, the position is deeply, personally earned. One reason that Coleridge continues to attract so many readers is that the world and our knowledge of it, as well as our realization of what it means to be human in that world, seem ever to present us with more, rather than less, to reconcile and to mediate.

As with other ideas vital to Coleridge—the mystery of language, the imagination, the nature of idea, image, and symbol—no one passage sets out fully what he means by the soul. From this seminal idea other ideas evolve and are generated. He treats the soul as if it were as real as the marrow of the bones or the translucent lens of the eye. Light, vision, and reflection are metaphors for the soul's being, perception, and exercise (see Beer, *AR* xciv–xcvi). The soul is an organ of spirit, and among all "organs of spirit" it is primary. To learn its method, its "language of spirits," is to acquire a strange power of speech, and to begin a journey in which language leads not only to knowledge of the world but also to knowledge of the self. For Coleridge, then, as Stephen Prickett concludes, "words are living powers *because* they are the tools of self-knowledge."[31] When Coleridge draws up early plans for a "philosophical" dictionary, which would, through the mediation of his grandson Herbert Coleridge, eventually become the *Oxford English Dictionary*, he notes that such a dictionary should treat "words as living growths, offlets, and organs of the human soul" (*Logic* 126). Especially in the study of language, he urges, it is vital to attend to the method of the soul, to the agonies it suffers, and to the story it cannot choose but tell.

Works Cited

Barfield, Owen. *What Coleridge Thought*. Middletown: Wesleyan University Press, 1971.

Barth, J. Robert, S.J. *Coleridge and Christian Doctrine*. 1969. New York: Fordham University Press, 1987.

———. *Coleridge and the Power of Love*. Columbia: University of Missouri Press, 1988.

———. "'A Spring of Love': Prayer and Blessing in Coleridge's 'Rime of the Ancient Mariner.'" *The Wordsworth Circle* 30 (1999): 75–80.

Bate, W. J. *Coleridge*. New York: Macmillan, 1968.

Beer, John. *Coleridge's Poetic Intelligence*. London: Macmillan, 1977.

Bostetter, E. E. "The Nightmare World of 'The Ancient Mariner.'" *Studies in Romanticism* 1 (1962): 241–254.

Boulger, James D. *Coleridge as Religious Thinker*. New Haven: Yale University Press, 1961.

Coleridge, Samuel Taylor. *Aids to Reflection*. Ed. John Beer. Princeton: Princeton University Press, 1993. *CC* Vol. IX.

———. *Biographia Literaria*. Ed. James Engell and W. J. Bate. 2 vols. Princeton: Princeton University Press, 1983. *CC* Vol. VII.

———. *The Collected Letters of Samuel Taylor Coleridge*. Ed. Earl Leslie Griggs. 6 vols. Oxford: Clarendon Press, 1956–1971.

———. *The Collected Works of Samuel Taylor Coleridge*. Ed. Kathleen Coburn. 16 vols. Bollingen Series 75. Princeton: Princeton University Press, 1969–. Cited as *CC*.

———. *Essays on His Times*. Ed. David V. Erdman. 3 vols. Princeton: Princeton University Press, 1978. *CC* Vol. III.

---

[31] *Poetry of Growth* 197.

———. *The Friend.* Ed. Barbara E. Rooke. 2 vols. Princeton: Princeton University Press, 1969. *CC* Vol. IV.

———. *Lay Sermons.* Ed. R. J. White. Princeton: Princeton University Press, 1972. *CC* Vol. VI.

———. *Lectures 1795: On Politics and Religion.* Ed. Lewis Patton and Peter Mann. Princeton: Princeton University Press, 1971. *CC* Vol. I.

———. *Lectures 1808–1819: On Literature.* Ed. Reginald A. Foakes. 2 vols. Princeton: Princeton University Press, 1984. *CC* Vol. V.

———. *Lectures 1818–1819: On the History of Philosophy.* Ed. J. R. de J. Jackson. 2 vols. Princeton: Princeton University Press, 2000. *CC* Vol. VIII.

———. *Logic.* Ed. J. R. de J. Jackson. Princeton: Princeton University Press, 1980. *CC* Vol. XIII.

———. *Marginalia.* Ed. H. J. Jackson and George Whalley. 5 vols. to date. Princeton: Princeton University Press, 1980–. *CC* Vol. XII.

———. *The Notebooks of Samuel Taylor Coleridge.* Ed. Kathleen Coburn. 4 vols. to date. Bollingen Series 50. Princeton: Princeton University Press, 1955–.

———. *Shorter Works and Fragments.* Ed. H. J. Jackson and J. R. de J. Jackson. 2 vols. Princeton: Princeton University Press, 1995. *CC* Vol. XI.

———. *Table Talk.* Ed. Carl Woodring. 2 vols. Princeton: Princeton University Press, 1990. *CC* Vol. XIV.

Dilthey, Wilhelm. *Selected Writings.* Ed. and trans. H. P. Rickman. Cambridge: Cambridge University Press, 1976.

Eichner, Hans. "The Rise of Modern Science and the Genesis of Romanticism." *PMLA* 97.1 (1982): 8–30.

Engell, James. "The Soul, Highest Cast of Consciousness." *The Cast of Consciousness: Concepts of the Mind in British and American Romanticism.* Ed. Beverly Taylor and Robert Bain. New York: Greenwood, 1987. 3–19.

Harding, Anthony John. *Coleridge and the Inspired Word.* Kingston and Montreal: McGill-Queen's University Press, 1985.

———. "Coleridge, Natural History, and the 'Analogy of Being.'" *History of European Ideas* 26 (2000): 143–158.

Hedley, Douglas. *Coleridge, Philosophy and Religion: "Aids to Reflection" and the Mirror of the Spirit.* Cambridge: Cambridge University Press, 2000.

Jackson, H. J. "Coleridge's Collaborator, Joseph Henry Green." *Studies in Romanticism* 21 (1982): 161–179.

Jasper, David. "The Two Worlds of Coleridge's 'The Rime of the Ancient Mariner.'" *An Infinite Complexity: Essays in Romanticism*. Ed. J. R. Watson. Edinburgh: Edinburgh University Press for the University of Durham, 1983. 125–144.

Ilie, Paul. Rev. of *Nature's Enigma: The Problem of the Polyp in the Letters of Bonnet, Trembley and Réaumur*, by Virginia P. Dawson. *Eighteenth-Century Studies* 24 (1991): 516–518.

Lockridge, Laurence. *Coleridge the Moralist*. Ithaca: Cornell University Press, 1977.

Miall, David. "Guilt and Death: The Predicament of the Ancient Mariner." *Studies in English Literature, 1500–1900* 24 (1984): 633–653.

Perkins, David. "The 'Ancient Mariner' and Its Interpreters: Some Versions of Coleridge." *Modern Language Quarterly* 57 (1996): 425–448.

Perkins, Mary Anne. *Coleridge's Philosophy: The Logos as Unifying Principle*. Oxford: Clarendon Press, 1994.

Perry, Seamus. *Coleridge and the Uses of Division*. Oxford: Clarendon Press, 1999.

Prickett, Stephen. *Coleridge and Wordsworth: The Poetry of Growth*. Cambridge: Cambridge University Press, 1970.

———. *Romanticism and Religion*. Cambridge: Cambridge University Press, 1976.

Spacks, Patricia Meyer. "The Soul's Imaginings: Daniel Defoe, William Cowper." *PMLA* 91 (1976): 420–435.

Taylor, Anya. *Coleridge's Defense of the Human*. Columbus: Ohio State University Press, 1986.

Vallins, David. "Self-Reliance: Individualism in Emerson and Coleridge." *Symbiosis* 5 (2001): 51–68.

Watson, George. *Coleridge the Poet*. London: Routledge & Kegan Paul, 1966.

Welch, Claude. *Protestant Thought in the Nineteenth Century*. 2 vols. New Haven: Yale University Press, 1972.

Wood, Barry. "The Growth of the Soul: Coleridge's Dialectical Method and the Strategy of Emerson's *Nature*." *PMLA* 91 (1976): 385–397.

9

The Gothic Coleridge: Mythos and the Real

Thomas Lloyd

I

THIS ESSAY will concern itself with Coleridge's practice of mythopoetic realism, which may be considered as a shadow-parallel to his metaphysical commitment to a Real Idealism, and to his theological foundation in the objective reality of God. When he wished to correct German Idealism's tendency to find meaning only in a subjective or speculative transcendental ground, he took two approaches: in metaphysics, by postulating a semi-Platonic view of the objective substantiality of the Ideas; and in his theological premises, by the distinctively Christian departure from the German school that is apparent in his reception of Schelling in the *Biographia Literaria*, where he proposes that the ultimate ground of Being, and therefore of the self, must be the self-existent Other of God. On either basis, the entirety of existence is more than the One Life, nor can it be encompassed in a monolithic conception of Nature, because the natural and the supernatural are each substantial and distinct realms. While a mythopoetic criticism would necessarily address both these dimensions, traditionally by seeking for archetypes in the poetry, it may also take a particular interest in a third realm equally valid in Coleridge's case, that of the "praeternatural" or the "transnatural," to use two of Coleridge's own terms. The transnatural territory is of special significance to his poesis, since it is not predicated directly upon abstract universals, nor on the concrete manifestations of *physis*, but is populated by a fecund throng of dramatized selves.

However, archetypes of Nature and of the celestial certainly do account for powerful moments in Coleridge's poetry. In "Frost at Midnight,"[1] the great natural Forms of lake, crag, and cloud mirror each other, and then become a further mirror for the celestial Archetype,[2] in which the sensitive soul synaesthetically "sees and hears" the "intelligible" and "eternal language" of God's communicative Logos. But all three domains lend "The Eolian Harp" its basic structure. Two are archetypes: Nature synthesizes as the "One Life," and the celestial as "The Family of Christ." But the third, transnatural domain provides the vital crux of the poem, in Gothic terms: "the coy Maid half-yielding to her Lover," accompanied by the "witchery of sound / As twilight Elfins make, when they at Eve / Voyage on gentle gales from Faery Land." While a very unenchanted and non-yielding maid will refute all this in the coda, nonetheless the transnatural middle of the poem provides the poem's most memorable mythodrama.

To use an old word, also sometimes used by Coleridge himself, his transnatural beings may be called "daemons," personal beings who may exist beyond the subjective finitude of human consciousness. One of the difficulties in dealing with these characters is that in his speculative thought, Coleridge was highly ambivalent about directly affirming the reality of daemonic beings. He encountered them frequently in his visionary flights, giving them life especially in his poems and in the raw poetic material of the *Notebooks*, but he would theorize them in quite the modern way, as aspects of the individual psyche. Yet, when he engaged in mythodrama, their objective otherness is necessarily assumed. Even so, the question must be asked: Are they simply aesthetic *données*? Are they considered to be aspects of "dramatic truth"; are they only conditionally real, operating only on a stage confined by strict subjective boundaries, outside of which the Real World exists? The answer is a qualified "no," the next step in support of which will be to take what I hope is a somewhat unusual approach to some very familiar material.

To do this, let us turn to the middle of the *Biographia Literaria* with the idea that this is also the crux of the work, involving incommensurate oppositions. The contrary implications of the meaning of the

---

[1] The basic text for the poetry is *The Complete Poetical Works of Samuel Taylor Coleridge*, ed. Ernest Hartley Coleridge. 2 vols. (London, 1912).

[2] Although Coleridge may have preferred the term "theosopheme," which he uses in a discussion of Homer and Aeschylus in the *Notebooks* 4.4832 (1821). *The Notebooks of Samuel Taylor Coleridge*, ed. Kathleen Coburn (Princeton, 1957–1990). Henceforth noted as *CN*.

Imagination represented in Books XIII and XIV embody Coleridge's ambivalence rather exactly. In the former, he begins by summarizing the metaphysical disquisition of the preceding chapters with his appreciation of "the venerable Sage of Koenigsberg," but then he presents his alter-egoic letter of complaint, in which his fictional friend complains about the vertigo he feels as he is spun in a wild series of alternations, from high metaphysical speculation into one of the largest of our Gothic cathedrals in a gusty moonlight night of autumn, 'Now in glimmer, now in gloom,'" and from "the Logos or communicative intellect in Man and Deity" to "the dark cave of Trophonius."[3] Both of these, the Gothic and the ancient chthonic/daemonic/prophetic loci, are highly significant, because they are repetitively important in Coleridge's mythopoetic, transnatural landscapes, so that the appearance of a phrase from *Christabel*, a poem that includes both these motifs, is therefore no accident. What is more, Coleridge the author will not heed the distress of his Platonic, epistolary persona, who recommends the separation of the two apparently contradictory domains, apparently because the shadowless *lumen siccum* of the *ratio* is not the only source of real revelation.

But, as strongly as Coleridge may *imply* a strange yet substantive basis for his transnatural characters and places, he cannot argue directly in their favor, nor is this the last ambivalence surrounding this matter here, at the crux of the *Biographia*. The epigraph from *Paradise Lost* that begins Book XIII and the famous definition of Imagination that concludes it posit the same objectively real basis for poetic production that underlies his famous definition of the Symbol in the *Statesman's Manual*,[4] all three of which would imply a real basis for the supernatural Gothic/chthonic beings that the inspired Imagination may produce. Despite this implication, however, he reverses his field again in Book XIV. In addressing the "supernatural incidents and agents" in the "Rime," he introduces equally famous concepts that undermine such an objective understanding. Now the truth in view is limited to "the dramatic truth of such emotions, as would accompany such incidents, supposing them real. And real in *this* sense they have been to every

---

[3] *Biographia Literaria*, eds. James Engell and W. Jackson Bate, in *The Collected Works of Samuel Taylor Coleridge*, ed. Kathleen Coburn (London and Princeton, 1969–), vol. VII (1984) 297–304. Henceforth, cited as *BL*. *The Collected Works* will henceforth be cited as *CC*.

[4] *The Statesman's Manual*, in *Lay Sermons*, ed. R. J. White, *CC* VI (1972) 29.

human being who, from whatever source of delusion, has at any time believed himself under supernatural agency." Such "shadows of the imagination" must be received by "that willing suspension of disbelief for the moment, which constitutes poetic faith."[5] Taken by itself, or supported by other passages in which Coleridge makes similar assertions, this may seem nothing more than an assertion of the familiar idea, part Platonic and part modern, that poetic creatures exist apart from reality, or, at least, apart from the rest of objective reality, but taken in the fuller context as I have suggested it here, there is reason to believe that this hedging is only one of the legs upon which Coleridge stands. The "shadows" here may suggest Plato's cave, but, as always, there is more to Coleridge than his Platonism, as Engell and Bate shrewdly suggest when they note the echo of Theseus' speech from *A Midsummer Night's Dream*. In truth, Coleridge spans Theseus, Hippolyta, Puck, and certainly the grotesque seer, Bottom, who knows that his experience was a "true dream."

A mythopoetic realist method, taking seriously the true dream, may be applied to Coleridge's speculative consideration of traditional myths and of Hebraic-Christian material, and even more strongly to his own poetic mythmaking, in which the third, transnatural category is especially relevant. In this realm, as might be suggested by its liminal positioning, Coleridge's characteristic rational desire for "distinction" and "reconciliation of apparent opposites" becomes unusually problematic, and so, such a method accepts the often unreconciled themes as they are, and sees in that lack of a rational conclusion an enterprise different from his rational mode of inquiry. As a part of this method, it is often necessary to attend to the center of a poem or discourse, rather than to its conclusion, to find the true crux of the drama that unfolds around it. This method is not intended to replace the findings of other methods of Coleridgean interpretation, which are more concerned with conclusive counters. For instance, the findings of critics who attend to a purely subjective basis, as in psychoanalytic criticism, or to material bases, political and social, constitute a solid contribution to an understanding of Coleridge the man, and Coleridge *in situ*, respectively. It is true that this analysis will depart from those who dismiss Coleridge's "ideology" in favor of other ideologies, since the purpose of this essay is to understand Coleridge himself, who believed in spiritual realities

---

[5] *BL*, II, 6.

and genuinely opposed either purely subjective or final material explanations for the world. However, this is not simply a method that accepts his *données* at face value, but examines those poetically created mythemes that sometimes pose an unanticipated challenge to his rational formulations, often in a highly threatening manner.

II

Christabel is a striking case of the threatening Coleridgean mytheme. Addressing the ongoing fractures in critical response to the poem, Anthony Harding, who has repeatedly addressed Coleridge's treatment of myth,[6] points out that, although the poem's characters, plot, and setting resemble those of Gothic prose tales, it will not be reduced to the same standard, because its "events and characters are polysemous in the way we usually expect myth to be polysemous." "*Christabel*," Harding says, is an instance "not of novelistic narrative, nor yet of parable or allegory, but of Romantic mythopoesis."[7]

While this observation may seem to apply most directly to the Mystery Poems, Coleridge's practice of mythopoesis, in fact, runs through his full career, influencing nearly everything he wrote. The difficulties facing any such theory are embodied by Harding's essay, which begins and ends on quite different notes. At the outset, although he has introduced the idea of "polysemous" meanings, he brings forward a concept

---

[6] In addition to the article about to be addressed, Harding has also on other occasions addressed Coleridge's mythicism, notably his long-standing interest in the Mysteries, especially the Samothracian, and his Schelling-derived theory that they include hermetic doctrines received, via the Phoenicians, from the "patriarchal," that is, pre-Mosaic, Jewish religion. See "Myth and the War of Ideas: Coleridge on the 'Prometheus' of Aeschylus," *Nineteenth-Century Contexts* 13 (1989): 177–196; "Coleridge, Subjectivity, and the 'Mirror of the Mysteries,'" *European Romantic Review* 5 (1995): 193–213; and "Imagination, Patriarchy, and Evil in Coleridge and Heidegger," *Studies in Romanticism* 35 (1996): 3–26. Harding sees that Coleridge found in the Mysteries and their "imaginative superstitions" a deeper understanding of origin than that of the "fanciful" official Greek polytheistic State religion, including the recognition of a primordial and extra-human origin for evil, and that in following this line of thought, he established authority for his own speculations along similar lines. I would suggest that such speculations may have been a theological response to the vivid and extrapersonal power of the mythic figures who emerged in his poetic creation, especially those of daemonic nature.

[7] Anthony John Harding, "Mythopoeic Elements in Christabel," *Modern Language Quarterly* 44 (1983) 39–40.

of myth that emphasizes its unitive force; at this point he follows Jane A. Nelson and adopts Edmund Leach's concept of myth as "the reunion of what in this world is divided." In this he sounds somewhat like J. Robert Barth, who, in responding to "Dejection," sees that

> The terrifying experience is thus sublimated to another level of reality, a mythic level, that is both meaningful and sustaining. For myth—the product of imagination, which brings together in a single vision "the general, with the concrete," "the individual, with the representative"—universalizes our experiences, showing them to be part of the larger experience of mankind; by binding us to each other through our common humanity, especially through our common experience of suffering, myth allows us to draw strength from each other.[8]

Barth's focus joins the idea of "myth" to Coleridge's own definitions of imagination in the *Biographia Literaria* and in the *Statesman's Manual*, based upon the imagination as a bridge between the psychological subject and universal objects, and it basically stands in agreement with Harding's belief that the intercalation of authorial consciousness and setting finally resolves "with nature internalized," if "nature" is understood to include a spiritual, transpersonal dimension, but is somewhat different from Harding's further suggestion that the characters are defined in terms of the poet's subjectivity: "Geraldine is surely an embodiment of mental, not of 'outward,' forms."[9] This idea, unlike Barth's, suggests a critical framework predisposed to psychoanalytic theorems, but this model of subjective subsumption does fit in rather well with an interpretation that would see Coleridge's speaking personae as akin to the post-Renaissance mage, the pantheist sage, and the utopian progressivist; and, in truth, Coleridge did adopt all these reconciling roles, especially in the earlier stages of his myriad minded course. Thus, operating in the "re-union" mode, Coleridge's mythopoesis would create symbolic congeners for his pursuit of ascending reason, free will, and philosophical system-building, and also for his political faith in progressive societal amelioration. All this implies a certain monism, and it is monism, the reduction of all things to a single substantial fabric under the control of the conscious will, that constituted the post-Enlightenment faith of Coleridge's era.

Yet we know that Coleridge became a severe critic of that faith, and,

---

[8] J. Robert Barth, S.J., *Coleridge and the Power of Love* (Columbia, Mo., 1988) 99.
[9] Harding, "Mythopoeic Elements in Christabel," 43, 41.

as Harding develops his analysis, he unexpectedly demonstrates that *Christabel* does not, after all, achieve its mythopoesis in a "unitive" manner, since he sees that Christabel's stymied condition, as it stands in the poem, is more meaningful than Coleridge's optimistic projections of a future version that would provide a rationally and theologically familiar resolution. Hazlitt's observation that *Christabel* "comes to no conclusion," is true, Harding observes,

> because the real subject of Christabel shows affinity not so much with traditional narrative poetry as with Blakean mythopoesis. Like *Visions of the Daughters of Albion*, Coleridge's poem depicts a strangeness in human experience; and instead of moving forward to an easy resolution, it ends with the dominant image of a human soul in its temporally divided and speechless state, as if recognizing that a miraculous hair's-breadth escape would be at best a weak palliative.[10]

The somewhat contradictory trajectory of Harding's essay, starting with unity and ending in polysemous arrest, is highly instructive, because it demonstrates two sides of Coleridge: the hope for unity and the threats to that hope. The reason for this outcome might be understood by departing from the idea that the poem is based upon a series of psychological counters, and instead, by taking an approach rooted in mythopoetic realism, by which beings that are "transnatural" (Coleridge's word, treated later in this essay), including both presences within the immediate person and beings dwelling beyond the subjective persona, have spontaneous life and power in and of themselves, and in fact can threaten to overpower and control the soul and the personal will. Thus, the poem is not only about the human soul, but about the soul confronted with a daemonic presence. Geraldine may be a vampire, or a less-terrible inhabitant of a mid-spiritual realm, but Stuart Peterfreund's suggestion that Geraldine is in fact Satan represents the most extreme possible suggestion of who she is, and also the most uncomfortable suggestion, in a Christian context, about the objective nature of the threatening reality.[11]

---

[10] Harding, "Mythopoeic Elements in Christabel," 46.

[11] "The Way of Immanence, Coleridge, and the Problem of Evil," *English Literary History* 55 (1988): 125–158. Peterfreund,, who combines expertise in the philosophy of science with literary criticism, is not addressing a specifically Christian context, but his analysis provides most interesting parallels to it. He frames his argument by pointing out that Coleridge, dissatisfied with Newton's "externalist" model of the universe because it made the mind too "passive," looked to immanentist models from Spinoza

However, a note of caution is in order here. Whereas Satan is independently real in the orthodox Christian conception of the world, Coleridge himself took a typically ambivalent position on the subject. J. Robert Barth has interesting light to shed in his examination of Coleridge's conception of Satan: "Although he generally does not want to accept the notion of Satan as an individual person, a fallen angel, he is confronted with Scriptural references to Satan and the devils," and, in a passage of biblical interpretation in Notebook 30 (1823–1824), ff. 34–37, Coleridge says:

> can any such Passage be adduced in the assertion of the existence of personal Intelligences, self-conscious Individuals, utterly yet responsibly wicked & malignant, of a diverse kind from the human, and neither men nor the disembodied Souls of Men?—I know of none.... On the other hand, I dare not deny the possibility of a finite Person *willing* evil irrevocably and beyond the powers of Repentance, & Reformation—Nay, the *Idea* is indispensable in Morality—or that this finite Person, or race of Persons, may have been invested with larger intellectual faculties, more enduring and subtle Bodies, than the Human Races.[12]

In one sense, this is a reasonably balanced critique, since he is careful to state that his purpose is to study the Scriptural Revelation, and that, although such a separate "Race" may exist, and is implied in many places in the Scripture, it cannot conclusively be proven from the Bible. But in another sense, he is protecting the Scripture from such knowledge, in a way entirely in keeping with his usual desire to protect the inviolate purity of the celestial Ideal from any daemonic incursion. Yet he allows that such knowledge might be accurate, although it would have to come from other sources. His own mythopoesis indeed suggests such a source. Mythopoesis, then, can be a healing and reconciling process, or a highly threatening one, both of them including a personal and an extrapersonal dimension. This is the transnatural territory, and it is there, especially in its dreadful mode, that the figure of the daemon appears.

---

to Humphrey Davy for a possible substitute. But, in "Christabel," he confronted the immanentist weakness: its inability to solve the problem of evil; thus, in the context of the immanentist worldview, Geraldine, who embodies Evil, is unstoppable. Certainly, in Leoline's domain there is no legitimate crucifix, or other sacred object, that would fend off the vampire.

[12] J. Robert Barth, S.J., *Coleridge and Christian Doctrine* (1969; New York, 1987) 119, n. 34.

Lawrence Kramer defines Coleridge's daemon on straightforwardly psychological grounds as an internal state in the imagination through which the self acts *like* a "hostile other," but in so doing, Kramer explains the history of the word in quite other terms, based on its original religious meaning:

> The self, in other words, acts like a hostile other, and the visions themselves appear, irresistibly, as a kind of negative inspiration.
>
> Perhaps the best term for this kind of experience, and for this kind of imagination, is the one most responsive to the sense of an alien presence: the term "daemonic." The word, referring metaphorically to beings neither human nor divine who sometimes enter into visionaries, is familiar enough; I use it here in a way that echoes Yeats's somber formulation, "I think of life as a struggle with the Daemon who would ever set us to the hardest work among those not impossible. . . . We meet always in the deeps of the mind, whatever our work, wherever our reverie carries us, that other Will." The daemon, it should be added, is not a demon, although it may act like one. Daemons, in other words, are not damned or malevolent spirits, nor are they actually supernatural in the Romantic tradition, though they are often represented in supernatural terms, particularly by Coleridge.[13]

While this is a useful model, recommended by Coleridge's own psychological interests and his repeated emphasis upon the powers of the will, nonetheless no search for a full understanding can leave things at that. Therefore, it may be helpful to leave out the "like," to emphasize that Coleridge in fact *does* represent the daemons "in supernatural terms," to side with Yeats' original implication that the "Daemon,"

---

[13] "That Other Will: The Daemonic in Coleridge and Wordsworth," *Philological Quarterly* 58 (1979): 299. Liddell and Scott's definitions and examples of the use of "daemon" and its cognates demonstrate its traversal of boundaries. In Homer, the word was used "most commonly of *the Divine power*," but it may be applied to a person "in some *astonishing* or *strange* condition." In Hesiod, it is used of "the souls of men of the golden age," as tutelary deities intermediary between men and the gods. It was also commonly used to mean "one's *daemon* or *genius*, and so one's *lot* or fortune," whether good or ill. By the time of Koine Greek, Plutarch and the New Testament, the term as used by Apuleius in *De daemone Socratis* illustrates a popular resolution of the conflict derived from Hesiod: they are spirits intermediary between the human and the angelic *animae*. Coleridge's representations, to the extent they permit such analysis (a large proviso), veer between the "intermediary" concept to the outright diabolic, at the same time that the boundaries between the *anima* and the supernal waver. But there is no divine Daemon in Coleridge to compare with Shelley's "Daemon of the World: A Fragment" (1815). Coleridge's own celestial mythemes demand a near-ascetic purity, far from the Abyss.

although found in "the Will," is nonetheless objectively "other," and thus to recognize that Coleridge's mythos sometimes treats the daemon as internal, and at other times as *other*. As this bilateral treatment suggests, this method does not at all preclude the inclusion of a psychological approach, as Paul Twitchell demonstrates when he reads "The Rime of the Ancient Mariner" by combining mythopoetic realism, based upon a Neoplatonic model, with a psychological approach: "Just as Coleridge has measured his way through a throbbing hierarchy of subhuman life until he reaches man, he continues, now working by inference, to suspect that there is also a 'new series' of powers that are superhuman."[14] Such an observation stands in close relationship with Coleridge's own remarks in Notebook 30. The third, or middle, daemonic world seems to be the place of transition, the threshold between self and Other.

III

The bilateral internality/externality of these supernatural powers, as Coleridge represents them, can be traced in his theorizing about aesthetic history, and in his own poetic work. Two aspects of the meaning of these "superhuman powers" might be characterized as: (1) the difference between his approach to the subject as a rational speculator and as an imaginative creator in poetry and poetic prose, and (2) his symbolic use of history to locate epochs with a particularly strong mythic culture, that is, in which supernatural powers were at an inspirational high tide This section will be devoted to the way that these features appear in his aesthetic theory, which discovers in European poetry a Gothic spirit quite outside of, and sometimes flatly opposed to, the personal consciousness, and, also, mysteriously indwelling the rationalistic outer body of the culture derived from noetic Greco-Roman roots.

---

[14] *Romantic Horizons: Aspects of the Sublime in English Poetry and Painting, 1770–1850* (Columbia, Mo., 1983) 93. Twitchell's immediate reference is to a passage in the *Theory of Life* that sees man the "Microcosm" at the "apex of the living pyramid." In "Coleridge and Turner: The Sublime at the Vortex" (85–108), Twitchell theorizes the characteristic realm of Coleridgean vision in the "vortex" between spheres, or between the rungs of the "ladder of life." His series of thresholds correspond to kinds of consciousness: the "liminal consciousness" with its celestial spirits, the "subliminal consciousness" with its Aquatic, Aerial, and Etherial Daemons, and the "normal consciousness" of the Ancient Mariner.

This section will include suggestions as to the impact of these elements on his purely creative mythos, especially in the poems, but a more precise analysis will, in the last section of this essay, be devoted to a crucial passage from the *Notebooks*, as an adumbration of future critical efforts which require a far vaster study.

Coleridge displays a strong predilection, as theologian, philosopher, and cultural historian, to leap back in time, in a series of gestures that employ history as a set of symbolic counters, to epochs that represent the sources of spiritual inspiration.[15] He leaps back over the Enlightenment to find linguistic and philosophical sustenance in the seventeenth century, back over the High Renaissance into the Gothic Middle Ages, and back over Greco-Roman classicism to the Presocratics and the Mystery Religions. The reason for the first of these leaps, back to Milton, Donne, and the Anglican divines, is put succinctly by Carl J. Friedrich, as he comments about the Baroque writers: "their most urgent concern was the depicting of human passions, seen as proliferations of supernatural powers rather than in the strictly human terms familiar to the renaissance and humanism."[16]

Even more relevant to Coleridge's poeticomythic project was his further leap backward from the Baroque over the High Renaissance, to find an important locus of spiritual history in the Gothic Middle Ages and its mystical Christianity. The fact that Coleridge was so memorably to visit the Middle Ages in the Mystery Poems and in other of his important works, such as "Love," "The Ballad of the Dark Ladie," "The Three Graves," and "The Mad Monk," indicates that this may be the most important historicopoetic locus of all; certainly, it provides a cultural landscape cross-fertilizing the Christian and the more ancient *mythoi*, where the ancient figures are, overtly or covertly, daemonic. Coleridge theorizes this source of inspiration in the historiography he proposes in his 1818 literary lecture series,[17] which is systematically founded on an interpretation of European history by which the northern Gothic peoples "re-unified" with the Southern

---

[15] Coleridge performs this imaginative act so frequently that he might be considered as having anticipated a characteristic passion in High Modernism, e.g., Yeats' Byzantium, the series of ideal locales in Pound's *Cantos*, Eliot's Little Gidding, and H. D.'s Helen.

[16] Carl J. Friedrich, *The Age of the Baroque: 1610–1660* (New York, 1952) 98–99.

[17] Lectures *1808–1819: On Literature*, ed. Reginald A. Foakes, *CC* vol. VI (1984) II. Henceforward, noted as *Lects 1808–1819*.

Greco-Romans to create modern civilization. Yet this turns out not to be a harmonious sort of unification, since he will go on to aver that the Gothic spirit and its art remained radically different from Greek and Roman classical aesthetics, that the result is a fertile tension between the two, and that the more potent is the Gothic "soul" that vitalizes the classical "body."

This is not to say Coleridge was no classicist, because so much of his philosophy depends upon that source, but to say that his non-classical side was the stronger component of his Muse. In the second lecture, he explained: "The Greeks were remarkable for complacency and completion . . . if we look upon any Greek production of art, the beauty of its parts, and the harmony of their union, the complete and complacent effect of the whole, are the striking characteristics." Coleridge here is attributing to the Greeks a definition of beauty that he was to expand in his aesthetic theorizing, heavily indebted to Neoplatonism, as in "On the Principles of Genial Criticism" and in "On Poesy, or Art." But in this lecture he provides an immediate demurrer from the classical modes, based not in philosophical ethos but in poetic mythos, by saying that the Goths were superior in pathos and sublimity. This was a belief that stayed with him; in 1832 he remarked: "Could you ever discover any thing sublime in our sense of the term in Greek Literature? I never could."[18] He believes that, in poetry, Homer has the Greek "pictorial" completion and its reasonable perfection: "as far as the eye and understanding are concerned, I am indeed gratified. But if I wish my feelings to be affected, if I wish my heart to be touched, if I wish to melt into sentiment and tenderness, I must turn to the heroic songs of the Goths, to the poetry of the middle ages." Not only feeling and sentiment, but a spiritual quality was involved, for, while the Greek statuary and epic poetry made the gods too human, the Goths had the opposite predilection: "but no statue, no artificial emblem, could satisfy the Northman's mind; the dark, wild imagery of nature which surrounded him, and the freedom of his life, gave his mind a tendency to the infinity, so that he found rest in that which presented no end, and derived satisfaction

---

[18] *Table Talk*, ed. Carl R. Woodring, 2 vols., *CC* vol. XIV (1990) I, 312 (July 21, 1832). He is most likely thinking of the majority of Greek works and their prime exemplar, Homer, as he theorizes in the terms he advanced in this lecture, and not including the tragedies. His lecture on Aeschylus' *Prometheus Bound* finds it a vast fund of sublimity, and its philosophy occupying a liminal space between the Greek and the Hebrew.

from that which was indistinct."[19] Both in pathos and in spirit, then, Coleridge declares his own Gothicism, and sets it in a "dark, wild" landscape familiar not only in the medievalizing poems cited above but also in "Dejection," "Mrs. Siddons," "To the Author of 'The Robbers,'" and, truly, in all of Coleridge's dark, stormy nights.

This "free," "wild," infinitely longing soul has its apposite form, a poetry characterized by "connexion without combination." The poems had no beginning, middle, and end, and no linear progression "to one purpose," and this structure is associated with a daemonic temper: "Imagine, then, that of images they had nothing like those of the Greeks. They had nothing but what was to be inward and sullenly refuse to disclose itself otherwise than in terrors," and in "fire-worship."[20] The Gothic cultural mode, then, represents two aspects notable in Coleridge's own work: its devotion to "terrors" which are not sentimental, but monitory of the presence of evil at a high level of reality, and the non-linear and sometimes fragmentary form of his productions, which must not be identified with the fragmentation of modern cultural institutions, but which, in their mythic "connectivity," actually stand in opposition to that development.

This last point requires some explanation, before we go on to complete the picture of Coleridge's speculative Gothicism, since the Coleridgean fragment is so often considered, not an opponent of modern sociopolitical fragmentation, but a harbinger of the postmodern *abîme*. A powerful fragment like "Christabel" is, in Coleridge's own terms, made up of the "*coarctation*" of time and space into personal "incarnational" image, but also includes a disintegrational process that Thomas McFarland calls "diasparaction," which means "torn to pieces." McFarland finds that "incompleteness, fragmentation, and ruin—the diasparactive triad—are at the very center of life."[21] McFarland sees the dispersive tendency of Coleridge's effective poems destroying his "old

---

[19] *Lects 1808–1819* II, 79–80 (Lecture 2, 1818).

[20] The *Philosophical Lectures of Samuel Taylor Coleridge*, ed. Kathleen Coburn (London and New York, 1949) Lecture X (March 1, 1819) 291. Given that Coleridge sees that the fire stolen by Aeschylus' Prometheus symbolizes Mind (Nous), and that Aeschylus' poetry is sublime, this play constitutes the underground element of Greek culture, founded in the sublime mystery cults. Coleridge's purpose is to attribute the virtues of the *Prometheus Bound* to a semi-Hebraic religious infusion, which constitutes a deeper faith than the official polytheistic religious institutions based on a native "Pelasgian" source.

[21] *Romanticism and the Forms of Ruin* (Princeton, 1981) 4–5.

dream" of harmony as a proof of his essential failure. But might we also compare this violent "tearing to pieces" with the *sparagmos* of Dionysus? After he is torn apart, a *coarctation* reconstitutes the god as a deity of mystical vision, ecstatic energy, and the tragic drama. Therefore, the tragic outcome of the Coleridgean *sparagmos* demands that Geraldine bear the scars of her violent transformative past, "this mark of my shame, this seal of my sorrow" (which she contagiously transfers to Christabel), as does the Ancient Mariner, like one of the lightning-scarred trees Coleridge had so admired in his walking tours.[22] If Coleridge does not explicitly provide the redemptive coarctation, well, then, neither did Sophocles.

In fact, there is a fellow-feeling relating the Greek tragedians to Coleridge's spiritual history of the Gothic, certainly in its melancholy, but also in two other specifically Gothic elements, as elucidated by Coleridge, which also play a central role in his own work: the non-monarchical, non-democratic Northern political organization that, like the poetry, was "connected without combination," and the unique "genius" of the greatest poets, especially Dante. A third, further element that seems to belong to the Gothic alone is the chivalric idea of love. Because these and all the other elements of the Gothic spirit are all based upon a fundamental spiritual love of infinity and high terrors, they all therefore interpenetrate and coadunate, making of them a great and vivifying contrast with the cultural fractures that had emerged in the nineteenth century, a model that perhaps provided a strong inspiration for his attempt to unify spiritual and political culture in *On the Constitution of Church and State*, and, too, might suggest a basic foundation for his opposition to the modern philosophy of "mechanism." The

---

[22] Coleridge wrote long notes recording his impressions of the natural landscapes he encountered on walking tours. One short section of a walking tour with the Wordsworths in Scotland follows: "The Rocks, by which we passed, under the brow of one of which I sate, beside an old blasted Tree, seemed the very link by which Nature connected Wood & Stone / The Rock Substance was not distinguishable in grain, cracks, & colors from old scathed Trees, Age- or Lightning-burnt / Right opposite to me the willowy Mountains with the broken wild craggy summits, & half way up one very large blasted Tree, white & leafless / —Here too I heard with a deep feeling the swelling unequal noise of mountain Water from the streams in the Ravines/" (*CN* 1.1469, August 26, 1803). The "blasted Tree" presides over the chthonic sounds; the last sentence may well be one source-text for the Simplon Pass and Snowden episodes in *The Prelude*, which had lain dormant since its 1799 first effort, and to which Wordsworth was to return the year following this note. It also strongly suggests the liminal scene on the vicarious mountain-ascent in "This Lime-Tree Bower."

English and Celtic love of independence as a concomitant of the "wild" and "infinite" Gothic soul may account for the opposition posed to Kubla Khan's tyranny, with its pseudo-Edenic, rationally planned landscape, by the subterranean and daemonic forces arrayed against it, and why this challenge is located in the dangerously, chthonically inspired prophet. This may not be so far removed from Sophocles' Antigone.

But in later European history, this same prophet, whose greatest inspiration is chthonic and unconscious, is represented by Dante, Petrarch, and Boccaccio, who internalize European history as a cultural conflict between its Gothic "soul" and its classical Roman "language." Coleridge was the first to say that Romanticism, in the medieval sense that would later be transferred *mutatis mutandis* to the early nineteenth century, was spiritually Gothic, whose powers "still retained the ascendant, whenever the use of their living Mother-language enabled the inspired poet to appear instead of the toilsome Scholar."[23] In the three Italian poets we see unconscious prophets in whom the culture war raged. They were, he says in the third lecture, under the "influences of the Greek and Roman Muse. . . . But happily for us and for their own fame, the intention of the writers as men is often at complete variance with the genius of the same men as poets." Coleridge is supplying a potent, if inadvertent, self-revelation of the "inspired poet" and lover in the "Verse Letter to Sara Hutchinson / Dejection," in opposition to the "toilsome Scholar" with his abstruse metaphysics.

If such an internal conflict is directed toward the possibility of and the obstacles to love, then that too is Gothic, because Coleridge also included "romantic" love as one of its specific marks: Gothic poetry's true merit lies in "the Love of the Marvelous, the deeper sensibility, the higher reverence for Womanhood, the characteristic spirit of Sentiment and Courtesy,—these were the heirlooms of Nature." The Gothic, then, is a spirit of love on several levels, and so the "higher reverence for Womanhood" extends to his idea of a Gothic "living Mother-language."[24] The Mother now is procreatrix of a free European culture, but also provides a genealogy for his own production that, as always, has another side. The mother-figure so prominent in his works

---

[23] *Lects 1808–1819* II, 91 (Lecture 3, 1818).

[24] *Lects 1808–1819* II, 93 (Lecture 3, 1818). Here the Gothic language-Mother appears as a bastion against the tendency of the classicized Italian writers after Dante, in whom "a foreign something . . . had been superinduced on the language instead of growing out of it."

is usually a paradisal locus, protecting the blissfully unconscious infant she holds. Yet Coleridge typically also figures the opponents of love in the same "marvelous" way when he dramatizes mythic, terrifying evil, since these daemons not only threaten love, but also mimic its procreative power. Hence, the series of maternal daemons in Coleridge's *oeuvre* on the terrifying side of non-conscious reality, such as Medea as mother of delusion and possession,[25] the prolific Hell-Hag who opposes the virginal Joan of Arc in "Destiny of Nations" (the title of this section also bore the telling title: "Joan of Arc, Book the Second [Preternatural Agency]"), the "Fiend-Hag" of "Ode to the Departing Year," or the "witches' home" in the "Verse Letter," where the "Mighty Poet, e'en to frenzy bold" rages.

Implied here is the aspect of "genius" that Coleridge finds in Dante, as a frankly unconscious force, and he treats this directly in some of his many definitions of genius, one of his favorite subjects. In his *Lectures on Literature* and in "On Poesy or Art," he said: "there is in Genius itself an unconscious activity—nay, that is *the* Genius in the man of Genius." Having said this, Coleridge adds a metaphor that repeats the dark mystery as death-symbolism, by giving a comprehensive primacy to the "Antinous," the beautiful but dead boy memorialized in art: "the Conscious is so impressed on the Unconscious, as to appear *in* it (ex. gr. Letters on a Tomb compared with Figures constituting a Tomb)."[26]

Here he again suggests the paradox that sees conscious "intention" at "complete variance with genius," whose fertility is so evident in his own mythopoetics. The speaker in Coleridge's poems is frequently a self-conscious poet who encounters unexpected and dreadful visitations. "Love," *Kubla Khan, Christabel,* and the "Verse Letter," as well as such poems as "Religious Musings," "The Destiny of Nations," and "France: An Ode," all play on this figure in complex ways that double and triple the poet-character and the singing voice as a dramatization of parallel personae, as is the relationship between *Christabel*'s protagonist, the fearful narrator, Leoline, and Bard Bracy. These poems, of course, also exemplify a strong backward extension in time, as with the troubadour and the mad Knight in "Love," that is also a gesture away from rational loci in intellectual history, whether that be nineteenth-

---

[25] CN 2.2930 (Oct–Nov 1802).
[26] See *Lects 1808–1819* II, 221–222 and n.18 (Lecture 13, 1818); and *CN* 3.4397. This text is the basis for "On Poesy, Or Art."

century England, the Renaissance, or classicist Greco-Roman civilization.

It is necessary to point out again that Coleridge's preference for Gothic sublimity is not always borne out in his theoretical writing, because, after all, this is the same man speaking who, in the *Friend*, was to inveigh against "indistinct conceptions" as the "poison in the cup of blessing,"[27] and it was the same man who, as critic, habitually took a very dim view of popular "Gothic" plays and novels of his own day, from Walpole to Lewis to Maturin. But, to apply the geographic terms of his own poetic historiography, it is as a Greco-Roman that he harmonizes and unifies, but as a Goth, in his larger sense of the word, that he writes much of his poetry and emotive notebook passages, and where his spontaneous, dreadful Muse invades the pristine, yet more passive, Reason.

IV

The connections between Coleridge's imaginative historiological theories and his poems already suggest that there is an ongoing mutual interchange between the individual and the broader realms of being, which takes on special urgency when we turn to the Coleridge's more direct encounters with daemonic afflatus, the energetic *limen* between them. In a recent essay, Anthony Harding makes new strides toward understanding what we are here calling Coleridge's mythopoetic realism, with respect to the nature of the imagination and the origin of evil: First, is the imagination purely an affirming and constructive force, or does it contain an opposing force; and then, is evil simply a psychological predisposition, or does it have its own independent being and even a primal Origin of its own? Harding follows the sometimes contradictory movements of Coleridge's thought, finding, for instance, a discontinuity between the publically promulgated *Aids to Reflection*, which sticks to the theologically less-suspect idea that evil is entirely of human origin and a matter of the will, and the more daring speculations to be found in the *Notebooks* and in the *Marginalia*. While in *AR* 256 Coleridge is to "brush the suprahuman origin of evil aside as a 'barren controversy,'" nonetheless his comments on the temptation of Eve in a

---

[27] The *Friend*, ed. Barbara Rooke, 2 vols., *CC* vol. IV (1969), I, 37.

marginalium upon Böhme, dating probably from 1819–1820, is radically different: "To the Adept it conveys the great mystery, that the origin of moral Evil is in the *Timeless*, εν τω αχρονω in a spirit, not comprehended in the consciousness—tho' revealed in the conscience of Man" (*CM* 1.685). The Adept, then, can pursue the inner sense of the myth to the point where the very 'origin of moral Evil' is seen to lie *outside* human consciousness."[28]

This question may take on more color if we turn to a confessional passage that sets out the permeable nature of the self/Other distinction, under the pressure of the daemonic, in the transnatural domain. In fact, mythopoesis can apply to figures perceived either as exogenously subsistent or as indwelling aspects of the personal psyche. Sometimes it is both, as in this note from 1812 which presents itself as a mythic personal history, first figured in confessional Christian terms, but then, marshaling terms from Greek, Latin, and Gothic daemonology, crosses over into a true mytho*drama*, which requires more than one persona:

> One of the strangest and most painful Peculiarities of my Nature (unless others have the same, & like me, hide it from the same inexplicable feeling of causeless shame & sense of a sort of guilt, joined with the apprehension of being feared and shrunk from as a something transnatural) I will here record—and my Motive or rather Impulse to do this, seems to myself an effort to †eloign and abalienate it from the dark Adyt of my own Being by a *visual* Outness—& not the wish for others to see it—
>
> It consists in a sudden second sight of some hidden Vice, past, present, or to come, of the person or persons with whom I am about to form a close intimacy—which never deters me but rather (as all these transnaturals) urge me on, just like the feeling of an Eddy-Torrent to a swimmer/. I see it as a Vision, feel it as a Prophecy—not as one *given* me by any other Being, but as an act of my own Spirit, of the absolute Noumenon / which in so doing seems to have offended against some Law of its Being, & to have acted the Traitor by a commune with full Consciousness independent of the tenure or inflicted state of Association, Cause & Effect &c &c—. . . .
>
> These occasional acts of The Ego noumenoς = repetitions or semblances of the original *Fall* of Man—hence shame & power—to leave the appointed Station and become Δαιμων‡

---

[28] Harding, "Imagination, Patriarchy, and Evil in Coleridge and Heidegger" 9. This is a large and fascinating topic, and an as yet undiscovered country in Coleridgean criticism.

† to eloign a eloigner, elongare, abire, fugere in longum,—in the imperative eloign thee! = make thyself distant/off with thee to moldary! Go to Hell & to the farthest end of it! &c &c

—In French e sounds as an English a, and the interchange between l and r is of notorious frequency in etymology—Hence, Aroynt thee, witch! . . . I suppose to be—Eloign thee, witch.

<‡ and perhaps invading the free will & rightful secrecy of a fellow-spirit—>[29]

Here, Coleridge first takes pains to iterate that he is exploring a primal depth in his own psyche, whose "visual Outness" is provided by himself in an attempt at self-exorcism, but the terms are curious in that they imply autonomous externals: "transnatural," Adyt, "the absolute Noumenon," and the "Δαιμων" (daemon) are all highly extreme, compared to any normal theological writing about the effects of "the original *Fall* of Man," in which the soul would not be allied with an absolute, nor would it transgress the boundaries between the strictly human and the daemonic. The word "transnatural" also has a double usage: in the note above, it invokes fear and aversion, located as it is in the *limen* above the "Adyt" or Abyss, but Coleridge could also employ the term in a benign, celestial way: "Not only my Thoughts, Affections extend to Objects transnatural, as Truth, Virtue, God. . . . I alone am Lord of Fire and Light. . . . Ergo, there is in me or rather *I* am praeternatural, i.e. supersensuous."[30]

The differing uses of these words are not careless, but mean that Coleridge's transnatural domain has a dark abyss of sin and fierce unredeemed passion, perhaps implied here by the loaded phrase "Lord of Fire," as it also holds the celestial Light of Truth, Virtue, God and immortality. The "absolute noumenal" self participates in both and, to create poetry, finds a series of symbols or analogies for them in physical life, but it is very significant that, in his desperate and guilty moments, Coleridge figures the chthonic attributes as absolutely as the celestial.

The elaborate footnotes for "eloign" and "abalienate" seem to be scholia, which follow a curious pattern of avoidance/approach. Since the obvious sense of the passage is that he is referring to a kind of exorcism, the scholia seem at first to shy away from this with a burst of

---

[29] CN 3.4166 (October 1812).

[30] CN 3.4060 (April 2, 1811); see also "Death and Grounds of Belief in a Future State," *Omniana* 372–374.

pedantry, but then to return irresistibly to the daemonic sense by writing "the farthest end of Hell," and "Aroynt thee, Witch!"

To "go to Hell & to the farthest end of it" carries a double meaning, first as exorcism, the banishment of the demon back to his abyss, and, second, as the act of the shaman or mythic hero who travels to the underworld in search of knowledge or love, like Aeneas or the "Hyperborean Wizard" in "Destiny of Nations" who is able to penetrate the caves beneath the primal ocean in ecstatic vision, as the agent of Torngarsuk, the Good Spirit, in order to engage the equally ancient Fiendhag, who lives beneath the oceanic Abyss, and who, strangely enough, is also the opponent of Joan of Arc herself. The Gothic phrase from *King Lear*, "Aroynt thee, Witch!" is ostensibly a philological exhibit, but it has directly to do with the subject of the passage at hand. As the Gothicizing poem "Mrs. Siddons" shows, the witch is a very important Coleridgean symbol, one figure in a long string of daemonesses who may alternatively represent either his own *anima* in its chthonic and original being, or the invading powers who bring his soul to that state. In "Mrs. Siddons," the witches are engaged in a sinful eroticism not only shocking by societal standards, but especially by the standards of Coleridge's own near-ascetic Idealism: "those hags, who at the witching time / Of murky Midnight ride the air sublime, / And mingle foul embrace with fiends of Hell." Like a witch, he sees himself as a "transnatural" being, and this is a "traitorous" departure from the good, a supernatural being that combines "shame & power," to result in an expressive/exorcistic mythopoetic production. Mythopoetic power resides in the daemon. Whereas he characteristically figures Reason and Imagination as timeless and *super*natural in origin, now in daemonic mode he is a *trans*natural. Reason has become Treason, and still, may yet have an exorcistic, redemptive value.

"Visual Outness" is mythopoesis itself, "recording" the vision compulsively and giving it body, even though it is laden with the chthonic afflatus and so much daunting sin and guilt that he fears its theurgic effect on "others." His desire to protect others from it is like his warning to the crowd around the ecstatic poet at the end of "Kubla Khan": "weave a circle round him thrice, / and close your eyes with holy dread." The sense of exile pervades this conflict: the producer stands apart, his production is an "eloignment" from his own abyss, and his anxious moralizing monitor also wants to keep a prudential distance between the devastating artifact and ordered society. The motif of the solitary that Coleridge so frequently advances as a requisite for the operation of the prophetic-poetic imagination is imbued with this conscience-driven and self-sacrificial morality.

The "Adyt" in which the fateful shift occurs might echo Dante's deepest Cocytus, where the great Traitors are immured, except that he is not immured; rather, he is "feared and shrunk from," like the pilot's boy responding to the resurgent Mariner, the Mad Monk, or the Kubla Khan poet. A better possibility is that the word has something in common with the *adytum* of the Cumaean Sybil (*Aeneid* VI.98) where she is beset by the terrors of the prophetic god.[31] This Abyss is the deep Origin supporting the transnatural realm, and shows that Coleridge himself is very much the poet of original apocalypse, remembered here first as the Fall, but then seeing deeply into a chthonic darkness still more ancient. To some extent, Coleridge is not alone in this. Anya Taylor has summarized the rise in the use of magical and oracular language in the poetry of the Ages of Sensibility and Romanticism as a rejection of materialism and a reiteration of the knowledge of spiritual powers beyond and against enlightened rationalism:

> Some intuition that the universe is alive, that unconscious attentiveness will allow the life to well up in the isolated, formerly rational, individual, and that it will rise in charms or incantations that can break down all rational barriers led these writers to think of poetry in a new way. They submit enthusiastically to being overwhelmed by oracles or invaded by powerful voices, hoping thereby to reach a revitalized center of force.[32]

However, Coleridge is different in that he was not "enthusiastic" about this incursion, but rather more like the Sybil in his terror, and more

---

[31] An *adytum* is both the inmost shrine of a temple and the depths of the earth, and Virgil uses it in both senses to describe the Sibyl's cave, where the oracular god spurs his prophetess to frenzy:

> Talibus ex adyto dictis Cumaea Sibylla
> horrendas canit ambages antroque remugit,
> obscuris vera involvens: ea frena furenti
> concutit, et stimulos sub pectore vertit Apollo. (VI.98–102)

> [In words like these the Sibyl from her shrine
> Sang riddles of terror and bellowed in her cave,
> Wrapping the truth in darkness; such the rein
> And spur Apollo gave her maddened heart.]

[32] *Magic and English Romanticism* (Athens, Ga., 1979) 16.

terrified still than she, because the "center of force" he was to encounter was not likely to be as kindly as Apollo, although perhaps just as distinctly Other. One is scarcely enthusiastic if one considers that submission brings a possible destruction. Thus, the "swimmer" on the dreadful "eddy" fears drowning, utter immersion in an oceanic "Abyss-figures" of apocalyptic dread much repeated across Coleridge's works.

Apocalypticism is surely implied in his description of the self as "Absolute Noumenon." Such nomenclature would not appear in Coleridge's theological writings, to be sure, where he wants to guard against implications of "Manicheanism," but, as "The Destiny of Nations" bears witness, the demands of mythodrama are different, and this struggle is taking place both inside and outside of finitude. As Harding is right to note, to place such drama in a "timeless" dimension is extremely significant. So, although Coleridge may have tried to present this passage as the description of an internal disposition, he has not fitted it out quite this way, as becomes especially apparent when the Absolute Noumenon is incarnated, as all mythodrama must be, in personae. Here, they are both the "swimmer" who sets out on his journey and the Daemon who appears at the climax, the dangerous figure who emerges after the swimmer has been immersed in the Adyt, and the boundary between internal and external being is violated: "perhaps invading the free will & rightful secrecy of a fellow-spirit." If the language at the outset has suggested exorcism, this implies possession. It may even be that the first figure, the swimmer, is all too finite, whereas his replacement, the Daemon, partakes of a more "absolute" nature. The dreadful contagions of the Mystery Poems proceed from such a source.

There is a two-sided possibility in the dramatization of the "daemon" given by Coleridge here, which reflects his unique mingling of the concepts of evil spirits as autonomous personal beings and as symbols of aspects of the individual psyche. There is no question that Coleridge the rational thinker tended to valorize the latter, typically modern explanation, but as mythopoet, he necessarily enacted the former. Anthony Harding addresses "two contradictory impulses" that Coleridge described in 1830 as the impulse to "'pass out of myself' and the opposite impulse 'not to suffer any one form to pass into *me* and to become a usurping *Self*.'"[33]

---

[33] *Coleridge and the Idea of Love* 88. Harding is discussing this comment in a different context, the celestial power of love as an "abstract Self" that Coleridge saw in dream as a "Universal personified" in the loved woman (87), but it shows how the daemonic power can also take on a personal force.

This usurpation may threaten treason and the Apocalypse, but it has its consolations. The wind on the chthonic Mount of prophecy, the "witches' home" at the center of the "Verse Letter to Sara Hutchinson" is a "Mighty Poet, even to frenzy bold," displacing dejection with its own energies, first external to the depressed watcher and then taking him by incursion, routing passivity but threatening the domestic peace. Here, like the woman "wailing for her demon lover" at the middle stage and crux of *Kubla Khan*, Coleridge encounters the Muse as Daemon.

Works Cited

Barth, J. Robert, S.J. *Coleridge and Christian Doctrine*. 1969. New York: Fordham University Press, 1987.

———. *Coleridge and the Power of Love*. Columbia: University of Missouri Press, 1988.

Coleridge, Samuel Taylor. *Biographia Literaria*. Eds. James Engell and W. Jackson Bate. 2 vols. Princeton: Princeton University Press, 1983. *CC* Vol. VII.

———. *The Collected Works of Samuel Taylor Coleridge*. Ed. Kathleen Coburn. 16 vols. Bollingen Series 75. Princeton: Princeton University Press, 1969–. Cited as *CC*.

———. *The Complete Poetical Works of Samuel Taylor Coleridge*. Ed. Ernest Hartley Coleridge. 2 vols. London: Oxford University Press, 1912.

———. "Death and Grounds of Belief in a Future State." *Omniana, or, Horae otiosiores*. Ed. Robert Southey. 2 vols. 1812.

———. *The Friend*. Ed. Barbara Rooke. 2 vols. Princeton: Princeton University Press, 1969. *CC* Vol. IV.

———. *Lay Sermons*. Ed. R. J. White. Princeton: Princeton University Press, 1972. *CC* Vol. VI.

———. *Lectures 1808–1819: On Literature*. Ed. Reginald A. Foakes. Princeton: Princeton University Press, 1984. *CC* Vol. VI.

———. *Marginalia*. Ed. H. J. Jackson and George Whalley. 5 vols. to date. Princeton: Princeton University Press, 1980–. *CC* Vol. XII.

———. *The Notebooks of Samuel Taylor Coleridge*. Ed. Kathleen Coburn. 4 vols. to date. Bollingen Series 50. Princeton: Princeton University Press, 1955–.

———. *On the Constitution of Church and State.* Ed. John Colmer. Princeton: Princeton University Press, 1976. *CC* Vol.X.

———. *The Philosophical Lectures of Samuel Taylor Coleridge.* Ed. Kathleen Coburn. London and New York: Philosophical Library, 1949.

———. *Table Talk.* Ed. Carl R. Woodring. 2 vols. Princeton: Princeton University Press, 1990. *CC* Vol. XIV.

Friedrich, Carl J. *The Age of the Baroque: 1610–1660.* New York, Evanston, London: Harper & Row, 1952.

Harding, Anthony John. *Coleridge and the Idea of Love.* London and New York: Cambridge University Press, 1974.

———. "Coleridge, Subjectivity, and the 'Mirror of the Mysteries.'" *European Romantic Review* 5 (1995): 193–213.

———. "Imagination, Patriarchy, and Evil in Coleridge and Heidegger." *Studies in Romanticism* 35 (1996): 3–26.

———. "Myth and the War of Ideas: Coleridge on the 'Prometheus' of Aeschylus." *Nineteenth-Century Contexts* 13 (1989): 177–196.

———. "Mythopoeic Elements in Christabel." *Modern Language Quarterly* 44 (1983): 39–50.

Kramer, Lawrence. "That Other Will: The Daemonic in Coleridge and Wordsworth." *Philological Quarterly* 58 (1979): 298–320.

McFarland, Thomas. *Romanticism and the Forms of Ruin.* Princeton: Princeton University Press, 1981.

Peterfreund, Stuart. "The Way of Immanence, Coleridge, and the Problem of Evil." *English Literary History* 55 (1988): 125–158.

Taylor, Anya. *Magic and English Romanticism.* Athens: University of Georgia Press, 1979.

Twitchell, Paul. *Romantic Horizons: Aspects of the Sublime in English Poetry and Painting, 1770–1850.* Columbia: University of Missouri Press, 1983.

Virgil. *Aeneid.* Trans. Frank O. Copley. Indianapolis and New York: Bobbs-Merrill, 1965.

10

"Sounding on His Way": Coleridgean Religious Dissent and Hazlitt's Conversational Style

Jonathan Mulrooney

LIKE OTHER INFORMAL ENCOUNTERS between figures of first- and second-generation Romanticism—Wordsworth's derision of Keats's "Hymn to Pan" comes to mind—Hazlitt's meeting with Coleridge in early 1798 represents a crucial point in the younger writer's career.[1] Coleridge had come to Shrewsbury to audition for a position as head of the Unitarian congregation there, and upon hearing him preach, Hazlitt relates later, he "could not have been more delighted if I had heard the music of the spheres. Poetry and Philosophy had met together. Truth and Genius had embraced, under the eye and with the sanction of Religion" (17.108).[2] As Hazlitt recalled in his 1823 *My First Acquaintance with the Poets*, Coleridge was a new kind of dissenting "poet-preacher" in whose voice "Truth had found a new ally in Fancy" (17.111). Seen next to Hazlitt's own father, a dissenting minister "who was a veteran in the cause, and then declining into the vale of years . . . no two individuals were ever more unlike than were the host and his guest" (17.110).

In his brief stay with the family, Coleridge demonstrated an independence of thought that had been personally and historically unavailable to Hazlitt's father. Unlike the Rev. Hazlitt, who had been "tossed about from congregation to congregation in the heats of the Unitarian

---

[1] That both encounters are charged with religious vocabulary reinforces Robert Ryan's recent claim that "religion was a critically important dimension of the public life" in Romantic-period Britain. See Ryan, *The Romantic Reformation: Religious Politics in English Literature, 1789–1824* (Cambridge, 1997) 1.

[2] All Hazlitt references are to *The Complete Works of William Hazlitt*, ed. P. P. Howe, 21 vols. (New York, 1967). Cited parenthetically with volume and page number.

controversy" (17.110), Coleridge exuded an imaginative force that transcended the limits of the institutional Church. As Hazlitt walked with Coleridge toward Nether Stowey at the conclusion of the visit, that force manifested itself as both physical and conversational mobility:

> The scholar in Chaucer is described as going "Sounding on his way." So Coleridge went on his. In digressing, in dilating, in passing from subject to subject, he appeared to me to float in air, to slide on ice. He told me in confidence (going along) that he should have preached two sermons before he accepted the situation at Shrewsbury, one on Infant baptism, the other on the Lord's Supper, shewing that he could not administer either, which would have effectually disqualified him from the object in view. (17.113)[3]

The implied connection here between stylistic and doctrinal freedom is one that would mark much of Hazlitt's own professionally itinerant career. Coleridge's "power of conversation" (17.114), his digressive rhetoric, and personal openness—manifested physically, too, in the way that Coleridge "continually crossed me on the way shifting from one side of the foot-path to the other" (17.113)—impressed upon Hazlitt the intellectual vitality that accompanied liberty from institutional constraints.

Daniel White has argued recently that Coleridge's dismissal of the Shrewsbury ministry represents a rejection of the politically limited "legacy of old middle-class Dissent" in favor of a community defined by a wider "mode of religious conversation."[4] For White, the 1790s conversation poems imagine an ideal public sphere in which the poet demonstrates an "ability to speak over the commotion of urban commerce and its interior correlate, self interest."[5] Conversation enables an intimate relation between poet and audience that is not only a rhetorical construction, but also a religiously inspired political vision of community. Poetry finds its power in an "involuntary social principle of

---

[3] For differing views of Coleridge's Unitarian commitments at this time, see J. Robert Barth, S.J., *Coleridge and Christian Doctrine* (New York, 1987), esp. 1–13; and Daniel E. White, "'Properer for a Sermon': Particularities of Dissent and Coleridge's Conversational Mode," *Studies in Romanticism* 40 (2001): 175–198.

[4] White 179, 188. The Wedgewood annuity, offered and accepted in the same month as the Shrewsbury post Coleridge rejected, enabled Coleridge to commit to a life of what White calls "dissident" Unitarianism (198).

[5] White 197.

concretion, the circular ripples expanding in a lake, the home-born feeling that in the absence of property could permanently transform sons of commerce into human beings pure and simple."[6] Hazlitt's own conversational style is a second-generation development of this Coleridgean "conversational mode"; his criticism has as its structuring principle a colloquial, digressive presentation of personal experience. Throughout Hazlitt's writing, but especially in his reviews of theatrical performances and other entertainments, public events initiate a psychological process that refigures the critic's imagined relation to the public world, both as a viewer and as a communicator of the event to the reader. Conversational criticism becomes a means of imagining an intimate connection between critic and reader, and of reworking both public and private experience in the face of a depersonalizing mass culture.

Two of Hazlitt's mid-career essays, *The Indian Jugglers* (1819) and *The Fight* (1822), are splendid examples of a periodical criticism that finds, even in the most popular of entertainments, potential for the reconstruction of the intimacy and ideal community modeled by the young Coleridge. In the years that followed the meeting at Shrewsbury, Hazlitt would become a strictly professional writer. Journalism provided both his central source of income and the field in which he achieved his public profile.[7] Sensitive to the exigencies of the publishing world in which he worked, Hazlitt developed a periodic style that negotiated a critical path between the poles of elitism and commercialism, even as he remained concerned with the ability of cultural experience to shape individual and collective subjectivities. For Hazlitt, the periodical essay becomes one link in a chain of ongoing conversation that transforms individuals into cultural communities. His criticism thus imagines a discursive community defined not by pre-existing categories of taste, but by a common interest among its participants in the critic's personal experience. Long after Coleridge had altered his political and religious allegiances, Hazlitt would cling to the critical style he began to fashion in Coleridge's "poet-preacher" image in January 1798.

Hazlitt's criticism is often read through the lens of the philosophical apparatus found in *An Essay on the Principles of Human Action* (1805),

---

[6] White 198.

[7] As Jon Cook states, "Hazlitt earned his living as a writer, and his living was precarious." See Cook, Introduction. *William Hazlitt: Selected Writings*, ed. Jon Cook (Oxford, 1992) xxx.

itself a document engaged with the philosophical legacy of Dissent. In that early text, Hazlitt argues that the disinterested imagination drives human behavior. Scholars have paid much attention to the anti-egotistical aspects of this project, and specifically to Hazlitt's assertion that the individual has as great an imaginative investment in other subjects as it does in its future self.[8] The related but more fundamental description of how collective experience helps to integrate individual identity has, however, been less closely examined. For Hazlitt, the subject's idea of a "self" with which it can identify imaginatively begins not in a recognition of existential difference, but in the process of perception:

> Personality does not arise either from the being this, or that, from the identity of the thinking being with itself at different times or at the same time, or still less from being unlike others, which is not necessary to it, but from the peculiar connection which subsists between the different faculties and perceptions of the same conscious being, constituted as man is, so that as the subject of his own reflection or consciousness the same things impressed on any of his faculties produce a quite different effect upon *him* from what they would do if they were impressed in the same way on any other being. (1.36)

But the peculiarity, or uniqueness, of an individual's mode of perception does not alone constitute conscious identity. For it is only through interaction with others that the subject's awareness of its peculiarity develops:

> It is by comparing the knowledge that I have of my own impressions, ideas, powers, &c. with my knowledge of the same or similar impressions, ideas, &c. in others, and with the still more imperfect conception

---

[8] Numerous critics have formed their studies around this central point, David Bromwich most recently. See Bromwich, *Hazlitt: The Mind of a Critic* (Oxford, 1983) 24–57. John Kinnaird connects the *Principles* to Hazlitt's development of "his sense of self as always in some mode or degree *intersubjective*, as existing and acting only in tension with real or imagined otherness." Kinnaird, *William Hazlitt: Critic of Power* (New York, 1978) 58. Tom Paulin likewise sees the *Principles* as the beginning of Hazlitt's exploration of the "social" imagination. Paulin, *The Day-Star of Liberty: William Hazlitt's Radical Style* (London, 1998) 34. For related discussions, see John L. Mahoney, *The Logic of Passion: The Literary Criticism of William Hazlitt* (New York, 1981) 74–75, and W. J. Bate, *John Keats* (Cambridge, 1963) 255–259. For a revisionary view of the *Principles*, see Uttara Natarajan, *Hazlitt and the Reach of Sense: Criticism, Morals, and the Metaphysics of Power* (Oxford, 1999). Natarajan argues that "the creations of genius, equally as the exercise of 'disinterestedness' in the *Essay on the Principles of Human Action*, are enabled by a powerful self, an egotistical sublime that Hazlitt does not apologize for, but celebrates throughout his writing" (7).

that I form of what passes in their minds when this is supposed to be essentially different from what passes in my own, that I acquire the general notion of self. If I had no idea of what passes in the minds of others, or if my ideas of their feelings and perceptions were perfect representations, i.e. mere conscious repetitions of them, all proper personal distinction would be lost either in pure self-love, or in perfect universal sympathy. (1.37–38)

"Self" is therefore a product of ongoing communication; instances of social activity call the mind's attention to the process by which it encounters "the minds of others." Sensory experience does not simply provide raw material for the imagination's associative powers. Rather, it is a prerequisite to the social, which is to say conversational, exchanges necessary for self-conception.[9] As experience becomes public, subject becomes self. Hazlitt writes in the later essay *Whether Genius Is Conscious of Its Powers?* that "no man is truly himself, but in the idea which others entertain of him" (12.117). Knowledge of that idea is produced by interaction, be it verbal conversation or the exchange both represented and facilitated by the printed page.

The relentless publicity necessary for the transformation of subject into self—what John Kinnaird has called "intersubjectivity"—informs Hazlitt's review criticism at the level of both form and content.[10] Stylistically, this dialectical procedure manifests itself in rapid (even Coleridgean) shifts between detailed description and affective reaction. Hazlitt's plain speaker often lapses into colloquial musings even as his prose retains the compact descriptive quality of the parliamentary reporting with which Hazlitt began his career. The opening of *The Indian Jugglers* provides an example: "Coming forward and seating

---

[9] Hazlitt will develop this idea further in the *Lectures on English Philosophy*, where he criticizes the Baconian school for restricting the interpretation of the word "experience, confining it to a knowledge of things without us; whereas it in fact includes all knowledge relating to objects either within or out of the mind, of which we have any direct or positive evidence" (2.124).

[10] The early roots of Hazlitt's notions of "intersubjectivity" can be found in Hume's *A Treatise of Human Nature*, Book 2, Part 2, Section 5: "We can form no wish, which has not a reference to society. A perfect solitude is, perhaps, the greatest punishment we can suffer.... Let all the powers and elements of nature conspire to serve and obey one man: Let the sun rise and set at his command; The sea and rivers roll as he pleases, and the earth furnish spontaneously whatever may be useful or agreeable to him: He will still be miserable, till you give him one person at least, with whom he may share his happiness, and whose esteem and friendship he may enjoy." Hume, *A Treatise of Human Nature*, eds. David Fate Norton and Mary J. Norton (Oxford, 2000) 235.

himself on the ground in his white dress and tightened turban, the chief of the Indian Jugglers begins with tossing up two brass balls, which is what any of us could do, and concludes with keeping up four at the same time, which is what none of us could do to save our lives" (8.77). This single sentence displays a subtle oscillation between description and reaction, with no explicit interruption indicating the shift. The rhetorical pattern drawn here intensifies as the sentence gives way quickly to an extended reflection on the relation between the thing seen and the imaginative act of seeing: "To conceive of this effort of extra ordinary dexterity distracts the imagination, and makes admiration breathless. Yet it costs nothing to the performer, any more than if it were a mere mechanical deception . . ." (8.78). The critic attempts to understand not only the act itself, but its effect on his imagination. "Seeing the Indian jugglers," he continues, "makes me ashamed of myself. I ask what there is that I can do as well as this? Nothing. What have I been doing all my life?" Against the juggler's "instance of exact perfection," Hazlitt's writings become simply "abortions." "What errors, what ill-pieced transitions, what crooked reasons, what lame conclusions! How little is made out, and that little how ill!" (8.79).

Despite its seeming spontaneity, Hazlitt's exasperated outburst is highly deliberate, a rhetorical performance designed to illustrate a relation between intellectual and mechanical power that is inexpressible through the form of conventional report or review. As his expression of feeling departs from traditional modes of address, the essay's inadequacy becomes a paradoxical measure of the writer's communicative power. The critic's imaginative failure—his inability to succeed as a writer to the degree of perfection embodied by the juggler—is communicated as an uncontained emotion that registers perfectly, and negatively, the limitations of the form it implicitly transcends and explicitly derides. The colloquial character of the outburst, its intimacy, and its intensity perform for the reader a depth of feeling beyond that which reporterly description can possibly convey. Not surprisingly, then, Hazlitt's spontaneous meditation ends when he begins to describe how his compositional method produces such fruitful lapses. When writing an essay, he asserts, "I endeavor to recollect all I have ever observed or thought upon a subject, and to express it as nearly as I can" (8.79). Recollection, by transforming the initial perception from sensation into memory, at once distances the witness from the moment of observation and enlarges the significance of that moment as an identity-shaping experience. To express recollection "as nearly as I can" is to construct a mediated return to the immediate; yet the review displays its "nearness" to the event by calling attention to its own incompleteness. The opening of *The Indian Jugglers* is thus a compact allegory of Hazlitt's position as a writer in a rapidly changing periodical field: perception and loss of the critical faculty are followed by the return of conscious reception, begetting a new form of criticism that finds its power not in reliance on a tradition of hierarchical evaluation, but in the critic's conversational authenticity.

For Hazlitt, in other words, the critic composes in, and the review's form represents, the indescribable temporal and psychological interstice between observation and expression. Further, review writing is the representation of a continually revised (and textually performed) negotiation between conflicting psychological states. A powerful external stimulus "distracts the imagination" from its critical office, divesting the viewer of the self-possession necessary to stanch the flow of feeling and enable composition (8.78). Yet though the sensory experience itself must end for composition to begin, writing cannot be divorced from the initial moment of sensation or it will fail to engage the reader's imagination. Like Wordsworth's "spontaneous overflow of powerful feelings," which "takes its origin from emotion recollected in tranquility," Hazlitt's composition registers the tension between the observer's immediacy of encounter and the writer's withdrawal into meditation. But unlike that great re-visionary Wordsworth, who often elides scenes of writing with his speaker's meditation on the feelings that occasioned them, Hazlitt's writing displays the need for concentrated labor in the production, and indeed imagination, of imaginative expression. Because he is self-consciously a periodical writer, Hazlitt's process of composition is performed *as compressed*—which is to say it is (conspicuously) not subsumed into a polished written form. His withdrawal into the reflection that enables writing can be only provisional. "I have also time on my hands to correct my opinions and polish my periods: but the one I cannot, and the other I will not do" (8.79). The shifting, colloquial style of the critic represents a nearness between observation and expression that excessive reflection will only diminish. Hazlitt's critical subject situates himself joyfully between, and is enlivened by the incommensurability of, the world of ideas and the unwieldy physical world that his writing brings into contact.

That the opening meditation of *The Indian Jugglers* is conspicuously occasioned by Hazlitt's vision of the juggler manifests, at the level of topical progression, an ongoing dialectic between mechanical and intellectual power that structures the essay as a whole. Compensation for the writer's imperfection is found as the witnessing "I" registers the experience of the event—as the event cannot register itself, nor even as the standardized language of report can convey it. For Hazlitt, "no act terminating in itself constitutes greatness," because the act's public effect ends when the act is finished (8.85). The critic's response to the act, however, has the potential to extend its power beyond the moment of first occurrence. For this reason, the critic must maintain contact with the experience he describes; otherwise the review becomes an exercise in cold philosophy:[11]

> To throw a barley-corn through the eye of a needle, to multiply nine figures by nine in the memory, argues infinite dexterity of body and capacity of mind, but nothing comes of either. There is a surprising power at work, but the effects are not proportionate, or such as take hold of the imagination. To impress the idea of power on others, they must be made in some way to feel it. It must be communicated to their understandings in the shape of an increase of knowledge, or it must subdue and overawe them by subjecting their wills. (8.84–85)

Without the critic's witness—the self-conscious transformation of event into a language that, like Coleridge's digressive talk, conspicuously transcends formulaic expression—the event exists only as a momentary diversion. Though the juggler's presentation of skill is a perfect one in mechanical terms, it is finite in time and space. By contrast, greatness for Hazlitt is "great power, producing great effects," which is to say that greatness is public: "It is not enough that a man has great power in himself, he must shew it to all the world in a way that cannot be hid or gainsaid. He must fill up a certain idea in the public mind" (8.84). Hazlitt's insistence on the public longevity of greatness is the political analogue of his insistence on the necessity of interaction for the integration of personal identity. Like the ordinary man, the great man cannot exist unto himself. Thus "no man is truly great, who is great only in his life-time. The test of greatness is the page of history" (8.84). Hazlitt's distinction between power and great-

---

[11] Roy Park has discussed at length Hazlitt's commitment to concrete description and detail over the "abstraction" and "generality" of his age (2). See Park, *Hazlitt and the Spirit of the Age* (Oxford, 1971) 1–6.

ness explains conversational criticism's social importance. In the temporal interstices between the occurrence of a perception and its annihilation from the memory, the critic transforms fleeting acts into text whose effects extend into the life-world of readers' "understandings."

The dialectic between mechanical and intellectual excellence that frames *The Indian Jugglers* makes its final turn when Hazlitt quotes his own previously published elegy for the deceased John Cavanagh, a player of the racket game "fives." The "willing tribute to his memory" that Hazlitt pays is another abrupt shift in the essay, for it appears just as Hazlitt has logically confirmed the primacy of intellectual over mechanical pursuits: "To return from this digression" (that is, from his consideration of greatness), "and conclude the Essay," Hazlitt explicitly remarks on the elegy's first publication without attributing it to himself: "[Cavanagh's] death was celebrated at the time in an article in the Examiner newspaper (Feb. 7, 1819)" (8.86). Because the unattributed elegy "falls in with my own way of considering such subjects, I shall here take leave to quote it" (8.86). Its extended and detailed description of Cavanagh's physical prowess raises his deeds to the status of art: "His blows were not undecided and ineffectual—lumbering like Mr. Wordsworth's epic poetry, nor wavering like Mr. Coleridge's lyric prose, nor short of the mark like Mr. Brougham's speeches, nor wide of it like Mr. Canning's wit, nor foul like the *Quarterly*, not *let* balls like the *Edinburgh Review*. Cobbett and Junius together would have made a Cavanagh" (8.87).

Thomas Talfourd argued that inclusion of the Cavanagh piece in *The Indian Jugglers* exemplified "the mass of personal feeling" that weakened Hazlitt as a philosopher and metaphysician: "He wrote elaborate essays to prove the superiority of physical qualifications to those of intellect—full of happy illustrations and striking instances . . . *but all beside the mark*, proving nothing but that which required no proof—that corporeal strength and beauty are more speedily and more surely appreciated than the products of genius."[12] Hazlitt is, in Talfourd's view, so carried away by a fascination with physical beauty that he misses the worth of his own criticism, which he "nobly vindicated at other times, when he shows, and makes us feel, that 'words are the

---

[12] Thomas Noon Talfourd, *Critical and Miscellaneous Writings* (Boston, 1854) 123.

only things which last forever.'"¹³ For Talfourd, the fault of *The Indian Jugglers* is Hazlitt's failure to see that "the links of living sympathy" . . . "[connecting] its author to distant times" are exemplified in "the very essay which would decry it."¹⁴ Talfourd, though, carried away himself by Hazlitt's descriptive powers, misses the crucial truth that the elegy is a quotation. When quoted within the context of *The Indian Jugglers*, the elegy's "willing tribute" honors in the same moment both the beauty of Cavanagh the player and the power of the words that memorialize him. What Talfourd mistakes for a diverting sentimentalism we can understand as Hazlitt's resolute commitment to representing the vital interdependence of the mind that writes and the life of real, which is to say public, experience.

On the one hand, then, the power of any action is determined, for Hazlitt, by its ability to "fill up a certain idea in the public mind." On the other, the fact that such an act enables written criticism reveals that the act's consequences can surpass its temporary existence. Hazlitt's means of "ending" his consideration of the efficacy of intellectual labor is to quote his own previously published valorization of a sporting hero's physical labor, a valorization accomplished by describing Cavanagh in the highest terms possible, as embodied language. The epitome of fleeting sporting elegance is the equal of "Cobbett and Junius together." The comparison of Cavanagh's "blows" with "Wordsworth's epic poetry," "Coleridge's lyric prose," "Brougham's speeches," and "Canning's wit," situates Hazlitt not merely as a spectator but also as a reader who transforms bodily action into a cultural sign. Combining emotional force and sinewy precision, the fives player's exploits affect those who have seen him. But because of the critic's witness, those who have not seen also may believe. Thus *The Indian Jugglers* does not finally emphasize the triumph of one form of activity, intellectual or physical, over the other. Instead, it offers the critic's coming-to-awareness of their interdependence as an allegory for the cultural experience of the early nineteenth-century reader.

The gestural rhetoric of *The Indian Jugglers*, which explicitly situates the critic as a communicator of cultural experience, develops in *The Fight* into a dramatic staging of the conversational critic's expanding

---

¹³ Talfourd 123. Talfourd quotes from Hazlitt's "On Thought and Action" (Hazlitt 8.107).
¹⁴ Talfourd 123.

social role. First published in the *New Monthly Magazine* in 1822, *The Fight* narrates Hazlitt's experience as a member of a provisional public sphere occasioned by the most illegitimate of entertainments, a boxing match outside the city limits. The critic depicts himself as one member of an audience of cultural consumers bound together not simply by attendance at the fight, but also by their interactions with one another before and after. The critic is therefore a subject within the historical event he reports, and this dual position calls attention to the ways in which the experience of viewership affects the critic's rhetorical presentation of the event. Hazlitt's anticipations of and reactions to the spectacle are all events in themselves, worthy of attention because they register the fight's ability to "fill up a certain idea in the public mind." Again, this is not to say that description of the event itself carries no weight in the review. On the contrary, it is, like the mechanical exploits detailed in *The Indian Jugglers*, the central point to and from which the essay's rhetorical trajectories radiate.

The combatants, the settings, and the action are all scrupulously described:

> The *swells* were parading in their white box-coats, the outer ring was cleared with some bruises on the heads and shins of the rustic assembly (for the *cockneys* had been distanced by the sixty-six miles); the time drew near, I had got a good stand; a bustle, a buzz, ran through the crowd, and from the opposite side entered Neate, between his second and bottle-holder. He rolled along, swathed in his loose great coat, his knock-knees bending under his huge bulk; and, with a modest cheerful air, threw his hat into the ring (17.81).

Hazlitt's criticism makes no attempt to contain the crowd's energy, instead raising their voyeurism to the level of Greek and Trojan soldiers watching "the modern Ajax" and "Diomed" in the *Iliad*'s mortal combat: "Who at that moment, big with a great event, did not draw his breath short—did not feel his heart throb?" (17.81).

Yet, while it is certainly a new kind of report, in which an illegitimate sporting battle takes on the qualities of a high cultural event, *The Fight* takes as its larger subject the public experience of the spectators, and, further, the critic's role in communicating that experience to his own "spectators," that is, his readers. Reports of conversational interactions make up more than half of the review. Like the descriptions of the fight, the conversational portions of the essay bring into contact "high" and "low" culture by depicting the intersection of written and verbal conversation. Each character is figured as a member of the community occasioned by the fight and maintained by the critic's central conversational role. Hazlitt's desire to see the fight ("*Where there's a will, there's a way.*—I said so to myself") is matched only by his need to share the experience of that desire. "We are cold to others only when we are dull in ourselves. Give a man a topic in his head, a throb of pleasure in his heart, and he will be glad to share it with the first person he meets" (17.73). Tellingly, his conversation is not restricted to interactions with others, but even emerges in his style of self-address. After debating with "Joe Toms" whether or not they could take one of the mail coaches to the fight, Hazlitt rushes off to Piccadilly: "The mail coach stand was bare. 'They are all gone,' said I—'this is always the way with me—in the instant I lose the future—if I had not stayed to pour out that last cup of tea, I should have been just in time'—and cursing my folly and ill-luck together, without inquiring at the coach-office whether the mails were gone or not, I walked on in despite . . ." (17.73).

Encountering the Brentford stage along the road, Hazlitt's musings to himself continue: "I argued (not unwisely) that even a Brentford coachman was better company than my own thoughts (such as they were just then), and at his invitation mounted the box with him. I immediately stated my case to him—namely, my quarrel with myself for missing the Bath and Bristol mail" (17.74). Hazlitt's critical persona is a subject defined internally by conversation. In a natural shift, then, his conversation extends easily both to the people he meets along the way and to the reader. Informed by the coachman that the mails had not in fact left yet, he bemoans that "The Bath mail I had set my mind upon, and I had missed it, as I missed every thing else, by my own absurdity. . . . 'Sir,' said he of the Brentford, 'the Bath mail will be up presently, my brother-in law drives it, and I will engage to stop him if there is a place empty'" (17.74).

Sliding among Hazlitt's imagined conversation with himself, his remarks to the coachman, quotations of the coachman, and descriptions of Hazlitt's own state of mind, the review positions the reader as an equal participant in the critic's experience. In *The Fight* there is little rhetorical distinction made between Hazlitt the fightgoer and Hazlitt the review critic; direct observations to the reader repeatedly interrupt reported conversations. Even as its depicted interactions confirm existing relationships (as between Hazlitt and "Joe Toms") and demonstrate the ever-expansive network of social relations that constitutes the public realm, the review's address to the reader adds another dimension to that public sphere. The critic's written review is presented as one element in a larger exchange that transcends the boundaries of print, enabling conversation to extend beyond the immediate moment of the fight's occurrence. Intersections between written and verbal communication occur throughout the review, highlighting the relationship between oral and textual conversation. When Joe reports to Hazlitt that he'd gotten a free ride on the mail (". . . It's a pity I didn't meet with you; we could then have gone down for nothing. But *mum's the word*."), Hazlitt's response to the request is not an apology to Joe, but an *apologia* before the reader, who is treated as the next member along the gossip chain: "It's the devil for any one to tell me a secret, for it's sure to come out in print. I do not care so much to gratify a friend, but the public ear is too great a temptation for me" (17.77).

Listening admiringly to the conversation of a fellow barfly passing the night before the fight in a pub, Hazlitt remarks to the man: "I said, 'You read Cobbett, don't you? At least,' says I, 'you talk as well as he writes.' He seemed to doubt this. But I said, 'We have an hour to spare: if you'll get pen, ink, and paper, and keep on talking, I'll write down what you say; and if it doesn't make a capital Political Register, I'll forfeit my head'" (17.78). Though the man does not accept the offer, the conversation that ensues is in fact recorded not by Hazlitt *in propria persona*, but by Hazlitt the critic:

> [He] told me soon afterwards, in the confidence of friendship, that 'The circumstance which had given him nearly the greatest concern of his life, was Cribbs beating Jem [Belcher] after he had lost his eye by racket-playing.'—The morning dawns; that dim but yet clear light appears, which weighs like solid bars of metal on the sleepless lids; the guests drop down from their chambers one by one—but it was too late to think of going to bed now (the clock was on the stroke of seven), we had nothing for it but to find a barbers. . . . (17.78)

Again, the narrative shifts repeatedly here between Hazlitt's quotation of the man (which, like a parliamentary report, retains the third-person description despite its enclosure in quotation marks) and direct observations of the conversation as an event. Shortly after this passage, Hazlitt addresses his reading audience directly: "Reader, have you ever seen a fight?" Everything that follows takes on the characteristics of friendly conversation with the reader:

> The crowd was very great when we arrived on the spot; open carriages were coming up, with streamers flying and music playing, and the country-people were pouring in over hedge and ditch in all directions, to see their hero beat or be beaten. The odds were still on Gas, but only by about five to four. Gully had been down to try Neate, and had backed him considerably, which was a damper to the sanguine confidence of the adverse party. About two hundred thousand pounds were pending. (17.79)

The paratactic clauses here strike a rhythm that underscores the critic's imaginative dialogue with the reader; conversational language situates the critic as experiential witness rather than aesthetic evaluator. His nearness to both the original event and the reader/auditor authorizes his description of the event's power, rendering the critical essay both a communication of, and initiator of, public experience.

On the way back to London, Hazlitt's role as facilitator of conversation continues as his sphere of personal contact widens. Meeting some strangers who "appeared a little sly and sore" on the subject of the fight, Hazlitt questions them, "and it was not till after several hints dropped, and questions put, that it turned out that they had missed it" (17.84). Meeting others, he remarks that "some inquiry was made by the company about the fight, and I gave (as the reader may believe) an eloquent and animated description of it" (17.85). Hazlitt closes the essay by returning to his friend Joe Toms, who "called upon me the next day, to ask me if I did not think the fight was a complete thing? I said I thought it was. I hope he will relish my account of it" (17.86). The closing word of the review is a postscript to the reader, who (in a final twist) very well may turn out to be Joe Toms himself. In *The Fight*, then, the social function of criticism is re-imagined as the formation of a community of reception through Hazlitt's self-positioning as both speaker and writer, character and critic. The essay not only memorializes the occasional public sphere brought into being by the fight, but aims to perpetuate that sphere by counting the essay's reader among its conversational initiates. As the perspective of a Carravagian scene draws the viewer into its circle of represented bodies, so the gestural rhetoric of Hazlitt's essay situates the reader as a participant in an ongoing conversation completed, but not finished, by the reader's presence as auditor.

In *The Fight*'s revision of criticism's social function, the perception of fleeting events is transformed through conversation into experience that alters the subjectivity of both critic and reader. The critic's subjective response to events calls attention to its own, and its reader's, dependence on conversational interaction. Stanley Jones has commented on Hazlitt's "disinclination to pontificate . . . his dislike of the egotistical; his views are commonly defined dramatically, on specific occasions, by opposition to those of others."[15] Though Hazlitt was certainly a member of the class of philosophical critics Jon Klancher describes emerging in the early nineteenth century, his criticism authorizes itself not with philosophical rhetoric, but through a performed affective reaction to the events he describes.[16] In communicating his experience, he is more an "unsettling observer," to employ David Bromwich's phrase, than a "resolute guide"(270). *The Indian Jugglers* performs this "unsettling" mode of criticism in Hazlitt's outburst of self-doubt and the extended meditation that follows, and *The Fight* stages it as an ongoing cultural conversation transcending the boundaries of the written text. Thus these essays elicit the reader's affective response even as they thematize the critic's affective experience.

By the time he composed *The Indian Jugglers* and *The Fight*, Hazlitt had given up on Coleridge politically. Reviewing Coleridge's 1816 *Lay Sermon*, he decried that "the whole of this Sermon is written to sanction the principle of Catholic dictation, and to reprobate that diffusion of free inquiry—that difference of private, and ascendancy of public opinion, which has been the necessary consequence, and the great benefit of the Reformation" (16.105). With his advocacy of an elite class of readers—an idea that would eventually develop into the "national clerisy" of *On the Constitution of Church and State*—Coleridge betrayed for Hazlitt precisely the intellectual freedoms he had modeled on his visit to Shrewsbury in 1798. In place of a public sphere of conversation, he imagined "a complete system of superstition without faith . . . and all the evils, without any of the blessings, of ignorance" (16.106).[17] Yet, despite his disenchantment with what Coleridge became, Hazlitt spent much of his career as an essayist translating into print the conversational intimacy represented by Coleridge's talk. Looking back after two

---

[15] Stanley Jones, *Hazlitt: A Life* (Oxford, 1989) 106.
[16] See Jon Klancher, *The Making of English Reading Audiences, 1790–1832* (Madison, Wis., 1987) 47–75.
[17] For a discussion of the differences between Coleridge's early and late conceptions of community, see Kelvin Everest, *Coleridge's Secret Ministry: The Context of the Conversation Poems, 1795–98* (Sussex, 1979).

decades, Hazlitt himself recognized the importance of his first meeting with Coleridge the "poet-preacher":

> I was at that time dumb, inarticulate, helpless, like a worm by the wayside, crushed, bleeding, lifeless; but now, bursting from the deadly bands that 'bound them, With Styx nine times round them' my ideas float on winged words, and as they expand their plumes, catch the golden light of other years. My soul has indeed remained in its original bondage, dark, obscure, with longings infinite and unsatisfied . . . but that my understanding also did not remain dumb and brutish, or at length found a language to express itself, I owe to Coleridge. (17.107)

The aim of the mid-career essays I have discussed is, like the aim of much of Hazlitt's theatrical criticism, to explore the ways that cultural experience engages "that trembling sensibility which is awake to every change and every modification of its ever varied impressions" (8.82). The youthful dissenter Coleridge was the first to teach Hazlitt this lesson, a lesson he would in turn wield in his critique of Coleridge's later political and religious allegiances. Against the cloistered virtues of a clerisy preserving the nation's cultural tradition, Hazlitt imagines a dissident subject, a conversational critic at large, bringing news of himself to the people.

Works Cited

Barth, J. Robert, S.J. *Coleridge and Christian Doctrine*. New York: Fordham University Press, 1987.
Bate, Walter Jackson. *John Keats*. Cambridge, Mass.: Belknap, 1963.
Bromwich, David. *Hazlitt: The Mind of a Critic*. Oxford: Oxford University Press, 1983.
Cook, Jon. Introduction. *William Hazlitt: Selected Writings*. Ed. Jon Cook. Oxford: Oxford University Press, 1992.
Everest, Kelvin. *Coleridge's Secret Ministry: The Context of the Conversation Poems, 1795–98*. Sussex: Harvester, 1979.
Hazlitt, William. *The Complete Works of William Hazlitt*. 21 vols. Ed. P. P. Howe after the edition of A. R. Waller and Arnold Glover. New York: AMS Press, 1967.
Hume, David. *A Treatise of Human Nature*. Eds. David Fate Norton and Mary J. Norton. Oxford: Oxford University Press, 2000.

Jones, Stanley. *Hazlitt: A Life*. Oxford: Clarendon Press, 1989.
Kinnaird, John. *William Hazlitt: Critic of Power*. New York: Columbia University Press, 1978.
Klancher, Jon P. *The Making of English Reading Audiences, 1790–1832*. Madison: University of Wisconsin Press, 1987.
Mahoney, John L. *The Logic of Passion: The Literary Criticism of William Hazlitt*. New York: Fordham University Press, 1981.
Natarajan, Uttara. *Hazlitt and the Reach of Sense: Criticism, Morals, and the Metaphysics of Power*. Oxford: Clarendon Press, 1999.
Park, Roy. *Hazlitt and the Spirit of the Age*. Oxford: Clarendon Press, 1971.
Paulin, Tom. *The Day-Star of Liberty: William Hazlitt's Radical Style*. London: Faber and Faber, 1998.
Ryan, Robert. *The Romantic Reformation: Religious Politics in English Literature, 1789–1824*. Cambridge: Cambridge University Press, 1997.
Talfourd, Thomas Noon. *Critical and Miscellaneous Writings*. Boston: Phillips, Sampson, and Company, 1854.
White, Daniel E. "'Properer for a Sermon': Particularities of Dissent and Coleridge's Conversational Mode." *Studies in Romanticism* 40 (2001): 175–198.

11

Coleridge and De Quincey on Miracles

Frederick Burwick

IN THE GREAT CONTROVERSY over David Hume's account "Of Miracles" in *An Enquiry Concerning Human Understanding* (1748), the response of Samuel Taylor Coleridge has received but little attention, and the response of Thomas De Quincey even less.[1] What has been written of De Quincey's deliberations on miracles has been no more than incidental—mere mention in passing that essays concerned with revelation were among his writings in the 1840s. In his manuscript essay "On Miracles" (June 7, 1847) De Quincey promises an extended treatment of the topic. In a marginal note he cites that scene from *Timon of Athens* in which the lords and senators are seated at the banquet table expecting a sumptuous meal and praising their host as "the old man still" (III.vi.61). De Quincey apparently plans to combine his former idealism and present disillusion in a dual "mission." He and "the original man" will be a team: "You shall see both of us," he tells the reader, "rendering the heart of some old nuisances."[2] It is also useful to reex-

---

[1] *An Enquiry Concerning Human Understanding*, ed. L. A. Selby-Bigge (Oxford, 1902), cited hereafter as *Enquiry*. Concerning Coleridge's response to Hume, see J. Robert Barth, S.J., *Coleridge and Christian Doctrine* (Cambridge, Mass., 1969), 6–7, 37–42; Stephen Prickett, *Romanticism and Religion* (Cambridge, 1976), 44–45, 51–55, 61–64; Stephen Happel, *Coleridge's Religious Imagination* (Salzburg, 1983), 782–85; and Anthony Harding, *Coleridge and the Inspired Word* (Montreal, 1985), 39–40, 64, 76–77, 82–83. Despite an anonymous reviewer's assertion in 1861 that De Quincey's "reply to Hume upon miracles [...] well deserves the attention of students of divinity" (*Quarterly Review* 110 [July 1861]: 17–18), there has been no sustained study of De Quincey's religious thought and only a few references to his essay "On Miracles as Subjects of Testimony"; see Edward Sackville-West, *Thomas De Quincey: His Life and Works* (New Haven, 1936), 180, 245; and Horace Ainsworth Eaton, *Thomas De Quincey: A Biography* (London, 1936), 447.

[2] "On Miracles," Ms. Author's collection, Claremont, California. Curiously, Alexander Japp omits this and other passages from his edition of the *Posthumous Works*, 2 vols.

amine the manuscripts in appraising Coleridge's deliberations on miracles. Previous studies of Coleridge have given primary attention to the work following *The Statesman's Manual* (1816), and justly so, for it was the later Coleridge who influenced theological developments throughout the remainder of the century. However, the crucial terms in his analysis of miracles, to be examined here, were formulated much earlier. When he turned his attention to the Gospel of John in 1807, Coleridge put forth those arguments on the Johannine *logos* which were to have been elaborated as a major section of the *Opus Maximum*.[3]

Coleridge and De Quincey were fully aware of the vigorous rebuttal of Hume that had been put forth in the eighteenth century by David Hartley, George Campbell, James Beattie, and Joseph Priestley. That debate, both pro and con, was conducted on Enlightenment ground. Both Coleridge and De Quincey, of course, were outspoken opponents of the materialist and mechanist assumptions of Enlightenment philosophy. Reinterpreting the argument in Romantic terms, they sought to clear the faith in supernatural mystery from all taint of weak-minded credulity. Hume approaches the miracle as if it had to be documented as an historical event. Coleridge answers Hume by arguing that a miracle works subjectively rather than objectively. Endorsing a doctrine of immanence similar to Coleridge's definition of symbol, De Quincey insists upon the semiotic mediation of all humanly intelligible manifestations of the divine.

The primary source of knowledge, Hume states, is experience: "the evidence for the truth of our senses." While experience "must be acknowledged," it "is not altogether infallible." A range of experiences must be compared, and the ratio of instances that confirm our expectations against those that oppose them provides our sense of probability. Because the range of our experience is limited, we rely on testimony to extend our knowledge. Testimony, of course, must be subjected to the same standard of proof and probability. We must judge its validity in relation to our own experience and observation. A miracle, as defined by Hume, is "a violation of the laws of nature." Any testimony regarding a miracle, therefore, presents a paradox: "As a uniform experience amounts to a proof, there is here a direct and full *proof* from the nature

---

(London, 1891); see I, 175. *Posthumous Works* will be cited parenthetically hereafter as *PW*.

[3] I thank Thomas McFarland for allowing me to consult the magisterial commentary to his edition of Coleridge's *Opus Maximum* now in preparation.

of the fact, against the existence of any miracle; nor can such a proof be destroyed, or the miracle rendered credible, but by an opposite proof, which is superior." The very circumstances that the witness must cite as evidence that a miracle has actually occurred are circumstances that render his testimony untenable. Hume concludes, then, that "no human testimony can have such force as to prove a miracle, and make it a just foundation for any system of religion" (*Enquiry* 109–131).[4]

When Coleridge delivered his Bristol lectures in 1795, he adhered closely to the refutation of Hume in David Hartley's *Observations on Man* (1749) and William Paley's *Evidences of Christianity* (1794). From Hartley he borrowed the argument that the "laws of nature" have yet to be fully discerned by science:

> Nothing is more common or constant than the effect of Gravity in making all Bodies upon the surface of our Earth tend to its centre—yet the rare and extraordinary Influences of Magnetism and Electricity can suspend this Tendency. Now before Magnetism & Electricity were discovered and verified by a variety of concurrent facts, there would have been as much reason to disallow the evidence of their particular effects attested by Eyewitness, as there is now to disallow the particular Miracles recorded in the Scripture. (*Lects 1795* 160–161)[5]

Experience and probability, Hume's criteria, are only relative and may require radically different interpretation as new evidence emerges. In reiterating Hartley's position, Coleridge challenges Hume's definition of a miracle as "a violation of the laws of nature." An act of the divine will may well demonstrate laws with which we are not yet acquainted. Even when he goes on to state that Christ's "system of morality . . . carries with it an irresistible force of conviction, and is of itself in the

---

[4] Antony Flew, in *Hume's Philosophy of Belief* (London, 1961), 196–197, acknowledges Hume's overconfidence in the knowledge and science of his own age and his failure to appreciate development and change. He cites, as example, Herodotus' account of the Phoenician sailors who claimed to have circumnavigated Africa (c. 600 BC). Herodotus discredited their story: "On their return they declared—I for my part do not believe them, but perhaps others may—that in sailing round Africa they had the sun upon their right hand." The detail about the change in the relative position of the sun, which seemed unbelievable to Herodotus, is precisely the evidence which, in light of subsequent knowledge, validates their account.

[5] Parenthetical citations refer to standard editions of Coleridge's collected works, letters, and notebooks (see list of Works Cited). Abbreviations are *Aids to Reflection* (*AR*); *Biographia Literaria* (*BL*); *Collected Letters* (*CL*); *The Friend* (*FR*); *Lectures 1795: On Politics and Religion* (*Lects 1795*); *Marginalia* (*CM*); *Notebooks* (*CN*); *The Statesman's Manual* (*LS*).

most philosophical sense of the word a Miracle," Coleridge repeats the arguments of Hartley and Priestley against Hume. Unlike his eighteenth-century predecessors, however, Coleridge is already thinking of the miracle not so much as the act or the expression, but more as the idea and the incumbent power. The evidence for the miracle of inspiration is its self-propagation. In a perfect "system of morality" resides a miraculous power. "Is it a Miracle," Coleridge asks, "that Jesus should be able to effect it? And no Miracle that Matthew or Luke or men of obscurer name should possess the Power?"

When Coleridge writes to George Fricker (October 4, 1806), he confesses his own past Unitarian or Socinian beliefs and describes his reply "to a sceptical friend, who had been a Socinian, and of course rested all the evidences of Christianity on miracles" (*CL* II, 1189). As he describes his "reconversion" in the *Biographia Literaria* (1817), he had been a "zealous Unitarian" only in respect to natural religion and had always deemed "the *idea* of the Trinity a fair scholastic inference from the being of God, as a creative intelligence" (*BL* I, 204). Natural religion, as argued by Grotius and Paley, he gradually recognizes as reductively mechanistic and too much at odds with his own "metaphysical notions."[6] Thus, in recounting to Fricker the advice to his Socinian friend, he argues that Grotius and Paley would never have been so influential "if thinking men had been habitually led to look into their own souls, instead of always looking out, both of themselves, and of their nature" (*CL* II, 1189). Even if the account of miracles had been bolstered by "delusion" and by "exaggeration," he asserts that Christian doctrine would not be altered by demonstrating their falsehood. In matters of doctrine, "the miracles are extra essential." In matters of faith, however, they are by no means "superfluous." Perception of a miracle is a demonstration of faith: "Even as Christ did, so would I teach; that is, build the miracle on the faith, not the faith on the miracle" (*CL* II, 1190).[7]

Coleridge clearly has adopted a mode of reasoning very different from what he had used in the 1795 lectures. He has already formulated the idea that miracles operate through a bond of faith. As Robert Barth

---

[6] Kathleen Coburn, editor of Coleridge's *Notebooks*, observes that he frequently levels a combined attack against Grotius and Paley (see *CN* II, 2640, 3135; III, 3911ff.) as well as against Priestley and Paley (see *CN* II, 2509, 2640; III, 3817, 3897, 4312).

[7] Cf. Coleridge's letters to Mary Cruikshank (September 21, 1807, *CL* III, 26–28) and J. Morgan (January 7, 1818, *CL* IV, 796–799).

has described the major themes in Coleridge's discussion of miracles in *The Friend* (1818) and in subsequent unpublished letters and notebook entries, Coleridge totally controverted the mechanist reasoning in eighteenth-century apologetics. For the apologists, from Samuel Butler's *Analogy of Religion* (1736) through Paley's *Evidences of Christianity*, miracles (1) were "departures from the ordinary course of nature"; (2) "prove that God is master of His creation and testify that His revealed word is true"; and (3) "were taken to be directed more to unbelievers than to believers." Coleridge, however, held that the contraries to these are true: "(1) the contravention of a law of nature is not the essence of a miracle; (2) the essential significance of a miracle is its sign value; and (3) faith *precedes* the perception of a miracle, that is to say, recognition of a miracle as such is a result of faith rather than its cause" (Barth 38).[8]

In rejecting the materialist and mechanist grounds of eighteenth-century apologetics, Coleridge reinterpreted the meaning of "law of nature," provided a new definition of the sign as symbol, and grounded faith in the intuitive reason. To forge a new metaphysics capable of fortifying Christian faith, he turned, as we know, to Benedict de Spinoza, Immanuel Kant, and Friedrich Wilhelm Joseph von Schelling. This was problematic. Hume, after all, spoke of the "true atheism . . . for which *Spinoza* is so universally famous."[9] Kant, too, had been accused of undermining traditional theology. And Schelling posited a "World-Soul" and an "Absolute Identity," yet refused to locate it in the Godhead and consequently reverts to pantheism. Nevertheless, Coleridge drew from all three in interpreting the gospels and formulating his new account of the miraculous. As Thomas McFarland has shown, the philosophy of Spinoza and Schelling, no less than Unitarian and Socinian thought, left Coleridge trapped in the metaphysics of externality, the "it is."[10] The revisions in his thinking are first articulated or, I should say, are first documented in August 1807 at the time of his meeting with De Quincey and his "warm conversation" with Thomas Poole.

The "eloquent dissertation"[11] with which Coleridge entertained his

---

[8] Asserting that "Coleridge treats of miracles (and we confine our discussion to scriptural miracles, as Coleridge does) in only one of the works published during his lifetime," Barth refers to passages in *The Friend*. Another published commentary on scriptural miracles appears in *The Statesman's Manual* (see *LS* 10).

[9] *A Treatise of Human Nature*, 2nd ed., rev. P. H. Nidditch (Oxford, 1978) 240.

[10] *Coleridge and the Pantheist Tradition* (Oxford, 1969) 155–157.

[11] *The Collected Writings of Thomas De Quincey*, ed. David Masson, 14 vols. (Edinburgh, 1889–1890), II, 152. Cited parenthetically hereafter as *DQ*.

youthful auditor (Coleridge was thirty-seven; De Quincey, twenty-two) commenced, in response to De Quincey's gift of Hartley's *De Ideis* (1746), with a discussion of Hartley. Describing himself as "a reverential believer in the doctrine of the Trinity," one whose "mind almost demanded mysteries in so mysterious a system of relations as those which connect us with another world" (*DQ* II, 154), De Quincey declared that he fully expected to encounter in Coleridge—whom he revered as a poet—a Unitarian, a Socinian, and therefore, to De Quincey's mind, not a Christian. Nor was it any comfort to learn that Coleridge by this time had stepped within the circle of "the *alles-zermalmender*, the world-shattering Kant" (*DQ* II, 155).[12] To De Quincey's surprise, Coleridge "penitentially" (*DQ* II, 156) disowned his former Unitarianism and now declared himself a believer in prayer, which he defined not as a passive rumination but as "the total concentration of the faculties." The act of praying, he informed De Quincey, is "the very highest energy of which the human heart was capable."[13] Coleridge's theme, then, was religious experience. "For about three hours he had continued to talk," De Quincey recollects, "and in the course of this performance he had delivered many most striking aphorisms, embalming more weight of truth, and separately more deserving to be themselves embalmed, than would easily be found in a month's course of select reading" (*DQ* II, 157).

During this visit with Coleridge in 1807, De Quincey had been cordially received by Poole, a "polished and liberal Englishman." Poole, who possessed "a good library, superbly mounted in all departments bearing at all upon political philosophy" (*DQ* II, 141), frequently hosted evening discussions with Coleridge.[14] One of Coleridge's fullest statements on miracles is an outline recapitulating ten propositions he

---

[12] De Quincey appropriates the epithet *"alles-zermalmender* Kant" from Coleridge; originally bestowed by Moses Mendelssohn in the preface to *Morgenstunden, oder Vorlesungen über das Dasein Gottes* (1790), it is repeated in *Biographia Literaria* (II, 89).

[13] Cf. Coleridge on prayer (*LS* 55). In her note to Coleridge's account of prayer in 1808 as "a guard against Self-delusion" and "the sole instrument of regeneration" (*CN* III, 3355), Coburn observes that prayer, "probably a frequent topic with him," was often the subject of discussions with Lady Beaumont (*CN* III, 3355n.)

[14] Coleridge was absent at the time of De Quincey's arrival; with no other company at dinner, Poole launched a discussion *tête-à-tête* of Coleridge's "unacknowledged obligations." The conversation apparently concerned only a borrowed source in Coleridge's elucidation of a passage from Pythagoras. De Quincey departs from the narrative of his visit to interpose a lengthy digression on Coleridge's borrowings, most notably the "real and palpable plagiarism" from Schelling in *Biographia Literaria*.

had considered on one such evening. Poole wrote at the top of the manuscript: "The following was written by Coleridge after a warm conversation between him and me concerning miracles. Tho Poole Augst 1807."[15] As the manuscript makes clear, their discussion of miracles had focused specifically on John's report of "one casting out devils" (Mark 9: 38) in Christ's name. The first six propositions, however, deal generally with supernatural powers and the possibility of a demonic as well as a divine origin of miracles. The discussion throughout concerns miracles as performed through the agency of a miracle-worker.

Coleridge begins with the definition of a miracle as "that which appears . . . beyond the power of unassisted man," and he goes on to state that "the only necessary & universal consequence of the belief in a miracle . . . is that the performer either is [himself,] or is assisted by powers[,] more than human." The question then arises whether the sources of power are divine or demonic. Although Coleridge elsewhere resists such incipient Manichaeism (see *BL* I, 205; *CN* III, 4424), he here indulges the possibility of Satanic forces of darkness. The grounds for discrimination rest partly with God, partly with man. God, for His part, "would not permit either conspiracies of men of very superior knowledge, or evil spirits to produce those appearances, which must to men in a given state of knowledge inevitably be received as miraculous." Man, for his part, has an intuitive capacity to recognize the traces of divinity. Manifestations of the divine are perceived, explains Coleridge, much in the same way the ear experiences harmony in sound: ". . . supposing the parations of the Heart towards Doctrines thereby welcomed as soon as heard, almost even as an Ear acknowledges & welcomes harmony in sounds, demanding no extrinsic proof that it is harmony." One such doctrine, Coleridge maintains, is the divinity of Christ, "the assumption of human nature by the Eternal Mind." Once the harmony of such a doctrine is felt, "miraculous actions would be naturally anticipated, not as a cause of Faith, but as the *result* of it." Here is Coleridge's key proposition that miracles are perceived through faith: "The great Truths of Christianity are directly declared to be [the] inward result of a certain moral state, incipient at least, and to be a revelation from God to minds in that state."[16]

From these propositions Coleridge turns to his argument (with ref-

---

[15] "Memorandum on Miracles," Ms. 34, 225 ff. 75–75ᵛ, British Museum, London.
[16] Ms. "Memorandum on Miracles"; and see *CN* III, 3278n.

erence to John 6:37, 44–45, 65) that Christ uses his miracles to mediate rather than to demonstrate: "Christ asserts that none come to him but immediately led by God—he no where attests miracles as proofs of Doctrine." That wonders might be wrought for the purposes of evil, as Coleridge had considered in his third and fourth propositions, is directly addressed when the question is put to Christ, "Can a devil open the eyes of the blind?" (John 10: 21). Christ himself warns against the "many who shall come in my name, saying I am *Christ*; and shall deceive many" (Mark 13: 6; see also 21–22). To guard against the deception, one must simply distinguish the ends from the means. As Coleridge points out, Christ "states indeed more than once the benevolent application of these extraordinary powers as a proof, that the supernatural worker was not malignant or anti-moral." This, he reminds Poole, is the significance of the text they had discussed from Mark's Gospel: Christ "in our passage (the message to John) enumerates these applications, as a strong presumptive argument that the supernatural power which worked them was identical with that which was to come." Because Christ had already warned of those who would come in his name to practice deception, John is troubled by one whom he has seen "casting out devils in thy name." Christ reassures him, "Forbid him not: for there is no man which shall do a miracle in my name, that can lightly speak evil of me" (Mark 9:38–39).

Coleridge sees in this passage, then, confirmation of the crucial element in his case for miracles. Christ often makes explicit that having faith makes the miracle possible, even if that faith is no larger than a mustard seed. By contrast, he says, Christ "no where assigns a miracle as an argument for Christian Faith, and so far from working miracles to produce Faith he uniformly demands pre-existing Faith in him as a requisite of the miracle." Coleridge refers as well to Peter's affirmation of faith (Matt. 16: 16; Luke 9: 20): "It was not Christ's intention broadly to inforce on John, further than his own heart led him, an actual faith in his Incarnation & consequent Divinity, but when Peter (first of all) declared,—Christ blesses him with fervour." Faith must assert itself from within; it cannot be imposed from without. Peter's faith came through revelation, not from beholding "all the miracles." Through faith the incumbent power passes from Christ to the Apostles and multiplies among "men of obscurer name." Christ concludes his parable of the fig tree with the caveat that "no man, no, not even the angels of heaven" could command a power capable of preventing "the coming of the Son of man" (Matt. 24: 36–37). In Coleridge's interpretation we are thus forbidden "to believe even an Angel of Heaven / whatever miracles and however astonishing he might perform, if in confirmation of new doctrines." Although the possibility of doctrines being founded on miracles is "absurd," Coleridge concludes that it would be a very dangerous absurdity: "the notion that miracles can prove doctrines" would indeed justify fears of evil deception, for it would expose "human nature to every species of delusion & sensuality."[17]

Because of his emphasis on the mediating power of faith, it may seem strange that Coleridge chose to elaborate his case for the intersubjectivity of religious experience by turning to the only gospel that makes no mention of faith.[18] The word *faith* does not appear in the Gospel of John because faith is actively predicated in the Word. When the Word becomes flesh, faith is possible only as an act of believing—that is, as active engagement in the doing and suffering, the *to poiein* and *to pathein*, of Christ. It was most probably only after Coleridge had been wrestling with Schelling's arguments on the reconciliation of subject and object[19] that he began to see the profound metaphysical implications of the "Word" and the "I am" as set forth in John's Gospel. His discovery of these implications is recorded in his notebook entries during June 1810. His later intention, announced in the *Biographia Literaria*, to write "a full commentary on the Gospel of St. John" as part of his demonstration of Christianity as "the one true Philosophy" (*BL* I, 136)[20] clearly has its inception in his recognition

---

[17] Ms. "Memorandum on Miracles"; and see *CN* III, 3278n.

[18] This is not just a peculiarity of the King James Version: *pistis*, the Greek noun for "faith," occurs eight times in Matthew, five in Mark, eleven in Luke, and not at all in John; the adjective *pistos*, "faithful," occurs three times in Matthew and five in Luke. John relies exclusively on the verb *pisteuo*, "believe" which occurs 98 times in his text, as opposed to 35 times in the other three gospels.

[19] See *CN* III, 3764 (April–June 1810) and 3764n. Coleridge's poetic lines about "the body / Eternal Shadow of the finite Soul / The Soul's self-symbol" are related by Coburn to Coleridge's marginal gloss on Schelling in *Jahrbücher der Medicin* (1805–1808). Coburn also notes Coleridge's response to Schelling's efforts to reconcile body/soul and subject/object (*CN* III, 3875, 4176, 4265).

[20] Cf. Coleridge's letters to Daniel Stuart (September 12, 1814) and to John May (September 27, 1815) describing the projected "*Logosophia:* or on the Logos, divine and human, in six Treatises," the fourth part of which was to provide " full Commentary on the Gospel of St. John" (*CL* III, 554; IV, 589–590). In the introduction to his forthcoming edition of the *Opus Maximum* for *The Collected Works of Samuel Taylor Coleridge*, McFarland provides thorough commentary on Coleridge and the *logos*. Cf. *Coleridge and the Pantheist Tradition* 191–195.

that, long before Schelling, John had succeeded in revealing how the "mysterious End" of Christianity consists "in tying together the two separate portions of one truth in the schemes of Materialism & Immaterialism."

One of the peculiarities that he notes in the Gospel of John is the apparent desynonymization of "miracle" and "sign." He finds "something very stupendous" in John 6:30. Following the feeding of the five thousand, the crowd seeks Christ on the opposite side of the sea. Christ reproaches them: "Ye seek me, not because ye saw miracles, but because ye did eat of the loaves, and were filled" (John 6:26). Since this is the crowd "whom he had fed miraculously the day or two before," Coleridge observes, it is strange that they should now ask him for a sign: "What sign shewest thou then, that we may see, and believe thee? what dost thou work?" (John 6:30).

> Was it not natural for him to have referred to his stupendous miracles, done in their own presence, but a day or two before? Was it not natural for him to have shewn what so many of the Advocates of Christianity, have since done—that he had not only given signs & works as great as any of their prophets, even the greatest, are related to have done, but even greater, & more frequent? When he refuses *a sign*, he does not refuse it merely to the persons tempting him and as such unworthy of having a miracle wrought for their sakes (which is the common but insufficient solution) but to *this generation*—Shall we say, that a *sign* meant something very different from *a miracle!* (*CN* III, 3846)

Although "sign" and "miracle" are used interchangeably in the Synoptic Gospels, Coleridge argues that John discriminates the terms in order to avoid the possibility of equating miracle-worker with thaumaturgist.[21] This would explain, Coleridge argues, the "apparent discord between different sentiments of Jesus himself concerning these miracles, and the evident discord between his general Language, & that of the Truth of Gospel History."

In contrast to the Synoptic Gospels, John has reduced the number of miracles to seven. John's gospel stipulates an active believing, as Coleridge has already argued, for a miracle to be perceived. Only under these conditions can the message of the miracle, its inherent sign, be

---

[21] C. H. Dodd, in *The Interpretation of the Fourth Gospel* (Cambridge, 1953), similarly emphasizes the sign as distinguished from the miracle, describing the central narrative of Christ's teaching (John 2: 1–12: 50) as the Book of Signs.

understood. Coleridge thus relates the *semeion* to the *logos*. Where Matthew, Mark, and Luke tell of Christ born of the Virgin Mary in a stable in Bethlehem, John defines Christ as born of the divine *logos*, the Word that was with God and was God, who becomes the Word made flesh (see 1: 1, 14). Thus John provides, as Coleridge recognized, a reconciliation of subject and object, idea and matter. Rather than standing in polar opposition to the "it is" of Spinoza and Schelling, as McFarland maintains,[22] the "I am" permeates and transforms the "it is." As the Word become flesh, Christ asserts his presence as "I am": "Before Abraham was, I am" (8: 58). Again in contrast to the Synoptic Gospels, the Christ of John's text teaches not in parables but in metaphors of the self. Self-presentation is the tool of his teaching: "I am the bread of life" (6: 35); "I am the light of the world" (8: 12); "I am one that bear witness of myself" (8: 18); "I am from above" (8: 23); "I am the door" (10: 7, 9); "I am the good shepherd" (10: 11, 14); "I am the resurrection, and the life" (11: 25); "I am the way, the truth, and the life" (14: 6); "I am the true vine" (15: 1).

Proposing that Christianity achieves its "mysterious End" by reconciling "the schemes of Materialism & Immaterialism," Coleridge claims that Christ in the Gospel of John gives primacy to the sign, not the miracle. The failure to see the sign is a persistent problem. The crowd that saw the miracle and ate the loaves still craved for the sign that they failed to see. Can there be any sign more profound or more self-evident, Coleridge asks, than Christ himself as the sign, the divine *logos* become flesh and blood?

> To give a flesh-and-blood reality to those processes of the rational and moral Being, which considered as abstractly intellectual, thin away into eternal notions, that remaining always the same, partake not of the life and change of material forms, which belong equally to all, faintly interest any, and from their very permanence and independence possess the weakest affinity with Fear, or Hope, or Love? (*CN* III, 3847)

Christ is that Word which is at once signifier and thing signified. His great task as teacher is to communicate that Word, to make the "I am" apparent and accessible. Thus he teaches in terms of his own body.

---

[22] McFarland continues to discuss the polarity of "it is" and "I am" throughout his chapter on "The Trinitarian Resolution." *Coleridge and the Pantheist Tradition* 191–255, esp. 195–197, 200–203, 210, 216; see also 373–374 for his note on the Gospel of John.

Christ's body, as the self-referential Word, is at once human and divine. In his effort to explain this notion of the word containing its own truth, Coleridge later, in *The Statesman's Manual,* defines "symbols" as "tautegorical" and "consubstantial with the truths, of which they are the conductors" (*LS* 29). Here, too, he discusses the "sign" as "symbol" mediating its own meaning. Christ's "body" does not simply refer to but *is* the life and the soul; moreover, because of the Word within the word, it *is* eternal life and salvation. He is "the Teacher and the Doctrine, the Giver and the Gift":

> Whether Christ's Discourses do not in a constant vein of peculiar Thought imply, that the growth, diseases, and restoration of the Soul are not merely analogous to those of the Body, as ideas to their appointed Symbols (i.e. by a factitious analogy, the work of association) but strictly so, as things of one class to things of another, in the linked ascent of creation?— Whether the plain purpose of John VI. be not to establish that *specific* difference between Christ and all other Delegates from Heaven, before & after him, that the faithful believe *them,* i. e. receive their *doctrines* as true and of divine Authority, but they not only are to believe Christ, but to believe in Christ—He is at once the Teacher and the Doctrine, the Giver and the Gift. (*CN* III, 3847)

In yet another contrast to the Synoptic Gospels, John omits the narrative of the Last Supper. Or rather, Coleridge argues, John replaces it with the eucharistic discourse beginning, "I am the bread of life" (John 6:35). The mediating Word absorbs whoever speaks it, knowing its meaning, into its meaning. The eucharistic mystery is not simply the presence of the body of Christ in the bread, but the presence of Christ in the body of whoever consumes it.

> These mysterious declarations in this Chapter so evidently connected with the miracle of the Loaves & Fishes narrated in the beginning of the Chapter, & seemingly, like the rest of Christ's miracles, bearing an intentional symbolical analogy to the declarations which follow as avowed comments on that miracle, and lastly, this Chapter considered as a *substitute for* the Texts in the three other Evangelists relating the institution of the Lord's Supper accounts for & alone can count for, the beloved Disciple's Silence on this institution. (*CN* III, 3847)

For Coleridge, then, John transcends the historical sequence of the Synoptic Gospels. The entire narrative of the Last Supper, crucifixion, and resurrection is subsumed in the discourse of the "living bread."

More important, that abyss between phenomenon and noumenon, which Kant had declared unbridgeable, is bridged.

> Remember, that flesh & blood as phenomena, must have a supporting Noumenon—that it does not follow, that the Noumenon remaining, the Phenomenon should likewise remain / that this is proved myriadfold in Chemistry & Physiology—and Scripturally evinced by the changes in the phenomena of Christ's Body after the Resurrection, which yet we are bound to believe *persisted* as his Body—. Remember too, that Christ's Body, as represented to the Eye, was a Phenomenon—but that the Body = Noumenon, with which the Logos was united, so becoming incarnate, was Human *Nature*—a mysterious thing, whose boundaries & laws of individualism we know not / assuredly, as a Noumenon, it is not bound to the conditions of Space. (*CN* III, 3847)

Although John affirms that in the Word made flesh the numinous becomes directly accessible through the phenomenal, the intuitive reason cannot reach beyond mere speculation into the mystery of God incarnate. The spiritual truth is accessible, even among the immediate witnesses of Christ, only to the willing believer. Scriptural evidence brings us this close, and no closer, to philosophical resolution.

The scriptural evidence, however, is at odds with the Socinian interpretation. Coleridge calls attention to the passage in which Paul tells Timothy that the "great . . . mystery" of God "manifest in the flesh" is "without controversy." God incarnate, writes Paul, was "seen of angels" (1 Tim. 3:16). If Christ was merely a man divinely inspired, "*psilos anthropos*," Coleridge asks, what could be the significance or purport of this passage? "What could the Angels *see* that men could not? But if it were *o theanthropos*, God incarnate, then indeed Angels *might* SEE, i.e. have a direct and *intuitive* knowledge of what men could only infer discursively & know by faith" (*CN* III, 3857). Throughout the notebook entries for June 1810 Coleridge grapples with scriptural references to miracles and Christ's divinity.[23] Although he acknowledges that a philosophical proof cannot be extrapolated from the Bible, he is firmly convinced that Hume's attack on miracles as well as the whole company of refutations, from Hartley to Paley, belabored the mere externalities. The true province of miracles is internal and subjective.

---

[23] See *CN* III, 3846–3847, 3886–3889, 3892–3893, 3897 (June 1810); also II, 3022 (February–March 1807), 3135 (September 1807), 3231 (1807–1810); III, 3278 (February–March 1808), 4249 (May 1815), 4381 (January 1818), and 4451–4452 (October 1818).

In *The Statesman's Manual* Coleridge describes the internalizing of the miracle as a necessary process of intellectual development. When superstitious credulity prevailed, man externalized his hopes and fears, seeking "the true cause and origin of public calamities in outward circumstances." The religion of superstition is idolatry. Thus "signs and wonders were requisite in order to startle and break down that superstition. This meant that miracles could not work as mere physical phenomena, but must also prompt revelation: "With each miracle worked there was a truth revealed, which thence forward was to act as its substitute." To think of a miracle only as a powerful and strange physical event is to "degrade ourselves," to succumb to the superstitious credulity that keeps us "mere slaves of sense and fancy" (*LS* 9). Revelation liberates. Miracles are properly understood, then, as a medium for communicating "spiritual truth." "It was only to overthrow the usurpation exercised in and through the senses, that the senses were miraculously appealed to." Once we see the meaning in the miracle, the language of the sense is fully translated into the language of symbols. This language, as Coleridge demonstrates in the Gospel of John, is self-referential: "Reason and Religion are their own evidence." Appropriating the language of symbol, Coleridge shows how "the natural Sun" reveals "the spiritual." Once the truth is revealed, miracles become superfluous:

> And if we neglect to apply truths in expectation of wonders, or under pretext of the cessation of the latter, we tempt God and merit the same reply which our Lord gave to the Pharisees on a like occasion. "A wicked and an adulterous generation seeketh after a sign, and there shall no sign be given to it, but the sign of the prophet Jonas": that is, a threatening call to repentance. (*LS* 10)

The great error in previous efforts to refute Hume had been the appeal to natural evidence which failed to give proper credence to the power of revelation. Because the great spiritual truths cannot be communicated in mechanical and material terms, the whole endeavor from Hartley to Paley to explain the prophecies and miracles was misdirected.

What were "the Wheels which Ezekial beheld, when the hand of the Lord was upon him"? Coleridge assures us that they were symbols, "at once Pictures and Ideals." As opposed to *allegory* (Coleridge retains the Greek sense of *allos* and *agoreuo* > to gather from elsewhere; *allegoreo* > to convey a meaning other than the literal one), a *symbol is* tautegorical—that is, it conveys its own meaning but with a difference. The difference is achieved by the "translucence" of the symbol which allows the "Ideal" to radiate through the "Picture." Thus the symbol reveals "the Special in the Individual," or "the Universal in the General, and, above all, "the Eternal through and in the Temporal" (*LS* 29–30, 73, 79). Now, this is a beautiful possibility, but how does it work? Coleridge seems to be begging the question: miracles reveal spiritual truths, symbols radiate ideal meanings; but to understand the one or the other, you must first have faith. Nor can it be a passive faith; you must actively believe in order to perceive. Upon what spiritual truth do you found the faith that will enable you to comprehend spiritual truths?

There is a spiritual truth, already resident in our intuition, which must be imparted to our consciousness or, to be more explicit, to our conscience. When Coleridge compared our recognition of truth to musical harmony, he had in mind the accord between intuition and the immanent workings of God in nature. This, of course, was the argument of "The Eolian Harp" (1796), in which the pantheistic implications are averted with Sara's look of "mild reproof" and the poet's disavowal. In his essay on "Spiritual Truths and the Understanding" (1818) he sustains orthodoxy by insisting upon the "I am" as focal point. The confluence, then, occurs not to passive "Harps . . . / That tremble into thought" when played upon by the "intellectual breeze." It results only from a willing conviction.[24] Coleridge asks "whether miracles can, of themselves, work a true conviction on the mind?" The answer is conditional, for "there are spiritual truths which must derive their evidence from within." The act of praying, he had told De Quincey, is "the very highest energy of which the human heart was capable." The "true *efficient* conviction of a moral truth," he writes in *The Friend*, "collects the energies of a man's whole being in the focus of the conscience." The spiritual truth that exists within asserts itself through our moral sensibility. Rising from the hidden regions of intuition, moral truth manifests itself with conviction in our conscience. And this, he declares, is "the one essential miracle"—the miracle of "that leading of the Father, without which no man can come to Christ" (cf. John 6: 37, 44–45, 65). Coleridge derives from the Gospel of John "that implication of doctrine in the miracle, and of miracle in the doc-

---

[24] Frederick Burwick, *The Damnation of Newton: Goethe's Color Theory and Romantic Perception* (Berlin, 1986), 249–254.

trine, which is the bridge of communication between the senses and the soul" (*FR* I, 431).

The bridge between "the senses and the soul," the "it is" and the "I am," does not connect two discrete spaces. The two are coincident. The bridge is merely a metaphysical bridge that enables thought to pass from one to the other. Coleridge explains the connection in his "Essay on the Principles of Method":

> Hast thou ever raised thy mind to the consideration of EXISTENCE, in and by itself, as the mere act of existing? Hast thou ever said to thyself thoughtfully, IT IS! heedless in that moment, whether it were a man before thee, or a flower, or a grain of sand? Without reference, in short, to this or that particular mode or form of existence? If thou hast indeed attained to this, thou wilt have felt the presence of a mystery, which must have fixed thy spirit in awe and wonder. The very words, There is nothing! or, There was a time, when there was nothing! are self-contradictory There is that within us which repels the proposition with as full and instantaneous light, as if it bore evidence against the fact in the right of its own eternity.
>
> Not TO BE, then, is impossible: TO BE, incomprehensible. (*FR* I, 514)

The intuition of the "it is" as "absolute existence" leads irresistibly to contemplation of an informing and sustaining power, the "I am." No mode or method of reasoning directs the steps by which we come to this truth. It is a truth that "manifests itself," a revelation. Coleridge repeats here his argument that the means to spiritual truth resides *a priori* within the intuition. He grants, nevertheless, that the truth must unfold historically and culturally. Relative to our state of learning, we "move progressively toward that divine idea." As truth is divine revelation, so progress is divine intervention.

When John Henry Newman some twenty-five years later proposed the relevance of historical to religious development, he emphasized the way in which man's learning could reveal more and more of the original truths of biblical revelation (Prickett 55–56, 161–170). Coleridge sees the historical progression itself as revelation. The laws which govern "man's development and progression" derive from the *a priori* structures of the mind. Understanding and fancy, directly stimulated through the senses, are the first to be nurtured. When they interpret the intuition of divinity, they inevitably "break and scatter the one divine and invisible life of nature into countless idols of the sense." Thus it was that "men sent by God have come with signs and wonders" to break down the superstitious idolatry of the senses (*FR* I, 518*)*. Reiterating this argument from *The Statesman's Manual*, Coleridge declares that "in the case of miracles . . . wisdom forbids her children to antedate their knowledge, or to act and feel otherwise, or further than they know." The idea may be derived from Hartley, as Coleridge had earlier used it in his lectures of 1795, but he has added a remarkable philosophical refinement. While natural phenomena at large reveal the laws of science, God's presence in nature reveals the laws of mind. As our understanding of both progresses, we will come to perceive miracles not in terms of external nature but as revelations of the capacities of intuitive reason:

> What we now consider as miracles in opposition to ordinary experience, we should then reverence with a yet higher devotion as harmonious parts of one great complex miracle, when the antithesis between experience and belief would itself be taken up into the unity of intuitive reason. (*FR* I, 519)

By appealing thus to historical development and a progressive maturation from faith to reason, Coleridge conveniently postpones the resolution of his argument. The history of philosophy remains conditional and inconclusive in recording the permutations of the essential spiritual truth, the "I am" in the "it is." Philosophy begins in wonder, Coleridge says, and ends in wonder. In the meantime we fill the interspace with admiration and content ourselves with symbols which seem to conjure the mystery of immanence.[25]

In contrast to Coleridge, De Quincey in his analysis of miracles never labors to construct an epistemology of intuition and intersubjectivity. As he had acknowledged on the occasion of his first meeting with Coleridge, his "mind almost demanded mysteries in so mysterious a system of relations as those which connect us to another world." Because he accepted the mind's impulsive quest of the mysterious *nexus* between the natural and the supernatural world, De Quincey never struggled with the metaphysics of the relationship. Himself a dedicated dreamer with "a constitutional determination to reverie," he was more inclined to perceive the dream as an external world rather than as an

---

[25] Cf. *FR* I, 519 and *AR* 185: "In Wonder all Philosophy began: in Wonder it ends: and Admiration fills up the interspace."

internal construct of the mind. Thus, too, supernatural manifestations of the divine belong to "another world" which is not merely connected to, but coincident with, and sometimes visibly manifest in this world. While Coleridge endeavors to bring all external traces of the miraculous into the internal space of "spiritual truth," De Quincey allows for a subtle cooperation between the internal and the external. He agrees with Coleridge, however, in attributing the essential power of miracles to the inherent "symbol" or sign.

De Quincey seems to have borrowed Coleridge's definition of the symbol as tautegorical—that is, "expressing the same subject but with a difference" (*LS* 30; cf. *AR* 199). For Coleridge, the symbol is akin to that "imperceptible infusion" of creative presence which distinguishes an "imitation" from a mere "copy" (*BL* I, 76; II, 43, 76, 212). For De Quincey, too, the co-presence of identity and alterity is a crucial attribute of all art. In his marginalia to Jacob Böhme, Coleridge explains the tri-unity of the Word that is God, the Word that is with God, and the Word become flesh (John 1:1, 14): "with God" is the copula which combines the first—itself God, or *Idem*—and the last, *Alter*, or God become Other (*CM* I, 690; cf. II, 33). Commenting on the connection of faith with power as proclaimed by Christ in the passage concerning "faith as a grain of mustard seed" (Matt. 17:20, Luke 17:6), Coleridge responds that there is "no proper allegorism in Scripture / *tauto en genei allo* solum in gradu *alla agoreī*" (*CM* I, 690). De Quincey similarly describes symbolic action as *idem in alio* (*DQ* I, 51; see also V, 237; X, 369; XI, 195–196). In its simplest formulation "sameness in difference" is the principle that renders a marble statue aesthetically more dynamic than Madame Tussaud's most lifelike wax figure. The wax mimics the flesh all too well: the difference is wanting. *Idem in alio* is what enables the whole to express more than the sum of its parts. A symbol reveals more than it means.

> One part of the effect from the symbolic is dependent upon the great catholic principle of the *Idem in alio*. The symbol restores the theme, but under new combinations of form or colouring; gives back, but changes; restores, but idealizes. (*DQ* I, 51)

The language of symbol thus has a power to transcend the limits of reason, to reach beyond experience, and to draw, like dreams, from a spiritual world. The "interlusory revealings of the symbolic" thus evoke *idem in alio*, "the solemn remembrances that lie hidden below."

What is involved in interpreting a report beyond the limits of reason and ordinary experience is explicitly developed in De Quincey's response to Hume's refutation of miracles. It has been said that De Quincey simply adapted the arguments against Hume from George Campbell's *Dissertation on Miracles* (1762). This opinion misses the deliberately precarious reasoning of "Miracles as Subjects of Testimony" (1839). The key word of the title is not "Miracles" but "Testimony"—not whether miracles occur but the presumptions of their record. De Quincey's essay, then, is about rhetoric. The crux of Hume's refutation, he says, is the problem of language: "Besides the objection to miracles that they are not capable of attestation, Hume's objection is not that they are false, but that they are incommunicable." To summarize Hume's argument in "Of Miracles," De Quincey uses a mathematical formula[26] of plus and minus factors as an apt, and perhaps ironic, way to reflect Hume's concern with measuring the credibility of any report, pro or con, on a supposedly miraculous moment of divine intervention:

> Assume the resistance to credibility in any preternatural occurrence as equal to x, and the very ideal or possible value of human testimony as no more than x: in that case, under the most favorable circumstances conceivable, the argument for and against a miracle, $+x$ and $-x$, will be equal; the values will destroy each other, the result will be $= 0$.
>
> But, inasmuch as this expresses the value of human testimony in its highest or ideal form,—a form which is seldom realized in experience,—the true result will be different: there will always be a negative result, much or little according to the circumstances, but in any case enough to turn the balance against believing a miracle. (*DQ* VIII, 157)

As De Quincey rightly points out, Hume does not deny the possibility of miracles. He denies, rather, the credibility of any witness seeking to give testimony that a miracle occurred. De Quincey's strategy is to shift the emphasis from historical to rhetorical, from verifying to persuading. There are only three circumstances, De Quincey notes, in which a miracle might be witnessed:

1. It might happen in the presence of a single witness,—that witness not being ourselves. . . .

---

[26] In his preface Masson apparently has this formula in mind when he objects that De Quincey's "counter-argument . . . is decidedly supersubtle,—too fine-spun and algebraic to be really effective" (*DQ* VIII, 4).

2. It might happen in the presence of many witnesses,—witnesses to a variable amount, but still (as before) ourselves not being amongst that multitude. . . .
3. It might happen in our own presence, and fall within the direct light of our own consciousness. (*DQ* VIII, 158)

Hume's argument addresses only the problems of communication attending the first of these three cases. The third case is irrelevant to Hume's argument because personal experience eliminates the need to determine the reliability of the witness or the validity of the communication. The second case seems to be pondered in Hume's fictitious example of the resurrection of Queen Elizabeth. Hume's supposed witnesses to this miracle are the Queen's physicians, who might well be suspected of collusion. De Quincey objects that Hume has thus excluded the strength of corroboration: "Though three or four nominally, virtually they are but one man." If Hume seriously wanted to entertain a case of multiple witnesses, why not, De Quincey suggests, "call in the whole Privy Council—or the Lord Mayor and Common Council of London, the Sheriffs of Middlesex, and the Twelve Judges?" (*DQ* VIII, 160).

In constructing his refutation De Quincey begins by noting that Hume has excluded corroborative testimony. He then observes that Hume has given no thought to various kinds of miracles. The basic discrimination, for De Quincey, involves internal and external miracles. By inner miracles he means those that occur "within the separate personal consciousness of each separate man." He lists three sorts of inner miracles: special providence, grace, and the efficacy of prayer. While many "philosophic Christians doubt or deny" special providence, the divine agency of both grace and prayer is basic to Christianity (*DQ* VIII, 163–164). Hume's argument, since it addresses only the communication of miracles among men, does not bother with miracles of spiritual communion. External miracles De Quincey divides into two sorts: "1. *Evidential* miracles, which simply *prove* Christianity; [and] 2. *Constituent* miracles, which, in a partial sense, *are* Christianity, as in part composing its substance." Of the latter order he insists upon "the miraculous birth of our Saviour, and his miraculous resurrection" (*DQ* VIII, 165).

The evidential miracles, De Quincey observes, were "occasional and polemic." Their whole function was "to meet a special hostility incident to the birth-struggles of a new religion." Hume's argument, therefore, is paradoxical and belated: paradoxical because, no matter how it might be judged by eighteenth-century criteria, the testimony as originally communicated was indeed highly effective; and belated because "a Christianised earth never can want polemic miracles again." Even if "Hume's argument were applicable in its whole strength to the evidential miracles, no result of any importance could follow." They have already worked their purpose in that early history when people of faith struggled under "a dominant idolatry" (*DQ* VIII, 166).

Although De Quincey thus dismisses the relevance of the argument against evidential miracles, an adequate answer to Hume still requires a defense of the constituent miracles, the miracles so essential to the faith that they are codified in the Nicene Creed. Hume held that the constituent miracles, however sacrosanct, were subject to the same criteria of analysis as any other claimed aberration of natural law. His fictitious resurrection of Queen Elizabeth is fully intended to duplicate the problems of witness and testimony accompanying the resurrection of Christ. Even in multiplying the factorial value of the testimony of the Apostles and reducing the testimony of the court physicians to a factor of one, De Quincey plays a game of numbers that leaves his rebuttal trapped by Hume's demand for material evidence. He seeks to avoid this trap by proposing two modes of valuation, *a priori* and *a posteriori*. In contrast to Coleridge, De Quincey does not avail himself of the Kantian application of these terms.

The *a posteriori* valuation of testimony, De Quincey asserts, derives from the detection of motives that influence our judgment. An "abstract resistance to credibility," De Quincey grants, has abundant historical justification in pagan cultures, where supernatural events were proclaimed on behalf of "ostentation" or "ambition." Magical phenomena, if not "blind accidents," were surely "blank expressions of power." The miracles of Christianity, by contrast, always have a moral purpose. As the temptations of Christ demonstrate, the miracles of his advent deliberately counter all claims to material power. Whereas the providence of Christ's miracles is exclusively moral, "to any other wielder of supernatural power, real or imaginary, it never had occurred, by way of pretence even, that he had a moral object" (*DQ* VIII, 169).

The *a priori* valuation also has abundant justification, not merely in the history of man but in the natural history of life itself.

> Upon any hypothesis, we are driven to suppose—and compelled to suppose—a miraculous state as introductory to the earliest state of nature. The planet, indeed, might form itself by mechanical laws of motion, repulsion, attraction, and central forces, but man could not. Life could not. (*DQ* VIII, 171)

God is "always already" present. This same sense of temporal priority informs Jesus' declaration: "Before Abraham was, I am." An *a priori* mode of apprehending events is relevant to the gradual unfolding of both natural history and human history. Thus the great prophets could predict accurately events to come because they perceived the divine purpose. De Quincey cites the desolation of Babylon, fulfilling Isaiah's prophecy, as an *a posteriori* miracle demonstrating an *a priori* miracle.

De Quincey's final argument in "Miracles as Subjects of Testimony" is his crucial argument against Hume, and it is the one to which he returns in subsequent discussions of miracles. The very definition of God is predicated on "a *power* to work miracles." The notion of God's "breaking" nature's law, which Hume had assumed as the necessary condition of miracles, is a paradox. Nature's laws are God's laws. The latter works through the former: the *natura naturans* is manifest in the *natura naturata*, to use the phrase Coleridge frequently quoted from Spinoza. Coleridge had followed Hartley in equating divine will and natural law.[27] De Quincey differs only in insisting upon the limits: advances in science can never allow more than a glimpse at the grandeur of infinite mystery. From a finite human vantage, science reveals only partially and obliquely those laws by which the divine will manifests itself. In terms of consequence, *a posteriori* the constituent miracles function "to revolutionise the moral nature of man"; in terms of origin, *a priori* the constituent miracles reveal an immediate and direct act of the divine will. They are manifest in the natural world yet independent of natural causality. Because they proceed from the will rather than from nature, the birth and resurrection of Christ are best understood as an *epigenesis*, as reaffirmation on behalf of the moral order of humanity of that very act of genesis which brought nature and man into being (*DQ* VIII, 173–175).

Even before Newman aroused the controversy over "development," De Quincey had already formulated his own notion on the progress of

---

[27] See David Hartley, *Observations on Man*, 3 vols. (1749; London 1801), II, 242; and Coleridge, *Lects 1795*, I, 11–16.

human intellect as an organic revelation of inherent and persisting truths. His conviction that man cooperates in expanding revelation prompts him to reverse the strategy that had informed Hume's *The Natural History of Religion* (1757). In tracing the development of man's beliefs, Hume acknowledged two sources of religion: "its foundation in reason" and "its origin in human nature" (24). A third source, God's revelation to mankind, is historically excluded by the "universal" polytheism of early religion. Even the second, human reason, must be deemed a fairly late addition to an historical record dominated by irrationality and corruption. De Quincey, although capable of little tolerance toward pagan and non-Christian cultures, looks far more approvingly than Hume upon man's irrationality.

"Modern Superstition," which appeared in *Blackwood's Edinburgh Magazine* (April 1840) ten months after "Miracles as Subjects of Testimony," continues the deliberation on miracles. "It is said continually that the age of the miraculous and supernatural is past," De Quincey states in a typically polemical opening. "I deny that it is so in any sense which implies this age to differ from all other generations of man except one." In response to God's continuing revelation, man has gradually strengthened his capacities to perceive the divine presence. Man's greatest asset in perceiving the divine has never been his reason but rather his superstition. Careful to rid the word of its grosser implications of credulity and delusion, De Quincey specifies that he means superstition "in the sense of sympathy with the invisible." As such, superstition is no hindrance to the progress of humanity. It is rather "the great test of man's grandeur" which enables him to reconcile the "earthly" and "celestial." Not only does it make available "the possibility of religion," De Quincey confidently declares, but as long as it is allowed to express itself superstition will always and inevitably "pass into pure forms of religion as man advances" (*DQ* VIII, 404). Nor is it easy to dismiss "all silent incarnations of miraculous power." Nature sometimes seems to mimic the human sympathies with peculiar precision as, for example, when "we see lineaments of faces and forms in petrifactions, in variegated marbles, in spars or in rocky strata, which our fancy interprets as once having been real human existences, but which are now confounded with the very substance of a mineral product. Taking on the characteristics of immanence which Coleridge attributed to symbols, such natural phenomena seem to occupy "a midway station between the physical and hyperphysical." Because the illusion of intelligent agency appears incontrovertible, De Quincey declares: "The stream of the miraculous is here confluent with the stream of the natural" (*DQ* VIII, 410).

Following the completion of *The Logic of Political Economy* (1844) and *Suspiria de profundis* (1845), De Quincey returned to the problem of miracles and divine providence. His thinking on these topics had been rekindled by Newman's *An Essay on the Development of Christian Doctrine* (1845). De Quincey wrote a series of papers on Newman's concept of "development," which he intended to bring together in a book on "Christianity in Relation to Human Development" (see *PW* I, xiv). In the manuscript "On Miracles" (June 7, 1847) De Quincey revealed his preparation for a major work on inspiration and development to be completed within five years. His chronic indigestion and loss of appetite, he tells his daughter Margaret (June 10, 1847), drive him to complete this new project:

> To be a great philosopher, it is absolutely necessary to be famished. My intellect is far too electric in its speed, and its growth of flying armies of thoughts entirely new. I could spare enough to fit a nation. This secret lies—not, observe, in my hair; cutting off that does no harm; it lies in my want of dinner, as also of breakfast and supper. Being famished, I shall show this world of ours in the next five years something that it never saw before.[28]

De Quincey, like Coleridge, constructed many more projects in his imagination than he ever brought to paper. But a good number of his essays, published and unpublished, clearly contributed to the planned work on inspiration and development. Among the first installments he wrote "On Christianity as an Organ of Political Movement" (April–June 1846) to examine the ways in which religion has shaped political history.

Just two years earlier Karl Marx had declared that "Religion . . . is the opium of the people,"[29] and others had blamed the Church for preaching passivity to the masses to render them docile to exploitation by the ruling class. De Quincey tries to turn the indictment around, not by denying corruption within the Church but by insisting that

---

[28] H. A. Page (pseud. Alexander H. Japp), *Thomas De Quincey: His Life and Writings with Unpublished Correspondence* (New York, 1877), I, 343.

[29] *Critique of the Hegelian Philosophy of Right*, Karl Marx and Friedrich Engels, *Collected Works*, vol. 3 (New York, 1975), 175.

the indictment itself is evidence of the moral benevolence of Christian doctrine: "Hence it has happened sometimes that minds of the highest order have entered into enmity with the Christian faith, have arraigned it as a curse to man, and have fought against it even upon Christian impulses (impulses of benignity that could not have had birth except in Christianity)" (*DQ* VIII, 207–208). The secret workings of Christianity, propagated as spiritual values, are always benevolent; the public workings, entangled in the material concerns of property and production, are often swayed by selfish interests. Even the latter, however, are held in check by the inspirational and doctrinal aspects of religion. Why, then, slavery? Why war among Christian nations? De Quincey confidently endorses the progress of social morality under Christian guidance. His own age had participated in the abolition of slavery, had contributed to the founding of charitable institutions, and had witnessed an expanding "*social* influence of woman" (*DQ* VIII, 233). He had no way of knowing, of course, that the twentieth century would be violently shaken by two global wars, but he did observe international tensions in his own day that required him to temper his optimism: "Shall I offend the reader by doubting after all, whether war is not an evil still destined to survive through several centuries?" To bring about "the final step for its extinction," De Quincey says, the world must cooperate in ratifying "a new and Christian code of international law" (*DQ* VIII, 236).

The essay "Protestantism" (November–December 1847) is a reply to *A Vindication of Protestant Principles* (1847), a tract by John W. Donaldson, which in turn is a response to Newman's *An Essay on the Development of Christian Doctrine*. Although he agrees with the author's position on inspiration, De Quincey takes him to task for his opposition to Newman's doctrine of development. Inspiration and development, De Quincey maintains, are fully compatible. Both the manner and matter of inspiration altered historically from the time of Moses and the Prophets to the time of Jesus and the Apostles. Not only the writing but also the interpretation of the text may be inspired and similarly subject to historical change. As Stephen Prickett (54–55) has shown, Coleridge preceded Newman in arguing the progressive unfolding of biblical thought. De Quincey, who had already adopted with Coleridge the basic hermeneutical idea that meanings could lie latent in a text until advances in knowledge made them accessible, readily endorses Newman's argument.

Donaldson's tract defines three basic attributes of Protestantism: "the sole sufficiency of Scripture, the right of private judgment in its interpretation, and the authority of individual conscience in matters of religion" (*DQ* VIII, 250). By insisting on individual rights, the Protestant Reformation gave intellectual dimension to the political concern with legal rights. These rights also required a new tolerance and a new intellectual responsibility. The problem, as Donaldson sees it, is that intellectual right and responsibility lead to an inevitable confrontation between religion and science.

> That we stand on the brink of a great theological crisis, that the problem must soon be solved how far orthodox Christianity is possible for those who are not behind their age in scholarship and science: this is a solemn fact, which may be ignored by the partisans of short-sighted bigotry, but which is felt by all, and confessed by most of those who are capable of appreciating its reality and importance. The deep sibylline vaticinations of Coleridge's philosophical mind, the practical workings of Arnold's religious sentimentalism, and the open acknowledgment of many divines who are living examples of the spirit of the age, have all, in different ways, foretold the advent of a Church of the Future.[30]

Such is the crisis. In confronting it, Donaldson apparently wants the Church of the Future to resist rather than build upon change. His "secret purpose," De Quincey observes, is to report "the latest novelties that have found a roosting-place in the English Church, amongst the most temperate of those churchmen who keep pace with modern philosophy." Tolerance toward these forces of change, Donaldson seems to be urging, should not be led to sanction change. He attempts to show, De Quincey says, "how far it is possible that strict orthodoxy should bend, on the one side, to new impulses, derived from an advancing philosophy, and yet, on the other side, should reconcile itself, both verbally and in spirit, with ancient standards" (*DQ* VIII, 262). The Church should remain, then, a repository of sameness amidst difference.

One means of holding onto that sameness is through the appeal to the inspiration of the Bible. Here De Quincey agrees with Donaldson in opposing "Bibliolatry," the fundamentalist insistence on the literal truth of "the Bible as the Word of God." He distinguishes between "inspiration as attaching to the separate words and phrases of the Scrip-

---

[30] *A Vindication of Protestant Principles* (London, 1847), ix; cf. *DQ* VIII, 259.

tures" and "inspiration as attaching to the spiritual truths and doctrines delivered in these Scriptures" (*DQ* VIII, 265). How is inspiration to be ascertained, De Quincey asks, in a collection of texts that has been strangely pieced together during its long history of transmission and translation? It is precisely in the harmony and coherence, in spite of the disrupted and fragmentary composition, that De Quincey finds the evidence of sustained inspiration.

> On such a final creation resulting from such a distraction of parts it is indispensable to suppose an overruling inspiration, in order at all to account for the final result of a most elaborate harmony. Besides,—which would argue some inconceivable magic if we did not assume a providential inspiration watching over the coherencies, tendencies, and intertesselations (to use a learned word) of the whole,—it happens that, in many instances, typical things are recorded, things ceremonial that could have no meaning to the person recording, prospective words that were reported and transmitted in a spirit of confiding faith, but that could have little meaning to the reporting parties for many hundreds of years. (*DQ* VIII, 265).

Although he thus describes a guiding rather than a literal inspiration, De Quincey also anticipates the argument for development. Meanings are evolved as part of the historical communication, gradual compilation, and ongoing reception of Scripture. The key passage, always cited as the Scripture's own declaration of "verbatim et literatim inspiration," is in Paul's letter to Timothy: "All scripture *is* given by inspiration of God, and *is* profitable for doctrine, for reproof, for correction, for instruction in righteousness" (2 Tim. 3:16). De Quincey has already called attention to the paradox that "Bibliolatry depends upon ignorance of Hebrew and Greek" (*DQ* VIII, 263). In keeping with his notion of the fragility and elusiveness of textual meanings, he provides a word-by-word exegesis of Paul's Greek. The crucial word, *theopneustos*, De Quincey translates literally as "God-breathed, or God-prompted." Whether it belongs to the subject or the predicate is ambiguous, for the Greek sentence has no copula. Thus God's breathing or prompting hovers indeterminately between *pasa graphē* (all writing) and *kai ophelimos pros didaskalian* (and/also serviceable toward doctrinal truth), between the text and the teaching. In his *Confessions of an Inquiring Spirit* (1825; published in 1840), Coleridge had also scrutinized this passage to argue that the truth of the Bible resides not in the literal sense of its words but in "its declared ends and purposes."³¹ No matter how Paul's words are syntactically construed, they cannot be made into a commandment of literalism. Elsewhere, as De Quincey reminds us, Paul preached that "the letter killeth, but the spirit giveth life" (2 Cor. 3:6). The *theopneustia* is better sought, therefore, not "in the corruptibilities of perishing syllables" but "in the sanctities of indefeasible, word-transcending ideas" (*DQ* VIII, 268). Inspiration is communicated through experience with the scriptural ideas. Through experience, too, the ideas may grow in individual consciousness and in the culture. Inspiration overrides the limits of language, enters into human actions, and thus contributes directly to development. This argument for development is opposed by Donaldson because he believes that it undermines the very origins of Christianity. Newman's doctrine, as he sees it, implies that "primitive" Christianity was in a state of error, or that Christ's own teachings were imperfect and have come into perfection only with the rise of modern learning.

De Quincey deftly corrects Donaldson's misapprehension by distinguishing "perfection" and "development": the former inheres in Christianity as "theory and system"; the latter is acquired by the Christian community through experience. Through "development" we perceive more and more of the original and abiding "perfection." De Quincey points out that Donaldson, when he is not condemning Newman, understands and endorses the idea of development: "At p. 33, when as yet he is not thinking of Mr. Newman, he says, 'If knowledge is progressive, the *development* of Christian doctrine must be progressive'" (*DQ* VIII, 294). De Quincey denies only the "must" in Donaldson's formulation. He goes on, however, to elaborate the modes of development, not in Newman's terms but in his own. He discusses the possibilities of philological, philosophical, and social development. Donaldson, he says, harbors paradoxically a surreptitious bibliolatry as well as a covert endorsement of development:

> The Scriptures must benefit, like any other book, by an increasing accuracy and compass of learning in the *exegesis* applied to them.... If all the world denied this, [Donaldson] is the man that cannot; since he relies upon philological knowledge as the one resource of Christian philosophy in all circumstances of difficulty for any of its interests, positive or negative.... He denounces development when dealing with the New-

---

³¹ *Confessions of an Enquiring Spirit*, ed. H. St. J. Hart (Stanford, 1957), 67–68.

manites; he relies on it when vaunting the functions of Philology (*DQ* VIII, 295).

Philosophical development, as "a mode of development continually going on, and reversing the steps of past human follies," may also be swayed by ideological fashions and made to waver in its quest for the good, true, and beautiful. De Quincey is optimistic, however, that philosophy is, in the long run, a reliable handmaid of religion: "All the texts and all the cases remain at this hour just as they were for our ancestors; and our reverence for these texts is just as absolute as theirs; but we, applying lights of experience which *they* had not, construe these texts by a different logic" (*DQ* VIII, 297). The best evidence of philosophical development is found in social development.

As in his essay "On Christianity as an Organ of Political Movement," he argues the benevolent influence on social progress. Scriptural inspiration nourishes man's spiritual and, indirectly, his intellectual development. The two, nevertheless, remain separate. While it stimulates the intellectual pursuits, the Bible neither reveals, nor can be countermanded by, scientific knowledge. The "divine mission" of revealing spiritual truth could not be disrupted by the "human mission" of unraveling the secrets of the material universe (*DQ* VIII, 282–283).[32] De Quincey thus circumvents the religion–science controversy which Donaldson had seen looming as the "great theological crisis" of the age. Galileo's excommunication for having proposed a scientific alternative to biblical cosmology is a prime example of the bibliolator's fanatical literalism. The Bible does not dictate scientific facts; it works, rather, through spiritual inspiration to excite intellectual inquiry into the riddles of the material world. By giving primacy to spiritual inspiration over intellectual inquiry, De Quincey inverts the Kantian postulate. After summarizing how Kant successfully collapsed the physico-theological proof, the cosmological proof, and the ontological proof "to demonstrate the indemonstrability of God," De Quincey observes that with the "same *apodeixis*, which he had thus inexorably torn from reason under one manifestation, Kant himself restored to the reason in another (the *praktische vernunft*)." Kant affirms God as a necessary "postulate of the human reason, as speaking though the conscience

---

[32] DeQuincey later elaborated this argument (see *DQ* VIII, 35–41) in "On the True Relations of the Bible to Merely Human Science" (1854), a postscript to "System of the Heavens" (1846).

and will, not proved *ostensively*, but indirectly proved as being *wanted* indispensably, and presupposed in other necessities of our human nature" (*DQ* VIII, 261–262). For Kant, reason is the given, from which follows a subjective need, and therefore a moral duty, to assume the existence of God. For De Quincey, a "sympathy with the invisible" is the given, from which follows the injunction to explore the unknown as far as reason will allow.

Inspiration means much more to De Quincey than scriptural revelation. He refers to "the pervading *spirit* of God's revealed command," to the efficacy of "the direct voice of God, ventriloquising through secret whispers of man's conscience." Development, as the reflex or reciprocal counterpart of inspiration, "is not so much a light which Scripture throws out upon human life as inversely a light which human life and its eternal evolutions throw back upon Scripture" (*DQ* VIII, 300–301). Inspiration intrudes upon consciousness as an irrational or suprarational presence. It may itself resist rational scrutiny, but it arouses the rational faculties, stimulating an activity of mind. In their reciprocity, inspiration and development bring about revelation, and revelation promulgates continuing interaction: "It cannot be the policy or true meaning of revelation to work towards any great purpose in man's destiny otherwise than through the co-agency of man's faculties, improved in the whole extent of their capacities" (*DQ* VIII, 307).

When De Quincey returns to Hume's attack on miracles, he reconciles what he had earlier called the internal and external miracles. The fragmentary manuscript "On Miracles" employs that mode of argument he had developed in his celebration of a "literature of power."[33] The biblical record was not intended as a "literature of knowledge"; its revelations excite the intuitive reason rather than convince the understanding. Hume was more right than he realized: miracles, however they are reported, bear no immediate relation to the event they pretend to describe. The appeal to probability and experience—the criteria by which we judge the credibility of a report—is irrelevant to the report of a miracle. The factors that compel us to believe that a given event is a miracle, Hume declares, compel us also to reject the likelihood that

---

[33] Although best known as formulated in "Letters to a Young Man" (1823; *DQ* X, 46–52) and "The Poetry of Pope" (1848; *DQ* XI, 53–59), De Quincey frequently repeats the critical distinction between the "literature of power" and the "literature of knowledge"; see Burwick, *Thomas De Quincey: Knowledge and Power* (London and New York, 2001), 1–23.

it occurred. He offers, therefore, a general maxim: "That no testimony is sufficient to establish a miracle, unless the testimony be of such a kind that its falsehood would be more miraculous, than the fact, which it endeavours to establish" (*Enquiry* 115–116). He means, of course, to leave the testimony of miracles trapped in paradox. De Quincey, with his new insight into inspiration and development, dissolves the paradox. The "falsehood" of testimony, as a kind of negative miracle, is no miracle at all, nor ever could be. The true miracle resides not in the event but in the testimony. The event is only a moment; the testimony endures.

De Quincey questions the purpose of "presenting Christ alive forever." By insisting on the physical presence of "Christ's going about and doing good" and "showing what commands one sense or other," mystery is bereft of its spiritual relevance. Quoting Christ's reply to the Pharisees and Sadducees when they desired "a sign from heaven" (Matt. 16:1), De Quincey asks: "What else is it than the case of 'a wicked and adulterous generation asking for a Sign'—laying such a stress on miracles?" (MS.; *PW* I, 173).[34] The purpose of a miracle is not to display physical power but to reveal moral truth. Were the Bible introduced in court, how could one use as evidence "the mere *facts* of the Gospel"? "Who knows anything of the contrivances, as to circumstances, persons, interests in which the whole narrative originated, or when? All is dark and dusty." The facts prove nothing. The miracle is the testimony, a means of saying what cannot be said: "Nothing in such a case *can* be proved but what shines by its own light. . . . Nay, God Himself could not attest a miracle, *but* (listen to this)—*but* (hear this my friend)—*but* by the internal revelation or visiting of the Spirit—to evade which, to dispense with which, a miracle is ever resorted to" (MS.; *PW* I, 175).[35]

The seemingly miraculous physical circumstances, then, are an evasion, a subterfuge, a sleight of God's hand. Or, if you prefer, an event "misapprehended" by the reporter. The real miracle is "the internal

---

[34] "Let Him Come Down from the Cross," Dove Cottage MS., cited hereafter as Dove C. MS.; and see *PW* I, 173. Japp's transcription (*PW* I, 174) omits the opening paragraph, approximately fifty-three words, and alters the word order of the sentence with the quotation from Matthew 16:4.

[35] Japp's transcription (*PW* I, 175) omits at the marked ellipsis 175 words including De Quincey's statement of his "mission" quoted in my opening paragraph as well as a passage on the impossibility of demonstration in religion and the necessity of compromise in moral compliance.

revelation or visiting of the Spirit." Thus he speculates on what would have happened at that moment when the priests were taunting, "Let Him come down from the cross," if Christ had actually descended.

> They would have been stunned and confounded for the moment, not at all converted in heart. Their hatred to Christ was not built on their unbelief, but their unbelief on their hatred; and hatred would not have been mitigated by another (however astounding) miracle. (Dove C. MS.; *PW* I, 174)

No more than the priests are we, or anyone, apt to experience a profound change merely at witnessing some surprising physical event. Something else must happen. Many of the physical events, De Quincey suspects, have been transformed by testimony too powerfully moved by the experience to attend to mere facts. What if Christ cured by *process* rather than by word or touch? The testimony may, then, report the awe and admiration, "since the *unity* given to the act of healing is probably (more probably than otherwise) but the figurative unity of the tendency to mythos." What happened to the multitude who followed Christ into the desert? Did they risk that journey with no thought of food or water? In his earlier reply to Hume, De Quincey had used this account as an example of the corroborated validity of many witnesses. Now he is quite willing to dismiss the physical circumstances as mere "gossip." Perhaps there was no physical miracle at all, but instead the more profound and invisible miracle of unselfish sharing.

> Such again as the miracle of the loaves—so liable to be utterly gossip, so incapable of being watched or examined amongst a crowd of 7000 people. Besides, were these people mad? The very fact which is said to have drawn Christ's pity—viz. their situation in the desert, surely cannot have escaped their own attention in going thither. Think of 7000 people rushing to a sort of destruction; for less than that, the mere inconvenience were not worthy of divine attention. (Dove C. MS.; *PW* I, 174)[36]

Physical miracles command awe. "How clearly do the villains betray their own hypocrisy about the divinity of Christianity, and at the same time the meanness of their own natures, who think the Messiah or God's Messenger must 1st prove his own commission by an act of

---

[36] The multitude, of course, is numbered 5,000, not 7,000, in Matthew 14: 21, Mark 6: 44, Luke 9: 14, and John 6: 10.

power" (Dove C. MS.; *PW* I, 176).[37] A philosophy of materialism and an ideology of power are at odds with religion as "a new revelation of moral forces." But what sort of religion is founded upon a display of power? Let Christ move a mountain: "This would have *coerced* people into believing." But it would not be a willing and spontaneous act of faith; indeed, it would be no belief at all. Whence came the power? By what agency? "This obstinately recurrent question remains," De Quincey says, and "the pretended belief would have left them just where they were as to any real belief in Christ."

Like Coleridge, then, De Quincey has defined the working of miracles as subjective. But for De Quincey the medium through which miracles are propagated is language. True testimony "shines by its own light." If counterfeited or falsified, it betrays its own imposture:

> Suppose the Gospels written 30 years after the events, and by ignorant superstitious men who have adopted the fables that old women had surrounded Christ with. How does this supposition vitiate their report of Christ's Parables? But, on the other hand, they could no more have invented the Parables than a man alleging a diamond mine could invent a diamond as attestation. The Parables prove themselves. (Dove C. MS; *PW* I, 176)

Thus he can proclaim in a subsequent note that miracles, even the constituent miracles, have their efficacy in the intuitive "power" inherent in their narration. Verification as documentary evidence ceases to be relevant. He again takes as his topic the priests' mocking taunt at the crucifixion: "Let Him come down from the cross."

In this note De Quincey explains why the profound influence of the spiritual resurrection could not have been accomplished by other means. A physical display, such as Christ's descending from the cross, would have failed to work, while the miracle of the disciples' testimony did work, and continues to work, most effectively. It would fail, De Quincey explains, because

> inverting the order of every true emanation from God, instead of growing and expanding for ever like a <, it would have attained its *maximum* at the first. The effect for the half-hour would have been prodigious, and from that moment when it began to flag it would degrade rapidly, until,

---

[37] Japp has altered the wording here to soften De Quincey's denunciation of hypocrisy. Instead of "How clearly do the villains," Japp has substituted "How dearly do these people."

in three days, a far fiercer hatred against Christ would have been moulded. (Dove C. MS; *PW* I, 177–178)

In elaborating his argument from "On Miracles," De Quincey lays the ground for the necessity of a spiritual rather than a physical miracle by establishing that the animosity of the priests sprang only from Christ's presumption of spiritual leadership, not from any doubts of the acts attributed to him. Thus the physical miracle of descending from the cross would not eradicate lurking suspicions "that He was an impostor in the sense that He pretended to a power of miracles which in fact He had not." This had never been the source of the priests' hatred. "The sense in which Christ had been an impostor for them was in assuming a commission, a spiritual embassy with appropriate functions, promises, prospects, to which He had not title." Greeted by the multitudes upon his arrival in Jerusalem, Christ commenced teaching in the temple, confuting the Sadducees, reproving the Pharisees. It was not for "miraculous impostorship" that the priests denounced him but for "spiritual impostorship." So successful were they in spreading their antagonism that the multitudes, given the choice, called for the release of Barabbas, not of Christ. Coming down from the cross, then, would be a stunning demonstration of power. The rivalry would be restored. The hatred would increase. No spiritual victory would be won. The indictment of Christ's "spiritual impostorship" could be answered only by a spiritual miracle, and that miracle is realized in "the sublimity of His moral system" (Dove C. MS; *PW* 1, 178).

For both Coleridge and De Quincey, miracles work subjectively. While Coleridge attempts to trace their apprehension through the intuition and the willing action of faith, De Quincey focuses attention on inspiration and development operating through language. Both emphasize the mediation of meaning through symbols; both define the symbol as combining identity with alterity; and both attribute to the symbol a capacity to represent the unknowable through the known. They agree that the alterity in the self-referential identity of biblical symbolism has its origin in the *theopneustia*, as word-embodied, word-transcending inspiration, and they devise similar schemes for reading symbols. While the practical reason compulsively pursues what lies beyond its boundaries, Coleridge states, an *a priori* intuition responds harmonically to the still unfathomed meaning. De Quincey describes a rational affinity with the irrational. He advocates a Higher Superstition, a "sympathy with the invisible," informed by intellectual curiosity rather than driven by taboo-ridden credulity. A symbol, for him, provides a convenient "midway station between the physical and hyperphysical."

Although Coleridge's deliberations on miracles can be traced throughout his career, it was his reading in 1810 that shaped his argument on intuition and the *logos*. De Quincey's examination of miracles belongs to a period thirty to thirty-seven years later. Coleridge discovered in the Gospel of John a resolution to the pantheist dilemma he had encountered in Spinoza, Kant, and Schelling. In recalling his first meeting with Coleridge, De Quincey lapsed into a diatribe against the "essentially destructive" influence of Kant, who, "let him say what he would *in* his books," privately professes "the horrid Ghoulish creed" (*DQ* II, 155) of atheism. Coleridge, of course, had also read Kant's *Tisch-Rede* but responded very differently:

> I can never without indignation read these most groundless attacks on Kant's System which I distinguish from Kant's own personal opinions respecting Prayer & Miracles. But his System is most friendly to the Christian Faith—were it only, that it proves the utter worthlessness of all the Grounds against its doctrines. (*CM* II, 185–186)[38]

De Quincey also grants as much to Kant (see *DQ* VIII, 260–261), but he does not elaborate, as Coleridge did, the intuitive reason as the effective ground for refuting the Humean claim that the "philosophical testimony on which the truth of the miracle rests is historical, that is, experiential."[39] To counter Hume, Coleridge turns to the Johannine gospel and interprets Christ's miracles in terms of the intersubjectivity of philosophical idealism. Following Newman, De Quincey emphasizes the reciprocity of inspiration and development, with the argument that

---

[38] Cf. Coleridge's marginal gloss to Edward Stillingfleet's assertion that "a power of miracles is the clearest evidence of a Divine Testimony." *Coleridge on the Seventeenth Century*, ed. Roberta Brinkley (Durham, N.C., 1955), 375–376.

[39] See Coleridge's *Logic* 191 on Hume's objection to "the truth of miracles": "Here one constituent only of the judgment is the legitimate or possible object of experience. The other half, the miraculous substitute of the antecedent, is not the possible object of human experience and therefore not a legitimate object of human history. Nay, even though the supersensual *A* were admitted to exist, there would nevertheless result no right of asserting a causal connection between it and the phenomenon *B*: for *this* would be an act of the judgment; but the necessity in the *causal* connection is, according to Mr. Hume, no act of the judgment, far rather, it is no act at all, but a mere *affection* of the animal sensibility, a passive *feeling*."

the progress of learning reveals more and more of the hidden mysteries of Christ's miracles. Although Coleridge, too, endorses a doctrine of historical development, he addresses that development primarily in terms of the individual mind.[40] De Quincey, however, observes a benevolent expansion of Christian ethics enlightening and transforming the culture as a whole. Confronting the failure of reason to reconcile the "it is" and "I am," Coleridge ultimately finds no better alternative than reliance on faith. Accepting supernatural mystery and the persuasive rhetoric of the irrational, De Quincey sought no better alternative.

Works Cited

Anon. Review of *Selections Grave and Gay, from the Writings, Published and Unpublished by Thomas De Quincey*. 14 vols. *Quarterly Review* 110 (July 1861): 1–35.

Barth, J. Robert, S.J. *Coleridge and Christian Doctrine*. Cambridge: Harvard University Press, 1969.

———. *The Symbolic Imagination: Coleridge and the Romantic Tradition*. 1977. 2nd ed. New York: Fordham University Press, 2001.

Beattie, James. *An Essay on the Nature and Immutability of Truth*. Edinburgh, 1770.

Burwick, Frederick. *The Damnation of Newton: Goethe's Color Theory and Romantic Perception*. Berlin: Gruyter, 1986.

———. *Thomas De Quincey: Knowledge and Power*. London; Palgrave; New York: St. Martin's, 2001.

Campbell, George. *Dissertation on Miracles*. London, 1762.

Coleridge, Samuel Taylor. *Aids to Reflection*. Ed. Derwent Coleridge. 7th ed. London: Edward Moxon, 1854.

———. *Biographia Literaria*. Ed. James Engell and W. Jackson Bate. 2 vols. Princeton: Princeton University Press; London: Routledge, 1983. *CC* Vol. VII.

———. *Coleridge on the Seventeenth Century*. Ed. Roberta Brinkley. Durham: Duke University Press, 1955.

---

[40] In *AR* 183 Coleridge writes: "Reason . . . either predetermines experience, or avails itself of a past experience to supersede its necessity in all future times; and affirms truths which no sense could perceive, nor experiment verify, nor experience confirm." On reason versus understanding see *AR* 167–185, 344–345; *Friend* I, 154–161.

———. *Collected Letters of Samuel Taylor Coleridge*. Ed. Earl Leslie Griggs. 6 vols. Oxford: Clarendon, 1956–1971.

———. *The Collected Works of Samuel Taylor Coleridge*. Ed. Kathleen Coburn. 16 vols. Bollingen Series 75. Princeton: Princeton University Press, 1969–. Cited as *CC*.

———. *Confessions of an Inquiring Spirit*. Ed. H. St. J. Hart. Stanford: Stanford University Press, 1957.

———. *The Friend*. Ed. Barbara E. Rooke. 2 vols. Princeton: Princeton University Press; London: Routledge, 1969. *CC* Vol. IV.

———. *Lay Sermons*. Ed. R. J. White. Princeton: Princeton University Press; London: Routledge, 1972. *CC* Vol. VI.

———. *Lectures 1795: On Politics and Religion*. Ed. Lewis Patton and Peter Mann. Princeton: Princeton University Press; London: Routledge, 1971. *CC* Vol. I.

———. *Logic*. Ed. J. R. de J. Jackson. Princeton: Princeton University Press; London: Routledge, 1981. *CC* Vol. XIII.

———. *Marginalia*. Ed. George Whalley. 6 vols. Princeton: Princeton University Press; London: Routledge, 1980–2001. *CC* Vol. XII.

———. "Memorandum on Miracles." MS. 34, 225, ff. 75–75V. British Museum, London.

———. *The Notebooks of Samuel Taylor Coleridge*. Ed. Kathleen Coburn. 4 vols. Bollingen Series 50. New York: Pantheon, 1957–1961; Princeton: Princeton University Press, 1973, 1990.

De Quincey, Thomas. *The Collected Writings of Thomas De Quincey*. Ed. David Masson. 14 vols. Edinburgh: Adam and Charles Black, 1889–1890.

———. "'Let Him Come Down from the Cross.'" MS. Dove Cottage Library, Grasmere, England.

———. "On Miracles." MS. Author's collection, Claremont, California.

———. *The Posthumous Works of Thomas De Quincey*. Ed. Alexander H. Japp. 2 vols. London: Heinemann, 1891.

Dodd, C. H. *The Interpretation of the Fourth Gospel*. Cambridge: Cambridge University Press, 1953.

Donaldson, John William. *A Vindication of Protestant Principles*. London: J. W. Parker, 1847.

Eaton, Horace Ainsworth. *Thomas De Quincey: A Biography*. London: Oxford University Press, 1936.

Flew, Antony. *Hume's Philosophy of Belief*. London: Routledge, 1961.

Happel, Stephen. *Coleridge's Religious Imagination.* Salzburg: Institut für Anglistik und Amerikanistik, 1983.

Harding, Anthony. *Coleridge and the Inspired Word.* Montreal: McGill-Queen's University Press, 1985.

Hartley, David. *Observations on Man.* 3 vols. 1749; London, 1801.

Hume, David. *An Enquiry Concerning Human Understanding.* Ed. L A. Selby-Bigge. Oxford: Clarendon Press, 1902.

———. *The Natural History of Religion.* Ed. H. E. Root. Stanford: Stanford University Press, 1957.

———. *A Treatise of Human Nature.* Ed. L A. Selby-Bigge. 2nd ed. Rev. P. H. Nidditch. Oxford: Clarendon Press, 1978.

Kant, Immanuel. *Werke.* Ed. Wilhelm Weischedel. 6 vols. Darmstadt: Wissenschaftliche Buchgesellschaft, 1966.

Marx, Karl. *Critique of the Hegelian Philosophy of Right.* Vol. 3 of Karl Marx and Friedrich Engel, *Collected Works.* 43 vols. New York: International, 1975.

McFarland, Thomas. *Coleridge and the Pantheist Tradition.* Oxford: Clarendon Press, 1969.

Newman, John Henry. *An Essay on the Development of Christian Doctrine.* London: J. Toovey, 1845.

Novalis. *Schriften.* Ed. Paul Kluckhohn and Richard Samuel. 5 vols. Stuttgart: Kohlhammer, 1960–1988.

Page, H. A. (pseud. Alexander H. Japp). *Thomas De Quincey: His Life and Writings with Unpublished Correspondence.* 2 vols. New York: Charles Scribner's Sons, 1877.

Paley, William. *Evidences of Christianity.* London, 1794.

Prickett, Stephen. *Romanticism and Religion.* Cambridge: Cambridge University Press, 1976.

Priestley, Joseph. *An History of the Corruptions of Christianity.* 2 vols. Birmingham, 1782.

———. *Institutes of Natural and Revealed Religion.* 3 vols. London, 1772–1777.

Sackville-West, Edward. *Thomas De Quincey: His Life and Works.* New Haven: Yale University Press, 1936.

12

Coleridge and Newman: The Centrality of Conscience

Philip C. Rule, S.J.

I

TO OUR MODERN SENSIBILITY the concept of individuality (inwardness, subjectivity, self-determination) is considered a great Romantic legacy of the late eighteenth and early nineteenth centuries, when many different voices spoke out on behalf of the individual. Mary Wollstonecraft argued that women had a right to education because they possessed reason, which is "the simple power of improvement; or, more properly speaking, of discerning truth. Every individual is in this respect a world in itself."[1] In a more overtly political context Coleridge asserted that "a people are free in proportion as they form their own opinions. In the strict sense of the word knowledge is power."[2] In his essay on the "Theory of Life," he applied the idea of individuality in the broadest philosophical sense when he said, "by life I everywhere mean the true Idea of Life, or that most general form under which life manifests itself to us, which includes all its other forms. This I have stated to be the tendency to individuation, and the degrees of intensities of life to consist in the progressive realization of this tendency."[3] A generation later, John Henry Newman in an 1838 Parochial Sermon imagined a town teeming with individuals and reflected that "every being in that great concourse *is his own centre*, and all things about are but shades, but a 'vain shadow,' in which he 'walketh and disquieteth

---

[1] *A Vindication of the Rights of Woman*, ed. Carol H. Poston (New York, 1988) 53.
[2] Samuel Taylor Coleridge, *The Watchman*, ed. Louis Patton, in *The Collected Works of Samuel Taylor Coleridge*, ed. Kathleen Coburn (Princeton, 1970) 4.
[3] Samuel Taylor Coleridge, *The Complete Works of Samuel Taylor Coleridge*, ed. W. G. T. Shedd, 7 vols. (New York, 1856) I, 391.

himself in vain.'"⁴ The highlighted phrase recurs in his writings until in 1870, in the *Grammar of Assent*, it became a philosophical principle: "everyone who reasons, *is his own centre*; and no expedient for attaining a common measure of minds can reverse this truth."⁵ Finally, in 1850, John Stuart Mill, fearing the encroachment of herd-like middle-class values and ideas on freedom of thought and action, stated that "in proportion to the development of his individuality, each person becomes more valuable to himself, and is therefore more capable of being of value to others."⁶ But "at present individuals are lost in the crowd" (62). Echoing Wollstonecraft and Newman, he asserted that "the unfailing and permanent source of improvement is liberty, since by it there are as many independent centers of improvement as there are individuals" (66).⁷

Freedom to choose, individuality, growth—these are ideas dear to the modern heart, but they were considered at best a mixed blessing by many contemporaries of Coleridge and Newman. In the political sphere such ideas could lead to subversive thoughts and actions, to an elevation of the individual over the community. Marilyn Butler, for example, has thoroughly documented the repressive, conservative anti-Jacobin influence on late eighteenth-century and early nineteenth-century English fiction and on Jane Austen in particular.⁸ There were also philosophical and theological fears that individuality could lead to subjectivism and relativism, and these in turn could lead to skepticism. The prophetic command of Thomas Carlyle's Diogenes Teufelsdröckh to "Close thy Byron, open thy Goethe"⁹ perhaps best sums up late

---

⁴ *Parochial and Plain Sermons*, 8 vols. (London, 1899) IV, 82. Emphasis added. This will be referred to hereafter as *PPS*.

⁵ *An Essay in Aid of a Grammar of Assent* (London, 1895) 345. Emphasis added. This will be referred to hereafter as *GA*.

⁶ *On Liberty*, ed. David Spitz (New York, 1975) 59–60.

⁷ Moral philosopher Charles Taylor sees a strong Coleridgean influence on Mill and considers "On Liberty" as "one form of a widespread attempt to integrate Romantic notions of personal fulfilment into the private lives of denizens of a civilization run more and more by the canons of instrumental reason." *Sources of the Self: The Making of Modern Identity* (Cambridge, Mass., 1989) 458. Taylor's study and J. B. Schneewind's magisterial *The Invention of Autonomy: A History of Modern Moral Philosophy* (Cambridge, 1998) have greatly enriched my reading of Coleridge's and Newman's efforts to develop a personalized proof for the existence of God. Regrettably, while Taylor recognizes Coleridge's role in the development of the modern sense of self, neither writer mentions Newman.

⁸ *Jane Austen and the War of Ideas* (Oxford, 1975), esp. ch. 4, "The Anti-Jacobins," 88–123.

⁹ *Sartor Resartus*, ed. Charles F. Harrold (New York, 1937) 192.

eighteenth-century and early nineteenth-century ambivalence about individuality. Turn away from the brooding and self-destructive inwardness of Byron's metaphysical heroes and turn outward to some altruistic, world-affirming purpose in life.

Coleridge and Newman, however, pressed the centrality of the individual and one's inwardness in examining religious experience by insisting that religion grows out of the concept of conscience, which is also central to individual growth in moral self-consciousness. Their focus on consciousness and conscience would provide for both of them a systematic structure of thought that would underlie writings often considered occasional and disparate in purpose; and it would give rise to a rhetorical style calculated to evoke personal response as much as to inform readers. The similarity of their approach is underscored by the fact that what we are about to look at are unpublished working papers that begin to spell out the central idea that permeates their respective published works. Here, regardless of any influence of Coleridge on Newman (and it was considerable, for all Newman's occasional denials), it is clear they were thinking along parallel lines in formulating a Christian apologetic tailored to the sensibilities of their age. The very individuality that caught the imagination of their contemporaries, favorably and unfavorably, would become the starting-point of their religious reflections.

II

At first glance the two men may seem to have little in common. There are, however, strong similarities, the foremost of which was an unusually heightened capacity for self-awareness and self-reflection and a rare capacity for describing the landscape of a reflecting self. In *The Prelude* Wordsworth addressed Coleridge as "one / More deeply read in thy own thoughts" than he was.[10] Newman's ability to make his inner life utterly transparent is poignantly exemplified by George Eliot's candid and plaintive admission that "the Apology now mainly affects me as the revelation of a life—how different from one's own, yet with how

---

[10] William Wordsworth, *The Prelude: 1799, 1805, 1850*, ed. Jonathan Wordsworth, M. H. Abrams, and Stephen Gill (New York, 1979), *1850* II, 210–211.

close a fellowship in its needs and burthens—I mean spiritual needs and burthens."[11]

Coleridge died a year after Newman published his first major work, *The Arians of the Fourth Century* (1833), but by the middle of the nineteenth century critics began to compare the two. In 1850 an anonymous reviewer of *Confessions of an Inquiring Spirit* violently attacked Coleridge's view of inspiration, saying that along with Parker and Newman he was one of "Satan's agents." In 1856, James Martineau published a major review essay of the writings of Coleridge, Carlyle, and Newman, pointing out the powerful personal influence each wielded, respectively, in his philosophical, literary, and religious responses to the age. From Martineau's time there has been a small but steady stream of scholarship comparing the thought of Coleridge and Newman.[12]

Both men underwent profound religious conversions as a result of grave illness. Coleridge fell seriously ill in 1805 during his stay in Malta when he was thirty-three. This illness marked a turning-point in his life; for his acceptance of the Trinity, previously held only on philosophical grounds, now helped him resolve his doubts about incarnation and redemption and satisfy his great personal need for redemption.[13] By sheer coincidence Newman's illness occurred in Sicily when he was thirty-two. In the *Apologia* he reflected, "I began to think I had a mission."[14] Upon recovering he returned to England and the beginning of the Tractarian Movement. In 1813, estranged from Wordsworth and struggling with opium addiction, Coleridge again found his religious consciousness agonizingly deepened. He said "a new world opened to me, in the infinity of my Own spirit!"[15]

Perhaps the most striking similarity between the two, indeed the focus of this essay, is the primacy of the moral order and the corollary

---

[11] Quoted in *The George Eliot Letters*, ed. Gordon Haight, 9 vols. (New Haven, 1954–1956), IV, 158–159.

[12] For these and other examples of conservative and progressive religious reactions to Coleridge see Philip C. Rule, "Coleridge's Reputation as a Religious Thinker: 1816–1972," *Harvard Theological Review* 67 (1974): 289–320.

[13] See J. Robert Barth, S.J., *Coleridge and Christian Doctrine* (Cambridge, Mass., 1969) 9–10.

[14] John Henry Newman, *Apologia pro vita sua*, ed. David DeLaura (New York, 1965) 40. This will be referred to hereafter as *Apo*.

[15] Samuel Taylor Coleridge, *Collected Letters of Samuel Taylor Coleridge*, ed. Earl Leslie Griggs, 6 vols. (Oxford, 1956–1971), III, 463–464. This will be referred to hereafter as *CL*.

that morality and religion are inseparable. The challenge of human existence is not just to speculate about the mystery of the universe but also freely to respond to it. To grasp the whole of human experience is, ultimately, to confront mystery, not as an evasion of intelligibility and reason but as the necessary horizon that grounds and makes possible our experience, understanding, judging, and choosing. To speak of the known is implicitly and necessarily to acknowledge the unknown and the unknowable. What John Stuart Mill observed about the difference between Bentham and Coleridge applies as well to Newman. Newman, like Coleridge, was more interested in the "why" of things than in the "what." Such an intellectual bias led inevitably to the moral dimension of human experience; and both had an implicit faith in the normal, healthy operation of the questioning process that structures our cognitive faculties. It was a line and style of questioning that led both men to be conscious of the existence and primacy of the will even in the process of intellection and to see the will as the starting point for explaining the ontological and cognitive orientation of human beings to God.

What led them along similar lines of thought? Questions of possible influences aside, there are clear signs that the originality of their insights into the role of conscience in knowing God is to be found in their respective analyses of their own personal religious experiences and self-awareness. Both had a strong sense of self. By this I do not mean merely that they were introspective or given to soul-searching. Rather, each was adept at the very difficult philosophical process of self-appropriation, a process whereby one becomes reflectively or explicitly aware of oneself in the act of knowing. Another striking parallel seems to account for the early beginning of this process. An almost precocious imaginative grasp of the single self existing in the vastness of the universe, if their recollections can be relied on, may well have grounded in them a strong, pre-conceptual religious sensibility.

Early childhood experiences seem to have produced in both of them a heightened sense of the unity of all things in God. In one of several autobiographical letters to Thomas Poole, Coleridge writes that from his "early reading of Faery Tales, & Genii, &c &c—my mind had been habituated *to the Vast*—& I never regarded *my senses* in any way as the criteria of my belief. I regulated all my creeds by my conceptions, not by my *sight*—even at that age. Should children be permitted to read Romances & Relations of Giants & Magicians & Genii?—I know all that has been said against it; but I have formed my faith in the affirmative.—I know of no other way of giving the mind a love of 'the Great' & 'the Whole.'"[16] Speaking of his childhood reading of the Arabian Tales and other such stories, Newman says "my imagination ran on unknown influences, on magical powers and talismans" (*Apo* 15). And he added that those "childish imaginations" were instrumental in "isolating me from the objects which surround me, in confirming me in my mistrust of the reality of material phenomena, and making me rest in the thought of two and only two supreme and luminously self-evident beings, myself and my creator" (*Apo* 18). Although Newman does not speak explicitly of "the vast" and "the Whole," they are implicit in his twofold grasp of self and creator. For as Coleridge's consciousness never led him to "regard my *senses* in any way as the criteria of my belief," so Newman confirmed himself in his "mistrust of the reality of material phenomena." This might sound as if both Coleridge and Newman belonged to the intuitionist camp; but both men disdained what Coleridge called "mechanistic materialism" and Newman branded as Liberalism, the arid, skeptical rationalism inherited from the eighteenth century.

Their sense of the wholeness of human experience and of the universe led them each to attempt a comprehensive synthesis of Christianity, a project interrupted for Coleridge, more often than not, by temperament and financial exigencies. As for Newman it was simply the case of ceaseless demands on his time: tutoring, preaching, writing for the specific needs of the Tractarian Movement, and becoming increasingly involved in his own process of conversion to Roman Catholicism. But despite the apparently "occasional" character of much of their writing, there was a constant, underlying drive toward synthesis. Coleridge had long envisioned a *Magnum Opus*, a sort of "Summa Theologica et Philosophica"; but he never got beyond a work entitled *Opus Maximum*, which still, in manuscript form, remains yet another of those monumental Romantic literary fragments.[17] Yet Thomas McFarland argues that the idea of the *Magnum Opus* was in fact the

---

[16] *CL*, I, 354.

[17] The manuscript, housed in the Victoria College Library, University of Toronto, consists of three vellum-bound volumes. This will be referred to hereafter as *Opus*. The Roman numerals refer to the volumes, the Arabic to the folio pages. The publication of the complete text, including other material, in *The Collected Works of Samuel Taylor Coleridge* is in progress.

organizing pattern of all his other writings.[18] Rarely mentioned, if even noticed, is the fact that Newman also contemplated what he called an *Opus Magnum* for which he sketched out some prologomena in 1857 and to which he never returned.[19] But the makings of a system are clearly seen in the mind of each man. Their respective "proofs" for the existence of God from conscience, together with Coleridge's concept of "Higher Reason" and Newman's concept of the "Illative Sense," provide the key, I believe, to understanding what they were about intellectually and how their individual works form a system of thought.

III

In the early 1820s Coleridge began dictating what is known as the *Opus Maximum* to Joseph Green and James Gillman. Some twenty-five years before, he had written to Thomas Poole describing a course of studies for young men that would cover "Man as Animal," "Man as an *Intellectual* Being," and "Man as Religious Being."[20] Thomas McFarland says these three headings "precisely denominate the idiosyncratic amalgam of scientific investigation, philosophy, and theology that characterize Coleridge's general commitment of thought and the detailed content of the *Opus Maximum* as we have it" (357). In Volume I he deals largely with cosmology and cosmogony in a very sketchy manner. But even here he is laying the groundwork for his reflections on human beings as spiritual, that is, intellectual and religious. His predilection for the organic over the mechanistic grounds a vital hierarchy rising from the senses, to the intellectual, and then the religious. In true Coleridgean fashion, these stages in a process of transcendence are distinct but not separate from one another. Only the move from the religious to an apprehension of God requires the mediation of Faith.

In moving in the next two volumes to the intellectual and religious (I would suggest "moral" is a better word than "religious" in this context), Coleridge lays down one assumption or postulate in his scientific analysis of the moral dimension of human experience. This postulate is "the

---

[18] *Romanticism and the Forms of Ruin: Wordsworth, Coleridge, and the Modalities of Fragmentation* (Princeton, 1981) 342–381.

[19] His earliest biographer, Wilfrid Ward, included a transcript of the prospectus in *The Life of John Henry Newman*, 2 vols. (London, 1912), I, 423–425.

[20] *CL*, I, 209.

Existence of the *Will*, which a moment's reflexion will convince us is the same as *Moral Responsibility*" (*Opus* II, 13). And it is precisely our consciousness of this responsibility that distinguishes human beings from animals, for "Brutes may be and are *scious* but not conscious" (*Opus* II, 138). But unlike the postulates of geometry or exact sciences, moral postulates can be demanded but not "extorted" (*Opus* II, 91). They cannot be extorted precisely because one is free to accept or reject them without being subjected to general ridicule. Because we are conscious of this free agency in moral choice, we implicitly assume the source of the agency. He makes the bold statement that "the consciousness of conscience is itself conscience" (*Opus* II, 32). I take this to mean that moral self-consciousness is the defining characteristic of a human being.

Two other assumptions emerge from this conscious self-appropriation. First, we implicitly trust our cognitive faculties, although we can be deceived and can deceive ourselves at times. Secondly, our intellectual or spiritual faculties are active. We freely choose to exercise them or not. They are not passive like the senses. And they are not mechanical or impersonal, operating in some kind of logical or mechanical manner. The whole person chooses to understand, reason, judge, and choose. We freely choose to believe or trust our human capacity to know and reason. This freedom is a belief in oneself. As theologian Karl Rahner says, "when freedom is really understood, it is not the power to do this or that, but the power to decide about oneself and to actualize oneself."[21]

Can one, however, argue from one's own "consciousness of conscience" to that of one's fellow human beings? Coleridge says that "these assumptions we have found comprised in one position—Man is a responsible agent & in consequence *hath a will*. Have I a responsible will?—Concerning this each individual must be himself the querist and respondent" (*Opus* II, 92). That many human beings are seemingly without conscience—do not reach real moral consciousness—is, Coleridge confesses, "a giant difficulty" (*Opus* II, 45). He points out, however, that "nothing can become an object of consciousness but by reflexion" (*Opus* II, 49). Turning to a point that he would develop at length in his *Aids to Reflection*, he says: "the solution to the problem

---

[21] *Foundations of Christian Faith: An Introduction to the Idea of Christianity* (New York, 1984) 38.

must be sought for in the genesis or origination of the *Thou*. But in order to do this I must require from the reader an energy of attention correspondent to the subtlety of the subject far beyond what I shall have occasion to require in any following part of the work" (*Opus* II, 144).[22]

In Volume III of the *Opus Maximum* Coleridge discusses the relationship between will and reason. In God, will and reason are identified; therefore "the reason in man is representative of the will in God. It follows therefore that the conscience is the specific witness respecting the unity or harmony of the will with the reason, effected by the self-subordination of the individual will, as representing the Self to the reason, as the representative of the will to God" (*Opus* III, 7). This voluntary submission of the human reason to the will of God subordinates will to reason and conscience, and is in fact constitutive of person. We are not just talking machines or animals; we are experiencing, understanding, reasoning, judging, choosing subjects. And since this fidelity or allegiance to a superior moral being is faith, it follows that "Faith in all its relations subsists in the synthesis of reason & the individual will, or reconcilement of the reason with the will by the self subordination of the will to the reason" (*Opus* III, 21). The fundamental importance of the will is no more clearly stated than in his dismissal of a posteriori proofs for God's existence from the sensible world. Coleridge agrees wholeheartedly with Luther that "without that inward revelation by which we know ourselves responsible & thus know, what no understanding can reach, the reality of the will, in vain should we endeavour to make the notion of a divinity out of any material which the senses can convey or the world afford" (*Opus* III, 33). Further on, he says even more emphatically, "To deduce a Deity wholly from nature is in the result to substitute an Apotheosis of Nature for a Deity" (*Opus* III, 61). The only cogent argument for the existence of God is a moral one. "All speculative distinction," he continues, "must begin with Postulates that derive their legitimacy, substance, and sanction from

---

[22] That the "energy of attention" required to arrive at moral consciousness is seldom applied is borne out by A. H. Maslow's sober assessment that self-actualization is achieved by no more than one percent of the human population. *Toward a Psychology of Being* (Princeton, 1962) 190. The question is further complicated, as Maurice Nédoncelle points out, because "this priority of the thou over the he and its power to bring the he into being are seldom admitted in philosophy: Coleridge, Martin Buber, and perhaps Gabriel Marcel have sketched the theory." *God's Encounter with Man* (New York, 1964) 39.

the *conscience*: and from which ever of the two points the reason may start, from the things that are seen to the One Invisible or from the idea of the absolute One to the things that are seen, it will find a chasm which the Moral Being only, which the Spirit and Religion of man alone can fill up or over-bridge" (*Opus* II, 38).

Coleridge has thus insisted over and over on the intimate relationship between the intellectual and the moral orders. The only bridge between a transcendent moral being and a finite moral being is the conscience, the consciousness of which constitutes a person. It is also the only bridge between the I and the Thou—between two subjects in their subjectivity—the ultimate expression of which is love. To love is to recognize the other as person or subject, not as thing or object, a distinction he called "sacred."

What about the truth-claim of such an argument for the existence of God? In an untitled chapter of the *Opus Maximum* on the origin of the idea of God in the human mind, Coleridge comes to grips with this vexing question. His answer is that there is a capacity in all human beings to recognize and experience radical freedom and responsibility. Using an analogy similar to one he had used earlier in *Biographia Literaria*, he says: "The young bull, ere yet its horns are formed, the stag-chafer in its worm state makes its bed chamber prior to its metamorphosis exactly as much longer as is required for the length of the horn which is yet to be produced. Throughout all of Nature there is a manifestation of power pre-existent to the product" (*Opus* III, 63)[23]

What realizes or actualizes this potency? Ultimately it is love, beginning with parental love. Love entails an "other," a Thou; and it ultimately involves a process of self-transcendence that enables the individual to transcend a given stage of knowing and being, in progressive steps, until a person possibly arrives at an explicit conception and affirmation of the supreme or absolute Other or Thou who is God. Describing the role of parents, especially the mother, in teaching the infant love and selfhood, Coleridge observes that "ere yet the conscience [*sic*] self exists the love begins & the first love is love to another" (*Opus* III, 65).[24] Even in the infant, faith is prior to intellection; for,

---

[23] Coleridge would use this same analogy again to argue that spiritual instincts are as indefectible as natural instincts. See *Aids to Reflection*, ed. John Beer, in *The Collected Works*, ed. Coburn (Princeton, 1993) 353.

[24] While the phrase "conscience self" may be a mistake in dictation ("conscious" is penciled in the margin by way of correction), two pages later "conscienceness" appears

"Faith implicit Faith the offspring of unreflecting love is an antecedent and indispensable condition of all its [the infant's] knowledge: the life is the light thereof" (*Opus* III, 66). There is in each human being a connatural potency, oriented toward God, which is activated first by love between parent and child. Returning to his analogy of a natural potency or capacity, he asks: "Why have men a faith in God, there is but one answer, the man & the man alone has a Father & a Mother. All begins in instinct but do all therefore begin alike? Oh no! each hath its own & the instincts of man must be human, rational instincts. Reason itself mutely here prophesying its own future advent" (*Opus* III, 67).[25]

Coleridge decried religion reduced to mere ceremonies and magic, which are signs of an inevitable descent into materialism because of undue stress on the visible. Human love is spiritual as well as physical; and when we substitute the latter for the former, the ills he constantly laments will ensue. "Hence for state-policy we have state-craft and the mockery of experience; for the fine arts a marketable trade; for philosophy a jargon of materialism and the study of nature conducted on such principles as place it in doubtful rivalry with the art and theory of cooking" (*Opus* III, 78).

The true beginning of both philosophy and religion, then, is love, which alone conditions a person to be responsive to that which ultimately corresponds to and actualizes the spiritual potential in each of us. "The reverence of the invisible, substantiated by the feelings of love, this which is the essence and proper definition of religion, is the commencement of the intellectual life, or humanity. If you love not

---

in the text and is corrected to "consciousness." In any event the expressions "conscience self" and "conscienceness" sound like felicitous Coleridgean neologisms, like his use of "tautegorical" to yoke together "tautological" and "allegorical" to describe "symbol." For he does it earlier in an 1807 Notebook entry where he reflects on "wide fellow-consciousness" and ends by saying, "Conceive a Bliss for Self-conscience, combining with a Bliss from increase of Action." *The Notebooks of Samuel Taylor Coleridge*, ed. Kathleen Coburn, 4 vols. to date (Princeton: 1955–) III, Series 3156, Entry 12.71. This will be referred to hereafter as *CN*.

[25] In a study that would certainly have pleased Coleridge, given his propensity to see the relatedness of all things, Alasdair MacIntyre suggests that the human capacity for moral life is rooted in our "vulnerability and affliction" and corresponding "dependence" on others, a trait that he sees in higher "intelligent" animal forms, suggesting a similarity of moral potentiality in both higher animals and human beings. He also lauds feminist philosophers for "their emphasis upon the importance of the mother-child relationship as a paradigm for moral relationships." *Dependent Rational Beings* (Chicago, 1999) 2–3.

your earthly parent how *can* ye love your father in heaven?" (*Opus* III, 79). Using a homely and touching example, Coleridge shows how parental presence affects the child's sense of subjective reality. One discovers the self in the consciousness of others. Feeling alone and alienated, a child cries out at night.

> In such a state of mind has many a parent heard the three years old that has awoke during the dark night in the little crib by the mother's bed entreat in piteous tones 'touch me, only touch me with your finger.' A child of that age under the same circumstances I heard myself using these very words, in answer to the mother's enquiries half hushing & half chiding: 'I am not here, touch me, Mother, that I may be here!' The witness of its own being had been suspended in the loss of the mother's presence by sight or sound or feeling. The form in the shape and the form affirmed for itself are blended into one, and yet convey the earliest lesson of distinction and alterity. (*Opus* III, 91–92)

Distinction and alterity, I and Thou, the self and the other—one grows into a sense of one's own individuality and uniqueness through a lifelong interplay between one's self and the other selves who are our fellow human beings. One becomes fully conscious of the self as subject not in knowing objects but in knowing and loving other subjects, other knowers, other lovers, other beings conscious of conscience.[26] What we would today call interpersonal or intersubjective relationships are premised, for Coleridge, on the existence of the will. He again reminds his reader that "the original postulates & their concession was that of a responsible will, from which the reality of a will generally became demonstrable, to convince him that his responsible will is the essential and indispensable ground & condition of his Personality" (*Opus* III, 158).

Another aspect of this process of becoming aware of oneself as a "spiritual" being, a being conscious of will or moral responsibility, is manifested in the kinds of reading in which a person engages. Coleridge draws a distinction between what one experiences in reading scientific or purely abstract matter and what one experiences in reading imaginative literature. "Try only to produce," he suggests, "the state of

---

[26] See J. Robert Barth, S.J., *Coleridge and the Power of Love* (Columbia, Mo., 1988), esp. the first two chapters; and Anthony John Harding, *Coleridge and the Idea of Love: Aspects of Relationship in Coleridge's Thought and Writing.* (London, 1974). Both books are richly illuminating about the importance of love in Coleridge's life and thought.

our consciousness, while we were following Euclid through the 37th proposition and then our state while we were perusing the pages of Tacitus or contemplating the creation of Milton" (*Opus* III, 168). The difference is that "in all purely scientific exertion of the mind there is no excitement of the sense of our own individuality, the mind acts, if I may use so bold yet so appropriate a metaphor, as verb impersonal. There is neither agent nor sympathy with any supposed agent; both agent and product are lost or contained in the act" (*Opus* III, 170). Euclid engages only the reason. I would suggest here, without expanding on the point, that the imagination enters in as the whole person is engaged and asked to respond not merely in a detached or notional way but in an involved and volitional (personal) way.[27] Such reading involves the "conscious will," as Coleridge calls it in the *Biographia Literaria*.[28] The personal nature of the imaginative text literally evokes an imaginative "attending" to the text. Since personhood is rooted in the will, the deepest response is moral. Thus we can see why he says about those who demand rational proofs in religious matters, that "the wiser plan, as we have before had occasion to remark is to say, or rather to remain silent and be content to know that the respondent must make himself a better man before he can become a more intelligent one" (*Opus* III, 151).

Coleridge's lengthy and fragmentary argument for God's existence from conscience boils down to this: the definition of what it is to be a person, a distinct, self-determining individual, and the definition of Christianity are two sides of the same coin. He says, quite simply, "there & only where a reason & a Will are co-present distinctly but in relation either of union or oppugnancy, a personality is affirmed" (*Opus* III, 188). Disciples like Green, Maurice, and Marsh would a generation later echo this view—no conscience (will and responsibility), no person. To be a person is to be a free, morally responsible being. Moral responsibility grounds the very possibility of a revealed religion based on the fundamental premise of human sinfulness. "Subjectively, or in relation to the order of conviction," Coleridge concludes, "the *responsibility* is assumed as the condition & staple ring in the chain of Chris-

---

[27] For a fuller study of this see Philip C. Rule, "Something of Great Constancy: Uses of the Imagination" (Regina, 1985).

[28] Samuel Taylor Coleridge, *Biographia Literaria*, ed. James Engell and W. Jackson Bate, 2 vols., in *The Collected Works*, ed. Coburn (Princeton, 1983) I, 103. This will be referred to hereafter as *BL*.

tian faith. This being denied directly or by a previous disbelief of the necessary inference from the fact of moral responsibility, namely the will, & therefore a power strictly spiritual, the concept of a corrupt and fallen nature is impossible, or rather the words are without meaning, and of course the whole scheme of redemption becomes equally hollow, first as having no object & 2ndly as having no conceivable agent" (*Opus* III, 193).

In the final analysis, Coleridge's conception of humans as animal (sensitive), intellectual, and religious (moral) implies that we are both historically and existentially religious beings—finite free spirits oriented by our nature to an absolute free spirit, God. To deny human freedom renders God unnecessary, indeed impossible to comprehend. To deny God is to rob human beings of any true meaning or dignity, to reduce them back to a sea of materialism. If there is no freedom, there is no true humanity. To be aware of oneself as free, as conscious of conscience, is to be, potentially at least, aware of God. According to theologian Bernard J. Lonergan, "as the question of God is implicit in all our questioning, so being in love with God is the basic fulfillment of our conscious intentionality."[29] This statement perfectly sums up not only Coleridge's position but also that of Newman, to whom we now turn.

IV

Newman's "Proof for Theism," written in 1859, would prove to be the center of his crowning work, *An Essay in Aid of a Grammar of Assent*, published in 1870. Only twenty-two manuscript pages in length, it stands by itself, unlike Coleridge's treatment, which is part of a larger, more ambitious exploration of human nature and religion. Newman seems to begin with the Kantian argument but points out immediately that "[W. G.] Ward thinks I hold that moral obligation is, because there is a God. But I hold just the reverse, viz. There is a God, because there is a moral obligation" (*PN*, II, 31).[30]

---

[29] *Method in Theology* (New York, 1972) 105.

[30] First published in *The Argument from Conscience to the Existence of God*, ed. Adrian K. Boekraad and Henry Tristram (Louvain, 1961) and later in *The Philosophical Notebook*, ed. Edward Sillem, 2 vols. (Louvain, 1969). All quotations are taken from Volume II of the 1969 edition, which will be referred to hereafter as *PN*.

Newman's starting point is phenomenological: "I am conscious of my own existence. That I am involves a great deal more than myself" (*PN* II, 31). His analysis of this consciousness reveals a number of "various faculties, which seem to be parts of my own being and to be at least as much facts as that being itself" (*PN* II, 31). They consist in such activities as "thinking (cogito ergo sum) or feeling, or remembering, or comparing, or exercising discourse" (*PN* II, 33). One does not have faith in these activities nor does one have direct knowledge of being, "because being is not known directly, but indirectly through these states" (*PN* II, 33–34). Thus Newman is neither a fideist nor an intuitionist—labels applied to him during his life and long afterward by critics of the *Grammar of Assent*. He explains further that "sentio ergo sum" like "cogito ergo sum" is neither argumentation nor deduction nor faith. "I do not advance from one proposition to another, when I know my existence from being conscious of my feeling, but one and the same act of consciousness brings home to me that which afterwards at leisure I draw out into two propositions, denoting two out of many aspects of one thing" (*PN* II, 35). One can proceed from "sentio ergo sum" to "cogito ergo sum" and the analysis is the same, for "consciousness and reasoning are those portions of the idea of being which are most essentially bound up with it" (*PN* II, 37). In denying that one has faith in one's cognitive processes Newman appears to differ from Coleridge; but the difference is merely verbal. Where Coleridge says, "to believe is the rule and to disbelieve an exception" (*Opus* III, 88), Newman says that as "there is no *faith* properly in these exercises of my being, so there is no skepticism about them properly—and it is as absurd to speak of being skeptical of consciousness, reasoning, memory, sensation, as to say I am skeptical whether I am" (*PN* II, 37). Newman is simply saying that we implicitly trust the integrity of human consciousness and human cognitive activity. Not bound up in the immediate reality of consciousness, however, is the reality of external objects or reality which "*is* an object of faith" (*PN* II, 37). Pressed hard, this begins to look like idealism or skepticism, both of which charges were leveled against Newman. What may cause some confusion is the fact that Newman does not distinguish between consciousness and experience. In a marginal annotation he says, "what is internal to the mind is an object of consciousness which external things are not. Thus the line is broad and deep between reliance on reason and conscience, and the trustworthiness of the impressions of the senses or the reality *or* existence of matter. Hence the being of God, arising out of what is internal, is an external fact different in evidence *or* proof from every other external fact" (*PN* II, 41). Newman's manner of speaking may suggest he actually takes all reality apart from God and himself on faith. I would suggest that what Newman is really saying is that the relationship between the person and God is fundamental to all other relationships.

Setting aside the existence of all other external reality, Newman says, "there is just one primary belief I have—not knowledge but belief—it is not in matter or space, or time, or any of this sort of outward thing—yet it is an external and outward being, or I should not talk of faith—it is belief in the existence of God" (*PN* II, 39). For Newman, God is an intimate part of his epistemology and, to the extent that he has one, his metaphysics. This is strikingly stated in the *Apologia pro vita sua* where, speaking of his deepest religious convictions, he mentions his early mistrust of the reality of material phenomena, a fact that made him "rest in the thought of two and only two absolutely and luminously self-evident beings, myself and my Creator" (16). In his "Proof" he says that "when I say that the external fact of the existence of God is an object of faith, and a primary object, I do not mean it is necessarily so in the order of history, but in the order of nature. I mean that it is more intimately connected with the nature of the human mind itself than anything else, and while it is to be received on faith hardly is it so in fact" (*PN* II, 43).

What is this link between our consciousness and the God who is external to us? Among the data of consciousness already considered—memory, sensation, reasoning—Newman also includes conscience, by which

> I mean the discrimination of acts as worthy of praise or blame. Now such praise or blame is a phenomenon of my existence, one of those phenomena thro' which, as I have said, my existence is brought home to me. But the accuracy or truth of the praise or blame in a particular case, is a matter not of faith, but of judgment. Here then are two senses of the word conscience. It either stands for the act of moral judgment, or for the particular judgment formed. In the former case it is the foundation of religion, in the latter of ethics. (*PN* II, 47)

In both instances, of course, reason is involved; but for Newman, as for Coleridge, it is practical rather than speculative reason at work.

In analyzing further this "feeling of conscience" Newman finds "it operates under a *special sanction*" (*PN*, II, 49). Although persons may conclude differently about what is concretely right or wrong, and while it is impossible to maintain "that there is any idea of moral right or wrong bound up in my primary consciousness of my existence," nevertheless "the sense of a special sanction remains one and the same in all men" (*PN* II, 49). What is the nature of this sanction? Why is it intimately bound up with the very nature of the mind itself, so intimately in fact that it is, like the existence of God, "more intimately connected with the nature of the human mind than anything else" (*PN* II, 49)? As with Coleridge, conscience is that which postulates the "Other" in our existence. Quoting from one of his University Sermons Newman explains that "conscience implies a relation between the soul & a something exterior, & that, moreover, superior to itself; a relation to an excellence which it does not possess, and to a tribunal over which it has no power" (*PN* II, 49–50). Newman sees conscience as that essential part of human nature that prompts us on in the process of self-transcendence. "This is conscience, and from the very nature of the case, its very existence carries on our minds to a Being exterior to ourselves; for else, whence did it come? And to a being superior to ourselves; else whence its strange, troublesome peremptoriness?" (*PN* II, 53). Here even the agnostic George Eliot found herself in agreement with Newman when, finding God "inconceivable" and immortality "unbelievable," she could still insist that duty was "peremptory and absolute."[31]

In his analysis of conscience Newman finds not only the idea of a lawgiver but also the idea of a future judgment. For these are not just laws of taste which are "attended to by no *sanction*," but rather laws which involve self-transcendence. For it is these feelings experienced in the imperatives of conscience which "carry the mind out of itself & beyond itself, which imply a tribunal in [the] future, & reward & punishment which are so special. The notion of a future judgment is thus involved in the feeling of conscience" (*PN* II, 59). Furthermore, the feeling that anticipates this "tribunal in [the] future" is personal in nature, and has as its object a personal God, since persons—free rational agents—could not reasonably feel responsible or accountable to an impersonal reality.

---

[31] Quoted in Gordon Haight, *George Eliot: A Biography* (New York, 1968) 464.

Newman compresses this entire argument into an enthymeme. "If then our *or* my existence is brought to me by my consciousness of thinking, and if thinking includes as one of its modes conscience or the sense of an imperative coercive law, and if such a sense when analyzed, i.e., reflected on, involves an inchoate recognition of a Divine Being, it follows that such recognition comes upon my recognition that I am, and is only not so clear an object as is my own existence" (*PN* II, 63). Like Coleridge, Newman sees conscience, i.e., moral self-consciousness, as prior in nature to all other forms of human knowing in that it grounds them and orchestrates all cognitive activity. "The being of a God brought home to me, illuminated, as it will be, in its various aspects by reflection, tradition, &c. &c., I have a guiding truth, which gives practical direction to my judgment & faith as regards a variety of other truths or professed truths which encounter me, as the trustworthiness of the senses, our social & personal duties, the divinity of Christianity &c. &c. It teaches me how to use evidence which is imperfect, and why I must not be sceptical" (*PN* II, 65). Newman, again like Coleridge, here articulates a theory of knowledge diametrically opposed to the rationalism and mechanism of the eighteenth century. Knowing (beyond the level of sensation) is active not passive; spiritual not material; and, most importantly, personal not impersonal. For Newman the whole person understands, reasons, and judges. The whole person has, in fact, an innate moral imperative to strive for the truth and in so doing trust the validity of one's cognitive operations. Implicit in this epistemology is the existence of the will and the corresponding moral responsibility of which Coleridge speaks.

The attention Newman gives to the question of reality and the external world attests to his concern about the matter. In an annotation made in 1864 he adds a fourth benefit of his "proof." The first three were its universality, its practicality, and its rejection of the "philosophical sin." The fourth is that "it forms the basis for the belief of the senses, for if there be a God, and I am his creature with a mission, He *means* me to *use* the senses—and I accept what they convey as coming from Him whatever be its intellectual & philosophical worth" (*PN* II, 66). In asking whether we have faith in our own existence he firmly rejects the idea. We have faith in the existence of the external world, but we have an intuition of self that is prior to this faith. "I have an intuition of three things prior to the knowledge of the fact of myself: 1. In consciousness. 2. in thought. 3. in a certain analysis, which becomes afterwards the principle of reasoning. These are involved in the words 'Cogito ergo sum.' Taking the acts of the mind to bits, therefore, knowledge of my existence is the fourth act; though I call all four one complex act of intuition. Here we have real intuition, but I have faith, not intuition, of the external world" (*PN*, II, 71). The objectivity, then, of the transcendent Other is discovered in one's own subjectivity. A fuller explanation of this proof would emerge in the *Grammar of Assent*, where Newman would develop his concept of the "illative sense" which leads one to make a "real" (or as he originally called it, "imaginative") assent to moral and religious truths.

V

Newman does not, like Coleridge, explain in any detail how conscience and consciousness are evoked by early interpersonal relationships between parent and child. But he does elsewhere in his writings allude to the role parents play in the development of the conscience. In an 1831 Parochial Sermon he says, "I had hitherto considered cultivation of domestic affections as the *source* of more extended Christian love.[32] In discussing the moral development of children he says they "cannot learn without the assistance of others the meaning of moral facts."[33] Discussing private judgment he writes that "our parents and teachers are our first informants concerning the next world; and they elicit and cherish the innate sense of right and wrong which acts as a guide coordinately with them."[34] In speaking of "eliciting" an "innate sense of right and wrong" Newman seems to agree with Coleridge in holding that conscience is instinctive or connatural. In a University Sermon Newman declares that, "so alert is the instinctive power of the educated conscience, that by some secret faculty, and without any intelligible reasoning process, it seems to detect moral truth where ever it lies hid, and feels a conviction of its own accuracy which bystanders cannot account for."[35]

---

[32] *PPS* II, 57.

[33] John Henry Newman, *Essays Critical and Historical*, 2 vols. (London, 1895) II, 250.

[34] John Henry Newman, *The Via Media of the Anglican Church*, 2 vols. (London, 1895) I, 132.

[35] John Henry Newman, *Fifteen Sermons Preached Before the University of Oxford* (London, 1899) 66.

In an 1810 notebook entry Coleridge makes a similar observation: "Providence has plac'd for the wisest purposes a religious instinct in our nature, which leads us to be ever credulous where *religious feelings* (i.e. the stern precepts & sublime hopes & fears of Morality are the declared moral of the miracle)."[36] In another notebook entry he says that religion and morality are secure and will endure "as long as anywhere in the partakers of human Nature there remains that instinctive craving, dim & blind tho' it may be, of the moral being after this unknown Bliss, or Blessedness—known only & anticipated by the Hollowness where it is."[37] This "hollowness" or receptivness echoes the two analogies described earlier, and appears again in *Aids to Reflection* where he says that "throughout animated nature, of each characteristic organ and faculty there exists a pre-assurance, an instinctive and practical application; and no pre-assurance common to the whole species does in any instance prove delusive. All other prophecies of nature have their exact fulfillment—in every other *ingrafted work* of promise, Nature is found true to her word; and is it in her noblest creature that she tells her first lie" (353)? These analogies echo a passage in the *Biographia Literaria* where he says that "only they can acquire the philosophic imagination, the sacred power of self-intuition . . . who can feel in their own spirits the same instinct, which impels the Chrysalis of the horned fly to leave room in its involucrum for antennae yet to come" (I, 241–242). But unlike animal instincts and potentialities, the human conscience requires interaction with others to evoke its activity. And activated it must be if a human being is to become not just an individual organism but an individual person.

This natural moral instinct is central to the "progressive," or what we would today call the developmental nature, of human growth. Since their development is not totally determined by biological structure or environmental influences, human beings grow as persons only by exercising will and reason. The human movement toward increasing individuation is a growth process. In plant and animal life genetic structure and environment control all growth. In human life moral choice is the distinctive source of growth. Even George Eliot, whose novels and other writings reveal a decidedly deterministic philosophy, has Mordecai tell Daniel Deronda that "the strongest principle of growth lies in human choice."[38]

---

[36] *CN* III, Series 3894, Entry 18.117.
[37] *CN* III, Series 3911, Entry 18.134.
[38] *Daniel Deronda*, ed. Barbara Hardy (Harmondsworth, 1967) 598.

Persons grow as persons only when they are actively making moral choices. At sixteen Newman took as his life motto the phrase "Growth the only evidence of life." Its influence is dramatically evident in all his major writings, *Arians of the Fourth Century, Essay on the Development of Christian Doctrine, Idea of a University,* and *Grammar of Assent.* Coleridge's preoccupation with growth and change, like Newman's, had both personal and philosophical dimensions. In 1826 Coleridge wrote Daniel Stuart that "within the last two years and more particularly within the last, my mind without sustaining any revolution in faith or principles has yet undergone a *change*; I trust, a progression—and I am more practically persuaded, that toward the close of our Lives, if we have been at any time sincere in cultivating the Good within us, events & circumstances are more & more working toward the maturing of that Good, even when they are hardest to bear for the moment."[39] He observed to Lord Liverpool that "with the Moderns, on the contrary, nothing grows; all is made—Growth itself is but a disguised mode of being made by the superinduction of jam data upon a jam datum. This habit of thinking permeates the whole mass of our principles, and it is in spite of ourselves that we are not like a herd of Americans, a people without a *History*: for the historic feeling is evanescent, even in the construction of history itself."[40]

For both these men human beings are not just made or created by God; they are constantly in the process of being created and made—prompted toward full individuation by the conscience. Coleridge once called God "Creator! (and Evolver!)"[41] The shaping metaphor of Newman's "Lead Kindly Light" implies a constant movement toward God. Human participation in this process of growth and development is predicated on the human capacity to respond to invitation and to accept responsibility for one's choices.

VI

The enterprise that engaged Coleridge and Newman is not mere ancient history. In the 1940s and 1950s, within Catholic theological cir-

---

[39] *CL* VI, 576.
[40] *CL* IV, 761.
[41] *CN* II, Series 25466, Entry 17.104.

cles, an issue arose that directly relates to their concerns and purposes, as the perennial question of the relationship between grace and nature divided theologians into two camps. "Extrinsicists" insisted on the radical separation of grace and nature. Since grace is not accessible to human experience apart from God's free overture, there can be no such thing as a "natural desire" for God that would obligate God to fulfill that desire. Among "Intrinsicists" the foremost was the French Jesuit Henri DeLubac. While holding the distinction between grace and nature, he also held that from the beginning of creation human beings have had a natural desire for God—and this view was condemned by the official Church. It was not until the 1960s that a theological position was developed that satisfied both sides of this dispute. Drawing on the phenomenology of Heidegger, Karl Rahner suggested the idea of a "supernatural existential," a capacity in human nature that was already supernatural. He argued that human beings are created with a supernatural capacity for desiring God that is distinct but not separate from human nature. In true Coleridgean fashion Rahner had conceived a supernatural connatural desire.

In retrospect one can see in this ongoing theological reflection—from Coleridge and Newman to Rahner—the beginning of what theologians now call "theological anthropology," an effort to develop a Christian apologetics that explains how the existence of a revealing transcendent being must be explained "from below" not "from above." It must begin with the finite concrete believer not with the transcendent revealer. This, I believe, is precisely what Coleridge and Newman set out to accomplish. Coleridge's many analogies illustrating the human capacity for knowing God and Newman's nuanced explanation of the "feeling" of conscience both move upward from human experience to transcendent reality. Like their twentieth-century successors they realized that Christian thinkers could no longer operate on a hermeneutic of assent in which explanation followed belief, and theology was simply "fides quaerens intellectum" (faith seeking understanding). Faced with the rigorous demands of radical critical thinking, they sought a common ground for discussion. Beginning with human experience as a methodologically acceptable starting-point, they went on to critique critical reason itself—Coleridge by the development of his idea of "Higher Reason" and Newman by the development of his idea of the "Illative Sense." As Coleridge brought together reason and faith, so Newman brought together reason (illative) and feeling (sense).

As "individuality" was the starting-point of this essay, it might fittingly end by pointing out that another current issue Coleridge and Newman tried to resolve was the growing dissociation of head and heart. A striking example of the relevance of this issue is Dickens's *Hard Times*, where Thomas Gradgrind, who assumes human beings are, in his own words, just "reasoning animals," destroys the life of his children and some of the students in his Utilitarian-inspired school by allowing only the reason to be trained. At the novel's end, seeing the ruined lives around him, he might have agreed with Newman that, "after all, man is *not* a reasoning animal; he is a seeing, feeling, contemplating, acting animal"(*GA*, 94). And Coleridge might have added that a person "must make himself a better man before he can make himself a more intelligent one" (*Opus* III, 51).

Works Cited

Barth, J. Robert, S.J. *Coleridge and Christian Doctrine*. Cambridge, Mass.: Harvard University Press, 1969.
———. *Coleridge and the Power of Love*. Columbia, Mo.: University of Missouri Press, 1988.
Butler, Marilyn. *Jane Austen and the War of Ideas*. Oxford: Clarendon Press, 1975.
Carlyle, Thomas. *Sartor Resartus*. Ed. Charles F. Harrold. New York: Odyssey, 1937.
Coleridge, Samuel Taylor. *Aids to Reflection*. Ed. John Beer. Princeton: Princeton University Press, 1993. *CC* Vol. IX.
———. *Biographia Literaria*. Ed James Engell and W. Jackson Bate. 2 vols. Princeton: Princeton University Press, 1983. *CC* Vol. VII.
———. *Collected Letters of Samuel Taylor Coleridge*. Ed Earl Leslie Griggs. 6 vols. Oxford: Oxford University Press, 1956–1971.
———. *The Collected Works of Samuel Taylor Coleridge*. Ed. Kathleen Coburn. Bollingen Series 75. Princeton: Princeton University Press, 1969–. Cited as *CC*.
———. *The Notebooks of Samuel Taylor Coleridge*. Ed. Kathleen Coburn. 4 vols. to date. Bollingen Series 50. Princeton: Princeton University Press, 1955–.
———. "Theory of Life," in *The Complete Works of Samuel Taylor Coleridge, with an Introductory Essay upon His Philosophical and Theologi-*

cal Opinions. Ed. W. G. T. Shedd. Volume I. New York: Harper and Brothers, 1856.

———. *The Watchman*. Ed. Lewis Patton. Princeton: Princeton University Press, 1970. *CC* Vol. II.

Eliot, George. *Daniel Deronda*. Ed. Barbara Hardy. Harmondsworth: Penguin, 1967.

———. *The George Eliot Letters*. Ed. Gordon Haight. 9 vols. New Haven: Yale University Press, 1954–1978.

Haight, Gordon. *George Eliot: A Biography*. New York: Oxford University Press, 1968.

Harding, John Anthony. *Coleridge and the Idea of Love: Aspects of Relationship in Coleridge's Thought and Writing*. London: Cambridge University Press, 1974.

Lonergan, Bernard J. *Method in Theology*. New York: Herder and Herder, 1972.

Maslow, A. H. *Toward a Psychology of Being*. Princeton: Princeton University Press, 1962.

McFarland, Thomas. *Romanticism and the Forms of Ruin: Wordsworth, Coleridge, and the Modalities of Fragmentation*. Princeton: Princeton University Press, 1981.

Mill, John Stuart. *On Liberty*. Ed David Spitz. New York: Norton, 1975.

Nédoncelle, Maurice. *God's Encounter with Man: A Contemporary Approach to Prayer*. New York: Sheed and Ward, 1964.

Newman, John Henry. *Apologia pro vita sua*. Ed. David Delaura. New York: Norton, 1965.

———. *The Argument from Conscience*. Ed. Adrian K. Boekraad and Henry Tristram. Louvain: Nauwelaerts, 1961.

———. *An Essay in Aid of a Grammar of Assent*. London: Longmans, Green, 1895.

———. *An Essay on the Development of Christian Doctrine*. London: Longmans, Green, 1894.

———. *Essays Critical and Historical*. 2 volumes. London: Longmans, Green, 1895.

———. *Fifteen Sermons Preached Before the University of Oxford*. London: Longmans, Green, 1899.

———. *Parochial and Plain Sermons*. 8 vols. London: Longmans, Green, 1899.

———. *The Philosophical Notebook.* Ed. Edward Sillem. 2 vols. Louvain: Nauwelaerts, 1969.

———. *The Via Media of the Anglican Church.* 2 vols. London: Longmans, Green, 1895.

Rahner, Karl. *Foundations of Christian Faith: An Introduction to the Idea of Christianity.* New York: Crossroads, 1984.

Rule, Philip C. "Coleridge's Reputation as a Religious Thinker: 1816–1972," *Harvard Theological Review* 67 (1974): 289–320.

———. "Something of Great Constancy: Uses of the Imagination." Regina: Campion College Press, 1985.

Schneewind, J. B. *The Invention of Autonomy: A History of Modern Moral Philosophy.* Cambridge: Cambridge University Press, 1998.

Taylor, Charles. *Sources of the Self: The Making of Modern Identity.* Cambridge, Mass.: Harvard University Press, 1989.

Ward, Wilfrid. *The Life of John Henry Newman.* 2 vols. London: Longmans, Green, 1912.

Wollstonecraft, Mary. *A Vindication of the Rights of Woman.* Ed. Carol H. Poston. New York: Norton, 1988.

Wordsworth, William. *The Prelude: 1799, 1805, 1850.* Ed. Jonathan Wordsworth, M. H. Abrams, and Stephen Gill. New York: Norton, 1979.

13

"All About the Heart": The Material-Theology of Maturin's *Melmoth the Wanderer*

Judith Wilt

BYRON's *Manfred* and Southey's *Thalaba the Destroyer* have blasphemous potency; Shelley's *Prometheus Unbound* and Blake's *The Marriage of Heaven and Hell* reach through and past the domain of the divine. Coleridge's "The Ancient Mariner" tells us of the spiritually unutterable, in terms so banal we must attend closely in order to unutter them. So does Blake's "The Tyger." And Mary Shelley's *Frankenstein*. But none of these masterworks displays its unutterance with more relish and reach and blasphemy, more enigmatic and desperate force, than Charles Maturin's *Melmoth the Wanderer* (1820), whose devilish protagonist, archpriest and Irishman, cavalier rebel and savage savant, bears in his body the "incommunicable condition" incapable of exchange, or change—the human condition.[1]

At once the God-licensed tempter of Job, the aristocrat self-licensed tempter of Richardson's eponymous heroine Clarissa, and the eloquent but outbargained rogue of a dozen romances and folktales from the Wandering Jew to *Paradise Lost*, Melmoth is a privileged voyeur of the human heart. The Irish peasant Biddy, half-sibyl, half-impostor, tells us early in the narrative frame that "it's all *here*; it's all *about the heart*" (13). To each of the hearts in extremity he visits, he offers what appears to be extrication from the prison of mortality, and each time he is rejected for the simplest of reasons. The "condition" he makes, the

---

[1] Charles Maturin, *Melmoth the Wanderer*, ed. Douglas Grant (London, 1968) 237. Maturin's novel directly quotes *Thalaba* and records its debt to the supernatural poetry of Byron and Coleridge in submerged language. The novel also refers directly to its Gothic inquisition-narrative forebear, Ann Radcliffe's *The Italian*, and has sly indirect fun with Matthew Gregory Lewis's *The Monk*.

condition he visibly is in, this mortal immortal, is torment. The condition cannot be relieved because it is everywhere. It cannot be "communicated" because you already have it. The Christian spin on this, as T. S. Eliot would later put it in "Little Gidding," goes: "We only live, or else suspire / Consumed by either fire or fire."[2] But "consumed" is inexact. We cannot bargain for immortality because that too we already have.

Charles Robert Maturin was an incoherent mix of passions and actions, a theologian and a dandy, a family man and misanthrope, a formidably well-educated elitist and at once a hater and a craver of popular approval. He was a member of the Anglo-Irish Ascendancy and also an Irish patriot, an ambitious artist vowed to clerical poverty and obedience. He wrote melodramas that blazed with incest and malice and violence. But his fables rode on a realist's assessment not just of the petty sins of people but of the paradoxical and systematic capture by institutional violence of human property—"real," national, intellectual and moral, while the humans, bewildered, erupted in rage or sank into torpor.

Like his Gothic-writing forebears, Horace Walpole and Ann Radcliffe, he transferred to precincts Mediterranean and historical his overpowering sense that the "castle" of human culture had somehow fallen into the hands of tyrants. Like his contemporary and would-be patron Walter Scott,[3] he wrote his usurped and now "British" home into his texts from his own equivocal position as Anglo-Irish. Missteps in Irish inheritance is a powerful motif in his novels *The Wild Irish Boy*, *The Milesian Chief*, and *Women Pour et Contre*; inheritance deflected, alienated, bankrupted, corrupted: in *The Milesian Chief* a former heir lives as his own land's steward. *Melmoth the Wanderer* opens as an Anglo-Irish inheritance passes from uncle to nephew while the landless natives watch their opportunity to continue to haunt the process.

But unlike Scott or Radcliffe (let alone Shelley or Byron), Maturin was an Anglican clergyman: his preface argues that the novel is actually an extension of a thought in one of his Sermons.[4] For him all these

---

[2] *The Complete Poems and Plays, 1909–1950* (New York, 1971) 144.

[3] Douglas Grant, the Oxford Edition's editor, tells us there that Scott tried to interest Lady Anne Jane Hatton, the Marchioness of Abercorn, in the financial plight of the Maturin family (543); Maturin hopefully dedicated the novel to her.

[4] One of the best modern treatments of the novel takes Maturin's rather tendentious claim seriously, broadly arguing that the novel in both theme and structure is a reflection on the text of the book of Job: "Maturin has shivered the text of Job . . . and then

issues of inheritance have a theological grounding as well as an historico-cultural aspect, one that hovers between gnostic elevation and Christian incarnation. The question, what are we heir to and how can we express our claim to it? becomes, what is the "incommunicable condition"? and (how) is it assuaged, or at least expressed, however incommunicably, in the Mysteries of original sin, atonement, and, especially, "faith." Descendent of Huguenots, ancestor of Oscar Wilde, Maturin throve addictively on paradox, and pursued both the theology and the "theater" of faith and good works beyond Reformation or Counter-Reformation solutions, into the incommunicable abyss. Here all actions, all passions, all desires, lead only to torment, including the desire-not-to-desire; all theories of suffering, from philosophers and theologians alike, founder on the same pointless "why?": the answer simply reports and redoubles the condition. Each man kills the thing he loves, dies of the desire he deplores.[5]

The "secret" Melmoth carries is in fact understood by the reader, in its orthodox vesture, its hapless "point," the moment it surfaces as a secret: the price of relief from mortality is immortal damnation. The heterodox core of the secret, however, is not a point but a fullness, a brilliant pleroma, a space of limitless depth and silence: "the secret of silence is the only secret. Words are a blasphemy against that taciturn and invisible God, whose presence enshrouds us in our last extremity," says the novel's most verbose and important theologian narrator (195), the Catholic Alonzo de Monçada. "What a difference," says a narrator within his narration, "between *words without meaning* and that *meaning without words* which the sublime phenomena of nature . . . convey to those who have 'ears to hear'" (321). Words are the business of the post-lapsarian sublime: words spun from the material of the body: tongue, lips, ears to hear, eyes to read. Words are the body's meanings, the "material-theological," the human condition. But the body and its words are also the gateway to the pleroma, the edge of the "only" secret, the dark material foundation which Christian incarnationalism stub-

---

challenged us to restore it." Kathleen Fowler, "Hieroglyphics in Fire: *Melmoth the Wanderer*," *Studies in Romanticism* 25 (1986): 538.

[5] As Carlo Testa points out, the pact-with-the-devil analysis of desire common before Goethe, which held that desire should and can be transferred from irregular object A to theologically sound point B, was being challenged by the time of Blake and Maturin: now the devil is a device for asking more broadly, "what is desire itself?" And all answers simply continue the problematization of the question. *Desire and the Devil: Demonic Contracts in French and European Literature* (New York, 1991) 15–16.

bornly weds to the realm of light. At this gateway one must resist the temptation to ask, or answer, what, or why.

Consider this exchange between the Master of the Inquisition and one of the novel's tersest theologians, who has just revealed the unconscious presumption of one of the city's best beloved and well-doing clerics:

> 'He sought the secret of discovering the presence or agency of the evil power.'
> 'Do you possess that secret?'
> 'My master forbids me to disclose it.'
> 'If your master were Jesus Christ, he would not forbid you. . . .'
> 'I am not sure of that.'
> 'You believe, then, it requires strength of mind to keep these abominable secrets?'
> 'No, I rather imagine strength of body.' (38)

The orthodox Anglican Maturin abominates orthodox Catholic Inquisitions, of course: the satire here is clear. Yet at another level this exchange, fathoms deep in the novel's Chinese boxes of buried narrative, represents a genuine passion to know, not the strength of the mind but strength itself, harbored unequivocally in the body.

It's true that the final wry comment acknowledges the Inquisitor's capacity to pry the Illuminated's secret out of the body's harbor, as he shortly does. But like "incommunicable condition," "strength of body" seems to float free of its sentence into that meaning without words which is the novel's paradoxical object of worship and curiosity. Strength *is* the body's, the body is the silence that grounds its words, and strength reclaims its own in the "enshrouding" presence of the divine. For though the tortured Illuminatus "uttered the following remarkable confession," what follows on the page is that blank space starred with asterisks which, under the tropes of "discoloured, obliterated and mutilated" (28) and above all "illegible" (39), unutters the secret every time. Unuttered, the secret origin of the felt and suffering "separateness" of humankind; unuttered the secret dynamic of the suffering reintegration, at-one-ment; ineffably unuttered the secret suffering action whose divine word is "faith," human word is "love."

In the design of the novel the moral action repeats a cycle of resurrection and reburial, disclosing and unuttering, while the plot travels from

Ireland through England to Spain and India, and circles back through Spain and England to Ireland. It travels also from theologies of faith to ontologies of love to a narratology still withholding its secret in the grammatical conditional. Melmoth himself can provide only a blizzard of "ifs" in his last prophecy of his end (537–538), and the frame narrator's grammar breaks down over the task of reporting it: footmarks on the turf to the edge of the Irish seacoast look "as if a person had dragged, or been dragged, his way through it" (542). In the frame story, an Anglo-Irish landlord, childless possessor of confiscated Irish estates gifted by Cromwell, lies dying, dreading the loss of the material comforts which his miserliness has already denied him. He dreads even more the visit of the elder brother of that confiscating ancestor, mysteriously unaged after 150 years, who represents in the historico-cultural register (take your pick) the intellectual counterpart of that ancestral religio-imperial avidity, and/or its avenging opposite.

"John Melmoth the Traveler" (26), student of ancient knowledges and connoisseur of suffering, is rumored a steady attendant at the deathbeds of guilty self-tormenters, but this is the dull routine of his "service" to his rumored diabolical master. The spice in the routine is presence, enabling presence, at the moment when the innocent, the not yet human, the always already human persons, first suffer the knowledge of their excruciating "condition." His true target is not the old miser but the new heir, his namesake and great-great-nephew John Melmoth, the timid and dependent university student, to whom he offers *himself* and his story as the fruit of the tree of knowledge.

Old Melmoth, it turns out, has by instinct hoarded, along with his wine and his rents, a blazing-eyed portrait of the Traveler and a disintegrating manuscript left about him by one of his obsessed targets from the seventeenth century, an English Restoration intellectual and dandy named Stanton, who first saw Melmoth convulsed in laughter as the shattering storm which both men had witnessed struck dead by lightning two innocent young lovers. The Traveler's countenance was—"here the manuscript was illegible"—and he told Stanton—"a long hiatus followed here" (31). And the relationship that followed, "the master passion . . . and master-torment of his life" (59), is set in motion as a fiery current flowing irresistibly between two poles, "the human condition" and "the Power" (31). This is the elemental force which the speaker of Shelley's "Mont Blanc" feels coming down the Arve, and Byron's Manfred went up the mountain to draw forth, the unnamable energy, mysteriously ordering, which dwells unfathomably behind all things.

Stanton's story provides the pattern for all the tales of the novel. From his eminence of philosophical reflection, intellectual mastery, and material freedom, he is reversed by human greed and institutional violence to incarcerated immobility, filth, and madness. This heart's extremity is Melmoth's cue; he appears, and delivers the incommunicable revelation of man's real condition. Stanton's "rejection" of the exchange of the human's condition for any other condition turns the screw of the master-torment a little tighter, makes the human more viscerally itself. The circumstances by which Stanton was freed from that particular extremity are irrelevant and hence unnarrated in the manuscript which he wrote as part of his obsessive pursuit of the bargainer he rejected. Tracing the Traveler to his Irish family home years before, he cast the text, with its pulsations of revelation and illegibility, into the house, as a shipwrecked captain commits his log in a bottle to the ocean (59), communicating his condition, but through a glass, darkly.

Two things besides the general pattern are important about this first tale. The first is a certain sardonic evenhandedness in the tales' depiction of religious madness. In the English madhouse Stanton hears a Puritan weaver repeat compulsively for hours the "points" of his Doctrine, and a Cavalier tailor monotonously recount the forms and costs of the garments he has made for the mighty. Much longer stays in Spain for other tales will license much more detailed descriptions of the iniquities of Counter-Reformation Catholicism so necessary to the nineteenth-century British imagination. But a brief visit to India will incriminate Hindu and Muslim cultural institutional religious practice as well. Indeed, *Melmoth* provides an interesting example of a process which Marilyn Butler has described, where radical thinkers using new knowledges of eastern religions contended with orthodox Christian thinkers for the "sacred" ground of the figures of Satan, and of that ambiguously animating/destroying "fire" which he represented.[6]

The second element of importance in this tale is its location of the

---

[6] "Romantic Manichaeism: Shelley's 'On the Devil, and Devils' and Byron's Mythological Dramas," *The Sun Is God: Painting, Literature and Mythology in the Nineteenth Century*, ed. J. B. Bullen (Oxford, 1989). Butler's essay does not consider *Melmoth*, but traces the fascination of poets and political philosophers with Zoroastrianism, "the thinking radical's form of religion," whose stylized worship of the sun and fire reinforces the primacy of flux and contrariety in being (15).

formal meeting of Melmoth and Stanton, who are the poles of the current between Power and the human condition, in a Restoration theater, one moreover showing plays that are a jumble of classical themes and contemporary costume, exotic characters and locales and English political intrigue, artificial emotion and real violence, even rapes (40). The educated Stanton deplores this jumbled communication until his gaze wanders from the spectacle to encounter the eyes of his long-sought interlocutor, when his "heart palpitates with violence" and his body reels in "nameless and deadly sickness" (43). The face of another spectator disrupts the safe boundaries of the theatrical; the stage overflows the boxes and vice-versa. In Counter-Reformation Spain "(the Catholic) religion is our national drama" (105); in Reformed England (Protestant) drama (and increasingly, as Ian Watt suggested long ago, the novel[7]) is the national religion.

The critical impulse that frames such comments, however, dies into the awe of fact, and "drama . . . nation . . . religion" also floats free of its sentence to join "strength of body" and "incommunicable condition" as the material-theological basis of the novel. For the vertiginous bilocation between spectator and spectacle, intrinsic to the human condition as Melmoth's instant presence to all his targets is to the nature of the Power, is fundamental to the theology of suffering, and so is the body's strength to admit and endure this vertiginous doubleness and the heart's capacity to circulate it.

The secular exploration of material-theological suffering begins when a powerful storm wrecks a vessel on the coast of young Melmoth's Irish property. Rushing down with a crowd of villagers equally powerless to help, he is pulled nearly in two by an irresistible attraction *both* to the tormented cry of the drowning men repeating the shrieks of wind and wave ("his senses reeled under the shock, and for a moment he echoed the storm with yells of actual insanity" [64]), *and* to the racking laugh of the unmoved spectator on the rock above him, which identifies the spectator as the Traveler described in the manu-

---

[7] See *The Rise of the Novel: Studies in DeFoe, Richardson and Fielding* (Berkeley [1957], 1967) 74–85. Michael McKeon has more recently complicated and challenged Watt's argument that a slowly secularizing English Protestantism generated in the eighteenth century a personal individualism fundamental both to the rise of the middle class and to the formal realism it preferred for its fiction: McKeon explores earlier genres of prose narrative, including the movement from medieval hagiography to Renaissance spiritual biography, to locate the origins of realism. *The Origins of the English Novel, 1600–1740* (Baltimore, 1987) 91–96.

script he has just read. Breaking out of his paralysis toward the stronger desire, he climbs after the Traveler, but falls into the sea to become one with the sufferers. Gripped by a fellow drowning man, he is carried to shore with him, where the two are found "locked in each other's hold, but stiff and senseless" (70).

The young boy would wish to credit himself and his fellow would-be rescuers with the received simplicities about the virtuous dynamic of suffering and empathy: "How much good there is in man . . . when it is called forth by the sufferings of his fellows!" (65). But the narrator cautions that the compound the young boy called "good" had in it elements of curiosity, pride of physical strength, and comparative consciousness of safety, not to mention the darker incitement to revel in the experience of the Absolute Worst, and the equivocal pleasure of storytelling to come. The young boy also tries to credit his rescuer directly, but Alonzo de Monçada, tempered in torture and as it turns out once targeted for temptation by the Traveler himself, reports impartially that he saved his own life, and that of young Melmoth, out of "instinct," that is the strength of the body, or, to use another more "polite" dialect, as he says, "the influence of my better genius" (71).

This linking of one body's suffering/strength with another body's life follows the line of Enlightenment empiricist thinking on association and sympathy. But as Steven Bruhm points out in his learned and provocative *Gothic Bodies: The Politics of Pain in Romantic Fiction*, there can be very dangerous surges and overloads in the currents of "sympathy." Tracing the arguments for the physiological basis of social sympathy and the pain/terror foundation of Burkean aesthetics, Bruhm shows how the "I know how you feel" experience of pain that shapes a community of sympathetic bodies can become a competitive and finally substitutional anti-ethic claiming "This hurts me more than it hurts you."[8] Here the empathetic spectator may even link with the torturer, co-opting, sympathetically, the virtuous space of the victim, the living space of the Other, erasing his interiority and even claiming his body, the strength of his body, as the spectator or torturer's own prosthesis. Such is the politics of the patriarchal male; such may be the politics of the revolutionary state, or the counter-revolutionary church. Such, closer to the bone, is the politics of the God of Abraham and Isaac, the God of the sacrifice of Christ.

---

[8] *Gothic Bodies: The Politics of Pain in Romantic Fiction* (Philadelphia, 1994) 15, 114.

It is no accident that the bulk of *Melmoth the Wanderer*, 460 of its 540 pages in the Oxford Edition, is narrated by the Spanish Catholic, Monçada, who has suffered in his (strength of) body an amount of experience equal in range, and nearly in pages, to what he has seen, read, and written of the sufferings of the Other—Jew, Puritan, and Catholic, male and female—and who has remained true to the faith of his culture. He has not turned aside from his suffering either to atheism or to conversion: he has never "exchanged" his condition (as Englishmen of the Reformation had done). Eagerly solicited by young Melmoth, the thirty-year-old Monçada first recounts his own history of familial and "Jesuitical" and Inquisitorial persecution in "The Tale of the Spaniard," climaxing with an encounter with the Traveler. He then reports, from a manuscript written in Greek (but in Hebrew characters) by a steadfastly unconverted Jewish scholar, which he translated into English, "The Tale of the Indian." The "Indian" is a young girl named Isadora, born in Spain but shipwrecked on an island off India, where as "Immalee," she begins her heart's true history with the same kind of encounter.

Maturin makes his two central targets Spanish and Catholic, partly as a bow to the general English national sense of having properly "left behind" a whole series of "ancient" tyrannies. More deeply, he wants to evoke in properly ambiguous Gothic style the pre-modern ferocity of the religious current flowing between the unutterable Divine Power and the incommunicable human condition, mediated and modernized by the Anglican *via media*, but also, of course, obscured and miniaturized by it. Further, while Alonzo and Immalee are in some respects both gendered humanly female to Melmoth's, the Power's, masculine pole, Maturin also needs Alonzo's specifically masculine body through which to stage the drama of faith in/as suffering—which generates narrative—as he needs Immalee's feminine sexuality to stage a similar drama for love in/as suffering—which generates, as we shall see, a more carnal product.

These two tales are related in another interesting way to two classics of eighteenth-century literature. They echo, translate, even plagiarize, the Gothico-Puritan drama of incarceration, temptation, torture, and no-exit extremity of Samuel Richardson's *Clarissa* (1748) and of the convent-captivity novel it inspired, Diderot's *La Religieuse* (1760), published in English as *Memoirs of a Nun* in 1796. Enthralled by Richardson's story of an independent-minded daughter undergoing a series of imprisonments designed as trials of her duty, virtue, character, and, finally, strength of body, the great French philosophe began a hoax tale of a daughter forced by family into convent life, in which she experiences the suffering of assault, seduction, maddening persuasions toward conversion, and equally maddening routine. Like Clarissa, Marie Suzanne in her intelligent self-awareness tries to discover the tiniest fragments of private space in her community of duty. She too makes a leap from intolerable duty into the fiery imprisonment of a seducer devil's phantom freedom.

Diderot, an outsider to the vexations of religious desire, was mainly interested in the exposure of institutional violence and the classic porno-sublime of the suffering and death of a beautiful woman: he solves, or rather abandons, the problem of the no-exit with a last-minute rescue of his heroine. Richardson, on the other hand, no stranger to the critique of institutions, or to the porno-sublime, *is* aflame with religious desire, and feels the no-exit dilemma with excruciating precision, forcing his characters into that exhausted extremity where the "enshrouding presence" of God finally awards them—the shroud.

The heroine of *Clarissa* accepts the incommunicable condition as a triumphant exit, and continues, rather as Melmoth does, in a postmortal narration that promises (threatens!) never to end. But the novel's antagonist, the trial-giver and tempter Lovelace, does not accept it; instead he sets out to claim her dead heart, still speaking its suffering, as though he could still wring from it that acknowledgment of himself that would keep them both immortal. In "The Tale of the Spaniard," Maturin, like Diderot, reworks this material into a convent captivity, transposing the tempter's passion-pursuit for the reluctant cleric into the masculine, homoerotic register. In "The Tale of the Indian" he returns to the structure of *Clarissa*, allowing the heroine this time *both* roles, displaying in the (hetero)sexual register the woman's flight but also the woman's enigmatic refusal to stop pursuing the heart's (Melmoth's heart, her idea of Melmoth's heart, her own heart's) extremity.

Mario Praz was the first to document fully the "plagiarisms" from Diderot's convent captivity tale in Maturin's "The Tale of the Spaniard," where Alonzo de Monçada is forced into monastic life to "buy" his parents indemnity from the illegitimacy that was their sexual sin.[9]

---

[9] Praz retells this story in *The Romantic Agony* (London, 1933) 177. Roving learnedly and eclectically among English and Continental writing both canonical and non-canonical, Praz in this book made the first twentieth-century argument for the impor-

Like his female counterpart in *Memoirs of a Nun*, Monçada suffered the mind-numbing monotony of the vocationless and workless conventual life, the spite lurking behind the theatrical competition in the performance of religious duties, the licensed same-sex overtures from the next "cell," the scene where freedom would mean trampling one's mother's body—all transposed from the bourgeois setting of Jansenist France to the convent of "ex-Jesuits" still impudently functioning in eighteenth-century Madrid despite the suppression of the order in 1767. But the most significant aspects of the tale are Maturin's own: the blasphemous playing at demonic possession and sacred miracle, the hinting at obscene Marian rites, the exquisitely appropriate entombment with the parricide monk who feasts on the cannibal moments of the human family in extremis—above all, the wrestling with an ethic of suffering and theology of atonement that a Christian can neither manage nor leave alone.

The theology is delivered early and insistently, in earnest debates between Monçada and other clerics, and both upholds and radically qualifies the standard accounts that legitimize human suffering with divine sanction. There was indeed *"one great Sacrifice"* (147) between the Father and the Son, but it remains, and should remain, Monçada argues, incommunicable and unduplicatable. Whatever its nature, the Sacrifice must be regarded as a deeply ambiguous index to the proper ethical relationship between human and human, or human and divine, and it certainly gives no warrant to any person or institution to deal in sacrifice, or to buy, or buy off, suffering, or to essay in one's inconceivable ignorance to move the levers of justice.

Faith, we come to understand, actually lives in the utter darkness of the meaning-without-words of that Sacrifice which figures the gap between the Power and the Human. But Faith maintains that great Sacrifice was One—we can't repeat it or take anything from it or give anything to it. We can't restage it in the body of the putatively erring or damned Other; we can only marvel at the damnable pleasure we take in his or her pain. We can't even restage it in our own body, where we experience the pain of our pleasures.

Faith, and theology as well, rather holds the mystery of the one great Sacrifice apart, if only by a hair's breadth, from the mystery of the

---

tance of *Melmoth*; see esp. chs. 2, "The Metamorphoses of Satan," and 3, "The Shadow of the Divine Marquis [De Sade]."

human body's mysterious cleaving to its own suffering as the vessel of its consciousness. Burke revived the Greek conception that suffering produces wisdom in the bodily registering of pain and terror as "the strongest sensation." Theologian Albert W. J. Harper comments this way on the complex dynamic of suffering and consciousness: "Conscious suffering suffers from at least a twofold conflict: the mind is desirous of bringing its suffering to an end and conquering it by coming upon a reason for its suffering, but the pride of consciousness also wants to make the most of the conscious state it feels it possesses in what has been described as the 'loquaciousness' of suffering."[10] Consciousness teeters between the desired "loquaciousness" of suffering and that "shattering" of language and identity which Elaine Scarry has noted is the true goal of the torturer, despite his putative quest for the words that would answer his questions.[11]

"You will be surprised to hear these sentiments from a Catholic," the Spaniard Monçada tells the Anglo-Irish Melmoth—Maturin here simultaneously reiterating the Reformers' claim that the whole mediating edifice of "theology" itself is a "Catholic" barrier to the true communication between God and man, while demonstrating that the communication does occur, in spite of theology. A similar intention governs his characterization of the man who guides Monçada out of his persecuting convent, and into the hands of the Inquisition. The "parricide monk" is an "amateur" of spectacles of suffering (207). By taking a hand in Monçada's life, planning a rescue by Monçada's brother which will actually bring Alonzo to cause Juan's death, the monk is restaging in the daylight the kin-murder that he insists made him the impenetrable and aridly skeptical "man" he is, trying to exorcise in this substitutional manner the memory of the patricide that visits him nightly.

---

[10] *The Theodicy of Suffering* (San Francisco, 1990) 39.

[11] *The Body in Pain: The Making and Unmaking of the World* (New York, 1985), see Introduction, esp. 3–11. Scarry's moving and broadly influential study introduced this dynamic between pain's agency in making the suffering body express the face of its "aliveness" or "sentience," and pain's capacity (especially in the hands of political torturers) to shatter the linguistic and pre-linguistic "voice" which is the body's personal extension of itself toward being, ultimately toward the Divine Power. In her reading, the Old and New Testaments record the distribution of voice, with its inevitable quality of embodiedness, as the current that flows between the human and the Divine, providing a new theology where the moral distance between man and God remains, but "no longer depends on a discrepancy in embodiedness" (184).

The parricide monk is doing this in cynical, and reverse, homage to the "theology" that makes promiscuously available to the "pride of consciousness," and blasphemously "substitutional" (224) for both pride and politics, the dynamic of the *one great Sacrifice*. The consequence, for the monk, is grimly logical: having adopted "the best theology" (225), that is, the substitute of every other suffering body for his own in a version of the Hobbesian war of each against all, he ventures out of the audience one day into the spectacle, a procession of high ecclesiastics, where his crime makes him the natural substitute for a superstitious crowd looking for a scapegoat for its own suffering, and his body is torn apart by them all until his loquaciousness shatters in formless cries and disappears.

Alonzo de Monçada is a careful religious thinker; the parricide monk is a keen theologian. But the subtlest theologian of them all is of course Melmoth the Traveler. In his brief appearance in "The Tale of the Spaniard," as a member and secret manipulator of the Inquisition, he makes only one contribution to the novel's theology of suffering, but it is a key one: "There is no error more absurd, and yet more rooted in the heart of man, than the belief that his suffering will promote his spiritual safety" (233). At first glance we would not be surprised to hear the person rumored to be the devil's agent begin his argument this way: detach man from this root, and "suffering" becomes merely a commodity, available for substitution, circulation, or, in the words of the devil's bargain, "exchange." Yet Melmoth's real role in the scheme of the things, as with every literary evocation of the devil, "the spirit that always wills the bad but always works the good," is to expose to scorn that very calculus of "spiritual safety"—without, however, uprooting the intimacy of the human heart and its suffering, the virtual equation of consciousness, wisdom, and suffering. Monçada may flee the Inquisition, as he swam from the wrecked ship to the coast of Ireland, by the instinctive strength of his body rather than from virtue, but he does not seek safety of any kind, nor does he seek, dangerously, to know the end (the fullness, or the goal) of the strength of his body.

This, we may speculate, was Melmoth's own original sin. The men to whom he offers "exchange of destinies" have refused the exchange but they cannot forget what they have glimpsed in him, the loquacity of *his* suffering. Each of them at some level still covets this loquacity, as they pursue him, the supremely narratable being. Stanton and Monçada remain alive after their meeting with Melmoth because they and their object *hold* one another in written and spoken narrative, narratives that always reach a space of blotted ink, unreadable words, lost pages, which testify to the incommunicable.

What is this but a classic metaphor for theology itself, a tense and paradoxical picturing of the science of the nature of God's Creation, where both poles of the current, both the Power and the human condition, are gendered male. The paradigm that grounds this one, however, the paradigm for strength of body spun into personal consciousness, is surely birth: the paradigm is sexuality, classically gendered as "woman." Melmoth's own hyperloquacious consciousness, we discover, can be exposed, and perhaps even redeemed, only in a narrative that admits (relocates him in) its origin in his body, a narrative whose agent is a woman.

The woman was born Isadora to a Spanish merchant family but was shipwrecked onto a prelapsarian Isle near India as a toddler, and worshipped as the goddess Immalee by native visitants to the Isle. She is a different story altogether for Melmoth the Traveler. The men he visits are targets because they are ripe with suffering; they are his duty, for he is, he says, assigned to conduct them to the logic of the last choice—the death of consciousness or the hyperconsciousness of the damned. But Immalee, her consciousness diffused throughout the natural streams and fruits and lights and leaves which feed and clothe and stimulate her as she grows like a plant on the Isle, seems to be a personal choice, not an assignment. Maturin creates Melmoth as a devil's disciple, but the line between Master and Servant is more blurred in this fable than in any of the other tales. Insofar as he is Satan to her Eve he has in a manner broken from his "service" to his dark master; he has gone back to the springs of creation to be *himself* the one to pull apart the poles of Divine and Human and make the lightning crackle between them. More deeply, he has gone to her out of desire, not just to give her the bitter inheritance of separation, suffering, consciousness and the last choice, but also to give himself the same gift again, to re-enter, through her innocent interlocutories and her infinitely alluring strength of bodily and spiritual endurance, that dynamic, round upon round, of pain and loquacious consciousness which is the condition of the human.

The first exchanges in the Isle are thus straight out of *Paradise Lost*. Melmoth's Satan engages Immalee's Eve in three quests—for knowledge not just of what is good but of what is; for "thought," which separates thinker from objects of thought, and, more dangerously, thought-objects of sense perception from thought-objects of imagination; and for language, the capacity to "talk thoughts" (287) and even "write thoughts" (318), which creates that artificial world which is most paradoxically the most human world. But their later exchanges on the Isle and in Madrid take "thought" in the direction of intersubjective (hetero)sexual passion. Looking upon the facts of natural and human life that Melmoth discloses, Immalee reasons, "To think, then, is to suffer" (288). But as she comes to recognize that lightning may strike from inside as well as outside, that the worm may fly in to devour the rosebud but the rose may also already be "sick" of a desire to fly from its stem, she learns to feel, and then to court, that "secret sentiment" (319) which the prudent would "banish" or "crush" (319), but the seeker or traveler would clasp and define herself by, Love.[12] The Love which thought forbids is the supreme teacher of suffering: the "mysterious terror which always trembles at the bottom of the hearts of those who dare to love" (321) stubbornly holds open the beating, bleeding muscle of the heart that thought would prudently close.

In all the exchanges between Melmoth and Immalee, whether on the Isle, or after she is rescued to resume the life of Isadora in Madrid, the woman, the human, grips this terror as her portion. And slowly, seeking as well as fighting the magnetic force of her terror/desire, Melmoth is drawn to re-experience human passion, human self-contradiction, human despair. He marshals against this force his weapons of "spoken thought" and perhaps even "written thought," blasting her alternately with fiery satire and icy disdain, but to no real avail. In the foreground of "The Tale of the Indian" we seem to read *her* story, as she moves through the "stages" of love (362–364), from active desire through the permanent paradox of absence or presence as "equally unsupportable," to that "profound and perilous absorption of the soul when it is determined to penetrate the mysteries" (365). In the back-

---

[12] Maturin brings Melmoth to Immalee as a virtual embodiment of Blake's lament in *Songs of Experience*, "O Rose, thou art sick, / The Invisible worm / That flies in the night / In the howling storm / Has found out thy bed / Of crimson joy, / And his dark secret love / does thy life destroy." On the Isle, Immalee has seen the worm destroy the flower, but argues to Melmoth that no horror attends this, for "the worm was not the native of the flower; its own leaves could never have hurt it." But he responds with an invitation to enter the human world of "forbidden passion," where the hurt is invisible, internal, self-generated, where one leaf on a stem may be poison to the next leaf (285–286).

ground of this narrative, however, we follow the story of Melmoth's *own* increasing absorption: in the mystery of her insistent attachment; in the command which lies beneath her constant plaint, "will he be there?" (287, 323, 533); above all in the tell-tale and utterly material sound and sight and feel of the mighty muscle of her heart, beating "like a wave against a rock" (353), throbbing "almost visibly in the white and palpitating bosom" (365), moving eerily "in his hand . . . like a bird with a string tied round its leg" (376).

In the foreground, we focus on Melmoth's blasphemous challenge to Immalee to wed him, in spite of her family, in the teeth of reason, and in the dead of night—with Death as the celebrant (394) and a voyage to hell as their wedding trip (355). In the background, however, we see his return to her, after every failure or reversal, after his every attempt to wither her by abandonment. Struggling with compassion (285), with a Hamlet-like tendency to "blunted purpose" (288), tempted by the cool "breeze" of her purity (309), both relieved and horrified by his success in driving her through the stages of the passion of love, Melmoth comes back again and again, and finally gets what he ought not to want—not an "exchange" of destinies in the abstraction of eternity but a mortal and profoundly carnal union, a mutual absorption in desire which produces incontrovertible evidence of the material-theological. Melmoth's encounters with Monçada and young Melmoth generate stories: his encounter with Immalee generates a child. Beneath the trinity of theology, the trinity of (hetero)sexuality.

This infant is a curious and profound glitch in the story of Melmoth as scripted by the myth of the devil's bargain. Behind this parabola of self-extension we see Maturin invoke the trinitarian theology of divine incarnation/extension, along with its Miltonic shadow trinity of Satan, Sin, and Death. But its formal premise is emphatically human and embodied. With the birth of his child, Melmoth is back in the original human bargain for immortality, where the corporeal and spiritual self continues in a trajectory of (hetero)sexuality, family, race, even nation, while the core of personhood, figured in the beating heart, casts its desire, its motion, its meanings without words, into the secret of silence, toward the taciturn and invisible God. From that perspective, when Melmoth looks upon his daughter, he looks upon his end, and so does Maturin's own narrative.

As Maturin's nest of stories unfolds toward its end, the narrative scatters into illegibilities and into multiple genres—the dream, the vision, the melodramatic scene. And theologies grow less readable too. Immalee is imprisoned with her child by the Inquisition as a way of entrapping the devilish figure who is usurping its Power: "if there be human elements in him, if there be anything mortal clinging to his heart, we shall wind round the roots of it and extract it" (524). This might have made an interesting ending, but Maturin bypasses it: Melmoth visits Immalee and his child, and departs, still untrapped. On the night of his visit, the night before mother and infant were to be separated, the infant died, with a black mark around its throat. But whether the mark of mortality is code for the original incommunicable human condition, or from the murdering hand of Immalee's "maternal despair" (530), or from the hand of an enraged father snatching back the sign of his renewed bargain with his own humanity, the narrative will not say.

Immalee's heart "breaks" after the death of her infant, but as her bodily death approaches, that mighty muscle still beats its command to love. For though she has, like all of Melmoth's targets, refused to "exchange" her redeemable mortal immortality for his unregenerate preternatural immortality, she is hoping to meet more than her God in that secret silence. Though at one level she plunges into the grave to escape the pursuing Melmoth, she also seeks him, accepting her deathbed confessor's promise of heaven only on a condition, the human condition of love-desire: "'Paradise!' uttered Isadora, with her last breath, '*will he be there!*'" (533).

The orthodox theology of Maturin's intention, properly immaterial, provides a final sequence on the Irish coast in which Melmoth returns to the frame story, to his original home, stricken in age but still frozen in preternatural Gothic outlawry, dreaming, and then apparently experiencing, a fall into hell. But the command of Immalee, italicized as an exclamation, not a question, to constitute a Paradise with the bodily "thereness" of her lover-tutor, beats like a wave against the rock of his self-narrated picture of flaming damnation. *Either* picture is a plausible context for the final moment of the novel, where "an overwhelming mass of conviction . . . falls upon the mind . . . and crushes out the truth from the heart" (542). It is a truth that can be "exchanged" only in "looks of silent and unutterable horror" between the two men, Monçada and young Melmoth, who are heirs to the communicable properties of their now-dead families, and to the incommunicable condition, always already communicated, of the human.

Works Cited

Bruhm, Steven. *Gothic Bodies: The Politics of Pain in Romantic Fiction.* Philadelphia: University of Pennsylvania Press, 1994.

Butler, Marilyn. "Romantic Manichaeism: Shelley's 'On the Devil, and Devils' and Byron's Mythological Dramas." *The Sun Is God: Painting, Literature and Mythology in the Nineteenth Century.* Ed. J. B. Bullen. Oxford: Clarendon Press, 1989.

Eliot. T. S. "Little Gidding," *T. S. Eliot: The Complete Poems and Plays.* New York: Harcourt, Brace & World, 1971.

Fowler, Kathleen. "Hieroglyphics in Fire: *Melmoth the Wanderer.*" *Studies in Romanticism* 25 (1986): 521–539.

Harper, Albert W. J. *The Theodicy of Suffering.* San Francisco: Mellen Research University Press, 1990.

Maturin, Charles Robert. *Melmoth the Wanderer.* Ed. Douglas Grant. London: Oxford University Press, 1968.

McKeon, Michael. *The Origins of the English Novel, 1600–1740.* Baltimore: The Johns Hopkins University Press, 1987.

Praz, Mario. *The Romantic Agony.* London: Oxford University Press, 1933.

Scarry, Elaine. *The Body in Pain: The Making and Unmaking of the World.* New York: Oxford University Press, 1985.

Testa, Carlo. *Desire and the Devil: Demonic Contracts in French and European Literature.* New York: Peter Lang, 1991.

Watt, Ian. *The Rise of the Novel: Studies in DeFoe, Richardson and Fielding.* 1957. Berkeley: University of California Press, 1967.

NOTES ON CONTRIBUTORS

JOHN ANDERSON is a Lecturer at Boston College. His research interests include the European epic tradition, the women poets of the British Romantic period, Emily Dickinson, and Wallace Stevens. His articles and reviews have appeared in such journals as the *Huntington Library Quarterly*, *SEL: Studies in English Literature*, *Pedagogy*, and the *Yearbook of Comparative and General Literature*. He is currently at work on a study of Emily Dickinson's literary influence.

J. ROBERT BARTH, S.J., is the James P. McIntyre Professor of English at Boston College. His research interests include the British Romantic poets, Gerard Manley Hopkins, Graham Greene, and the relationship between literature and religion. His books include *Coleridge and Christian Doctrine* (1969; new edition 1987); *The Symbolic Imagination: Coleridge and the Romantic Tradition* (1977; new edition 2000), which won the Book of the Year Award of the Conference on Christianity and Literature; and *Coleridge and the Power of Love* (1988). He is also editor of *Religious Perspectives in Faulkner's Fiction: Yoknapatawpha and Beyond* (1972) and co-editor (with John L. Mahoney) of *Coleridge, Keats, and the Imagination: Romanticism and Adam's Dream* (1990). His articles and reviews have appeared in such journals as *America*, *Christianity and Literature*, *English Language Notes*, *Journal of English and Germanic Philology*, *Keats-Shelley Journal*, *Literature and Belief*, *Renascence*, *Studies in Romanticism*, *The Coleridge Bulletin*, *The Wordsworth Circle*, and *Thought*, as well as in a number of books. A forthcoming book is entitled *Of Fabric More Divine: Wordsworth, Coleridge, and the Religious Imagination*.

FREDERICK BURWICK is Professor of English at the University of California at Los Angeles. He is co-editor, with Grant Scott, of the *European Romantic Review*, published quarterly by Routledge Press. Among the twenty books he has authored and edited, his most recent works are *Mimesis and Its Romantic Reflections* (2001) and *Thomas De Quincey:*

Knowledge and Power (2001). His book *Poetic Madness and the Romantic Imagination* (1996) won the Outstanding Book of the Year Award of the American Conference on Romanticism. He has been named Distinguished Scholar by both the British Academy (1992) and the Keats-Shelley Association (1998).

JAMES ENGELL, Gurney Professor of English and Professor of Comparative Literature at Harvard University, has explored several connections between religion and literature. His essays in this vein include studies of Coleridge's "This Lime-Tree Bower My Prison" and of Coleridge's "First Postulates, Final Causes." He has also written on the importance of Robert Lowth's *Lectures on the Sacred Poetry of the Hebrews*. His *Creative Imagination: Enlightenment to Romanticism* (1981) traces, among other themes, the ways in which imagination has influenced religious thought. His other books include *Forming the Critical Mind, Dryden to Coleridge* (1989) and *The Committed Word: Literature and Public Values* (1999), which calls for a return to the study of rhetoric. He has edited four books, including *Coleridge: The Early Family Letters* (1994) and (with W. J. Bate) *Biographia Literaria* (1983) for the *Collected Works of Coleridge*. His latest project, with Anthony Dangerfield, is *Higher Education in the Age of Money*.

ROBERT KIELY is Loker Professor of English and American Literature at Harvard University, where he teaches courses in the modern and postmodern novel, the English Bible, and Christian literature. His books include *Robert Louis Stevenson and the Fiction of Adventure* (1964), *The Romantic Novel in England* (1972), *Beyond Egotism: The Fiction of James Joyce, Virginia Woolf, and D. H. Lawrence* (1980), and *Reverse Traditiion: Postmodern Fictions and the Nineteenth-Century Novel* (1993). He has also edited *The Good Heart: The Dalai Lama's Commentary on the Gospels* (1996). His most recent book is *Still Learning: Spiritual Sketches from a Professor's Life* (2000). His current research is on literary aesthetics and Italian religious art, with an emphasis on Ruskin, James, and Pater.

DAVID LEIGH, S.J., is Professor of English at Seattle University, where he recently completed fifteen years as Director of the Honors Program, Core Curriculum Director, and then Chair of the English Department. In addition to *Circuitous Journeys: Modern Spiritual Autobiography* (2000), he has published numerous articles in the area of literature and religion. Besides serving as co-editor of the journal *Ultimate Reality and Meaning* (published by the University of Toronto), he is currently working on a book on apocalyptic patterns in modern fiction.

THOMAS LLOYD, after years in the great city pent, took his Ph.D. as a late vocation under the direction of John L. Mahoney. He now teaches in the English Department of Christendom College in sylvan Front Royal, Virginia, where he is rekindling his love of Nature and teaching great literature to undergraduates.

JONATHAN MULROONEY, who studied as an undergraduate with John Mahoney, is an Assistant Professor of English at the University of Vermont. His scholarly interests include the public culture of the Romantic period, William Hazlitt, and John Keats. His essays have appeared in *Studies in the Novel* and *Profession*, and others are forthcoming in *Nineteenth-Century Contexts* and *Studies in Romanticism*. He is currently at work on a book entitled *Romanticism and the Subject of Theater*, which explores the relationship between theatrical experience and lyric subjectivity in early nineteenth-century Britain.

DAVID PERKINS is the Marquand Professor of English and American Literature at Harvard University, Emeritus. He has also taught at the University of Göttingen and at the University of California. His research interests include English Romanticism, modern and contemporary poetry, and the theory of literary history. He is the author of *The Quest for Permanence: The Symbolism of Wordsworth, Shelley, and Keats* (1959), *Wordsworth and the Poetry of Sincerity* (1964), *A History of Modern Poetry*, vol. I: *From the 1890s to the High Modernist Mode* (1976), vol. II: *Modernism and After* (1987), and *Is Literary History Possible?* (1992). He has edited two anthologies, *English Romantic Writers* (1967; 2nd edition 1995) and (with W. J. Bate) *British and American Poets: Chaucer to the Present* (1986). He also edited *Theoretical Issues in Literary History* (1991) and (with James Engell) *Teaching Literature: What Is Needed Now?* (1988). His articles and reviews have appeared in such journals as the *ADE Bulletin, African American Review, Blake Quarterly, CIEFL Bulletin, Clio, Eighteenth Century Life, English Literary History, European Romantic Review, Harvard Library Bulletin, Harvard Review, JEGP, Keats-Shelley Journal, Modern Language Quarterly, New*

Literary History, Poetry, Nineteenth-Century Literature, Southern Review, Studies in English Literature, Studies in Romanticism, Texas Studies in Literature and Language, and *The Wordsworth Circle,* as well as in a number of books. He is currently writing about the campaign for animal rights in Romantic England.

PHILIP C. RULE, S.J., is Associate Professor of English at the College of the Holy Cross. His research focuses on several nineteenth-century British writers and topics: the Romantic poets, British women writers, the Bildungsroman, John Henry Newman, and nineteenth-century religious thought. His articles and reviews have appeared in *America, Christianity and Literature, Christian Scholar's Review, Harvard Theological Review, Journal of the American Academy of Religion, New Scholasticism, Nineteenth-Century Prose, Renascence, Theological Studies,* and *The Wordsworth Circle,* as well as in several books. He is currently writing a book on Coleridge, Newman, and the centrality of conscience in their writings; and is working on a critical edition of the corrrespondence of Charles Kingsley.

CHARLES RZEPKA is Professor of English at Boston University. He has written extensively on William Wordsworth, Thomas De Quincey, and other authors and poets of the Romantic period, as well as on popular literature and culture. He is currently working on a cultural history of detective fiction in England and America.

DENNIS TAYLOR is Professor of English at Boston College, as well as editor of the journal *Religion and the Arts*. He is a scholar of Victorian literature, Victorian philology, and Victorian and modernist metrical theory. His books include *Hardy's Poetry, 1860–1928* (1981, 1989), *Hardy's Metres and Victorian Prosody* (1988), *Hardy's Literary Language and Victorian Philology* (1993), and an edition of *Jude the Obscure* (1998). He has also published articles on Wallace Stevens, the OED, Wordsworth, Thomas Gray, James Joyce, and the "confidence man." He has lectured and published on spiritual autobiography, and his current work concerns "Shakespeare and the Reformation" and "Wordsworth and Catholic Remnants"—parts of a larger study of Protestant/Catholic relations in English literature.

JUDITH WILT is Professor of English at Boston College. She writes and teaches in the fields of Victorian fiction, popular culture genres,

Women's Studies, and religion and literature. She is the author of *The Readable People of George Meredith* (1975), *Ghosts of the Gothic: Austen, Eliot, and Lawrence* (1980), *Secret Leaves: The Novels of Sir Walter Scott* (1985), and *Abortion, Choice, and Contemporary Fiction: The Armaggedon of the Maternal Instinct* (1991). She is the editor of the forthcoming New Riverside Edition of *Frankenstein* and *The Island of Doctor Moreau*, and her current work is a book-length study of the novels of Mrs. Humphry Ward.

A BIBLIOGRAPHY OF THE WORKS OF JOHN L. MAHONEY

PUBLICATIONS

1958

"The Classical Tradition in Eighteenth-Century Rhetorical Education." *History of Education Journal* 9 (Summer 1958): 93–97.

1959

"Thomas Trollope: Victorian Man of Letters." *University of Rochester Library Bulletin* 14 (Spring 1959): 39–42.

1960

"Captain Cox: Ballad and Book Collector Extraordinary." *University of Rochester Library Bulletin* 15 (Winter 1960): 25–28.
"Dr. Johnson at Work." *Columbia University Library Columns* 10 (November 1960): 20–23.
"Child's *English and Scottish Popular Ballads and Ballad Scholarship*." *Catholic Library Association Journal* 4 (1960): 126–131.

1961

"Foundations of Introductory Courses in Literature." *The Catholic Educational Review* 59 (January 1961): 40–42.
"Ovid and Medieval Courtly Love Poetry." *Classical Folia* 15 (1961): 14–27.
"Theme and Image in a Keats Sonnet on Fame." *English Record* 12 (Fall 1961): 24–25. Reprinted in *Creative Writing* 13 (November 1962): 25–26.
"The Quest for Objectivity in Hazlitt's Dramatic Criticism." *Drama Critique* 4 (November 1961): 132–136.

1962

"Donne and Fulke-Greville: Two Christian Attitudes Towards the Renaissance Idea of Mutability and Decay." *CLA Journal* 5 (March 1962): 202–212.

"Byron's Admiration of Pope: A Romantic Paradox." *Discourse: A Review of the Liberal Arts* (Summer 1962): 309–315.

"Platonism as Unifying Element in Spenser's Foure Hymnes." *Bulletin de Faculté des Lettres de Strasbourg* 52 (December 1962): 211–219.

1963

"Symbolism and Calvinism in the Novels of Kafka." *Renascence* 15 (Summer 1963): 200–207.

"Keats and the Metaphor of Fame." *English Studies* 44 (October 1963): 1–3.

"Burke and India." *The Burke Newsletter* 4 (1963): 210–219.

1964

William Duff's Essay on Original Genius. Selected with an introduction. Gainesville, Florida: Scholars' Facsimiles and Reprints, 1964.

1965

An Essay on Dramatic Poesy and Other Critical Writings by John Dryden. Indianapolis: The Bobbs-Merrill Company, 1965.

"Sheridan on Hastings: The Classical Oration and Eighteenth-Century English Politics." *The Burke Newsletter* 6 (Spring 1965): 210–219.

Introductory "Note on Eighteenth-Century English Literature." *Sublimity and Sensibility in English Romanticism*. Cambridge, Mass.: Fogg Art Museum, Harvard University, 1965.

1966

"Addison and Akenside: Psychological Criticism and Romantic Poetry." *British Journal of Aesthetics* 6 (October 1966): 365–374.

"Imitation and the Quest for Objectivity in English Romantic Theory." *Proceedings of the Fourth Congress of the International Comparative Literature Association*. Paris and The Hague, 1966, pp. 774–780.

1967

"The Real in the Romantic Theory of William Hazlitt." Abstracted in *Le Réal dans la littérature et dans la langue.* Paris, 1967.

1970

"Classical Form and the Oratory of Edmund Burke." *Classical Folia* 24 (1970): 46–81.

1972

Rev. of Robert M. Cooper, *Lost on Both Sides: Dante Gabriel Rossetti—Critic and Poet.* Athens: Ohio University Press, 1970. *Thought* 47 (1972): 136–137.

"The Deadlock of the Universities." *Intellect* (November 1972): 93–94.

1973

"Higher Education: The Challenge and the Possibilities." *Improving College and University Teaching* (Fall 1973).

1975

"In the Walks of Real Life: Hazlitt on the Restoration and the Eighteenth Century." *Modern Language Studies* 5 (1975): 21–30.

"The Futuristic Imagination: Hazlitt's Criticism of *Romeo and Juliet*." *British Journal of Aesthetics* 19 (1975): 65–67.

Rev. of *Aesthetics and the Theory of Criticism: Selected Essays of Arnold Isenberg.* Ed. William Callaghan et. al. Chicago: The University of Chicago Press, 1973. *Thought* 50 (1975): 96–97.

1976

Rev. of Richard B. Schwartz, *Samuel Johnson and the Problem of Evil.* Madison: University of Wisconsin Press, 1975. *Thought* 51 (1976): 216–217.

1977

"The Reptile's Lot: Theme and Image in Coleridge's Late Poetry." *The Wordsworth Circle* 8 (1977): 349–360.

"Shelley's *Defense of Poetry*: The Poet and Moral Education." *Inscape: Essays and Studies in Honor of Rev. Charles Donovan, S.J.* Boston College, 1977, pp. 108–113.

Rev. of J. Robert Barth, *The Symbolic Imagination: Coleridge and the Romantic Tradition*. Princeton: Princeton University Press, 1977. *America* (September 1977): 174–175.

1978

The English Romantics: Major Poetry and Critical Theory. Edited with introductions, critical essays, and notes. Lexington and Toronto: D. C. Heath and Co., 1978. Reissued by Waveland Press, 1997.

"New Dimensions in Hazlitt's Aesthetics." *The English Romantics: Major Poetry and Critical Theory*, pp. 786–794.

"Writing and the University: Some Immodest Proposals." *Publications of the Governing Boards of Universities* 20 (September–October 1978): 46–47.

1979

"Reynolds's Discourses on Art: The Delicate Balance of Neoclassical Aesthetics." *British Journal of Aesthetics* 18 (Spring 1979). Abstracted in the *International Repertory of the Literature of Art* and *The Philosopher's Index*.

1980

The Enlightenment and English Literature. Edited with critical introductions and notes. Lexington and Toronto: D. C. Heath and Co., 1980. Reissued by Waveland Press, 1999.

"Addison and Akenside: Psychological Criticism and English Romantic Poetry." *The Enlightenment and English Literature*, pp. 745–750.

Review Essay. *The Letters of William Hazlitt*. Ed. Herschel Moreland, assisted by William Hallam Bonner and Gerald Lahey. New York: New York University Press, 1978; and John Kinnaird, *William Hazlitt: Critic of Power*. New York: Columbia University Press, 1978. *Studies in Romanticism* 19 (1980): 142–150.

1981

The Logic of Passion: The Literary Criticism of William Hazlitt. New York: Fordham University Press, 1981.

"Coping with Change at Chestnut Hill." *Boston College Magazine* 44 (Winter 1981): 8–12.
Rev. of James Engell, *The Creative Imagination: Enlightenment to Romanticism*. Cambridge Mass.: Harvard University Press, 1981. *America* (December 1981): 385–386.

1982

Rev. of M. Jadwiga Swiatecka, *The Idea of the Symbol: Some Nineteenth Century Comparisons with Coleridge*. Cambridge: Cambridge University Press, 1980. *The Wordsworth Circle* 13 (1982): 124–125.
"Samuel Johnson." *Funk and Wagnalls Encyclopedia*. 1982.

1984

"The Problem of Mimesis in Shelley's *Defense of Poetry*." *British Journal of Aesthetics* 24 (Winter 1984): 59–64.
"The Anglo-Scottish Critics: Toward a Romantic Theory of Imitation." *Johnson and His Age*. Ed. James Engell. Harvard English Studies 12. Cambridge, Mass: Harvard University Press, 1984, pp. 255–283.

1985

The Persistence of Tragedy: Episodes in the History of Drama. Boston Public Library—National Endowment for the Humanities, 1985.
The Whole Internal Universe: Imitation and the New Defense of Poetry in British Criticism and Aesthetics, 1660–1830. New York: Fordham University Press, 1985.
"The Problem of Imitation in Neoclassic and Romantic Criticism and Aesthetics." *Proceedings of the Tenth Congress of the International Comparative Literature Association*. New York: Garland Press, 1985, pp. 135–145.

1986

"Imagination and the Ways of Genius." *Approaches to Hazlitt*. Ed. Harold Bloom. New Haven: Chelsea House, 1986, pp. 92–95.
"Teaching the 'Immortality Ode' with Coleridge's 'Dejection: An Ode.'" *Approaches to Teaching Wordsworth's Poetry*. Ed. Spencer Hall.

New York: The Modern Language Association of America, 1989, pp. 92–95.

1987

"Trouble in Paradise: Liberal Education and Its Best-Selling Critics." *Boston College Magazine* 46.4 (Fall 1987): 25–32.

1988

"William Hazlitt, 1778–1830." *Book of Days 1988*. Ann Arbor, Michigan: Pierian Press, 1988, pp. 207–208.

Review Essay. William Wordsworth, *The White Doe of Rylstone; or, The Fate of the Nortons*. Ed. Kristine Dugas. Ithaca and London: Cornell University Press, 1988; *Coleridge's "Dejection": The Earliest Manuscripts and the Earliest Writings*. Ed. Stephen Maxfield Parrish. Ithaca and London: Cornell University Press, 1988; *A Selection of Hebrew Melodies, Ancient and Modern by Isaac Nathan and Lord Byron*. Edited with introduction and notes by Frederick Burwick and Paul Douglass. Tuscaloosa and London: University of Alabama Press, 1988. *Nineteenth-Century Contexts* 12:2 (1988): 107–113.

Rev. of Jeffrey Cox, *In the Shadow of Romance: Romantic Tragic Drama in Germany, England, and France*. *South Central Modern Language Association Review* (Winter 1988): 115–118.

1989

"Teaching Shelley's 'Skylark' and *The Defense of Poetry*." *Approaches to Teaching Shelley's Poetry*. Ed. Spencer Hall. New York: The Modern Language Association of America, 1989, pp. 82–85.

Rev. of *William Wordsworth, Shorter Poems, 1807–1820*. Ed. Carl Ketcham. Ithaca and London: Cornell University Press, 1989. *Nineteenth-Century Contexts* 13 (1989): 249–251.

1990

Coleridge, Keats, and the Imagination: Romanticism and Adam's Dream. Edited with J. Robert Barth, S.J. Columbia: University of Missouri Press, 1990.

"'We Must Away': Tragedy and the Imagination in Coleridge's Later

Poems." *Coleridge, Keats, and the Imagination: Romanticism and Adam's Dream*, pp. 109–134.

1991

"William Hazlitt: The Essay as Vehicle for the Romantic Critic." *Charles Lamb Bulletin* (July 1991): 92–98.

"Hazlitt as Critic of Gusto." *Nineteenth-Century Literary Criticism*. Ed. Laurie DeMauro. New York: Gale Research Inc., 1991, pp. 178–181.

Rev. of Janet Ruth Heller, *Coleridge, Lamb, Hazlitt, and the Reader of Drama*. Columbia and London: University of Missouri Press, 1990. *The Wordsworth Circle* 22 (1991): 204–205.

1992

"Reynolds and Wordsworth: The Development of a Post-Enlightenment Aesthetic." *European Romantic Review* 3 (1992): 147–158.

"The Rydal Mount Ladies' Boarding School: A Wordsworthian Episode in America." *The Wordsworth Circle* 23 (1992): 43–48.

Essays on "Disinterestedness," "Organic Unity," "Wise Passiveness." *Encyclopedia of Romanticism*. Ed. Laura Dabundo. New York: Garland Publishing, 1992.

Rev. of Frederick Burwick, *Illusion and the Drama: Critical Theory of the Enlightenment and Romantic Era*. State College: Pennsylvania State University Press, 1991. *The Wordsworth Circle* 23 (1992): 216–220.

Rev. of Stanley Jones, *Hazlitt: A Life—From Winterslow to Firth Street*. Oxford: Clarendon Press, 1989. *Studies in Romanticism* 31 (1992): 108–112.

1993

Essays on "Intensity," "Spontaneity," "Subjectivity and Objectivity." *The New Princeton Encyclopedia of Poetry and Poetics*. Ed. Alex Preminger and T.V.F. Brogan. Princeton: Princeton University Press, 1993, pp. 610–611, 1207–1208, 1229–1230.

"On Don Bialostosky's *Wordsworth, Dialogics, and the Practice of Criticism*." Cambridge: Cambridge University Press, 1992. *Nineteenth-Century Contexts* 17 (1993): 269–275.

1994

Rev. of Jean Hall, *A Mind that Feeds Upon Infinity: The Deep Self in English Romantic Poetry*. Cranbury, N.J.: Associated University Presses, 1991. *Studies in Romanticism* 33 (1994): 169–172.

1995

"Intersection: The Poetry of Religious Experience." *The Catholic World* 238 (July–August 1995): 148–152.

1996

Rev. of Richard Holmes, *Dr. Johnson and Mr. Savage*. New York: Pantheon Books, 1993. *Southern Humanities Review* 30 (1996): 181–184.
Rev. of Vijay Mishra, *The Gothic Sublime*. Albany: State University of New York Press, 1994. *Southern Humanities Review* 30 (1996): 393–396.

1997

William Wordsworth: A Poetic Life. New York: Fordham University Press, 1997.
"Literature and Religion: Theory to Practice." *Perspectives on the Unity and Integration of Knowledge*. Ed. Ronald Glasberg. New York: Peter Lang, 1997, pp. 153–160.
"Critical Methodology and Writing about Religion and Literature." Review Essay. Nancy Easterlin, *Wordsworth and the Question of "Romantic Religion."* Cranbury, N.J.: Associated University Presses, 1996; and Ronald Wendling, *Coleridge's Progress to Christianity: Experience and Authority in Religious Faith*. Cranbury, N.J.: Associated University Presses, 1996. *Religion and the Arts* 1.4 (Winter 1997): 89–96.
"William Hazlitt." *Encyclopedia of the Essay*. Ed. Tracy Chevalier. London: Fitzroy Dearborn, 1997.

1998

Seeing Into the Life of Things: Essays on Literature and Religion. Edited with introduction. New York: Fordham University Press, 1998.

"Stevie Smith: Skepticism and the Poetry of Religious Experience." *Seeing Into the Life of Things*, pp. 319–330.

"The Burden of the Mystery: Excerpts from a Conversation on Religion and the Arts with Walter Jackson Bate." *Religion and the Arts* 2 (1998): 82–85.

"Integrating Religion and the Arts: Developing a Discourse." *URAM: Interdisciplinary Studies in the Philosophy of Understanding* 21 (1998): 230–241.

"The Rydal Mount Ladies' Boarding School: Wordsworthian Education in America." *Cultural Interactions in the Romantic Age.* Ed. Gregory Maertz. Albany: State University of New York Press, 1998, pp. 105–122.

2000

Rev. of Stephen Gill, *Wordsworth and the Victorians.* Oxford: Clarendon Press, 1998. *Studies in Romanticism* 39 (2000): 330–333.

2001

Wordsworth and the Critics: The Development of a Critical Reputation. Woodbridge, Suffolk, England, and Rochester, New York: Camden House, 2001.

"The True Story: Poetic Law and License in Johnson's Criticism." *1650–1850: Ideas, Inquiries, and Aesthetics in the Early Modern Era.* Ed. Kevin Cope. New York: AMS Press, 2001, pp. 185–198.

"Contemporary Attitudes Toward Biography and the Case of W. J. Bate's *Samuel Johnson.*" *1650–1850: Ideas, Inquiries,* and *Aesthetics in the Early Modern Era.* Ed. Kevin Cope. New York: AMS Press, 2001, pp. 333–347.

Review Essay. John Worthen. *The Gang: Coleridge, the Hutchinsons, and the Wordsworths in 1802.* New Haven: Yale University Press, 2001; Keith Hanley. *Wordsworth: A Poet's History.* Houndsmills, Basingstroke, Hampshire and New York: Palgrave, 2001. *The Wordsworth Circle* 32:4 (Autumn 2001): 185–187.

INDEX OF NAMES

Abrams, M. H., 51, 54n, 57, 61, 68, 74n
Addison, Joseph, 13, 59
Aeschylus, 135, 153n, 163n, 164n
Anderson, John M., 96n
Apuleius, 160n
Austen, Jane, 232

Bacon, Francis, 132, 180n
Baker, Herschel, xiii
Barbauld, Anna, 93
Barfield, Owen, 136
Barker, Juliet, 24n, 25n
Barth, J. Robert, S.J., 50n, 54n, 74n, 79n, 139n, 141n, 143n, 144, 145n, 157, 159, 177n, 193n, 196–197, 234n, 242n
Barth, Karl, 139
Bate, W. J., xiii, 131n, 155, 179n
Beattie, James, 194
Beaumont, Margaret, Lady, 198n
Beaupuy, Michel, 24, 25, 47
Beckett, Samuel, 112
Beer, John, 143n, 148
Bentham, Jeremy, 140, 235
Beuno, St., 121
Birnbaum, Ben, xi, xiv–xv
Blake, William, 2n, 6, 14, 15, 16, 56, 69, 138, 141, 158, 256, 258n, 270n
Blom, T. E., 54–55n, 56n, 67n
Bloom, Harold, 56–57, 68
Boccaccio, Giovanni, 166
Böhme, Jakob, 169, 210
Bostetter, Edward E., 144n
Boswell, James, 10
Boulger, James D., 131
Bourdieu, Pierre, 83n
Brantley, Richard E., 3n, 55, 57, 63n, 65, 68, 74n, 78
Bridges, Robert, 121, 124
Brier, Peter A., 37n

Bromwich, David, 179n, 190
Brooke, Stopford A., 56
Brougham, Henry Peter, 184–185
Brown, Marshall, 54–55n
Bruhm, Steven, 263
Buber, Martin, 239n
Buchan, Peter, 9
Bultmann, Rudolf, 139
Buonaparte, Napoleon, 141
Burke, Edmund, 267
Burwick, Frederick, 207n
Bush, Douglas, xiii
Butler, Joseph, 10
Butler, Marilyn, 232, 261
Butler, Samuel, 197
Byron, George Gordon, Lord, 232–233, 256, 257, 260, 261n

Caesar, Julius, 100
Campbell, George, 194, 211
Canning, George, 184–185
Carlyle, Thomas, 232
Carravaggio, Michelangelo da 189
Cavanagh, John, 184–185
Célan, Paul, 112
Chaplin, Charles, 141
Chaucer, Geoffrey, 24
Clare, John, 2n
Clarke, Samuel, 8
Clarkson, Thomas, 131, 133, 138
Cobbett, William, 184–185, 188
Coburn, Kathleen, 196n, 198n, 201n
Coleridge, George, 145
Coleridge, Herbert, 149
Coleridge, Samuel Taylor, 2n, 5, 10, 14, 15, 17, 33, 34, 56, 57, 61, 108, 128–151, 152–175, 176–192, 193–230, 231–255, 256
Coleridge, Sarah (Fricker), 207
Cook, John, 178n
Cowper, William, 2, 6, 14, 16, 54–72, 137n

INDEX OF NAMES

Cromwell, Oliver, 260
Cruikshank, Mary, 196n

D'Alembert, Jean le Rond, 129
Dante Alighieri, 99, 144, 166, 172
Darwin, Charles, 131, 147
Davidoff, Leonore, 2n, 7n, 8n
Davy, Humphrey, 159n
Dawson, P. M. S., 54n
Dawson, Virginia P., 128n
Dean, Richard, 9, 10
Defoe, Daniel, 137n, 262n
De Levie, Dagobert, 2n
DeLubac, Henri, S. J., 252
De Quincey, Thomas, 193–230
Dickens, Charles, 253
Dickinson, Emily, 90, 91, 97, 106, 109
Diderot, Denis, 129, 264
Digby, Kenelm, 133
Dilthey, Wilhelm, 133
Dixon, R. W., 112
Dodd, C. H., 202n
Donaldson, John W., 217–218, 220–221
Donne, John, 104, 162
Doolittle, Hilda ("H. D."), 162n
Drummond, William, 6
Duffy, Eamon, 42–43

Easterlin, Nancy, 74n, 78
Eaton, Horace Ainsworth, 193n
Eichner, Hans, 133n
Eliot, George, 26, 55, 233, 247, 250
Eliot, T. S., 257
Elizabeth I, 93, 99–102, 212–213
Ellis, David, 78
Emerson, Ralph Waldo, 137, 138n
Engell, James, 141n, 155
Engels, Friedrich, 83n, 216n
Euclid, 243
Evans, Bill, xii
Everest, Kelvin, 190n
Ezekiel, 206

Fenwick, Isabella, 118
Fichte, Johann, 134, 137
Fielding, Henry, 262n
Flew, Antony, 195n
Fowler, Kathleen, 258n
Fox, Charles, 56
Franchot, Jenny, 43

Francis of Assisi, St., 22–36
Free, William, N., 54n
Freud, Sigmund, 77, 82, 87
Fricker, George, 196
Friedrich, Carl J., 162
Fulford, Tim, 54n

Galilei, Galileo, 221
Gill, Frederick C., 55
Gill, Stephen, 80n, 114
Gillman, James, 237
Gilpin, William, 37, 44, 50
Goethe, Johann Wolfgang von, 26, 207n, 232, 258n
Granger, James, 2
Grant, Douglas, 257n
Green, Joel B., 95n
Green, Joseph Henry, 132, 138, 237, 243
Greenwood, Robert, 82–83
Griffin, Dustin, 54n
Grob, Alan, 114–115, 117–118
Grotius, Hugo, 196
Guillory, John, 83n

Haight, Gordon, 247n
Hall, Catherine, 2n, 7n, 8n
Happel, Stephen, 193n
Harbage, Alfred, xiii
Harding, Anthony John, 133, 138, 139n, 147n, 156–158, 168, 169n, 173, 193n, 242n
Harper, Albert W. J., 267
Hartley, David, 60, 194–196, 198, 205–206, 209, 214
Hartman, Geoffrey, 45, 50, 62–66, 114–115
Harwood, Dix, 2n
Hatton, Anne Jane, Lady, 257n
Hawthorne, Nathaniel, 43
Hazlitt, William, xiii, 158, 176–192
Heaney, Seamus, xii
Hedley, Douglas, 130n, 139n
Heidegger, Martin, 252
Heller, Deborah, 54n
Helmont, Jean-Baptiste van, 128
Hemans, Felicia, 17, 90–110
Herodotus, 195n
Hervey, James, 56, 57n
Hesiod, 160n

INDEX OF NAMES

Hobbes, Thomas, 268
Holme, Ann, 80n
Homer, 1, 153n, 163
Hopkins, Gerard Manley, S. J., 111–127
House, Humphrey, 54–55n
Hume, David, 11–12, 180n, 193–197, 205–206, 211–215, 222–223, 224, 227
Hutchinson, Mary, 75–76
Hutchinson, Sara, 166, 174

Ilie, Paul, 128
Iscariot, Judas, 105

Jackson, H. J., 132n
James, Henry, 42
Jasper, David, 146n
Jesus Christ, 4, 7, 23, 27, 33, 58, 79, 95, 102–105, 124, 138, 143, 145, 153, 196, 199–205, 207, 210, 213–214, 217, 223–228, 263
Joan of Arc, 167, 171
John the Baptist, St., 32
Johnson, Don, 77
Johnson, Lee M., 92–93, 100n, 108n
Johnson, Samuel, xii, xv, 10, 57, 129
Jonas, 206
Jones, Myrddin, 54n
Jones, Stanley, 190
Junius, 184–185

Kafka, Franz, 112
Kant, Immanuel, 10, 134, 137, 138, 197–198, 205, 221–222, 227, 244
Kean, Hilda, 2n
Keats, John, 15, 16, 23, 26, 138, 176
Kendall, Edward Augustus, 5, 7
Kierkegaard, Søren, 34–35, 112, 139
Kinnaird, John, 179n, 180
Klancher, Jon, 190
Kramer, Lawrence, 160

Lacan, Jacques, 82
Lamb, Charles, 50
Lamb, Mary, 50
Leach, Edmund, 157
Leigh, David J., S. J., 63n
Levinson, Marjorie, 37n
Lewis, Matthew "Monk," 168, 256n
Liverpool, Robert, Lord, 251

Locke, John, 8, 58, 60, 130, 136
Lockridge, Laurence S., 137n, 145n
Lonergan, Bernard J., S. J., 244
Longfellow, Henry Wadsworth, 43
Lonsdale, Roger, 93
Lovejoy, A. O., 8
Lowes, John Livingston, 136
Loyola, Ignatius, St., 123
Luther, Martin, 239
Lynch, David, xii

MacIntyre, Alisdair, 241n
McCarthy, William, 93
McConnell, Frank D., 54n
McFarland, Thomas, 7n, 164, 194n, 197, 201n, 203, 236–237
McKeon, Michael, 262n
McPartland, Marian, xii
Magdalene, Mary, St., 91, 94, 99, 102, 104
Mahoney, John L., xi–xv, 27n, 43n, 66n, 80n, 92, 100, 107, 179n
Marcel, Gabriel, 239n
Marcuse, Herbert, 141
Mariani, Paul, 123
Marsh, James, 243
Marshall, W. G., 54n, 65
Martineau, James, 234
Marx, Karl, 83n, 216
Mary, the Blessed Virgin, 39, 91, 92, 94–99, 100–101, 203
Maslow, A. H., 239n
Masson, David, 211n
Matlak, Richard E., 78, 82n
Maturin, Charles Robert, 168, 256–273
Maurice, F. D., 243
May, John, 201n
Mayhew, Henry, 17
Melnyk, Julie, 91, 94
Mendelssohn, Moses, 198n
Miall, David, 145n
Mill, John Stuart, 140, 232, 235
Miller, Perry, xiii
Milton, John, 26, 27, 29–30, 55, 56, 57, 61, 68–69, 135, 140, 143, 162, 243, 271
Moorman, Mary, 76n, 92
Morgan, John, 196n
Moses, 103, 130, 217
Musser, Joseph F., Jr., 54n

INDEX OF NAMES

Natarajan, Uttara, 179n
Nédoncelle, Maurice, 239n
Needler, Henry, 13
Nelson, Jane A., 157
Neri, Philip, St., 26
Newey, Vincent, 54–55n, 56, 59n, 68n
Newman, John Henry, 208, 214, 216, 217, 220–221, 227, 231–255
Newton, Isaac, 158n, 207n
Newton, John, 58, 59n, 60, 65
Nicholson, Norman, 55

Onorato, Richard J., 77
Owen, W. J. B., 54n

Page, Judith W., 108n
Paine, Thomas, 5
Paley, William, 4, 11–13, 14, 195–197, 205–206
Park, Roy, 183n
Parrish, Stephen, 84–85
Pattison, Mark, 112
Paul of Tarsus, St., 103, 124, 205, 219–220
Paulin, Tom, 179n
Perkins, David, 2n, 17n, 145n
Perkins, Mary Anne, 142
Perry, Seamus, 134n, 145n
Peter, St., 200
Peterfreund, Stuart, 158
Petrarch, Francesco, 96, 166
Pickering, Samuel Jr., 5n
Piper, H. W., 56
Plato, 112, 130, 134, 137, 147, 154–155
Plumptre, James, 2, 4
Plutarch, 160n
Poe, Edgar Allan, 38
Poole, Thomas, 197–200, 235, 237
Pope, Alexander, 9, 14
Potts, A. F., 54–55n
Pound, Ezra, 162n
Praz, Mario, 265
Price, Martin, 56
Price, Richard, 57
Prickett, Stephen, 133, 145n, 148, 149n, 193n, 208n, 217
Priestley, Joseph, 7, 57, 194, 196
Priestman, Martin, 54–55n, 56n, 57n, 59n, 66n

Primatt, Humphrey, 2
Pythagoras, 198n

Quinlan, Maurice, 55n

Radcliffe, Ann, 15, 31, 256n, 257
Rahner, Karl, S. J., 238, 252
Reid, Thomas, 7
Reynolds, John Hamilton, 15
Richardson, Alan, 78n
Richardson, Samuel, 256, 262n, 264
Robinson, Henry Crabb, 25–27, 28, 29
Robinson, Mary, 15
Rule, Philip C., S. J., 234n, 243n
Ryan, Robert M., 74n, 176n
Ryder, Richard D., 2n
Rylestone, Anne L., 92n, 107n
Rzepka, Charles J., 76n, 84n

Sackville-West, Edward, 193n
Scarry, Elaine, 267
Schelling, Friedrich Wilhelm Joseph von, 134, 135, 137, 138, 139, 152, 156n 197, 198n, 201–203, 227
Schiller, Friedrich von, 138
Schleiermacher, Friedrich, 139
Schneewind, J. B., 232n
Schulz, Max F., 55n
Scott, Walter, 257
Severn, Joseph, 26
Shaftesbury, Anthony Ashley Cooper, Earl of, 7, 8
Shakespeare, William, 33, 38, 97, 136
Shelley, Mary Wollstonecraft, 256
Shelley, Percy Bysshe, 14, 16, 17, 23, 160n, 256, 257, 260, 261n
Shepherd, T. B., 55
Siddons, Sarah, 164, 171
Smart, Christopher, 17–18
Smith, Charlotte, 15
Smith, Stevie, xii
Sophocles, 166
Southey, Robert, 9
Spacks, Patricia Meyer, 137n
Spence, Joseph, 9
Spenser, Edmund, 101
Spinoza, Benedict de, 132, 158n, 197, 203, 214, 227
Steiner, George, 111
Stephen, Leslie, 144
Stillingfleet, Edward, 227n

INDEX OF NAMES

Stoppard, Tom, xii
Stuart, Daniel, 201n, 251

Talfourd, Thomas, 184–185
Taylor, Anya, 10n, 132, 172
Taylor, Charles, 232n
Taylor, Dennis, 52n
Tennyson, Alfred, Lord, 114
Testa, Carlo, 258n
Thales, 147
Thelwall, John, 148
Thomas, Keith, 2n
Thomson, James, 13
Thompson, T. W., 80
Tillich, Paul, 139
Tindal, Matthew, 8
Traherne, Thomas, 56
Trickett, Rachel, 55n
Trimmer, Sarah, 1, 5, 7, 8
Turner, Ernest S., 2n
Turner, James, 2n
Tussaud, Madame, 210
Twitchell, Paul, 161

Ulmer, William A., 68n

Vallins, David, 138n
Vallon, Annette, 47, 75
Vaughan, Henry, 56
Virgil, 172n
Voltaire, François, 129

Walpole, Horace, 168, 257
Ward, Wilfrid, 237n

Ward, W. G., 244
Warren, Robert Penn, 144n
Watson, George, 144n
Watson, J. R., 46n, 74n
Watt, Ian, 262
Weiskel, Thomas, 82n
Welch, Claude, 139n
Wesley, John, 3, 10
White, Daniel, 177, 178n
White, R. J., 134
Whitehead, Alfred North, 147
Whiting, B. J., xiii
Wilde, Oscar, 258
Willey, Basil, 7n
William, Prince of Gloucester, 2
Winefred, St., 112, 120–121
Wolfson, Susan, 90
Wollaston, William, 8, 9
Wollstonecraft, Mary, 3, 7, 231–232
Wood, Barry, 137n
Woof, Robert, 80
Wordsworth, Dora, 26, 93
Wordsworth, Dorothy, 42, 49–50, 74
Wordsworth, John, 84–85, 87
Wordsworth, William, xii-xv, 2n, 5, 12, 13–14, 15, 16, 22–36, 37–53, 54–72, 73–89, 90–110, 111–127, 128, 138, 141, 145–146, 165n, 176, 182, 185, 233, 234

Yeats, William Butler, 160, 162n
Young, Thomas, 5

www.ingramcontent.com/pod-product-compliance
Lightning Source LLC
Chambersburg PA
CBHW051419290426
44109CB00016B/1365